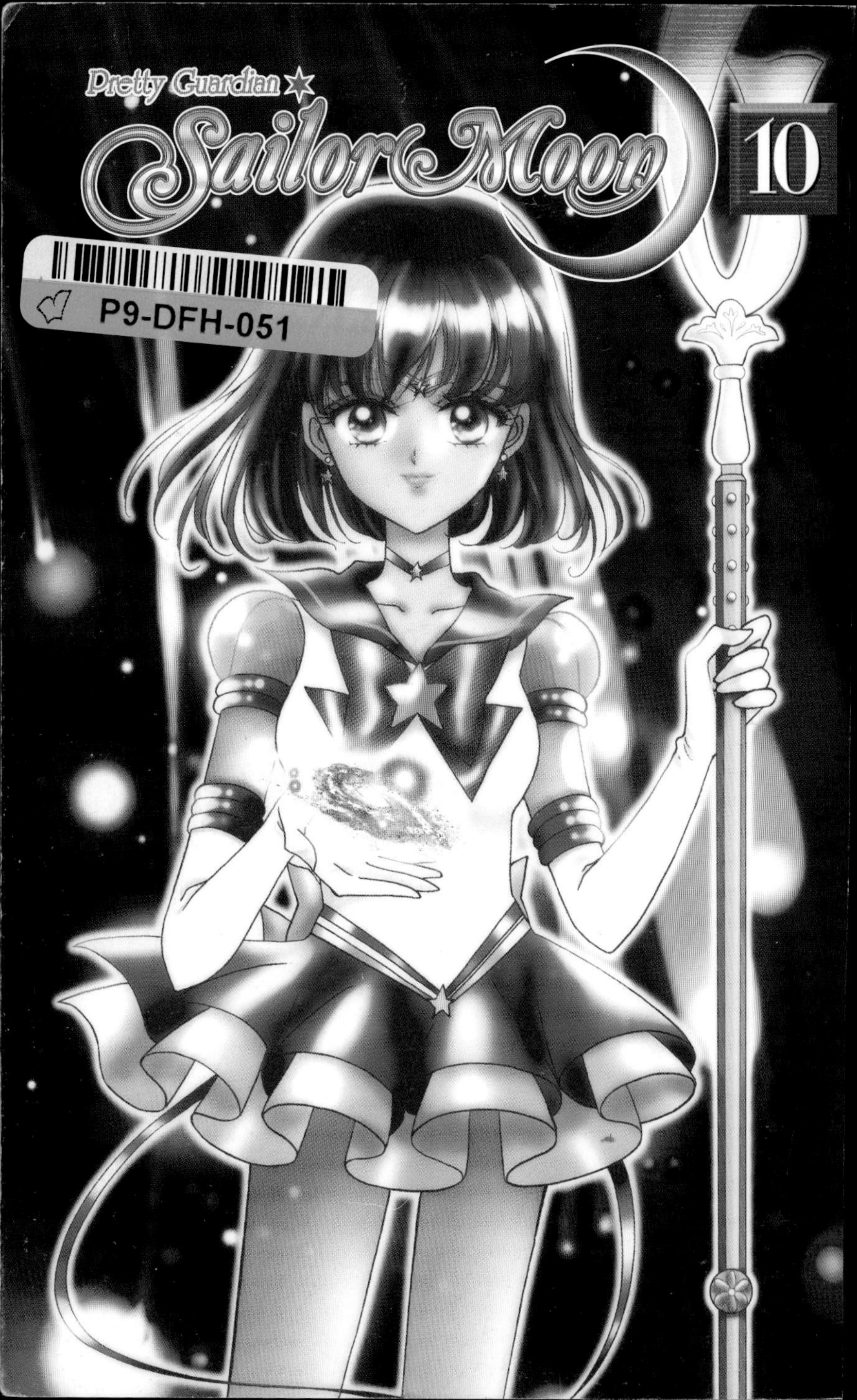
Pretty Guardian
Sailor Moon
10

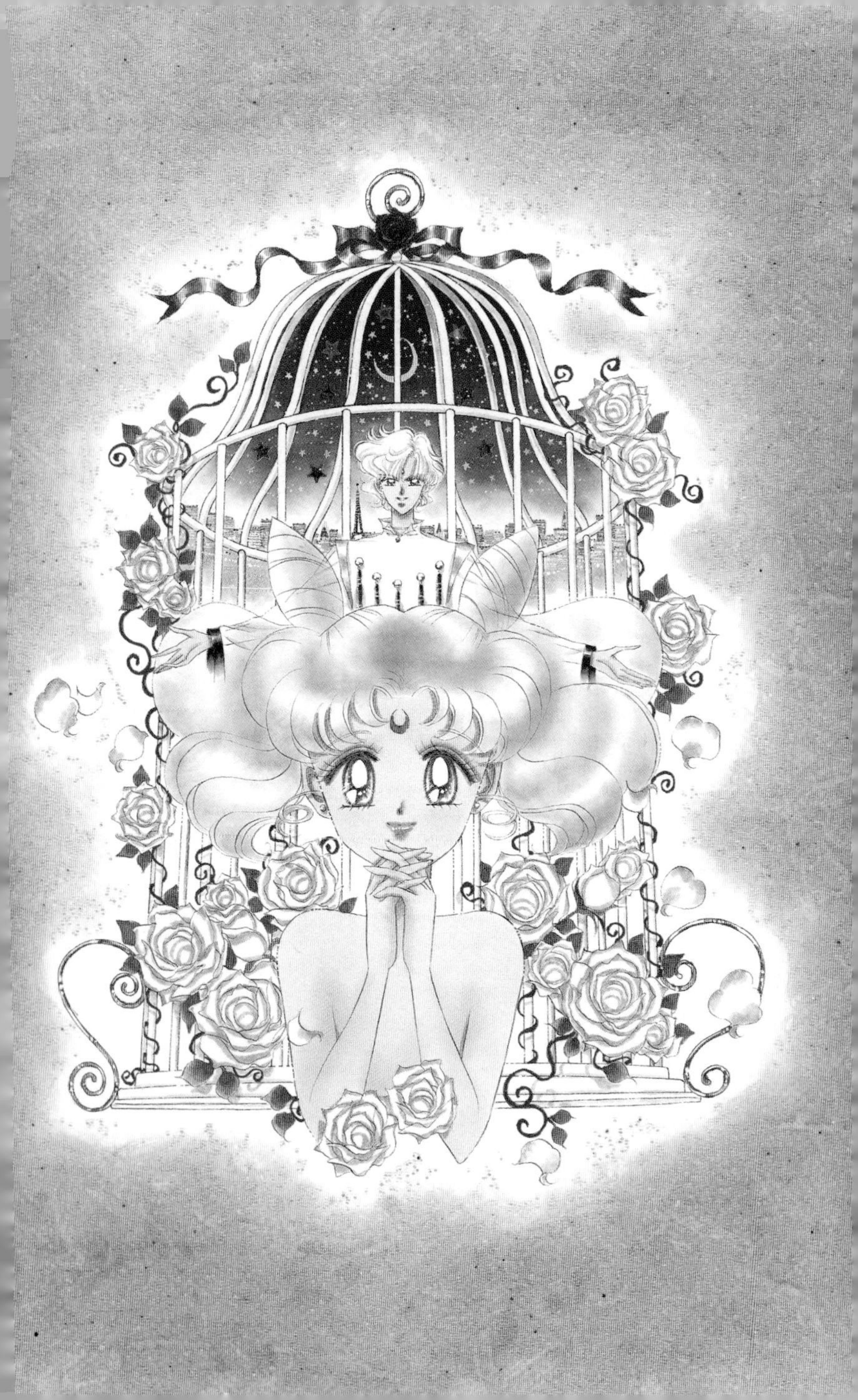

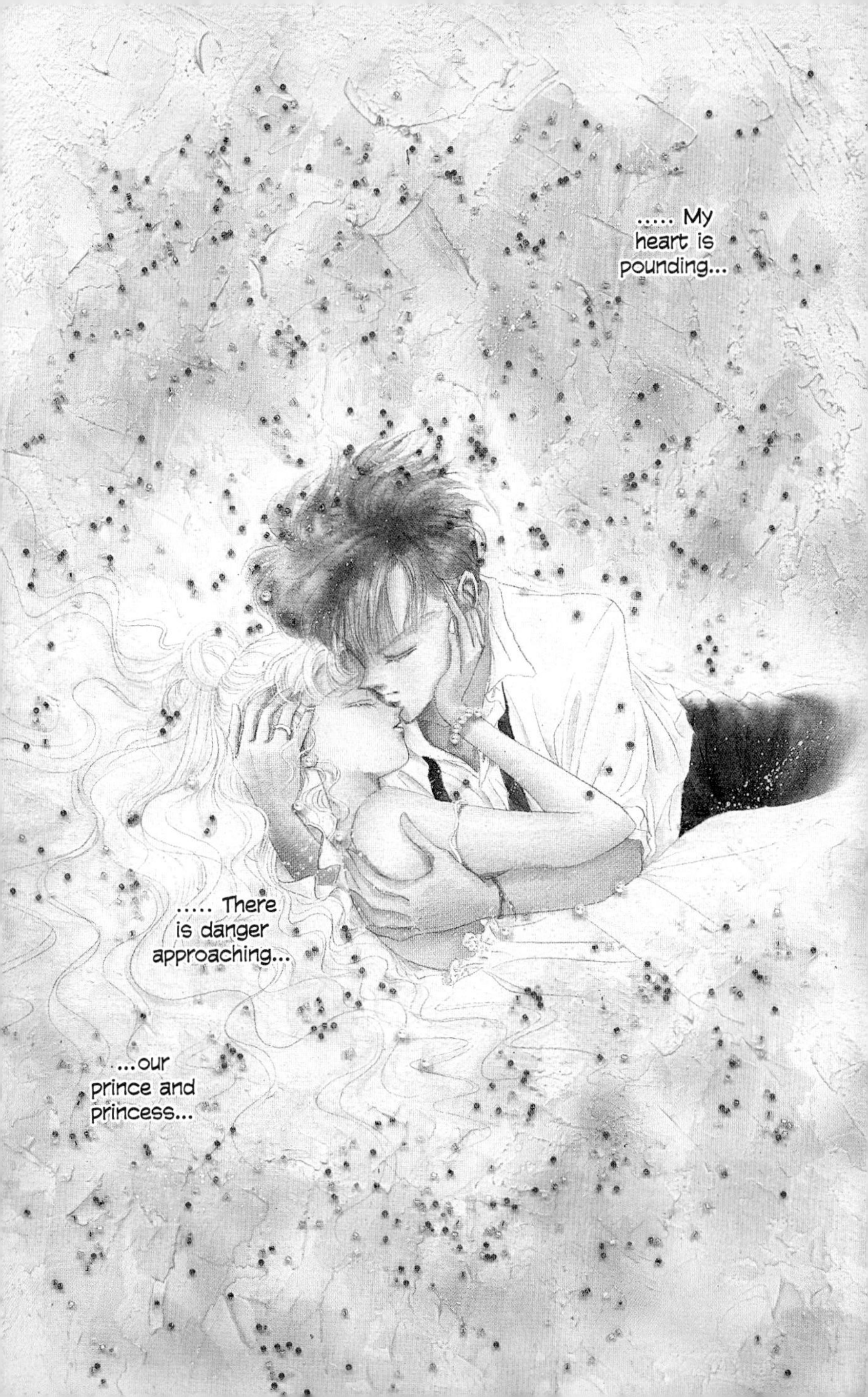

..... My heart is pounding...
..... There is danger approaching...
...our prince and princess...

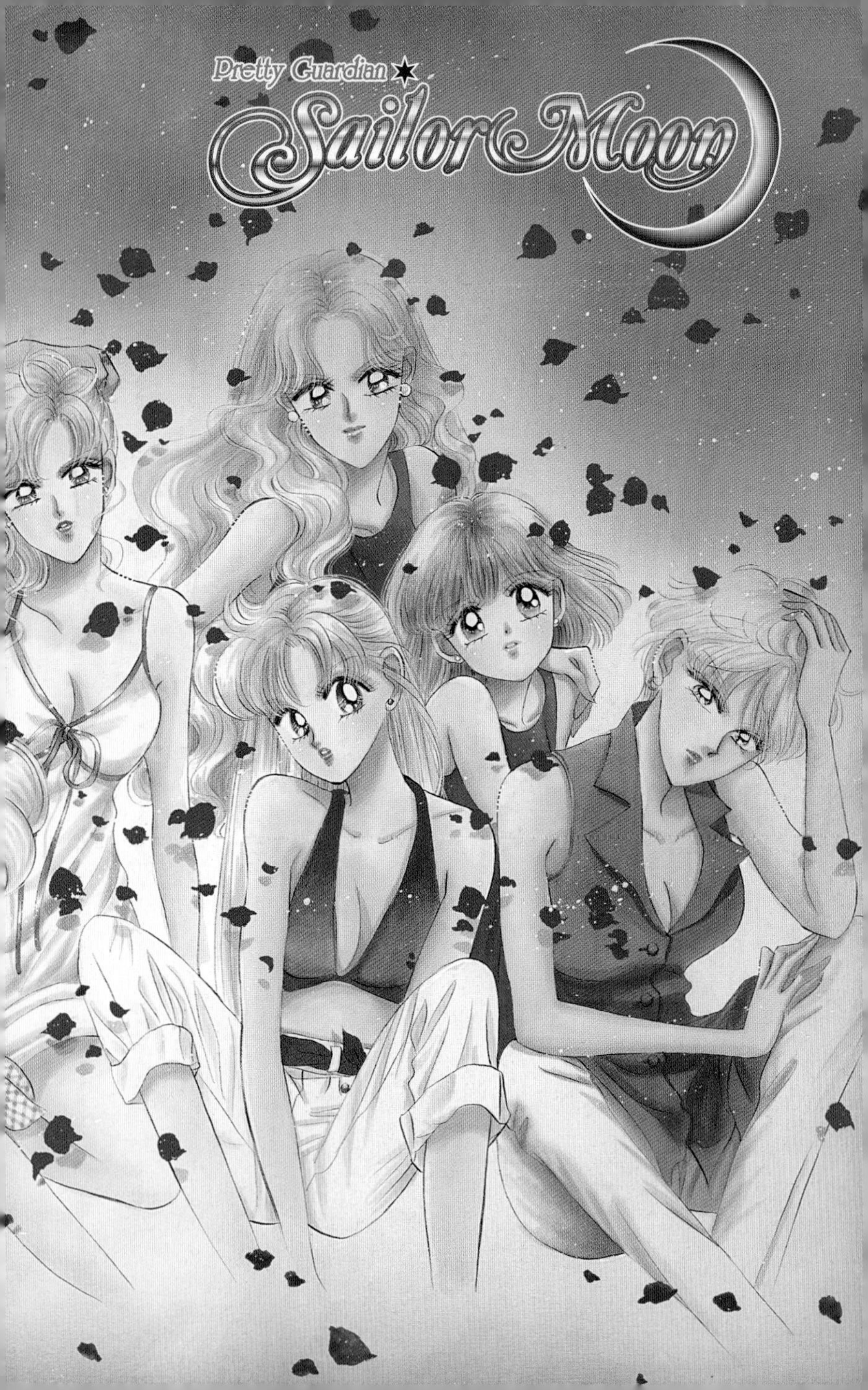
Pretty Guardian
Sailor Moon

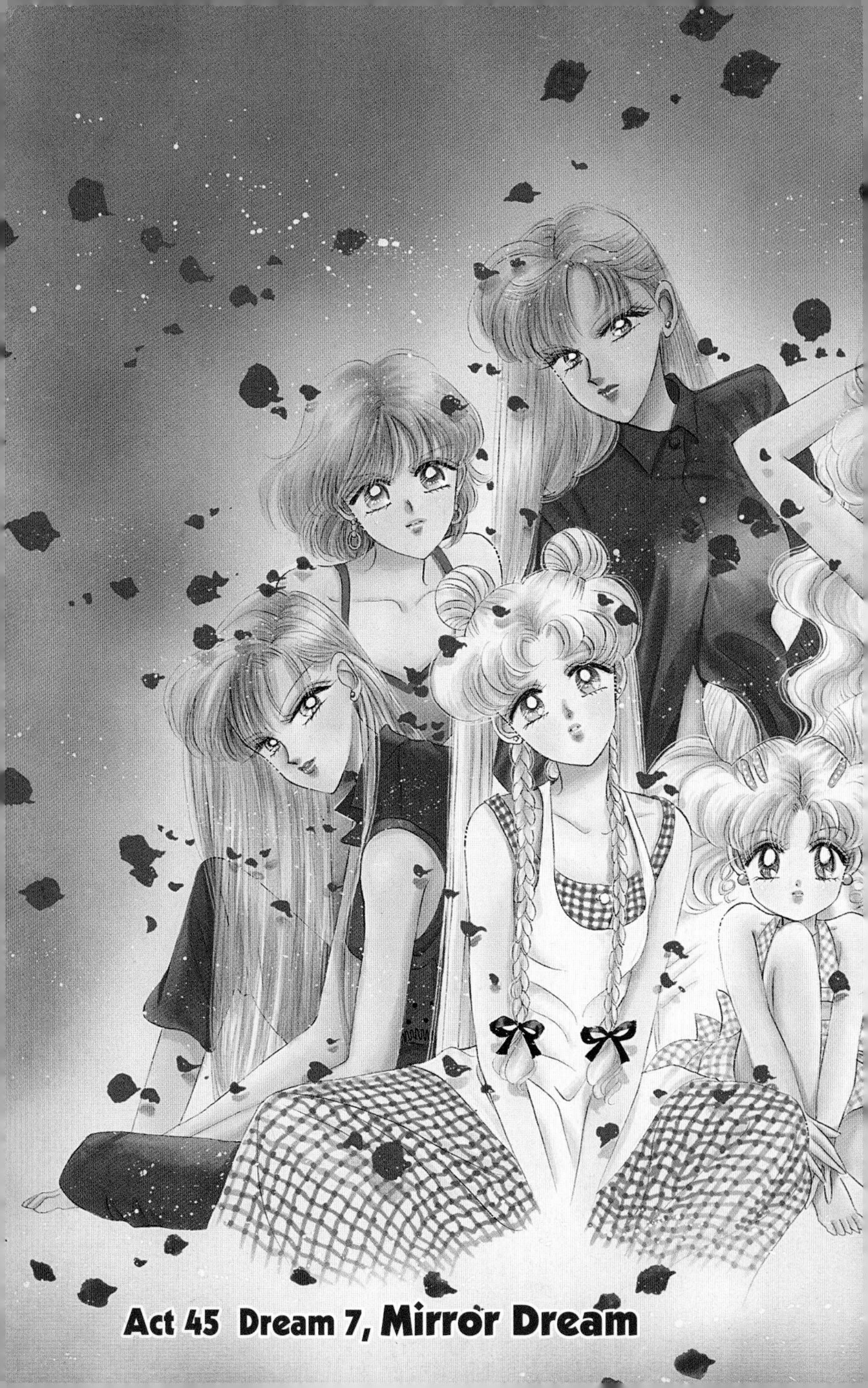

Act 45 Dream 7, Mirror Dream

CONTENTS

Pretty Guardian SAILORMOON

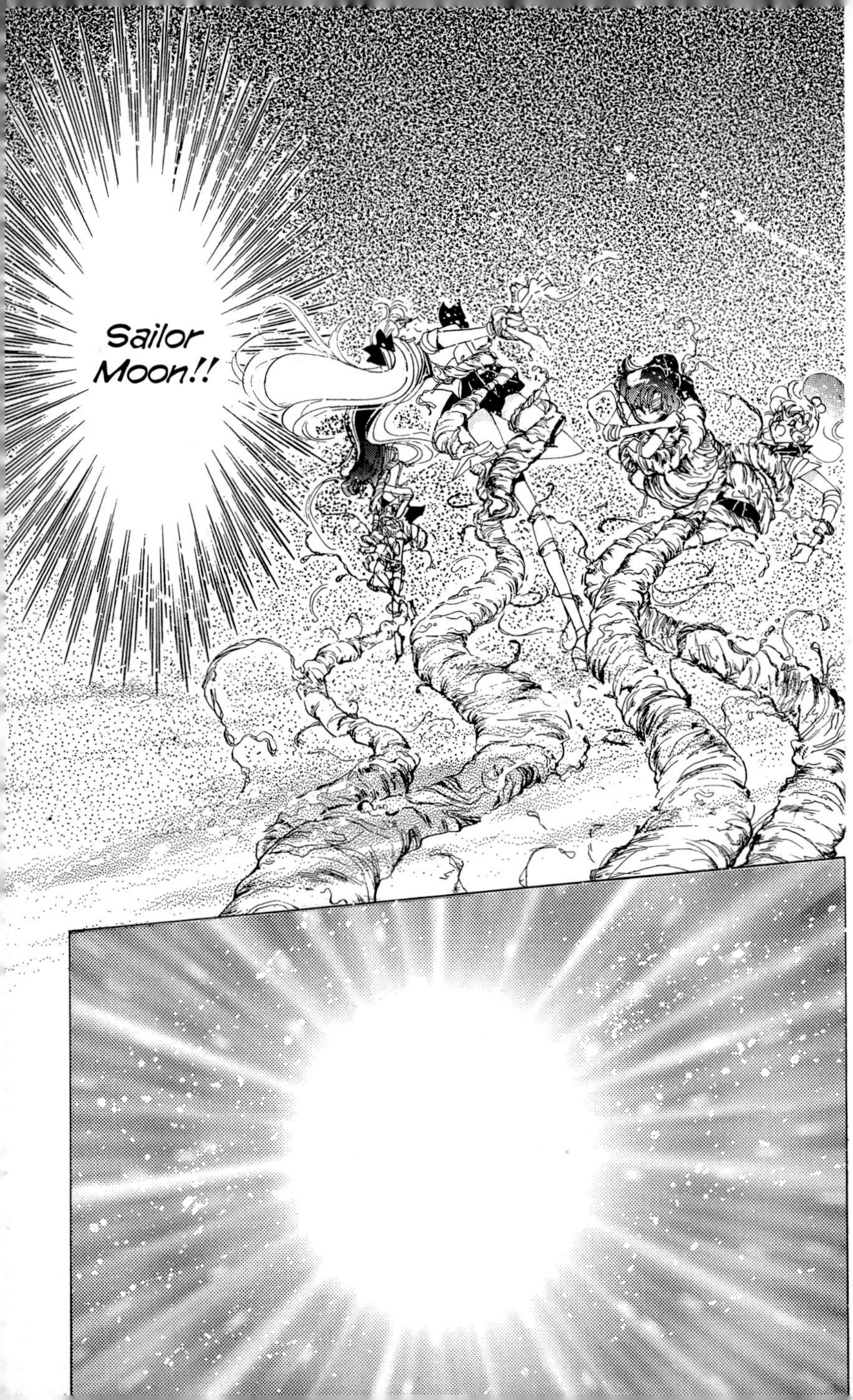
Sailor Moon!!

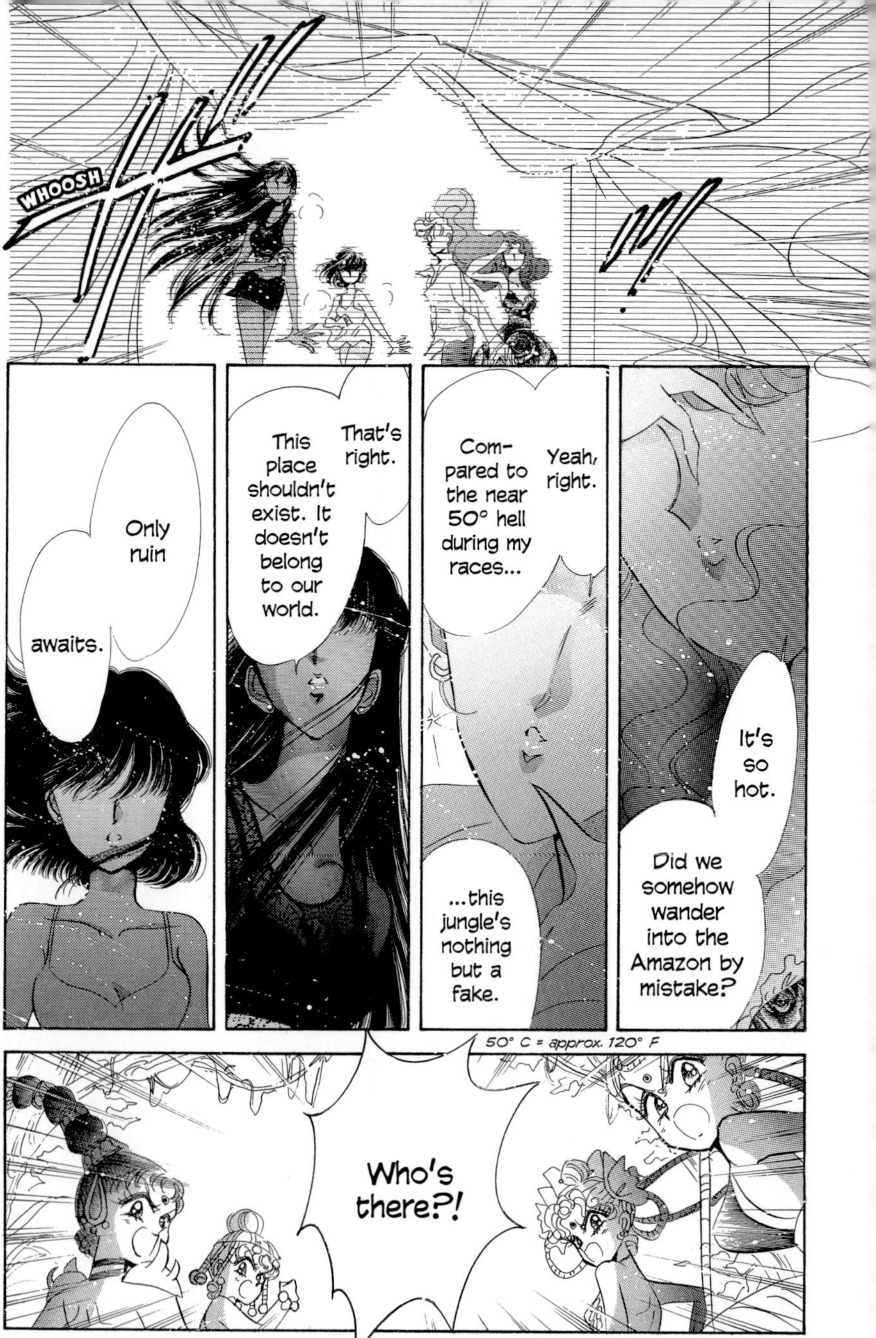
WHOOSH
It's so hot.
Did we somehow wander into the Amazon by mistake?
Yeah, right.
Compared to the near 50° hell during my races...
...this jungle's nothing but a fake.
That's right.
This place shouldn't exist. It doesn't belong to our world.
Only ruin
awaits.
Who's there?!

50° C = approx. 120° F

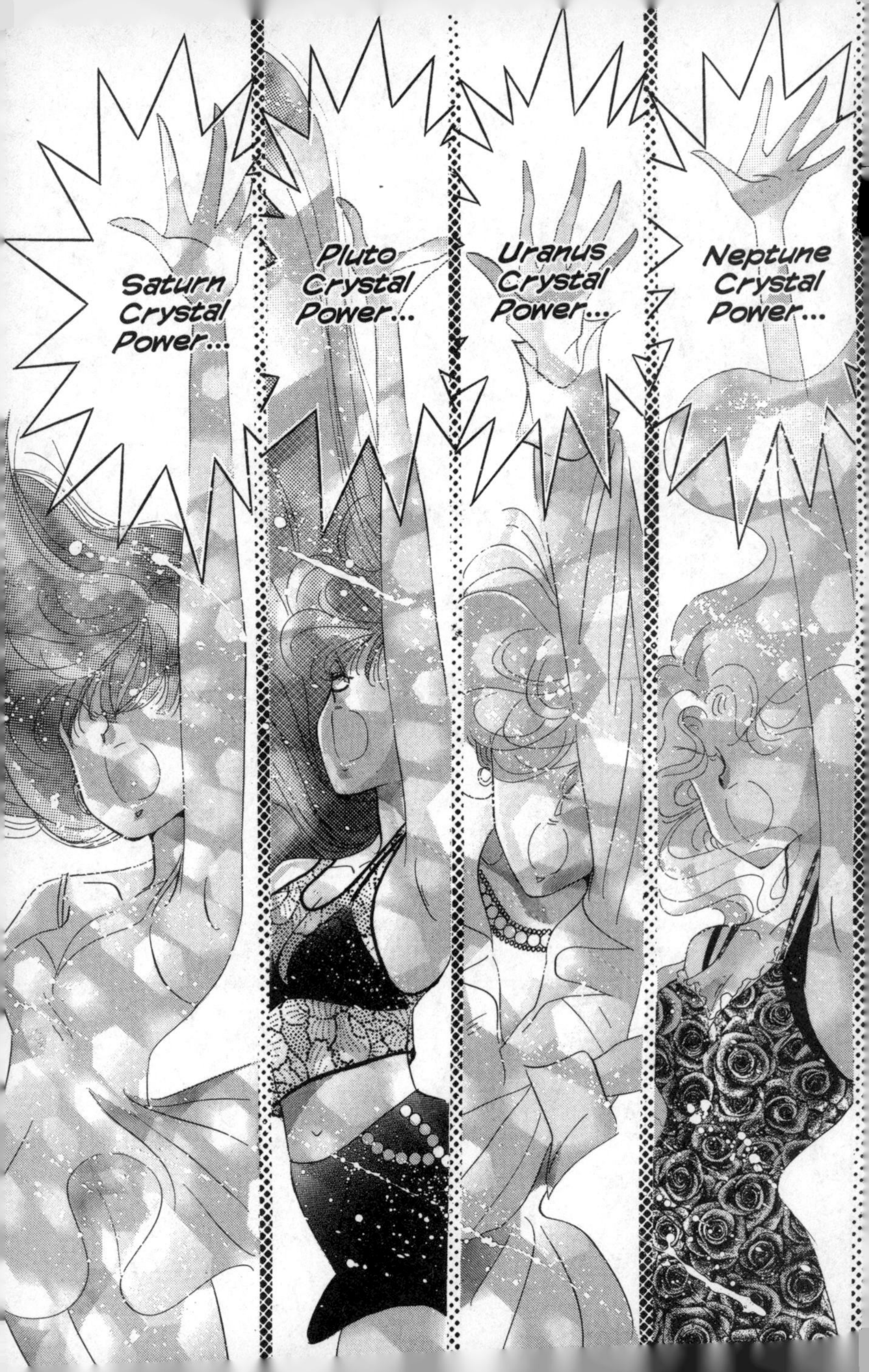
Neptune Crystal Power...
Uranus Crystal Power...
Pluto Crystal Power...
Saturn Crystal Power...

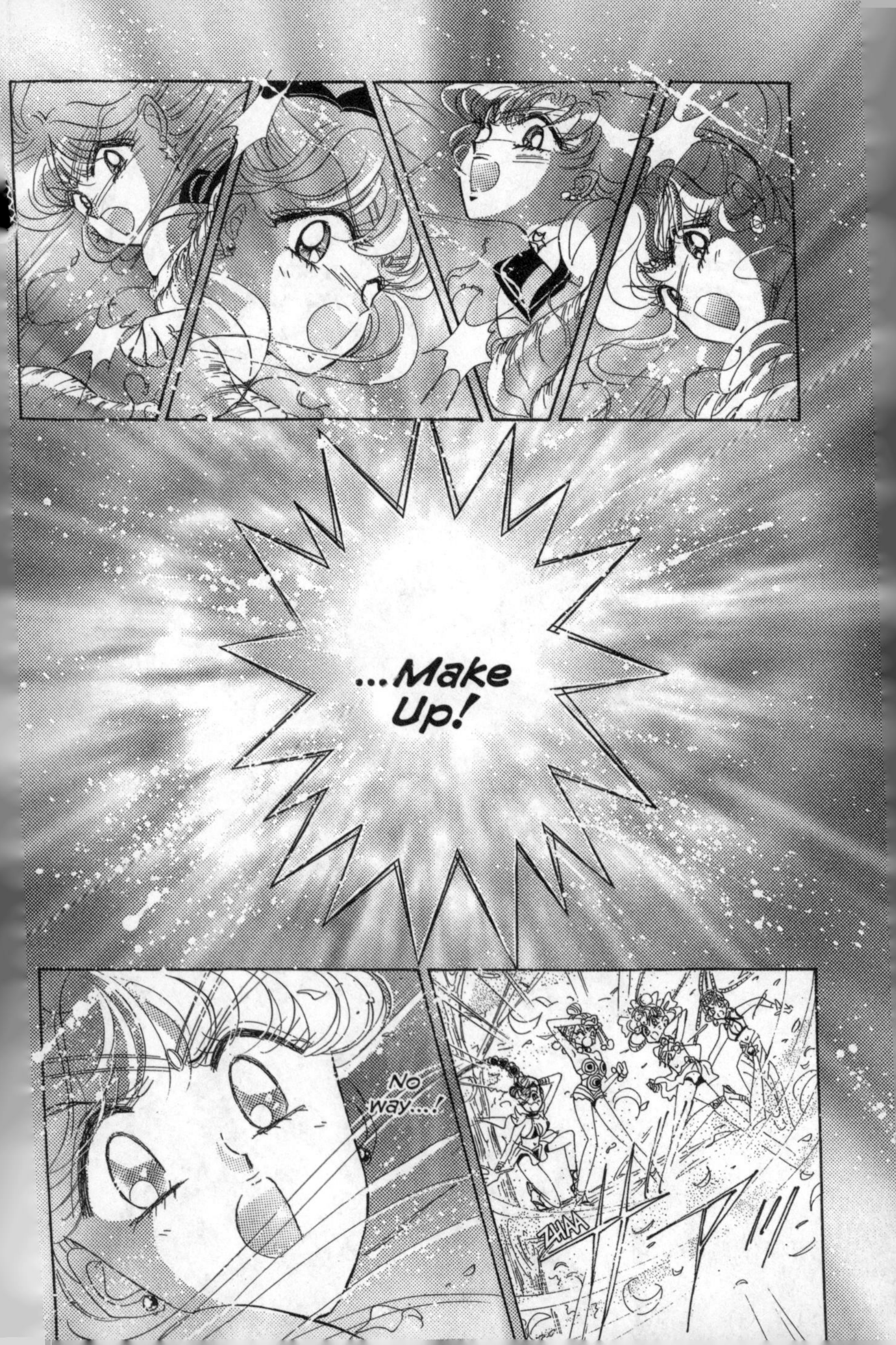
...Make Up!
ZHAA
No way...!

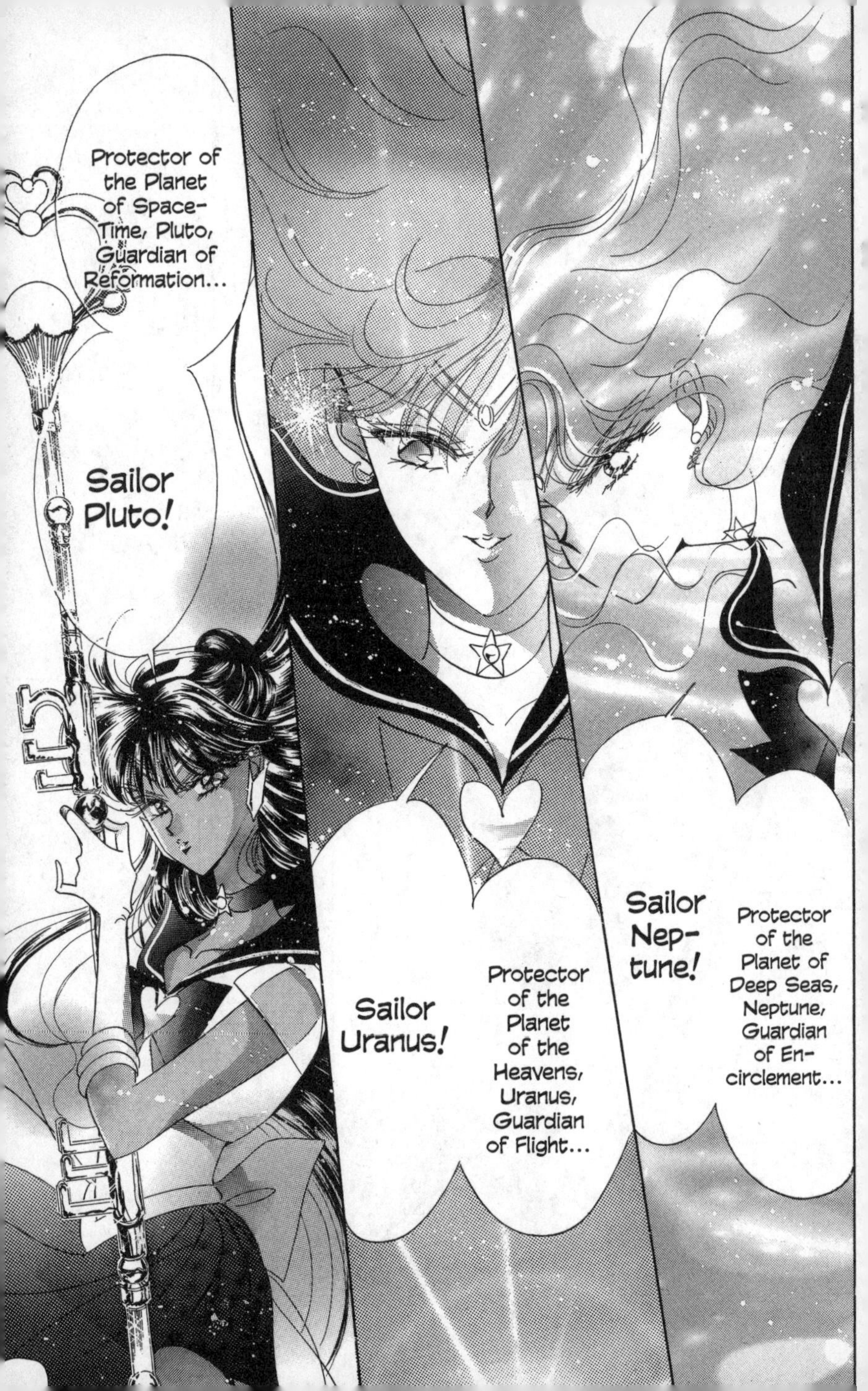
Protector of the Planet of Deep Seas, Neptune, Guardian of En-circlement...
Sailor Nep-tune!
Protector of the Planet of the Heavens, Uranus, Guardian of Flight...
Sailor Uranus!
Protector of the Planet of Space-Time, Pluto, Guardian of Reformation...
Sailor Pluto!

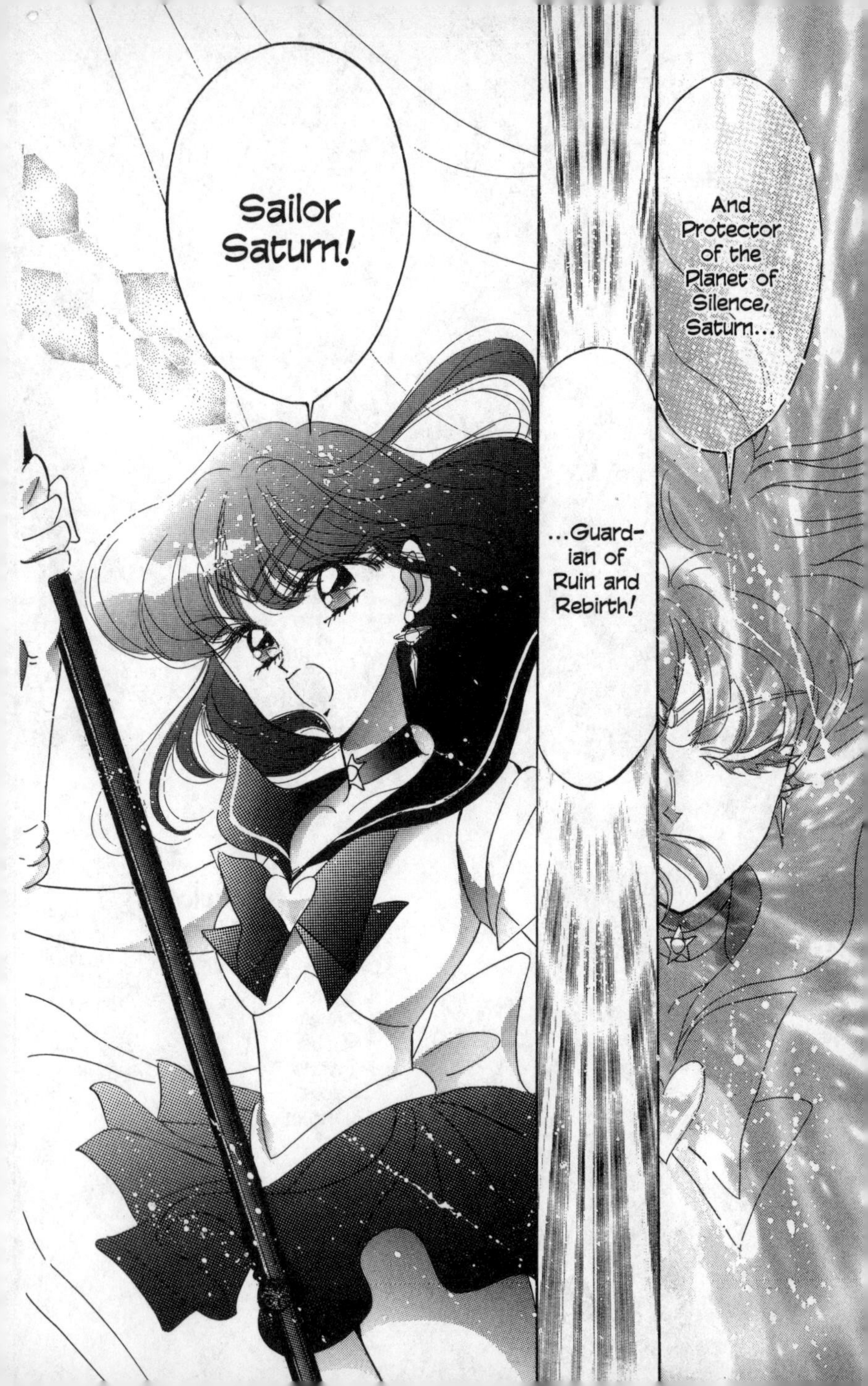
And Protector of the Planet of Silence, Saturn...
...Guard-ian of Ruin and Rebirth!
Sailor Saturn!

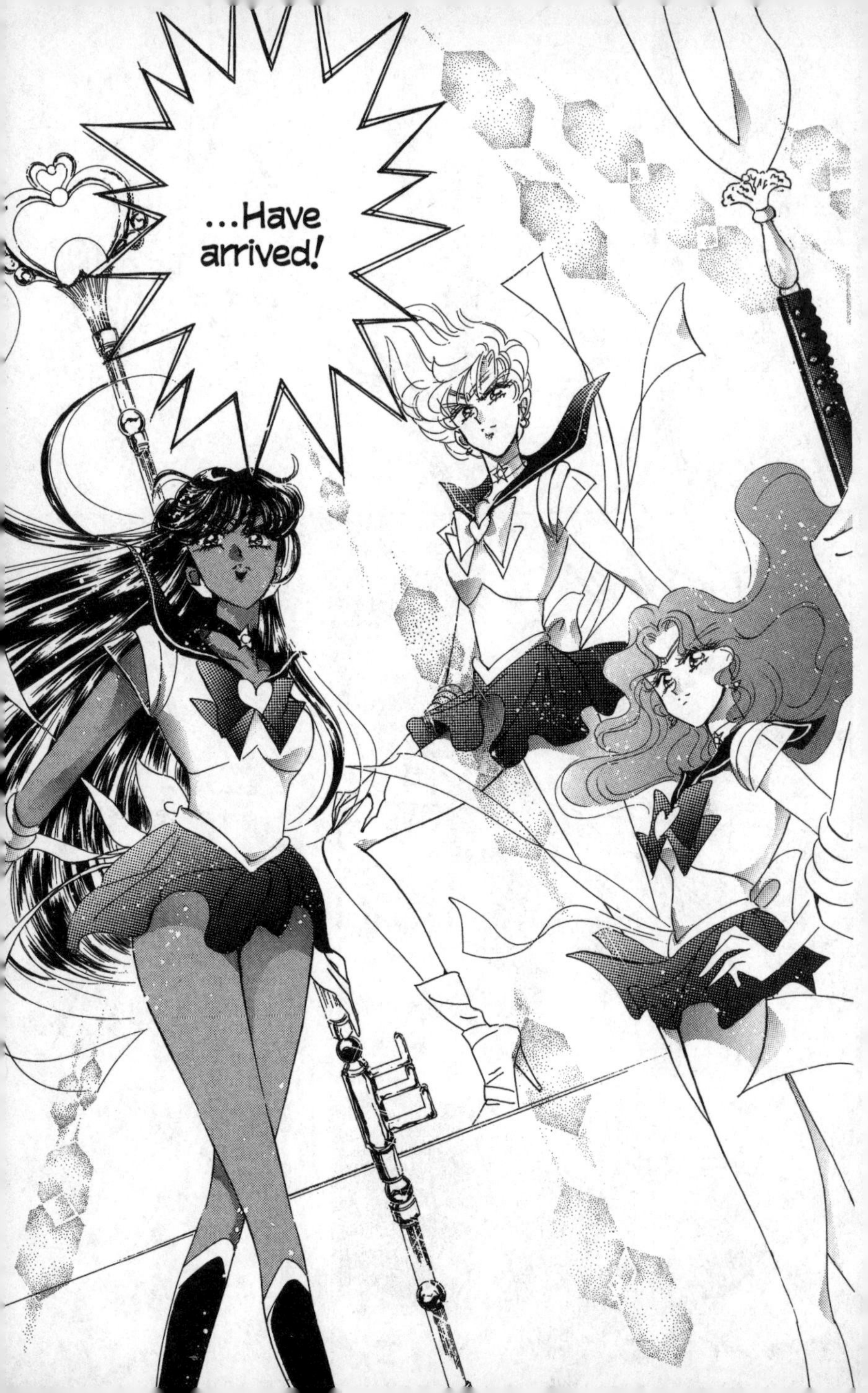
...Have arrived!

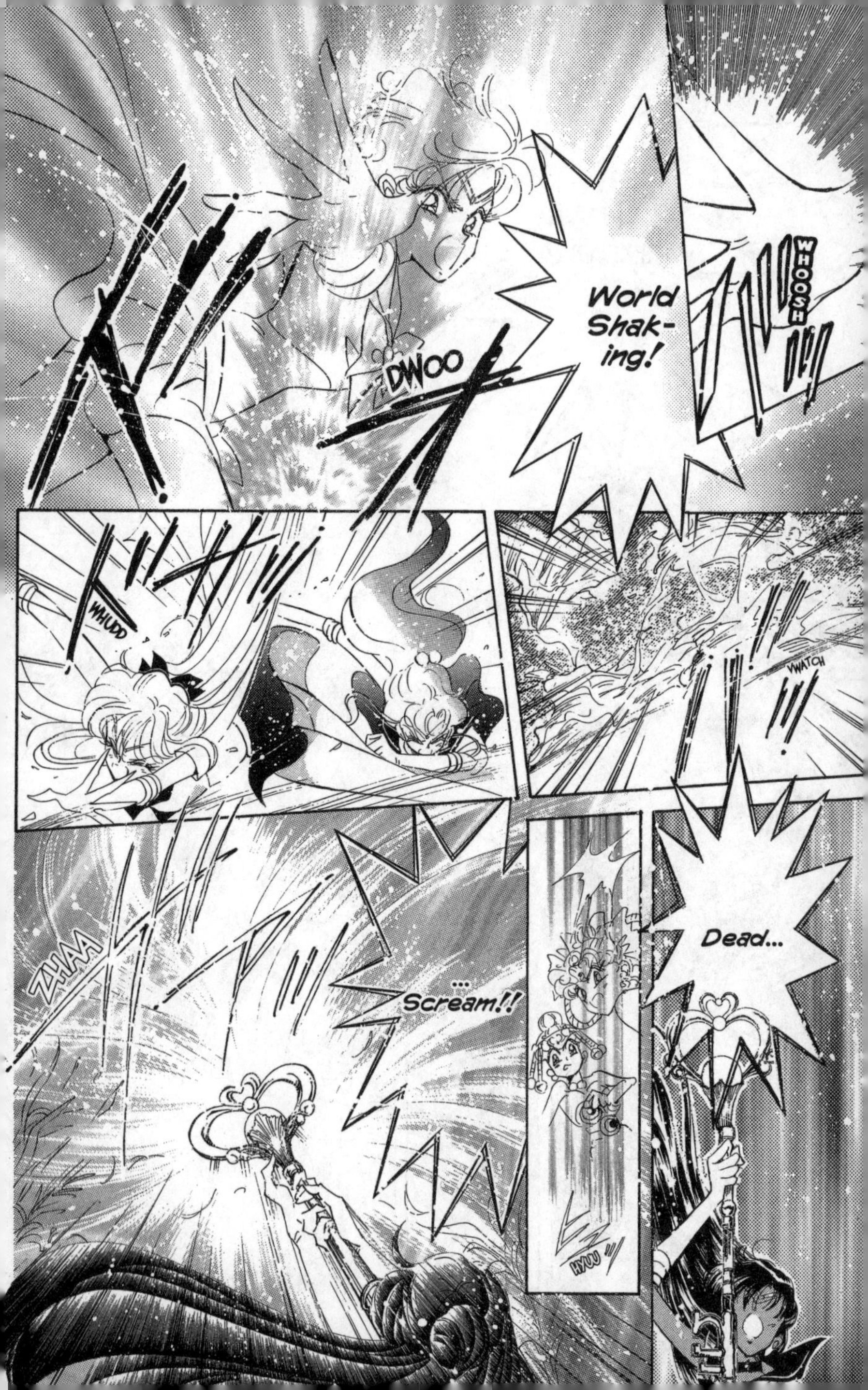
WHOOSH
World Shak-ing!
DWOO
VWATCH
WHUDD
Dead...
HYUU
...
Scream!!
ZHAA

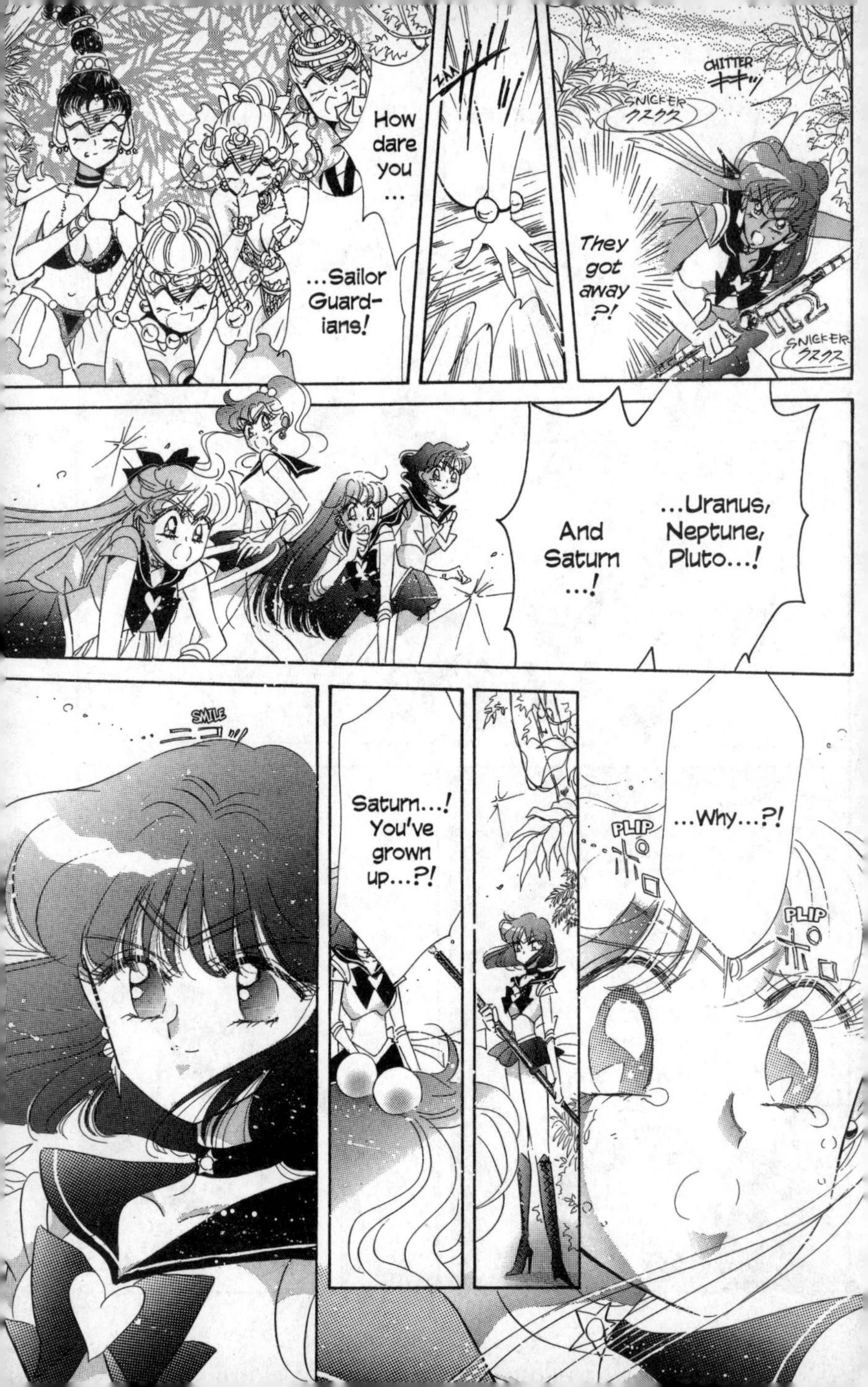
CHITTER
キキッ
SNICKER
クスクス
They got away?!
SNICKER
クスクス
How dare you ...
...Sailor Guard- ians!
...Uranus, Neptune, Pluto...!
And Saturn ...!
...Why...?!
PLIP
ポロ
PLIP
ポロ
Saturn...! You've grown up...?!
SMILE
ニコッ

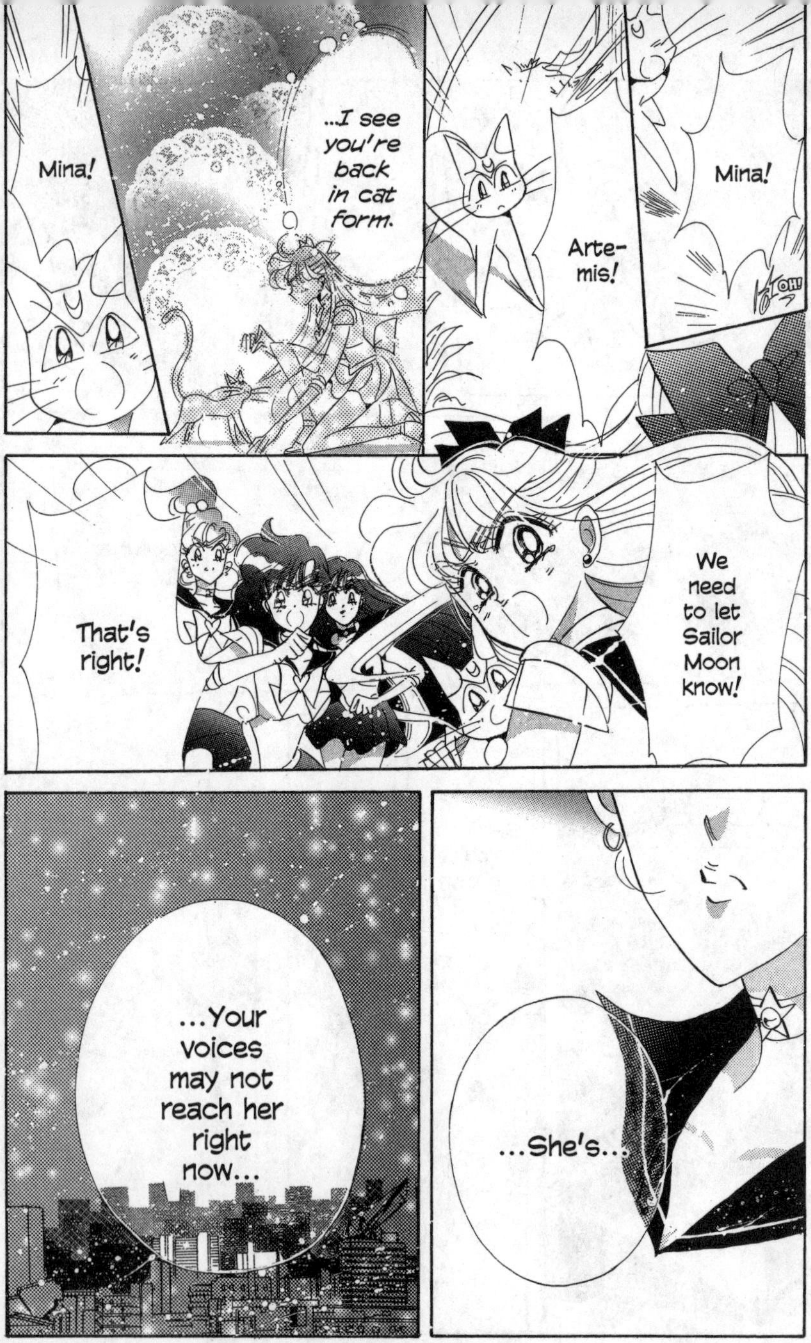
Mina!
OH!
Arte-mis!
...I see you're back in cat form.
Mina!
We need to let Sailor Moon know!
That's right!
...She's...
...Your voices may not reach her right now...

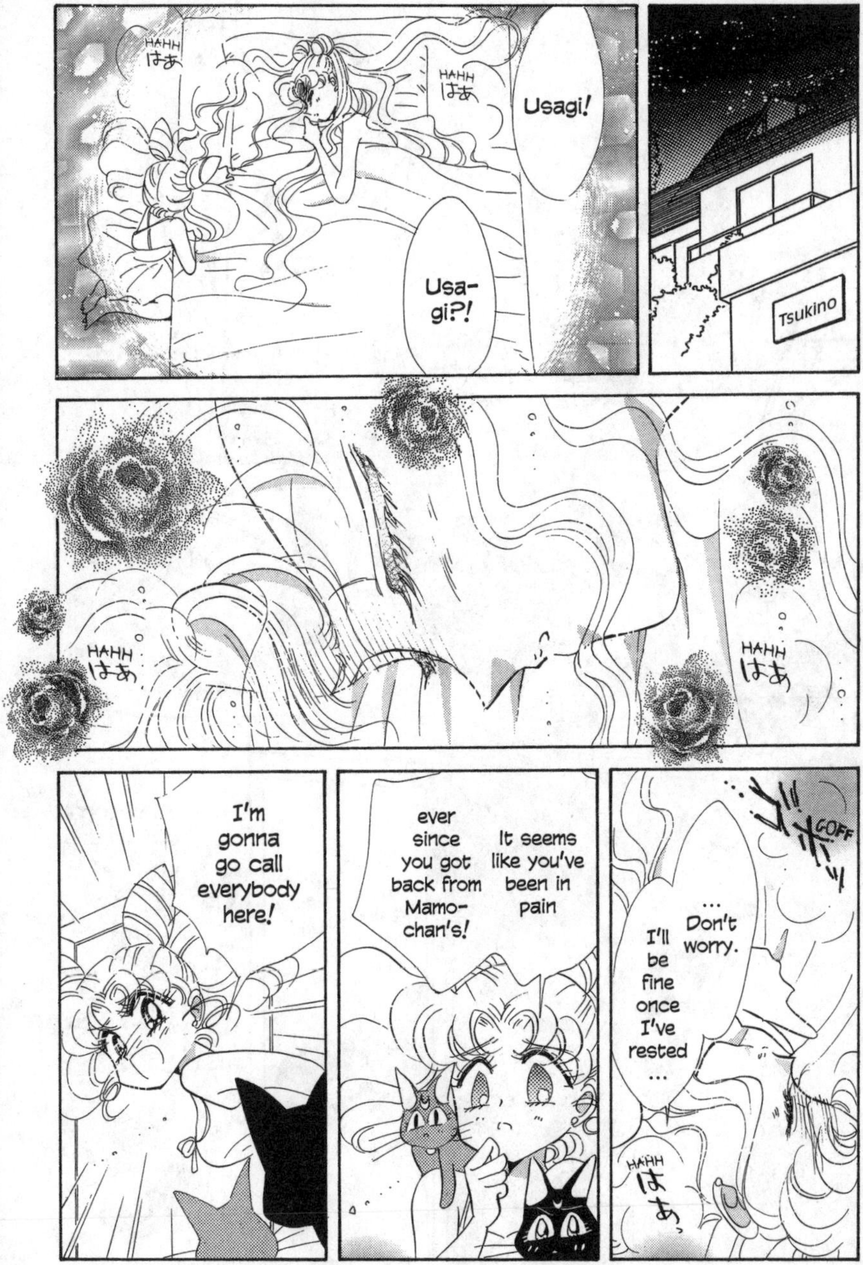
Tsukino
Usagi!
HAHH
はあ
Usa-gi?!
HAHH
はあ
HAHH
はあ
HAHH
はあ
GOFF
ゴホッ
... Don't worry.
I'll be fine once I've rested ...
HAHH
はあっ
It seems like you've been in pain
ever since you got back from Mamo-chan's!
I'm gonna go call everybody here!

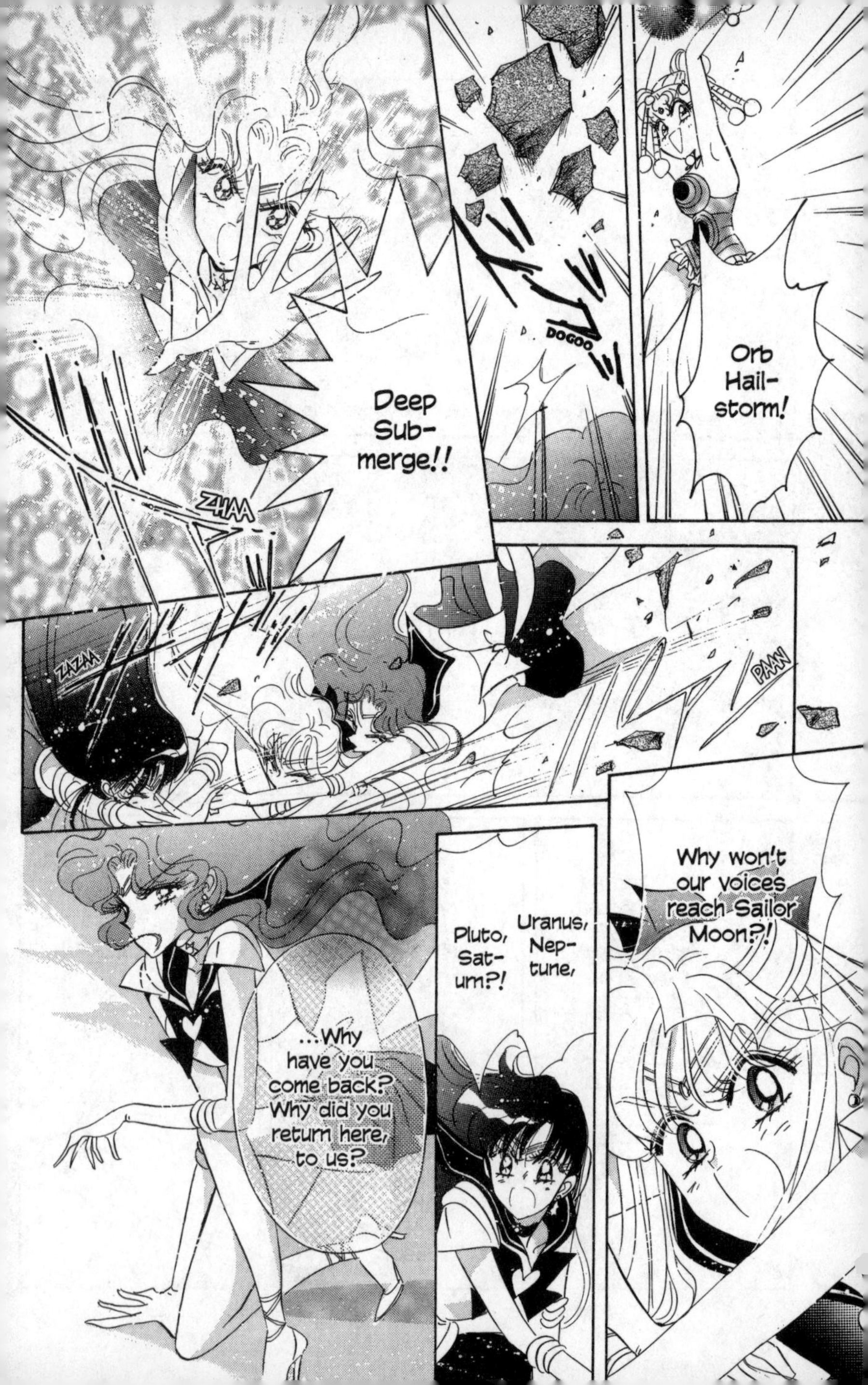
Orb Hail-storm!
DOGOO
Deep Sub-merge!!
ZHAA
PAAN
ZAZAA
Why won't our voices reach Sailor Moon?!
Uranus, Nep-tune,
Pluto, Sat-urn?!
...Why have you come back? Why did you return here, to us?

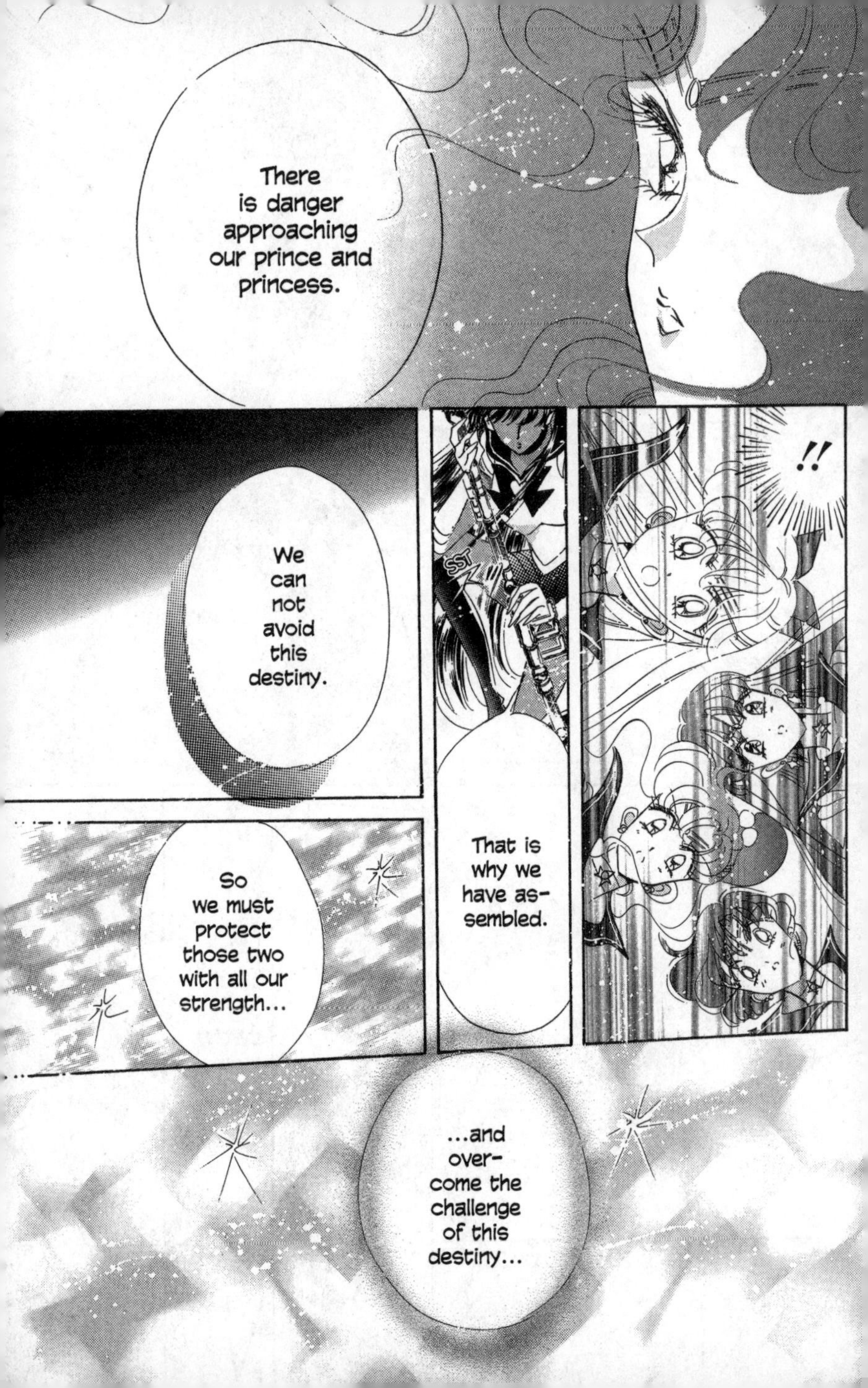
There is danger approaching our prince and princess.
!!
SST
That is why we have as-sembled.
We can not avoid this destiny.
So we must protect those two with all our strength...
...and over-come the challenge of this destiny...

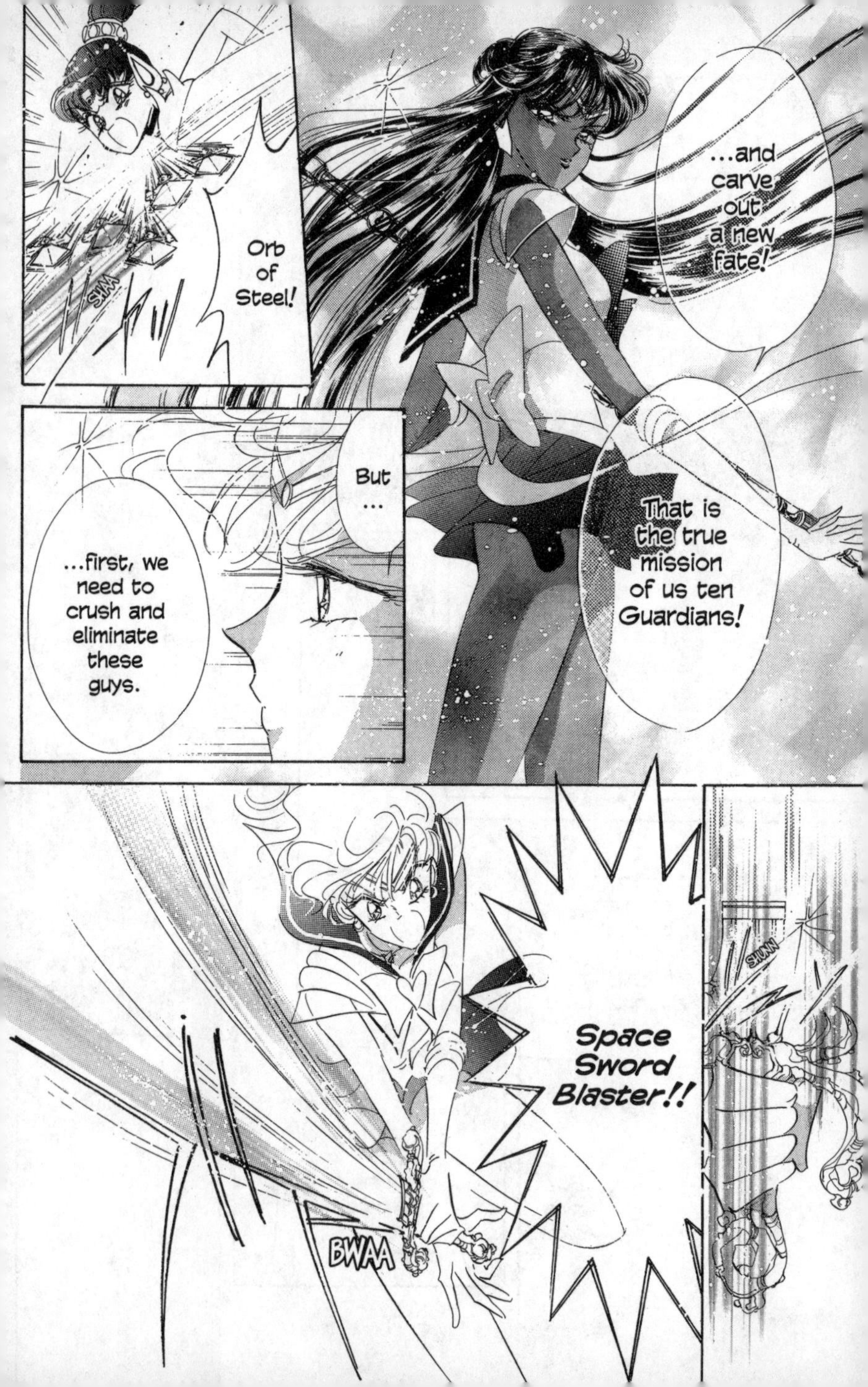
...and carve out a new fate!
That is the true mission of us ten Guardians!
Orb of Steel!
But ...
...first, we need to crush and eliminate these guys.
SHUNN
Space Sword Blaster!!
BWAA

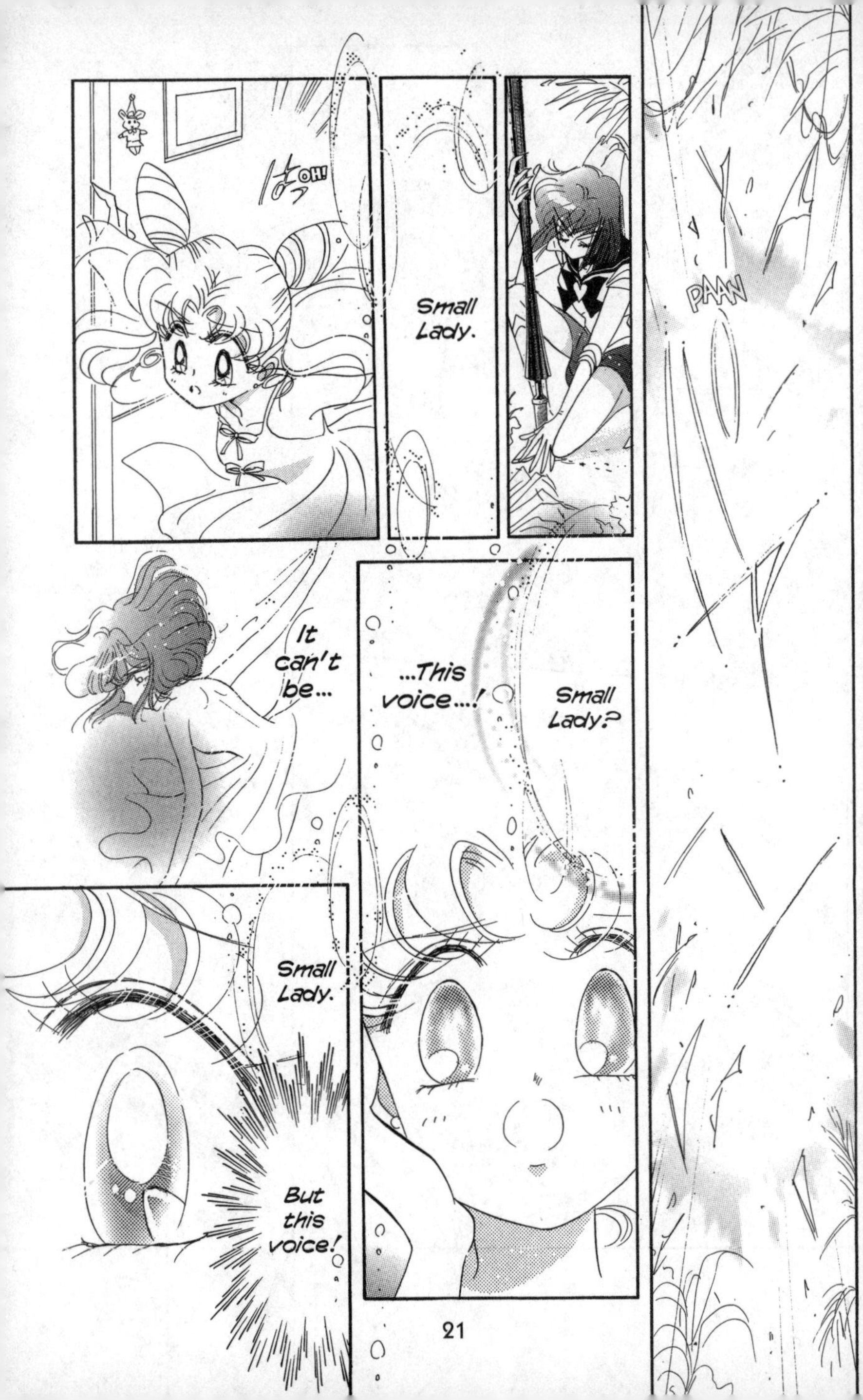
PAAN
Small Lady.
はっ OH!
Small Lady?
...This voice...!
It can't be...
Small Lady.
But this voice!

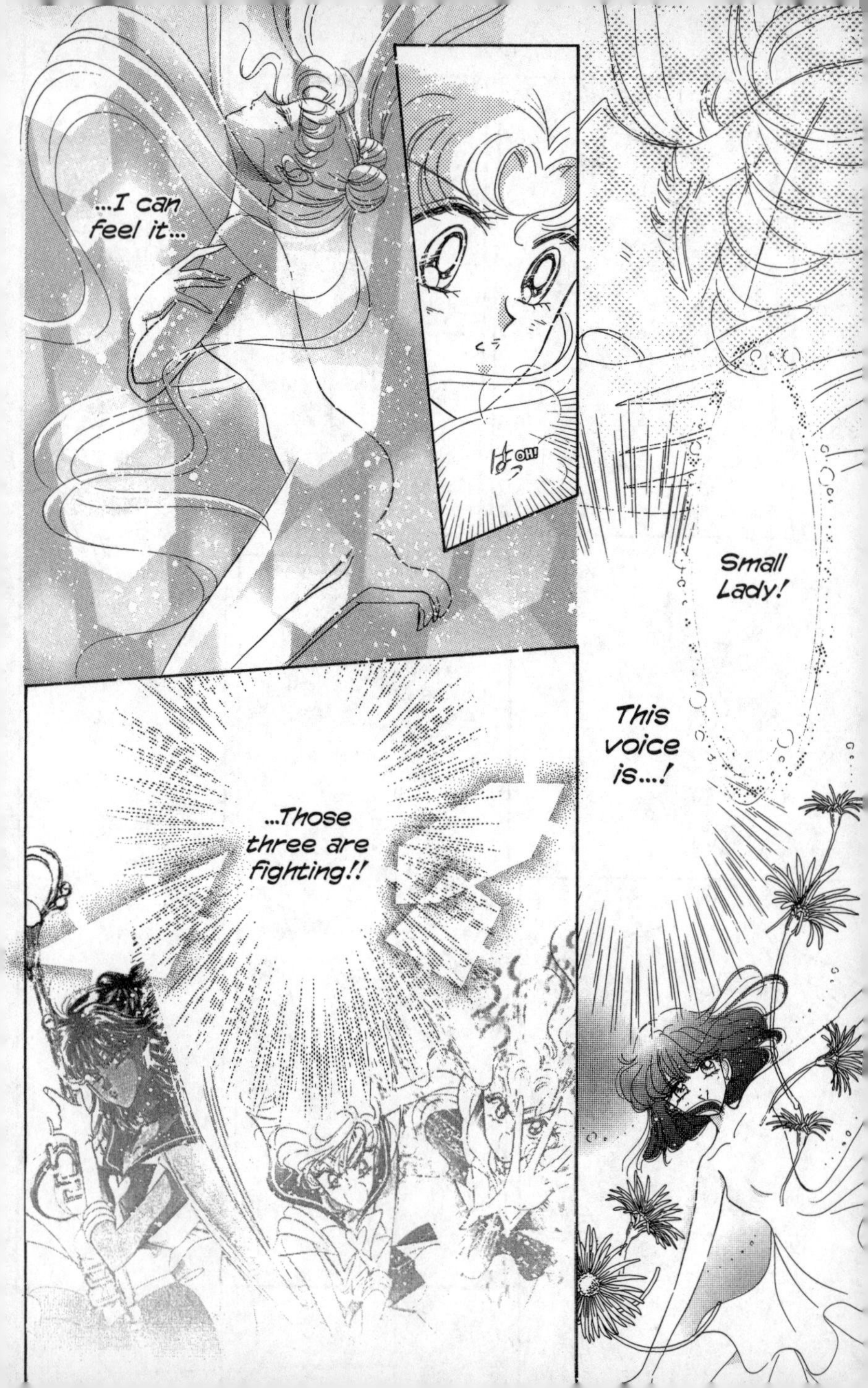
Small Lady!
This voice is...!
はっ OH!
...I can feel it...
...Those three are fighting!!

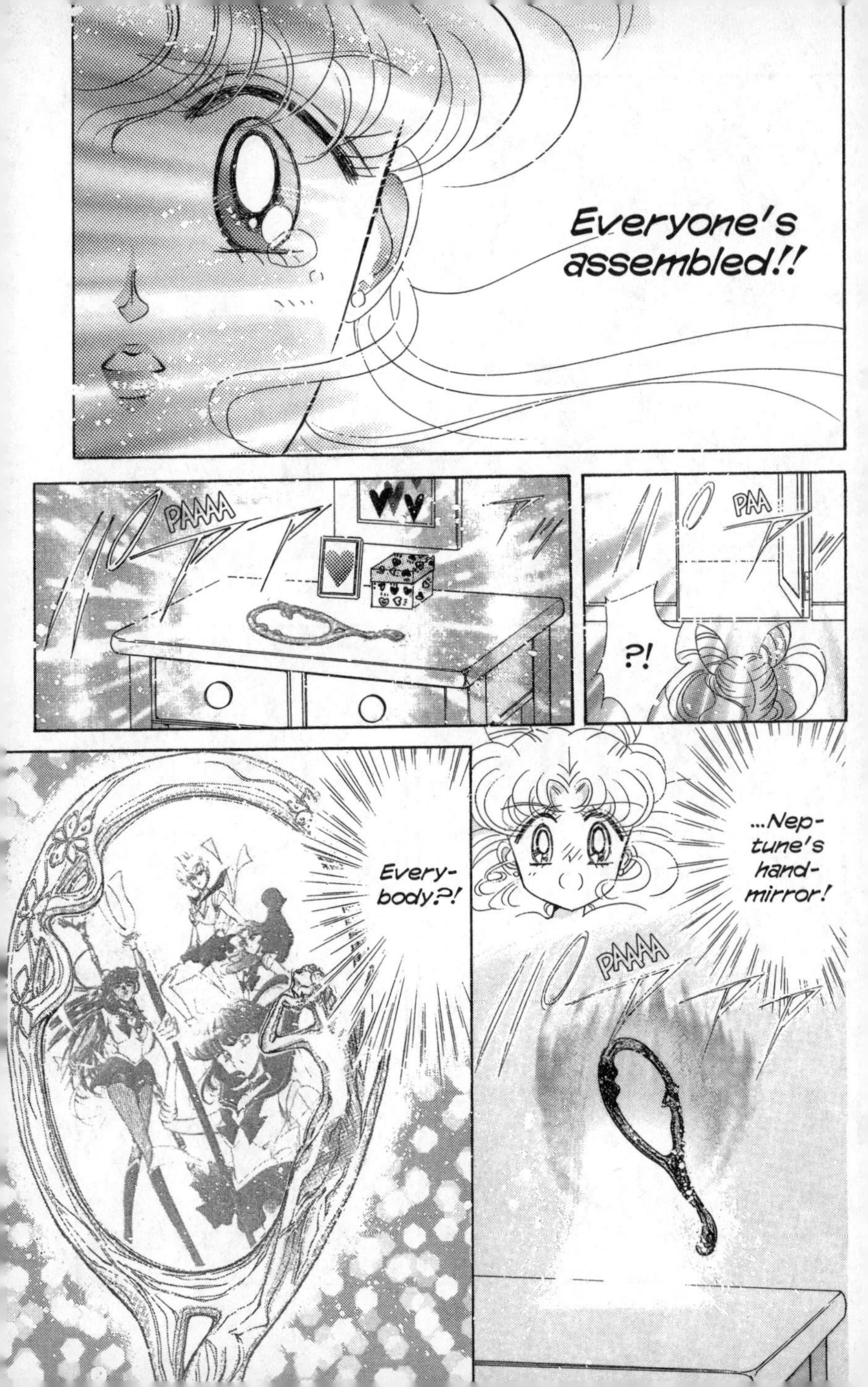

Everyone's assembled!!
PAA
?!
PAAAA
...Nep-tune's hand-mirror!
PAAAA
Every-body?!

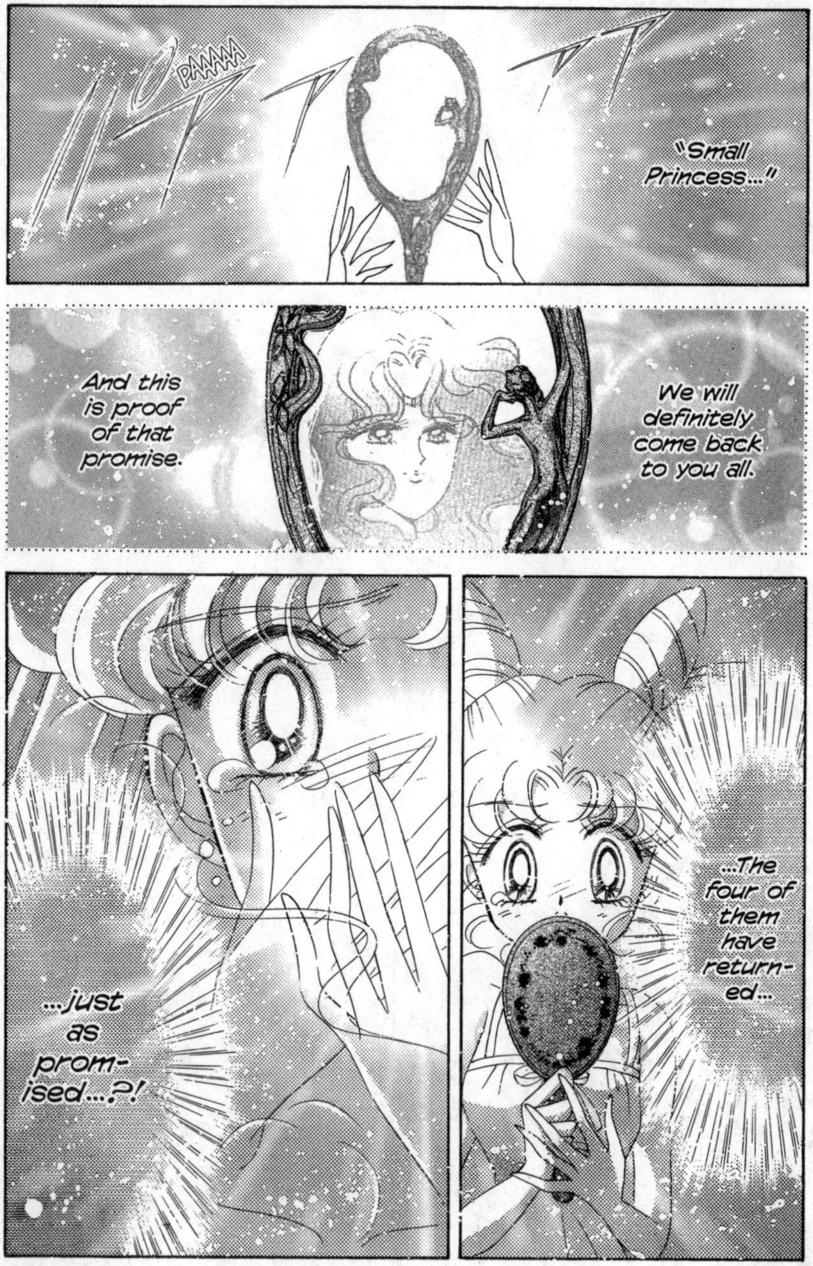
PAAAAA
"Small Princess..."
We will definitely come back to you all.
And this is proof of that promise.
...The four of them have returned...
...just as promised...?!

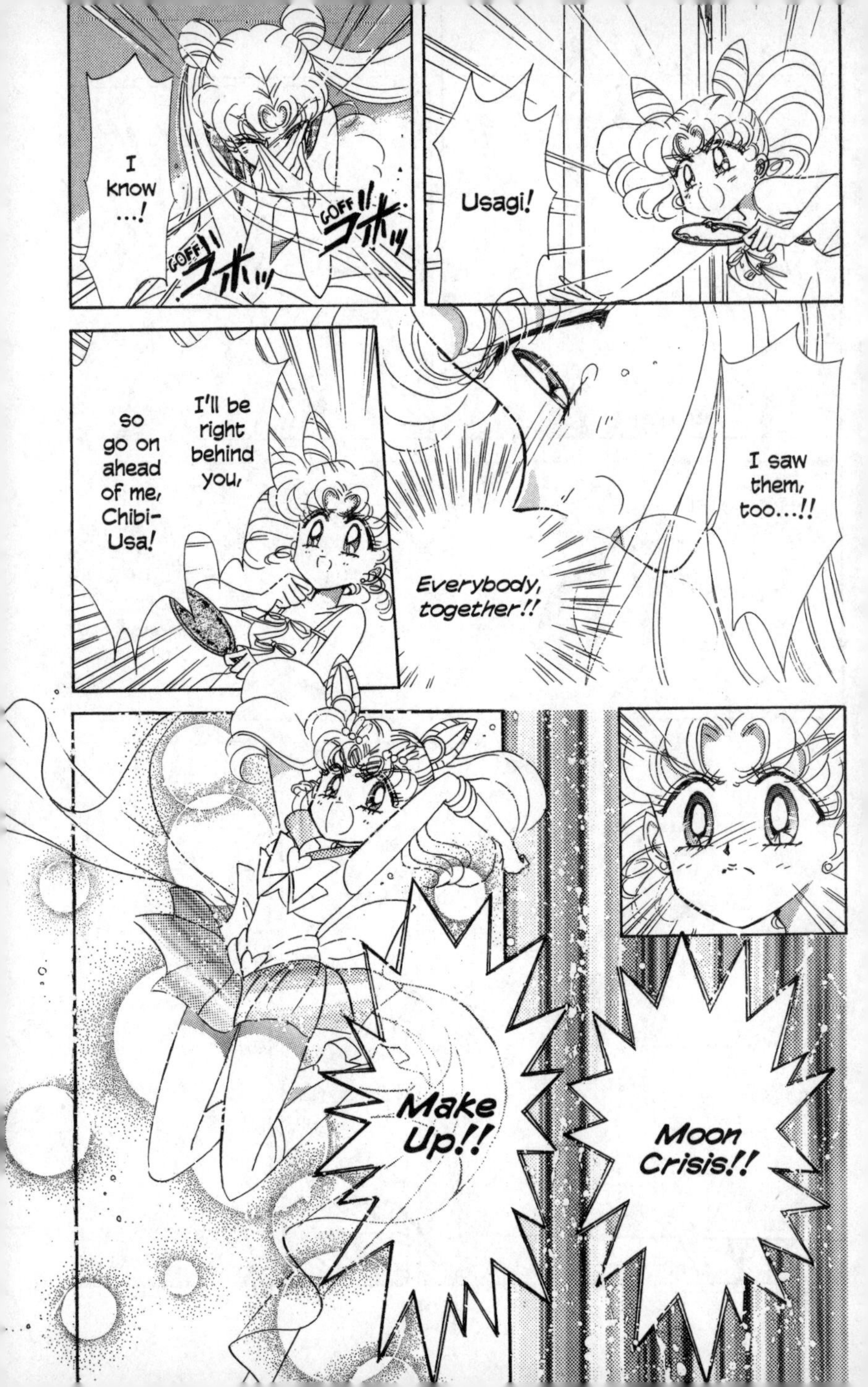
Usagi!
I know ...!
GOFF コホッ
GOFF コホッ
I saw them, too...!!
Everybody, together!!
I'll be right behind you,
so go on ahead of me, Chibi-Usa!
Moon Crisis!!
Make Up!!

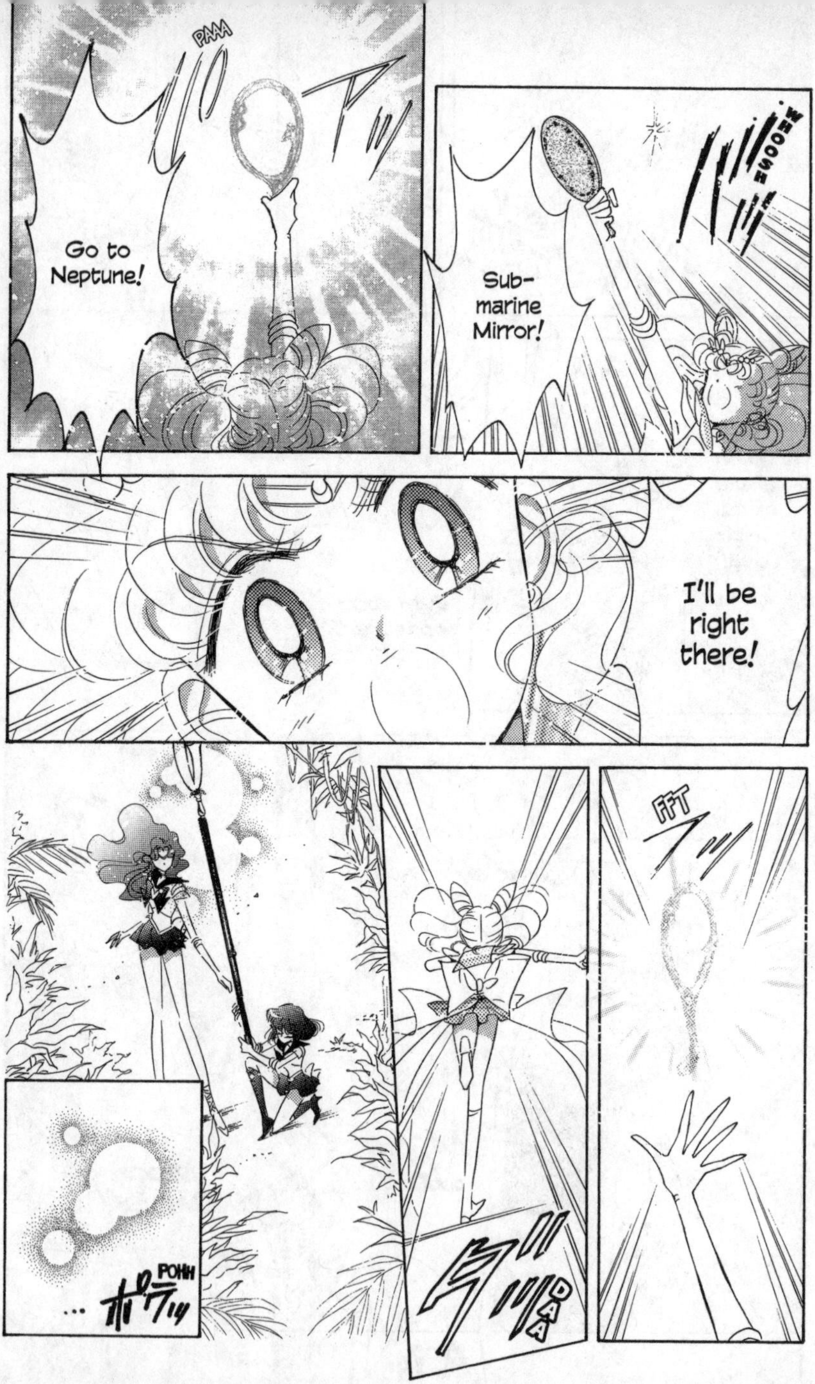
WHOOSH
Sub-marine Mirror!
PAAA
Go to Neptune!
I'll be right there!
FFT
DAA
POHH
...

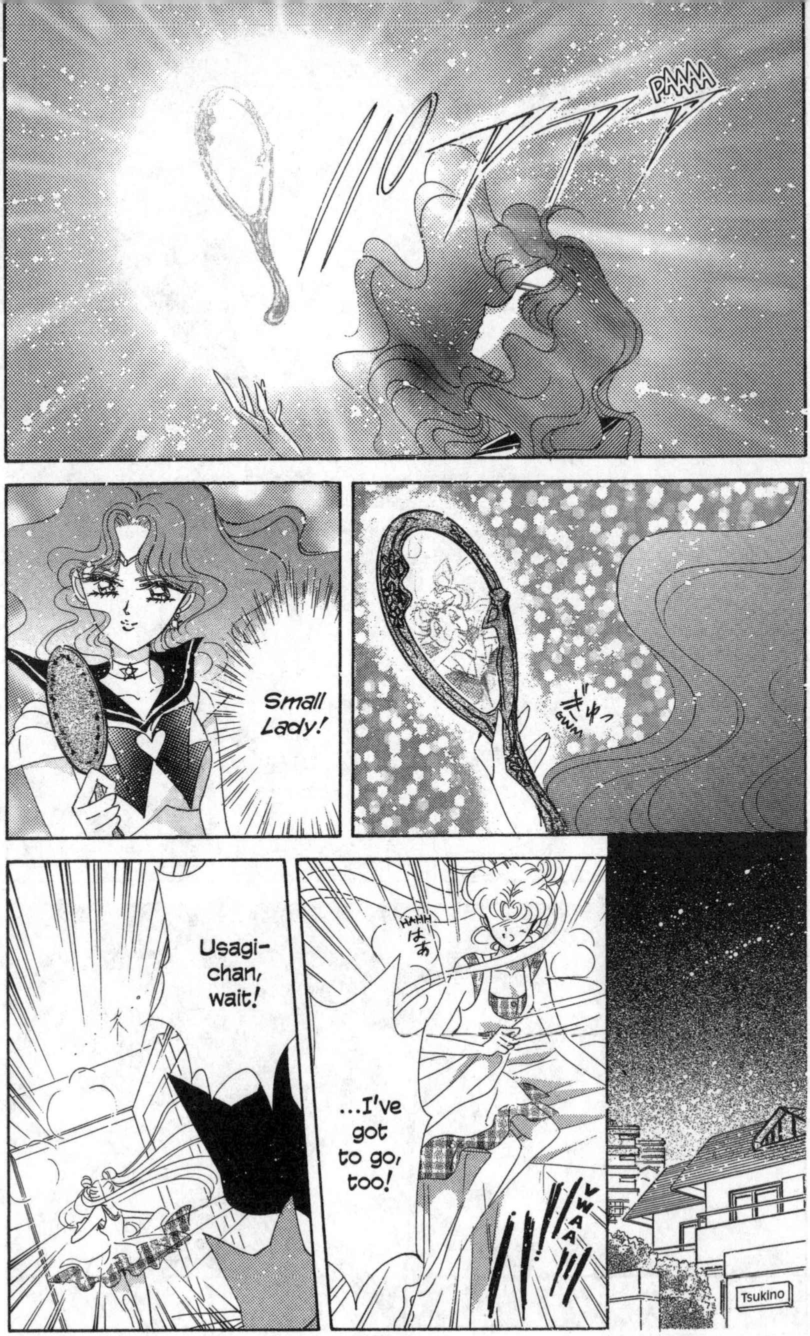
PAAAA
ぎゅっ
GWMM
Small Lady!
Tsukino
HAHH
はぁ
...I've got to go, too!
VWAA
Usagi-chan, wait!

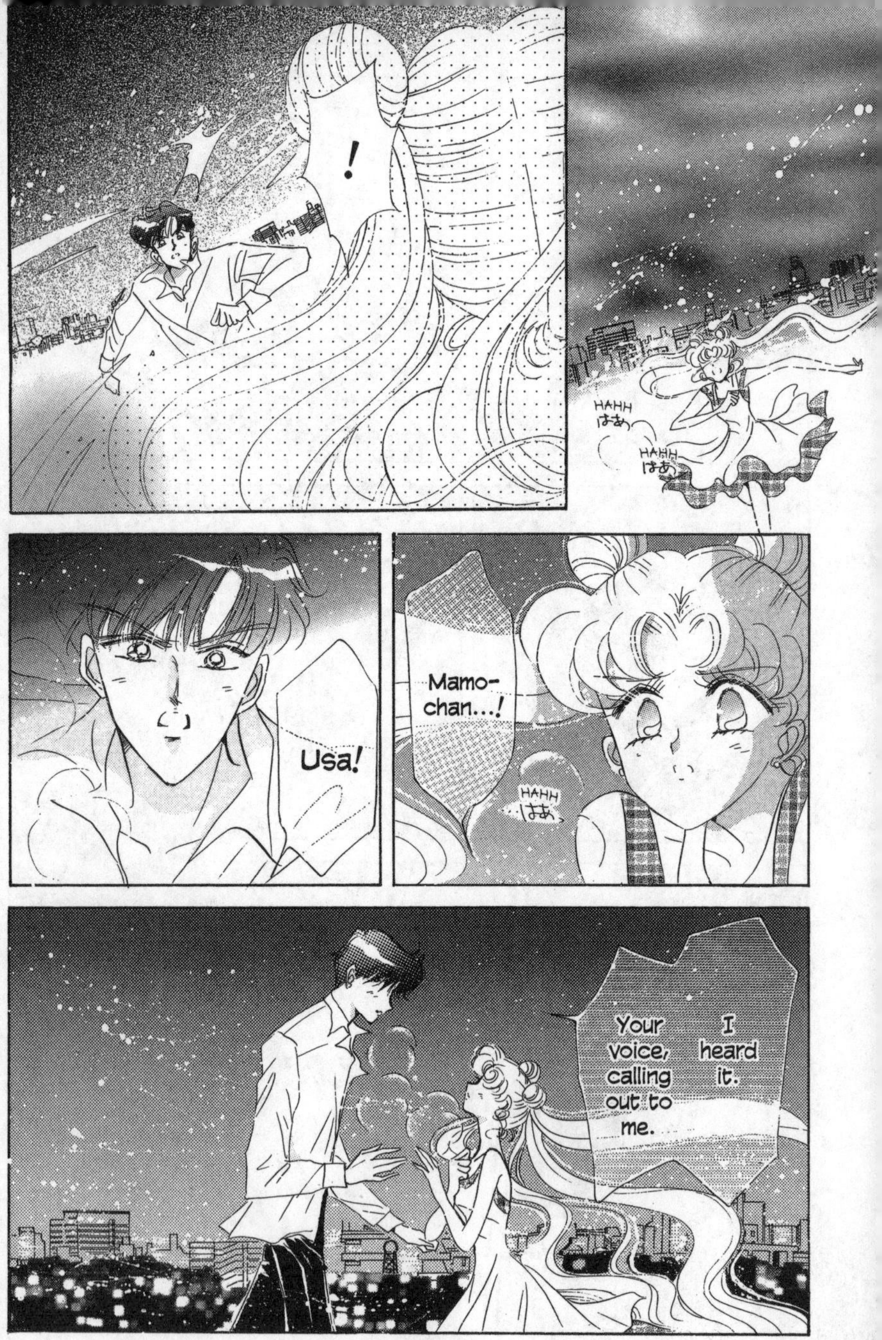
HAHH はあ
HAHH はあ
!
HAHH はあ
Mamo-chan...!
Usa!
I heard it.
Your voice, calling out to me.

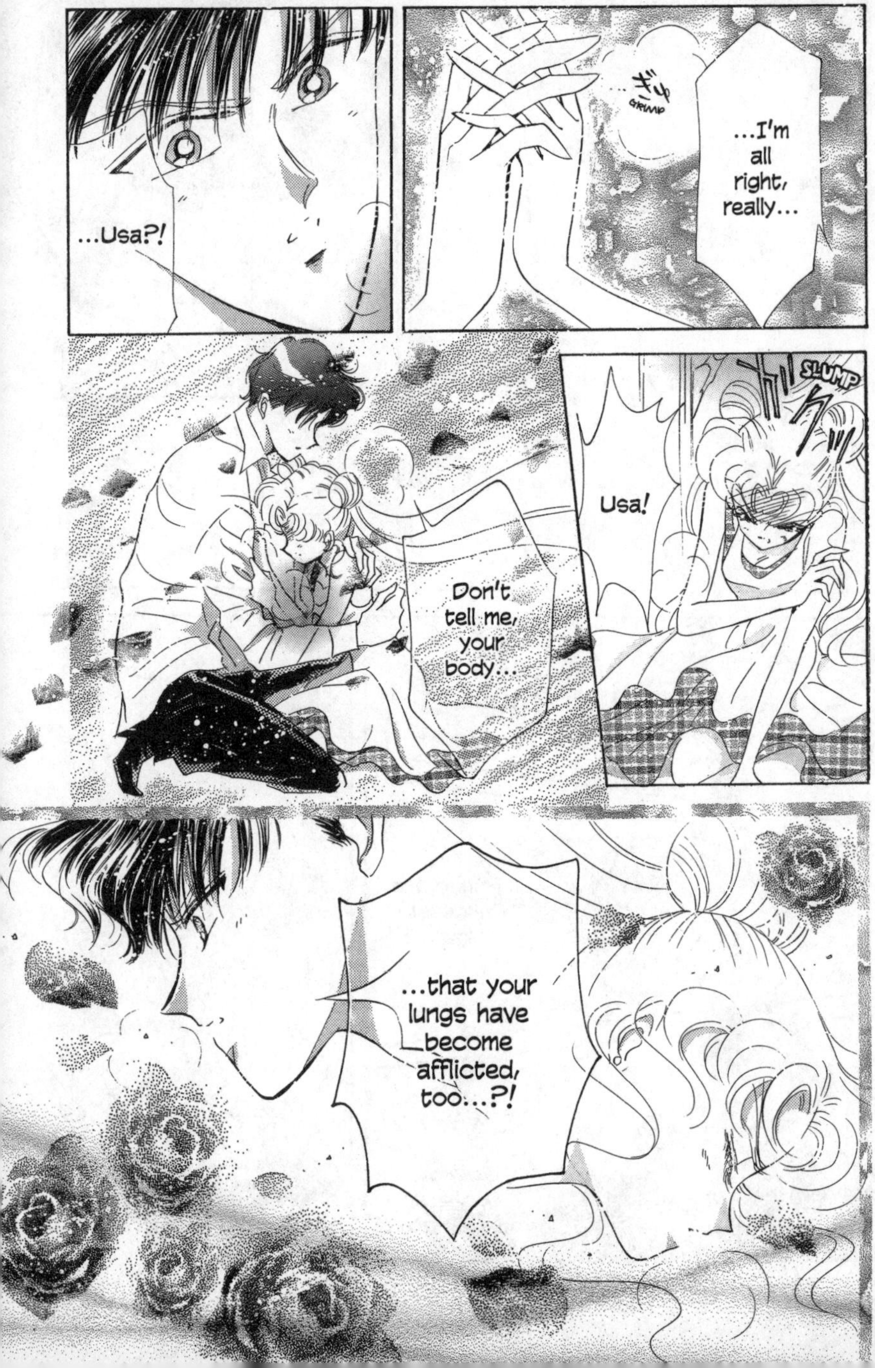

GRMP
...I'm all right, really...
...Usa?!
SLUMP
Usa!
Don't tell me, your body...
...that your lungs have become afflicted, too...?!

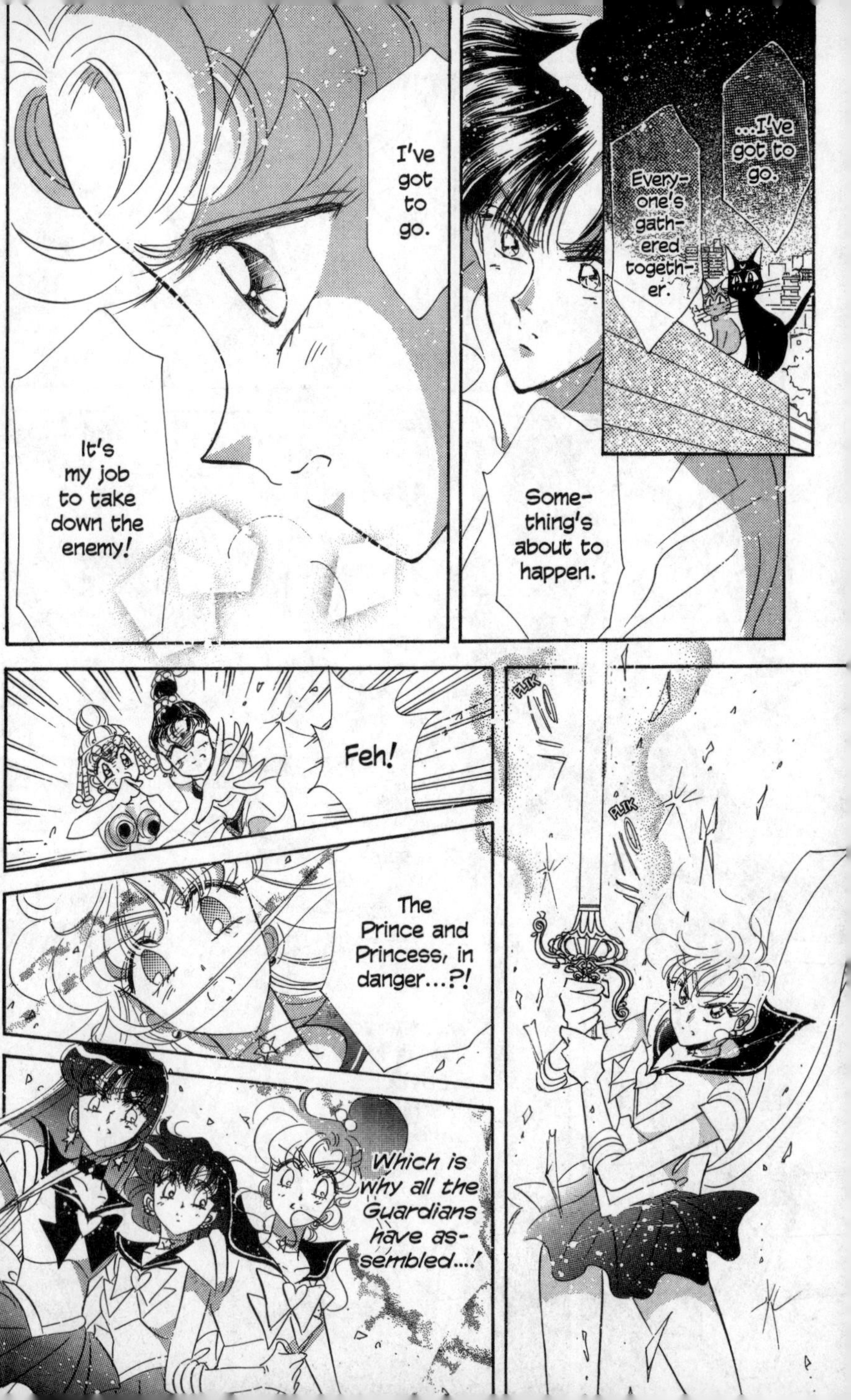
...I've got to go.
Every-one's gath-ered togeth-er.
Some-thing's about to happen.
I've got to go.
It's my job to take down the enemy!
PLIK
PLIK
Feh!
The Prince and Princess, in danger...?!
Which is why all the Guardians have as-sembled...!

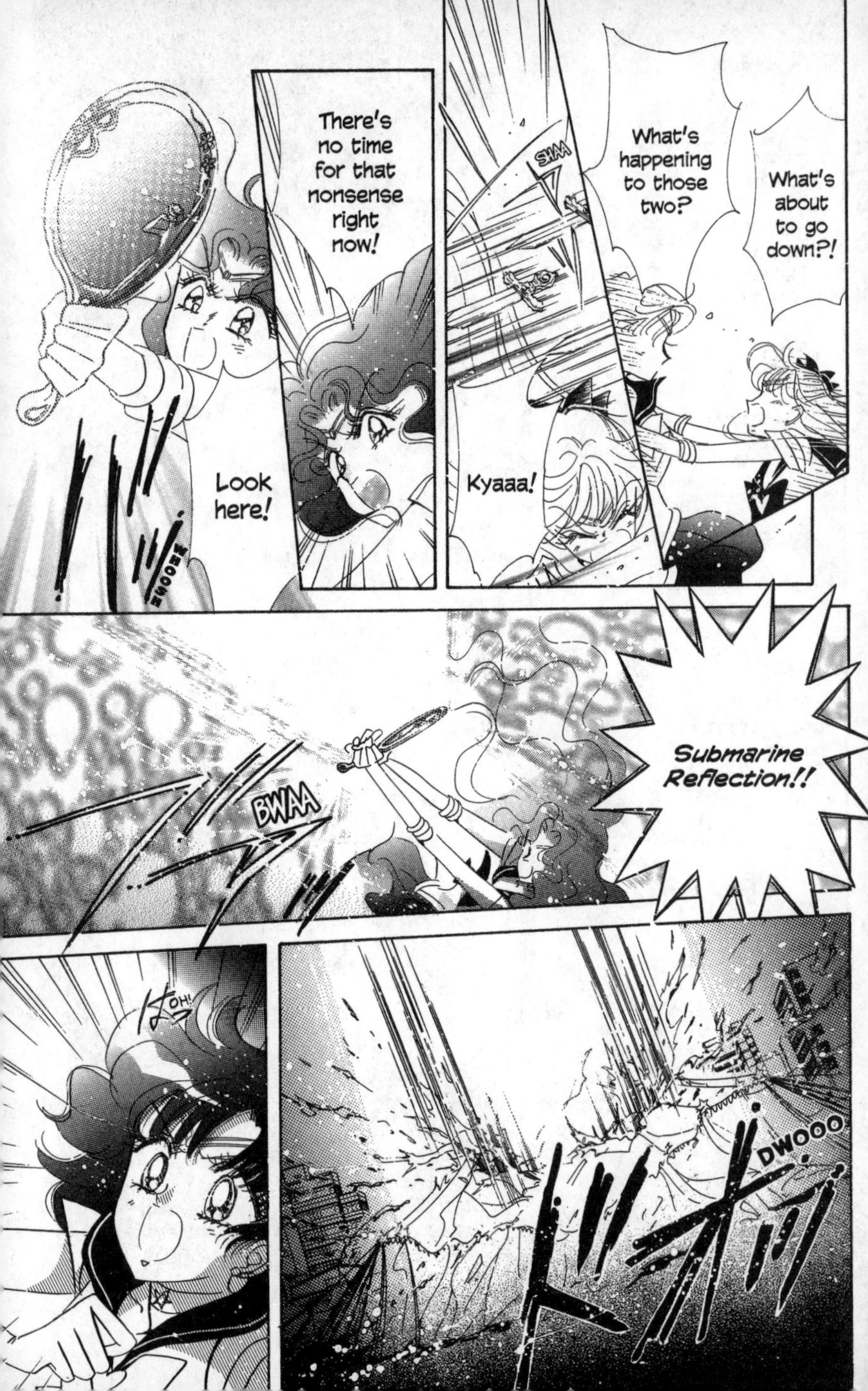
What's about to go down?!
What's happening to those two?
SHAA
Kyaaa!
There's no time for that nonsense right now!
Look here!
WHOOSH
Submarine Reflection!!
BWAA
DWOOO
OH!

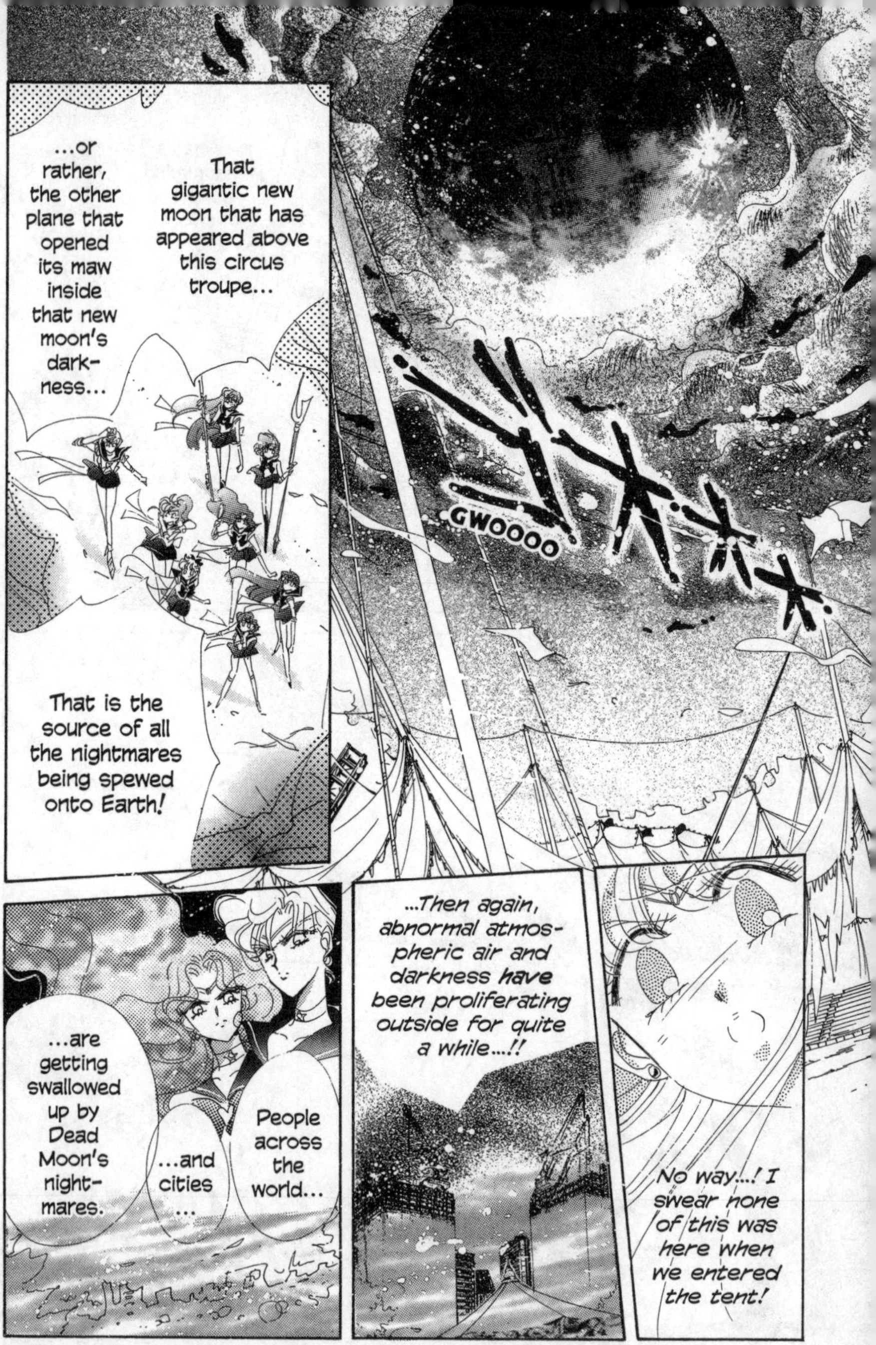

GWOOOO
That gigantic new moon that has appeared above this circus troupe...
...or rather, the other plane that opened its maw inside that new moon's darkness...
That is the source of all the nightmares being spewed onto Earth!
No way...! I swear none of this was here when we entered the tent!
...Then again, abnormal atmospheric air and darkness **have** been proliferating outside for quite a while...!!
People across the world...
...and cities...
...are getting swallowed up by Dead Moon's nightmares.

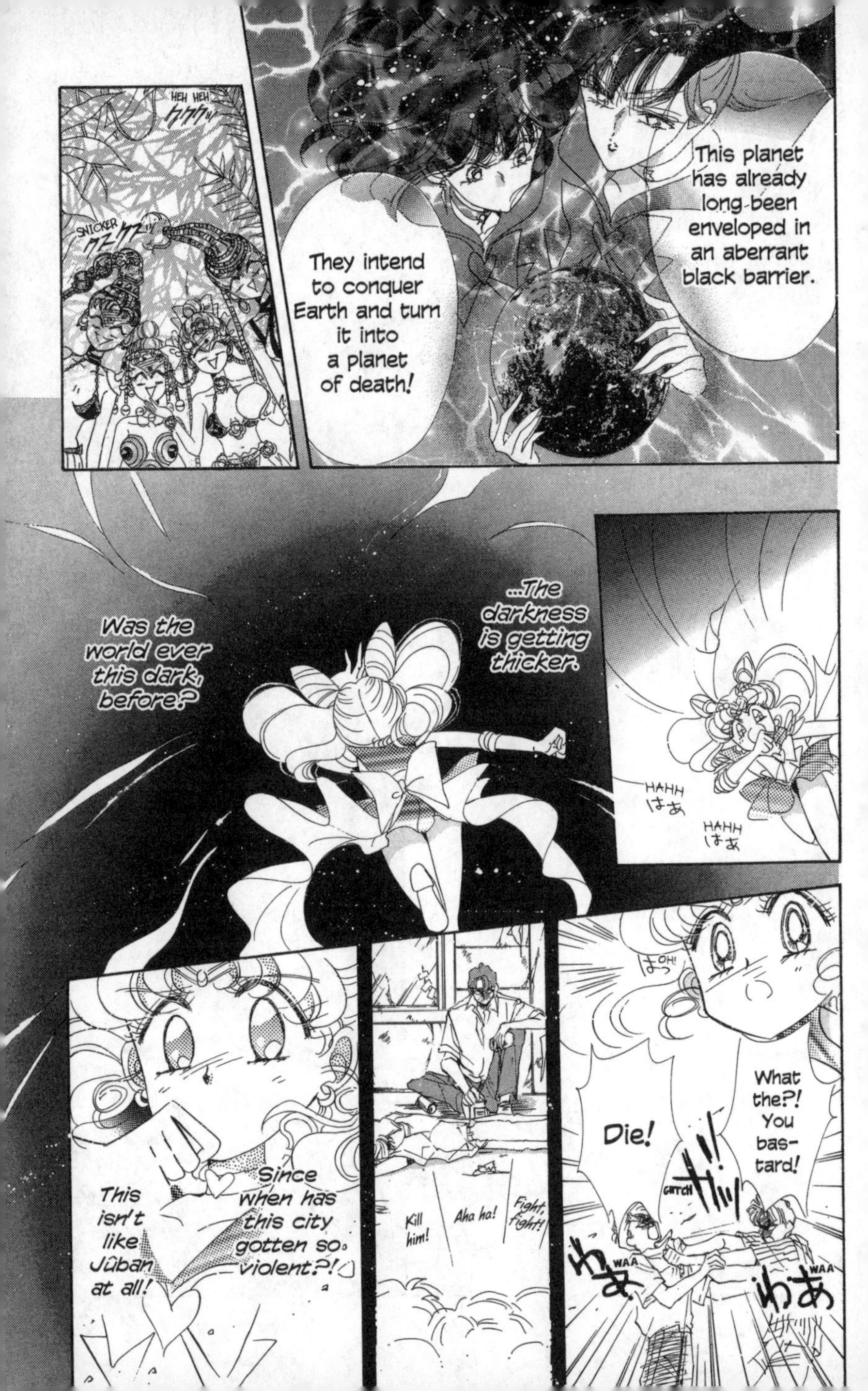
This planet has already long been enveloped in an aberrant black barrier.
They intend to conquer Earth and turn it into a planet of death!
HEH HEH
SNICKER
HAHH はあ
HAHH はあ
...The darkness is getting thicker.
Was the world ever this dark, before?
OH!
What the?! You bastard!
Die!
GRTCH
WAA わあ
わあ WAA
Fight, fight!
Aha ha!
Kill him!
Since when has this city gotten so violent?!
This isn't like Jûban at all!

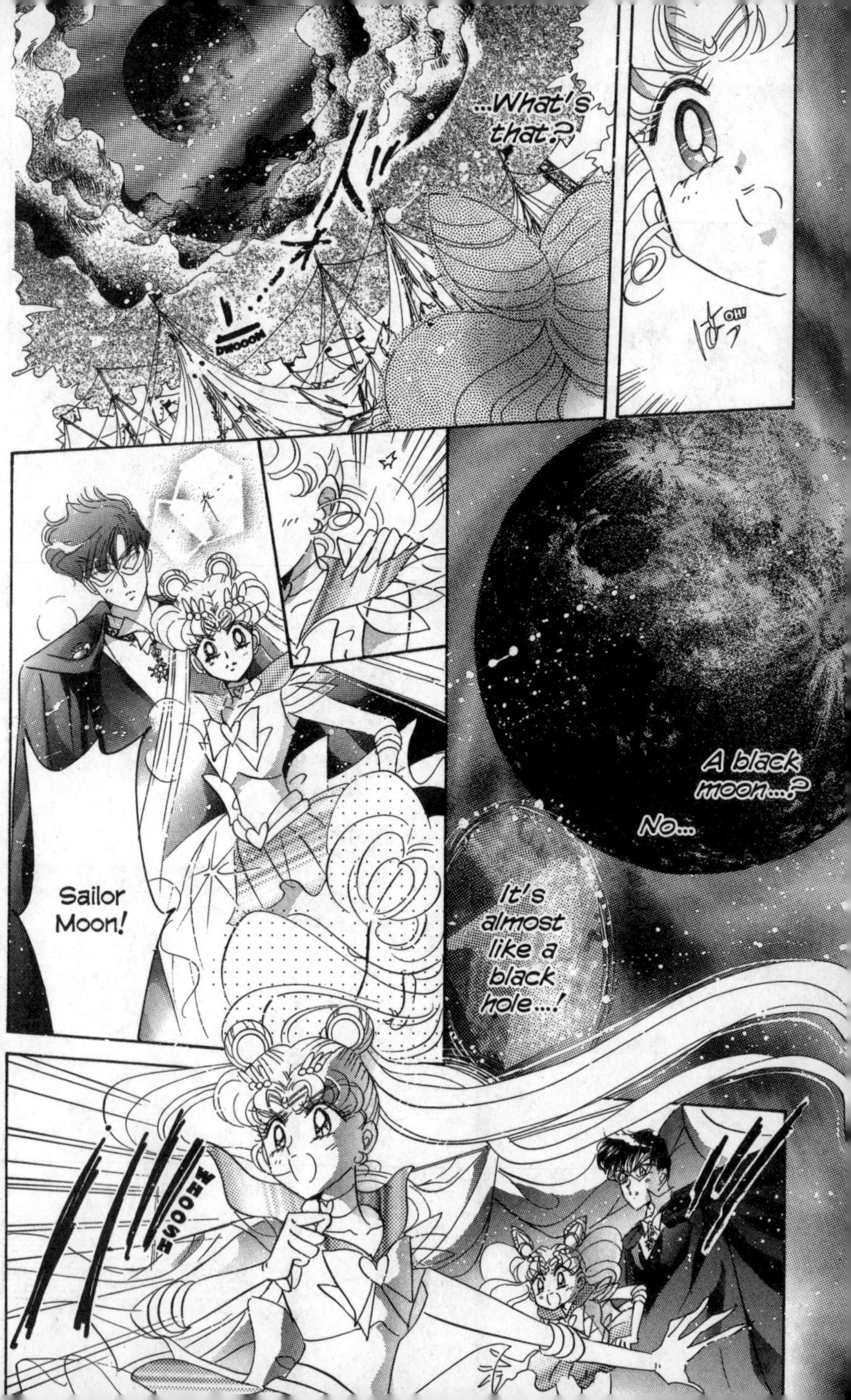
OH!
...What's that?
DWOOOM
A black moon...?
No...
It's almost like a black hole...!
Sailor Moon!
WHOOSH

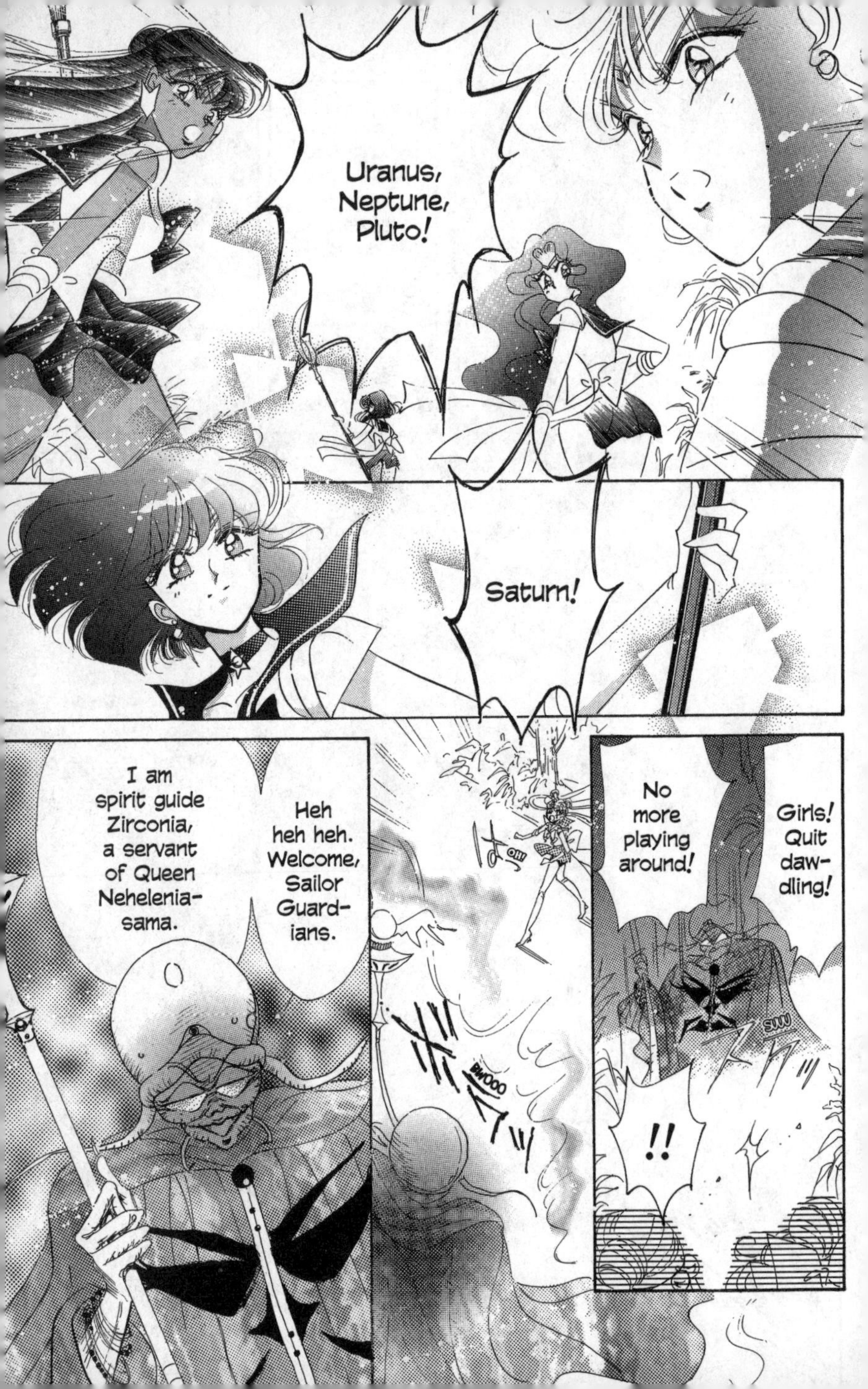
Uranus, Neptune, Pluto!
Saturn!
Girls! Quit dawdling!
No more playing around!
SUUU
!!
OH!
BWOOO
Heh heh heh. Welcome, Sailor Guardians.
I am spirit guide Zirconia, a servant of Queen Nehelenia-sama.

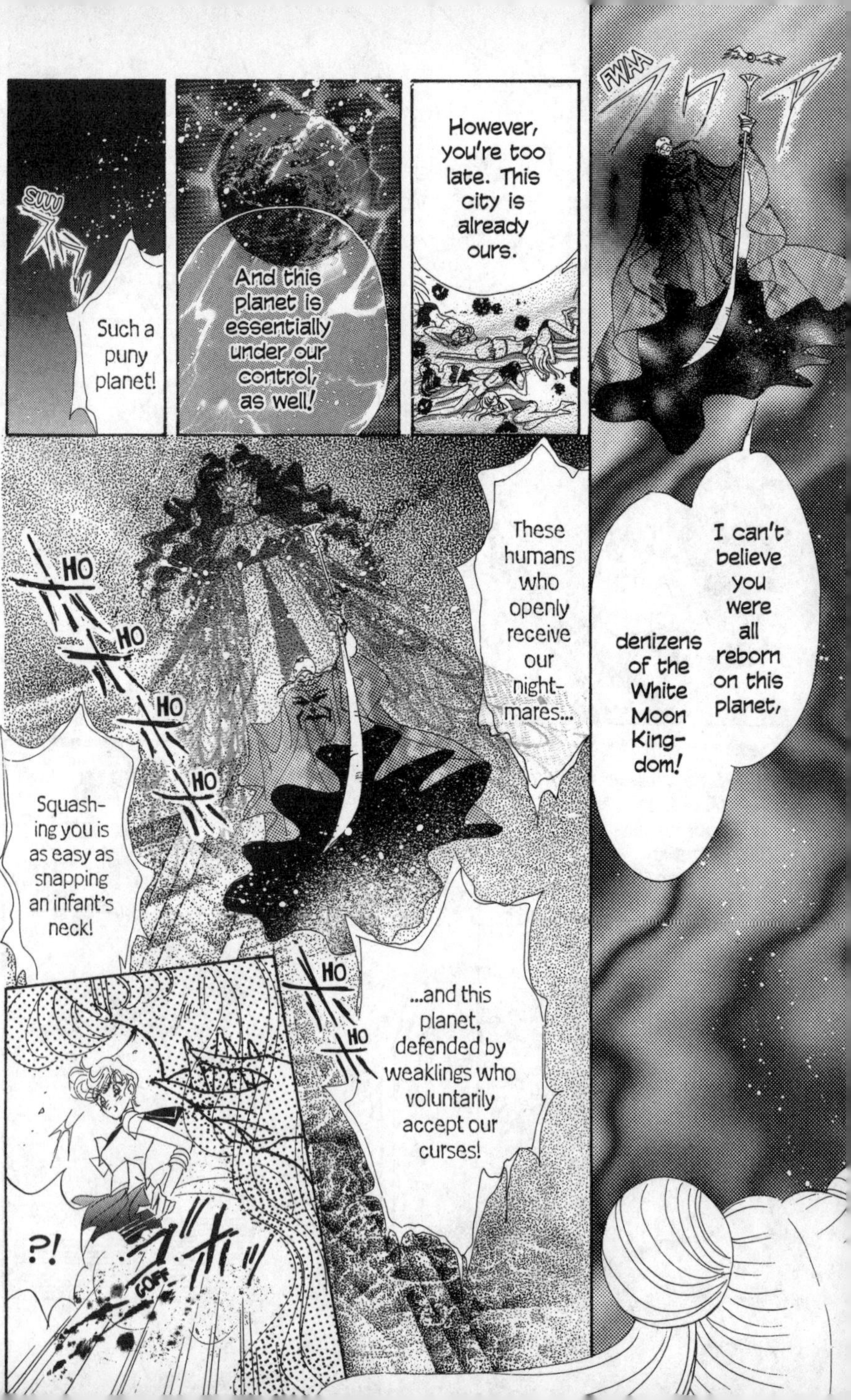
FWAA
I can't believe you were all reborn on this planet,
denizens of the White Moon Kingdom!
However, you're too late. This city is already ours.
And this planet is essentially under our control, as well!
SWW
Such a puny planet!
These humans who openly receive our nightmares...
HO
HO
HO
HO
Squashing you is as easy as snapping an infant's neck!
...and this planet, defended by weaklings who voluntarily accept our curses!
HO
HO
?!
GOFF

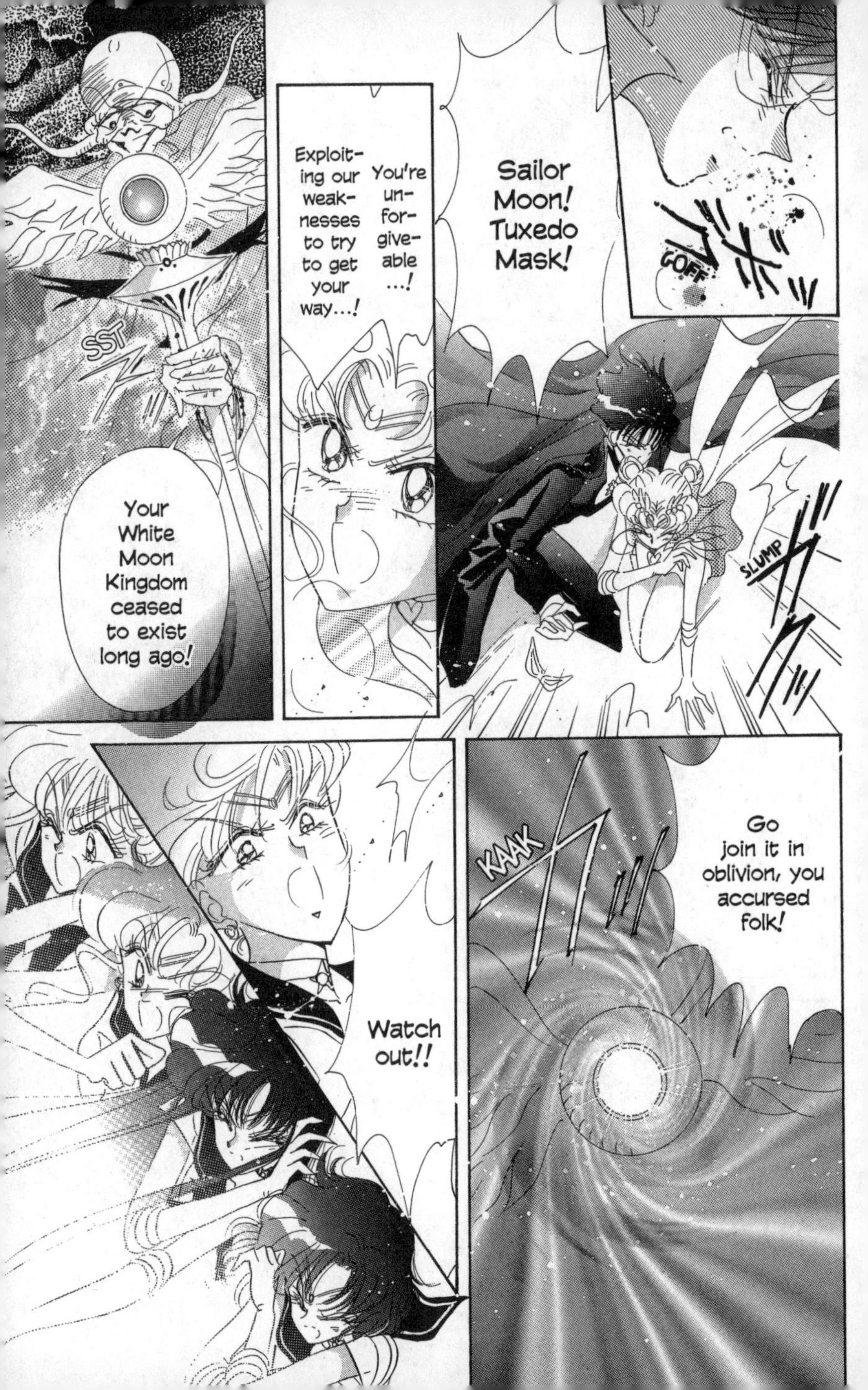
GOFF
Sailor Moon! Tuxedo Mask!
SLUMP
You're unforgive-able...!
Exploit-ing our weak-nesses to try to get your way...!
SST
Your White Moon Kingdom ceased to exist long ago!
Go join it in oblivion, you accursed folk!
KAAK
Watch out!!

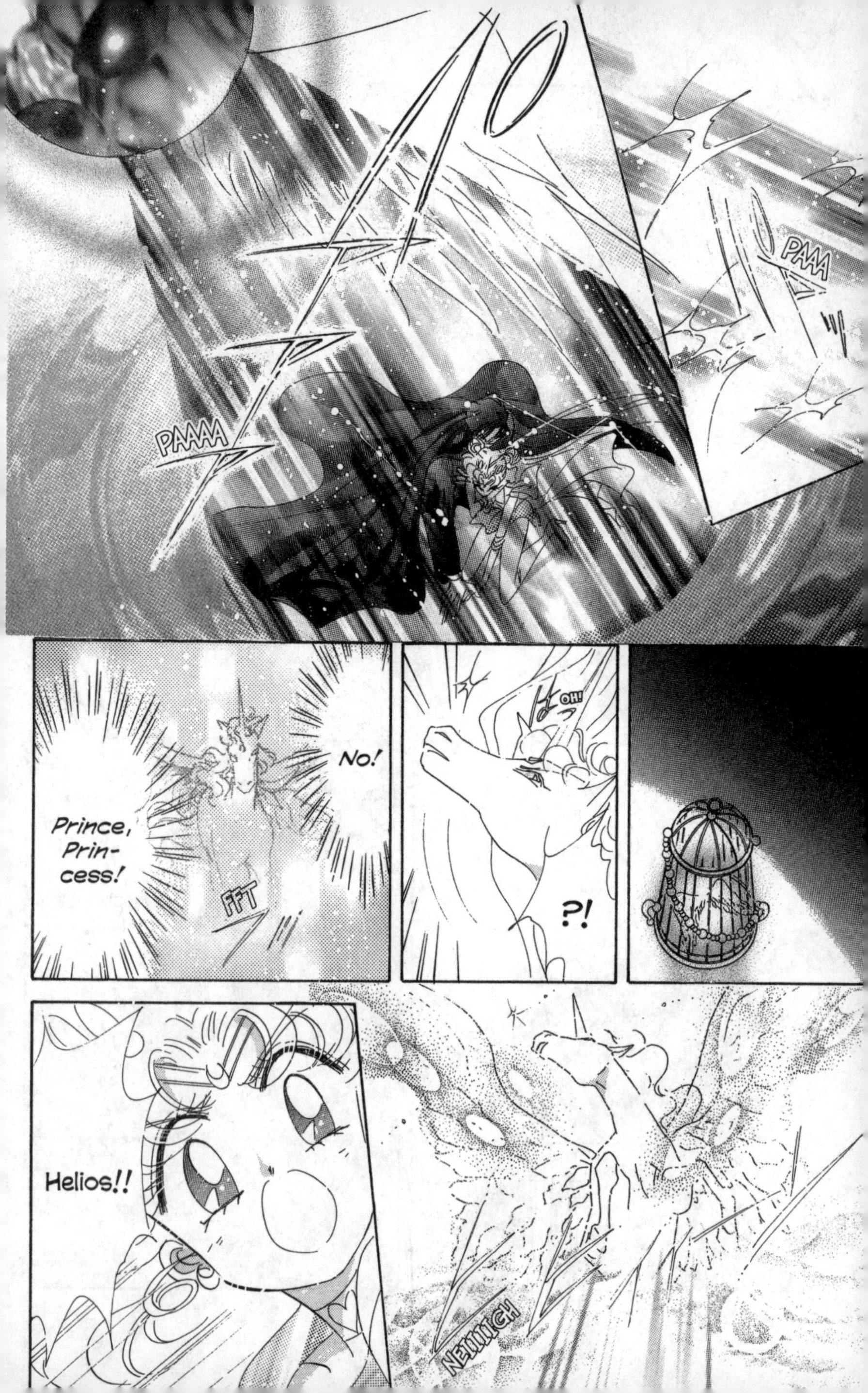
PAAA
PAAAA
OH!
?!
No!
Prince, Prin-cess!
FFT
NEIIIICH
Helios!!

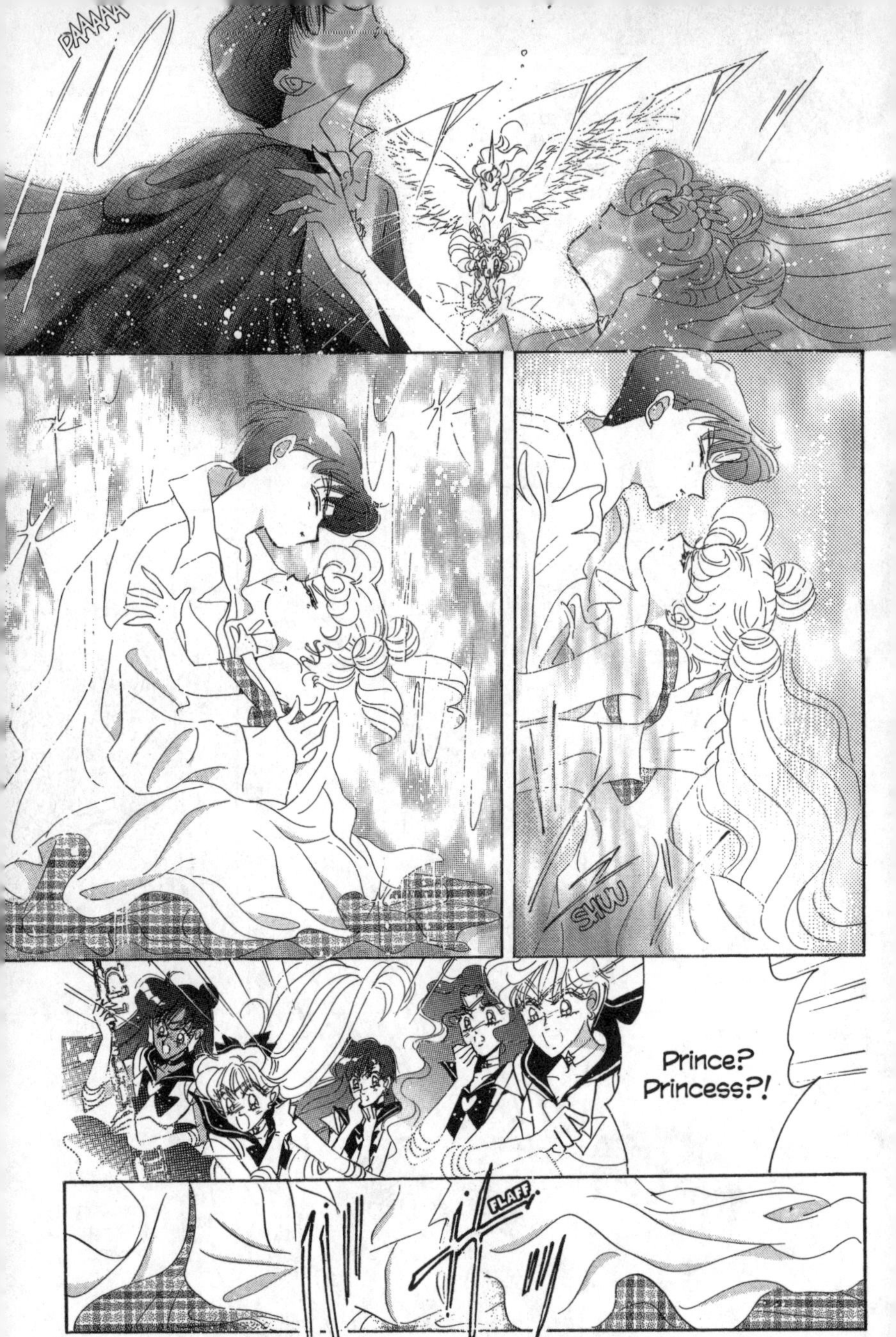
PAAAAA
SHUU
Prince?
Princess?!
FLAFF

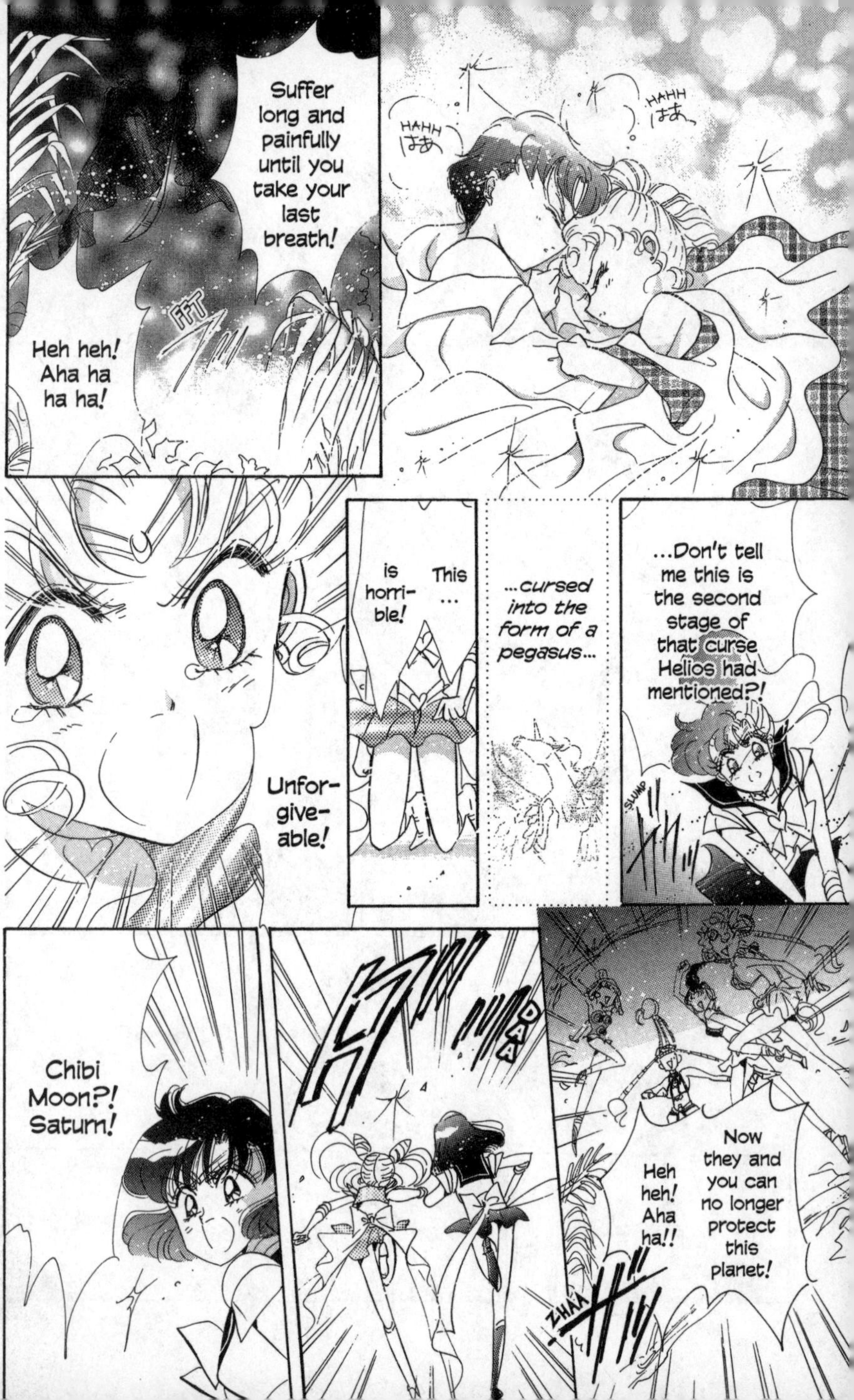
HAHH はあ
HAHH はあ
Suffer long and painfully until you take your last breath!
FFT
Heh heh! Aha ha ha ha!
...Don't tell me this is the second stage of that curse Helios had mentioned?!
SLUMP
...cursed into the form of a pegasus...
This ...
is horrible!
Unfor-give-able!
Now they and you can no longer protect this planet!
Heh heh! Aha ha!!
ZHAA
DAA
Chibi Moon?! Saturn!

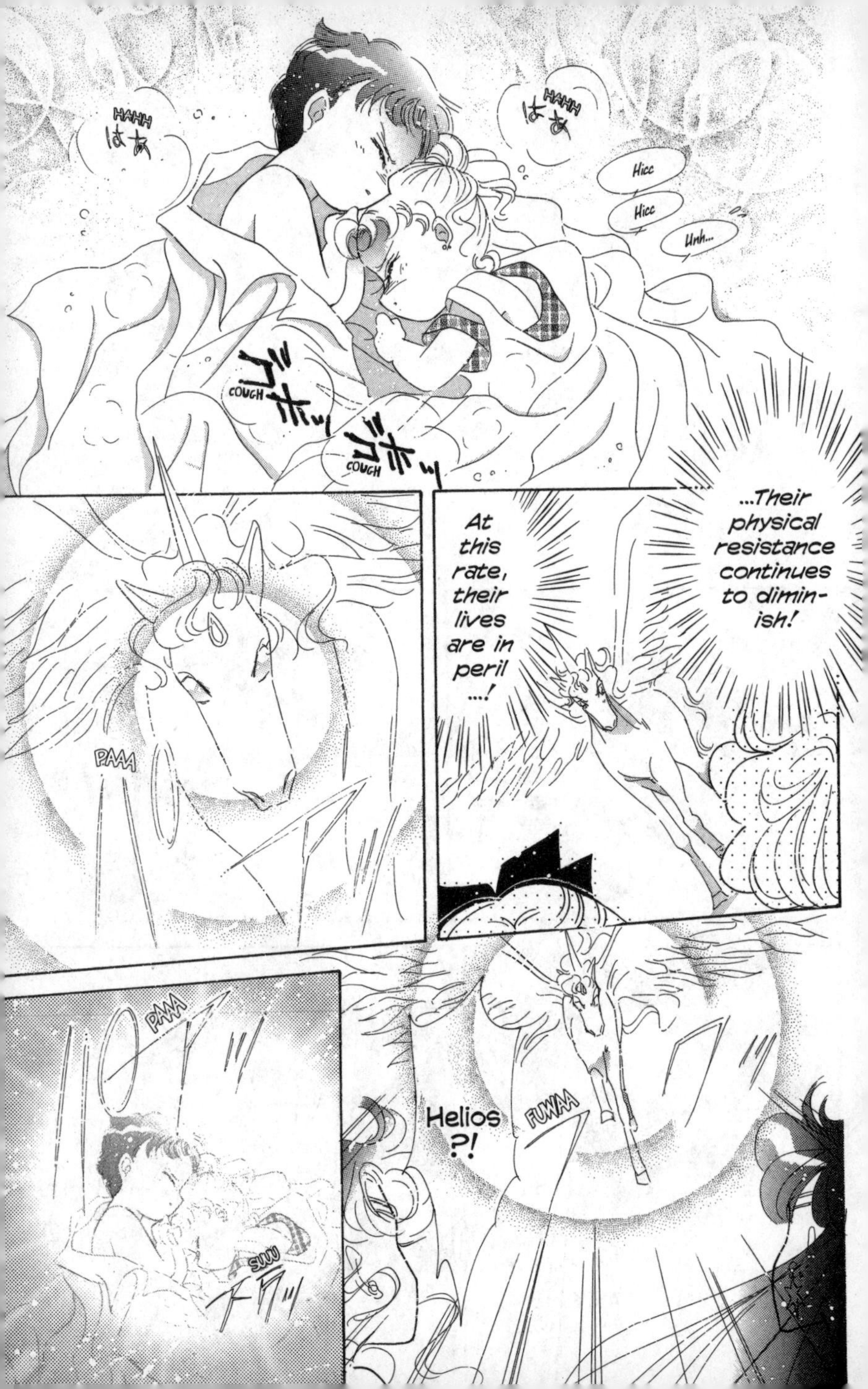
HAHH
はぁ
Hicc
Hicc
Unh...
HAHH
はぁ
COUGH
ゴホッ
COUGH
ゴホッ
...Their physical resistance continues to diminish!
At this rate, their lives are in peril ....!
PAAA
FUWAA
Helios ?!
PAAA
SUUU

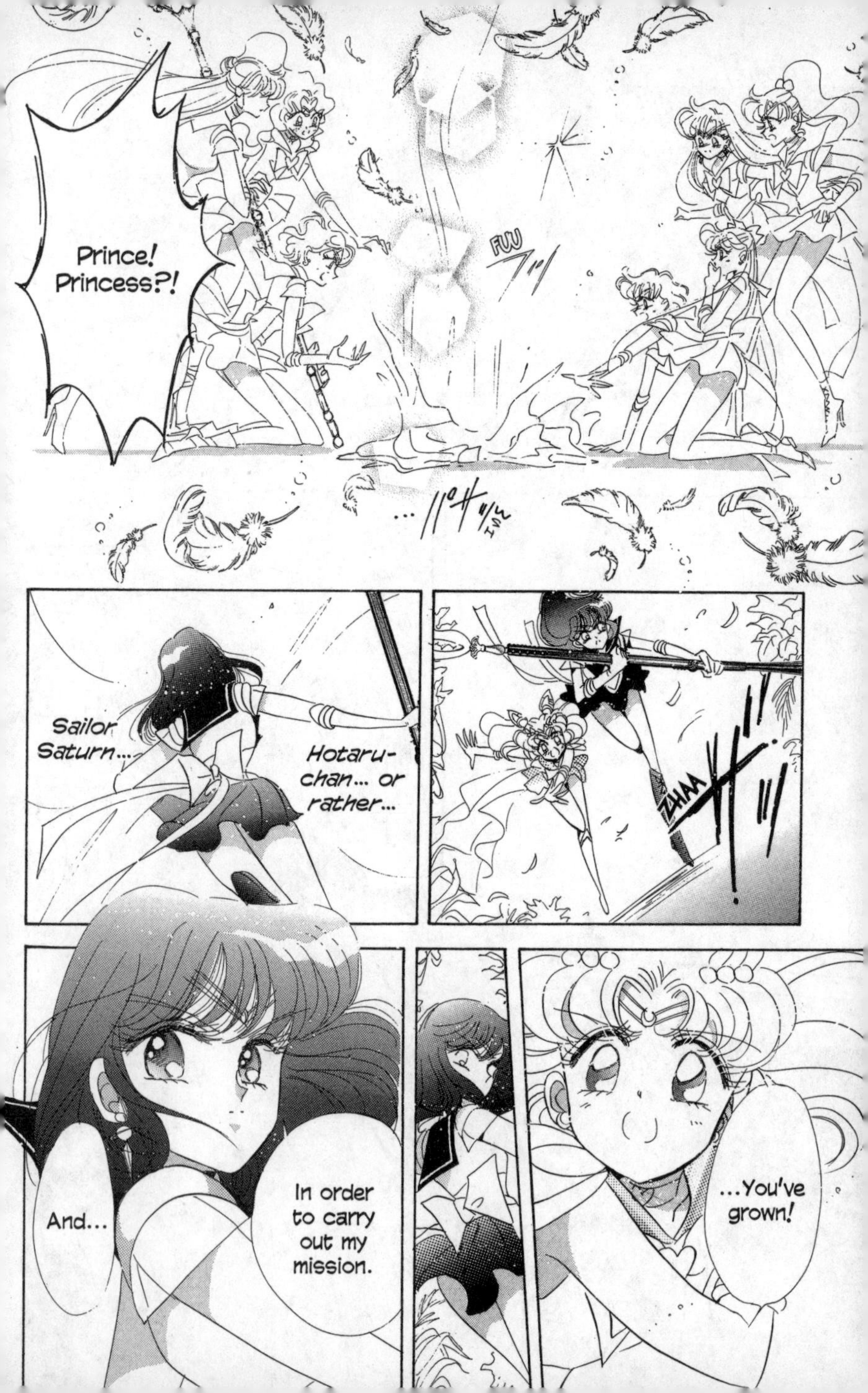
FUU
Prince!
Princess?!
ZHAA
Hotaru-chan... or rather...
Sailor Saturn...
...You've grown!
In order to carry out my mission.
And...

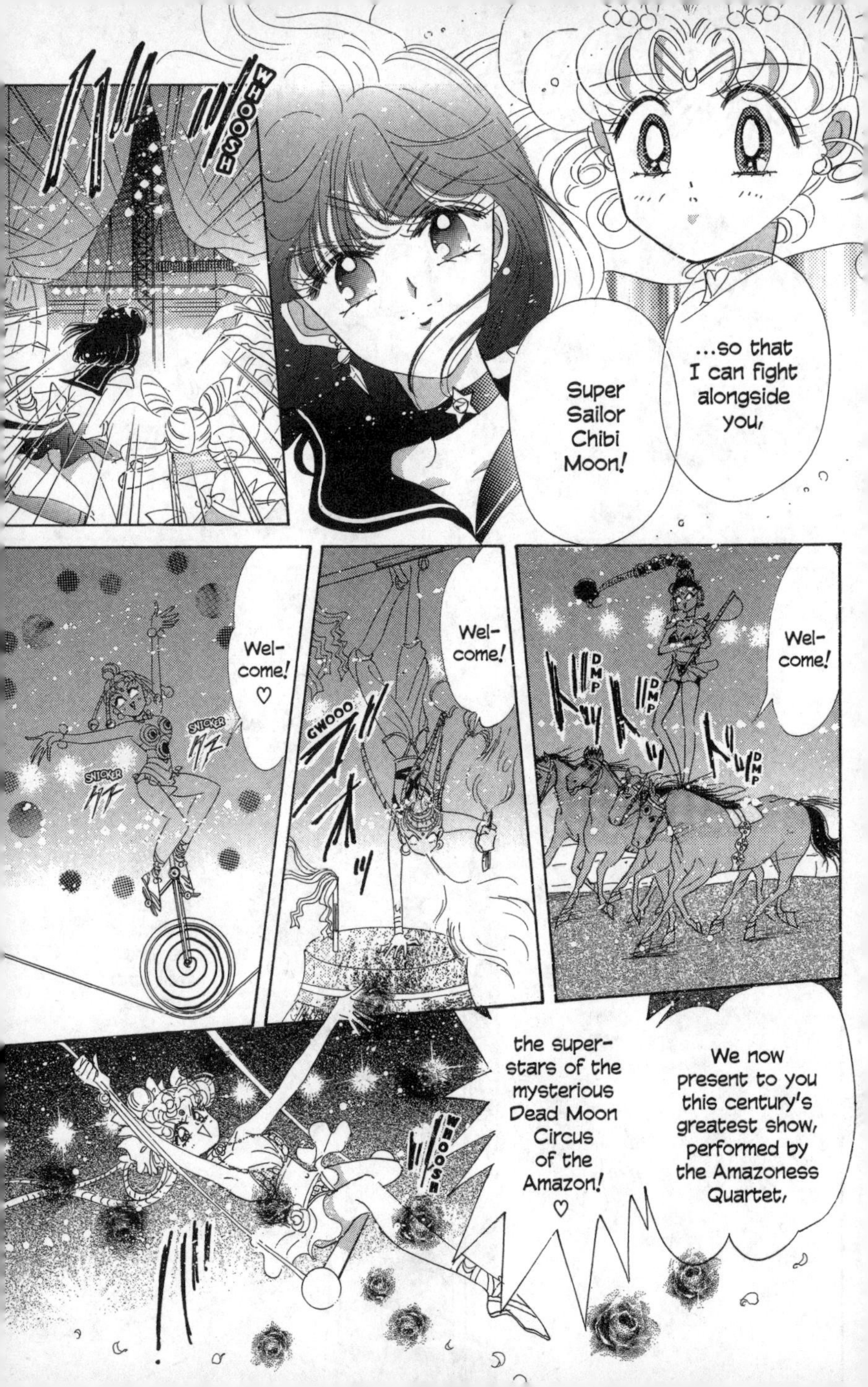
...so that I can fight alongside you,
Super Sailor Chibi Moon!
WHOOSH
Wel- come!
DMP
DMP
DMP
Wel- come!
GWOOO
Wel- come! ♡
SNICKER
SNICKER
We now present to you this century's greatest show, performed by the Amazoness Quartet,
the super- stars of the mysterious Dead Moon Circus of the Amazon! ♡
WHOOSH

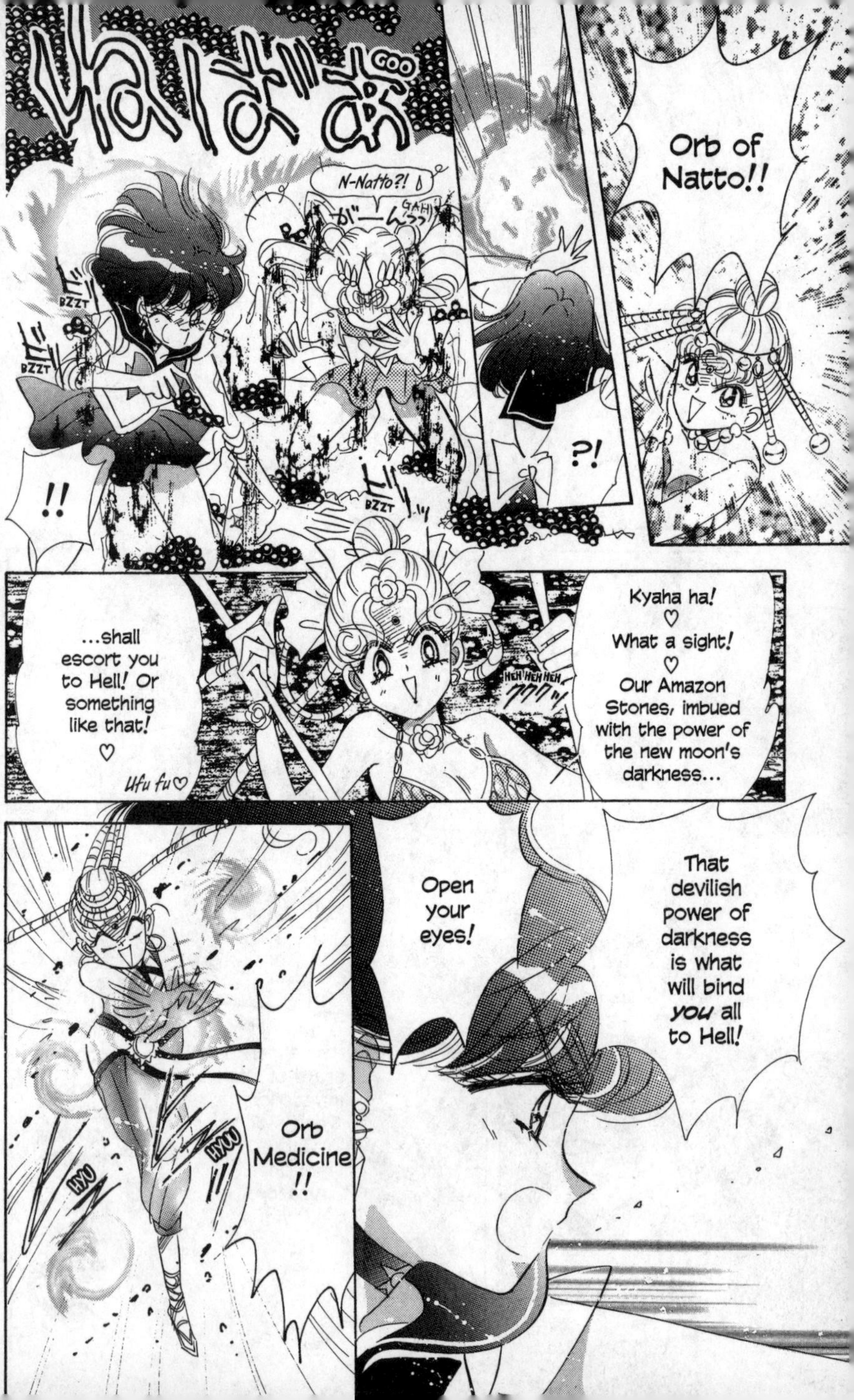

Orb of Natto!!
?!
GOO
N-Natto?!
GAH!
BZZT
BZZT
BZZT
!!
Kyaha ha! ♡ What a sight! ♡ Our Amazon Stones, imbued with the power of the new moon's darkness...
HEH HEH HEH
...shall escort you to Hell! Or something like that! ♡
Ufu fu♡
That devilish power of darkness is what will bind *you* all to Hell!
Open your eyes!
Orb Medicine!!
HYUU
HYU

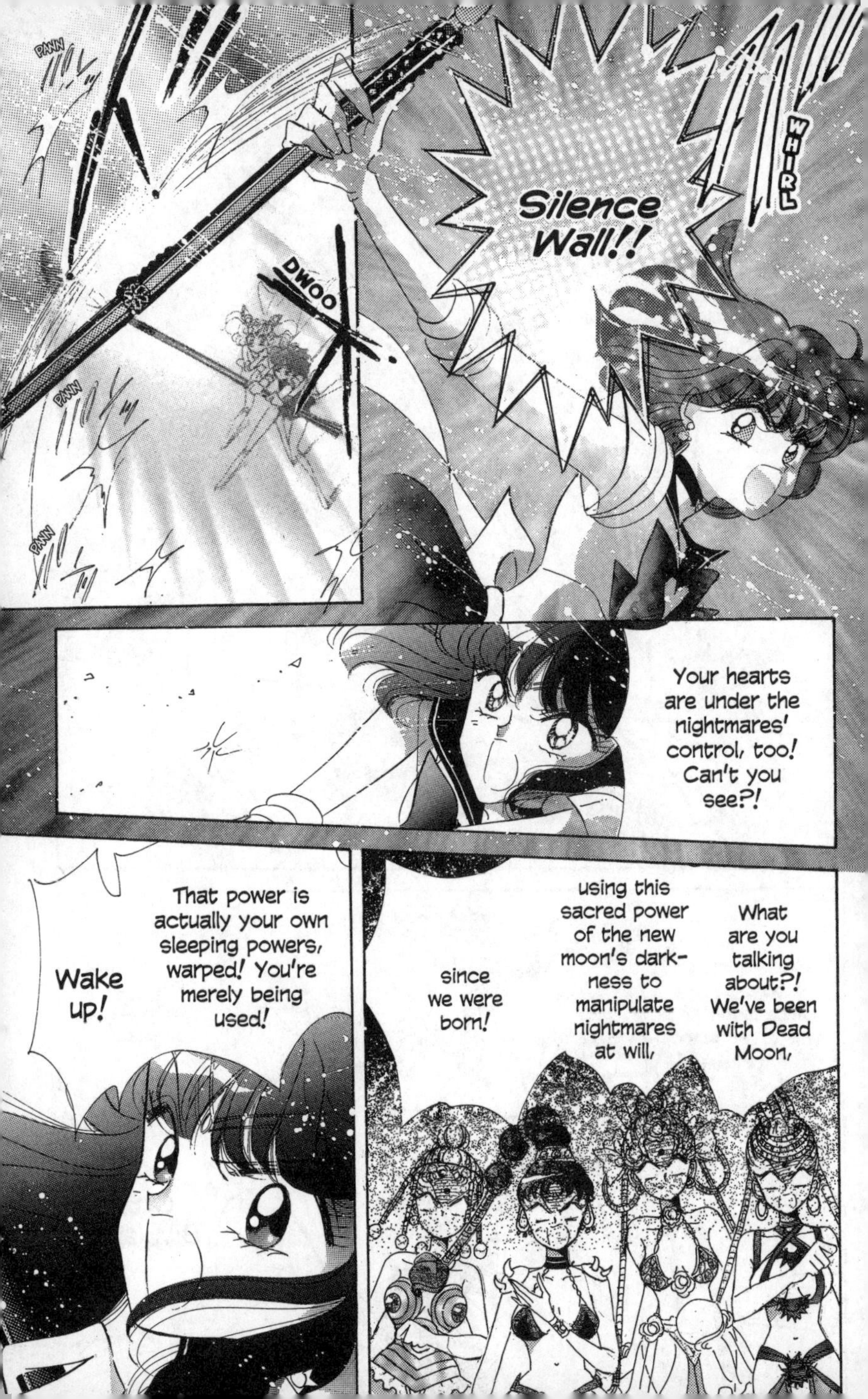
WHIRL
Silence Wall!!
PANN
DWOO
PANN
PANN
Your hearts are under the nightmares' control, too! Can't you see?!
What are you talking about?! We've been with Dead Moon,
using this sacred power of the new moon's dark-ness to manipulate nightmares at will,
since we were born!
That power is actually your own sleeping powers, warped! You're merely being used!
Wake up!

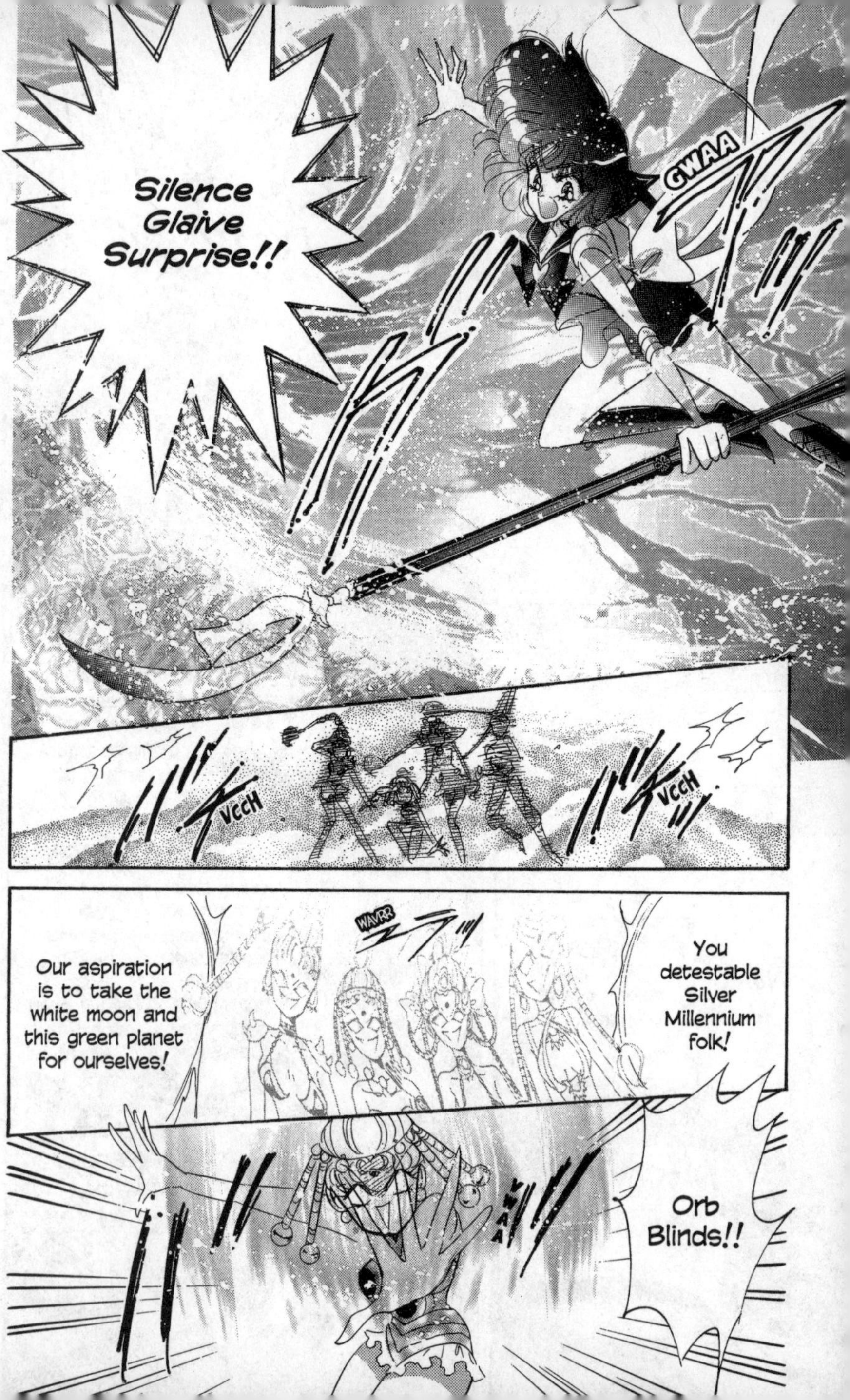
GWAA
Silence Glaive Surprise!!
VCCH
VCCH
WAVRR
You detestable Silver Millennium folk!
Our aspiration is to take the white moon and this green planet for ourselves!
Orb Blinds!!
VWAA

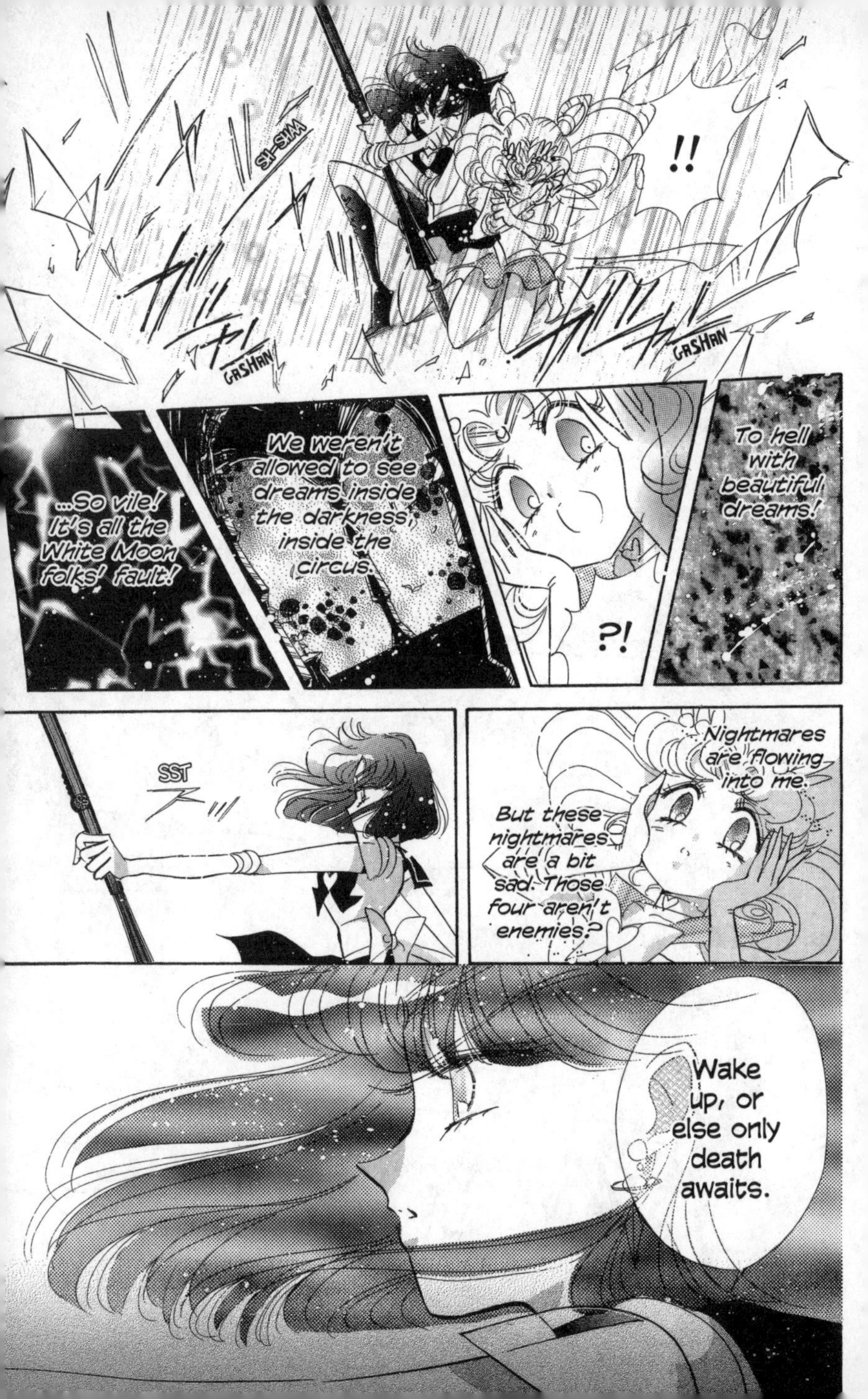
!!
GASHAN
SH-SHA
GASHAN
To hell with beautiful dreams!
?!
We weren't allowed to see dreams inside the darkness, inside the circus.
...So vile! It's all the White Moon folks' fault!
Nightmares are flowing into me.
But these nightmares are a bit sad. Those four aren't enemies?
SST
Wake up, or else only death awaits.

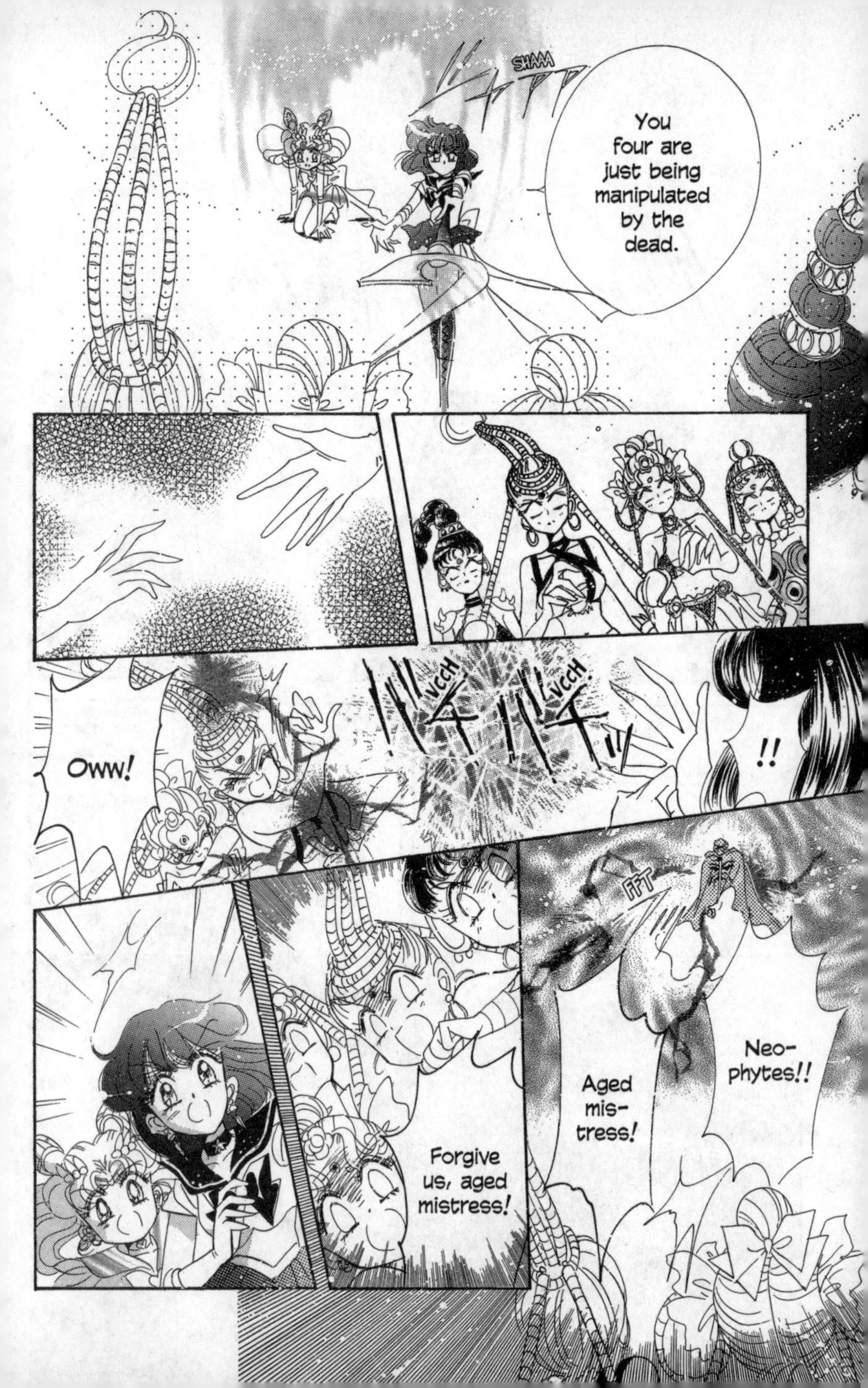
SHAAA
You four are just being manipulated by the dead.
!!
VCCH
VCCH
Oww!
FFT
Neo-phytes!!
Aged mis-tress!
Forgive us, aged mistress!

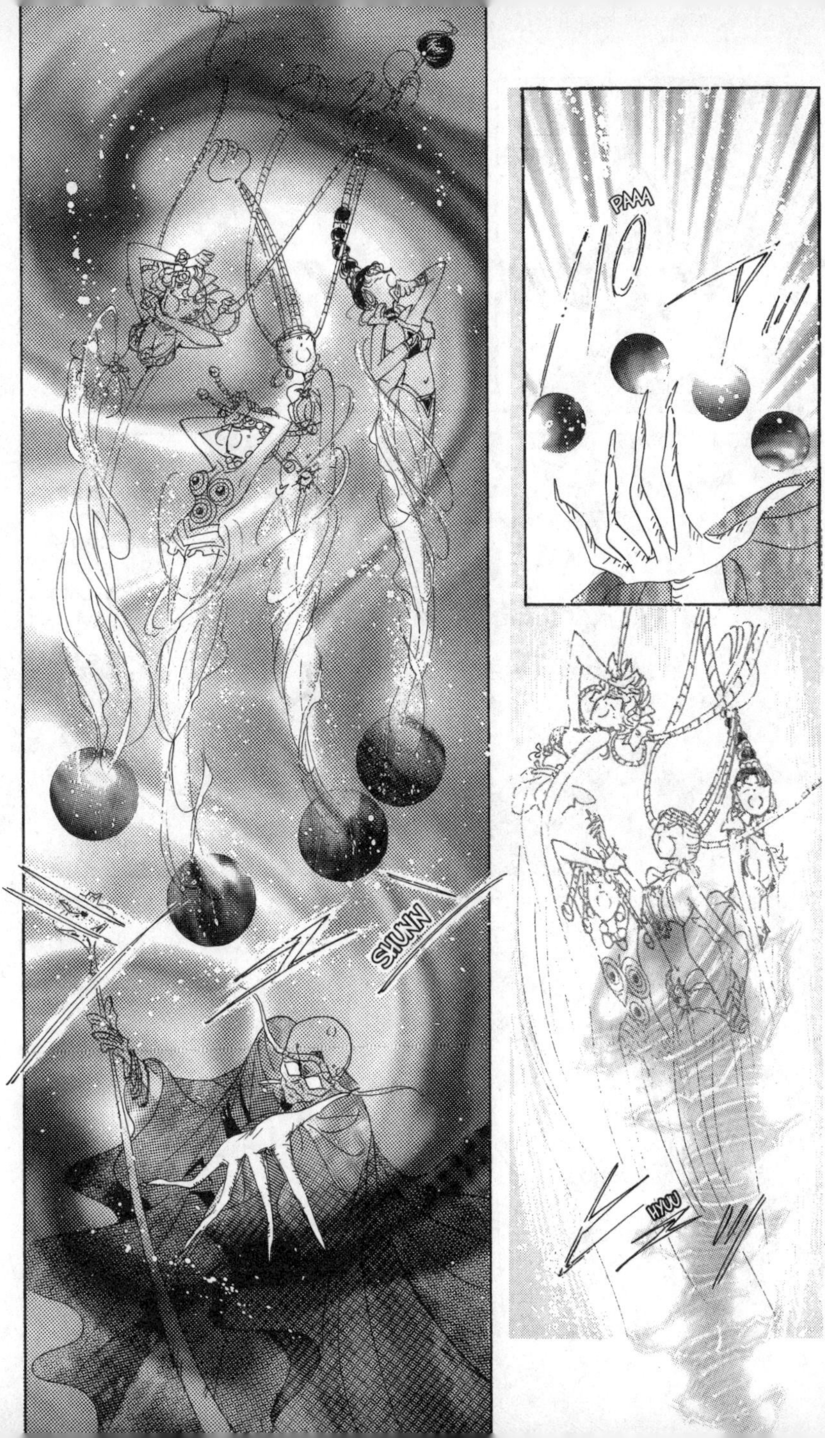
PAAA
HYUU
SHUNN

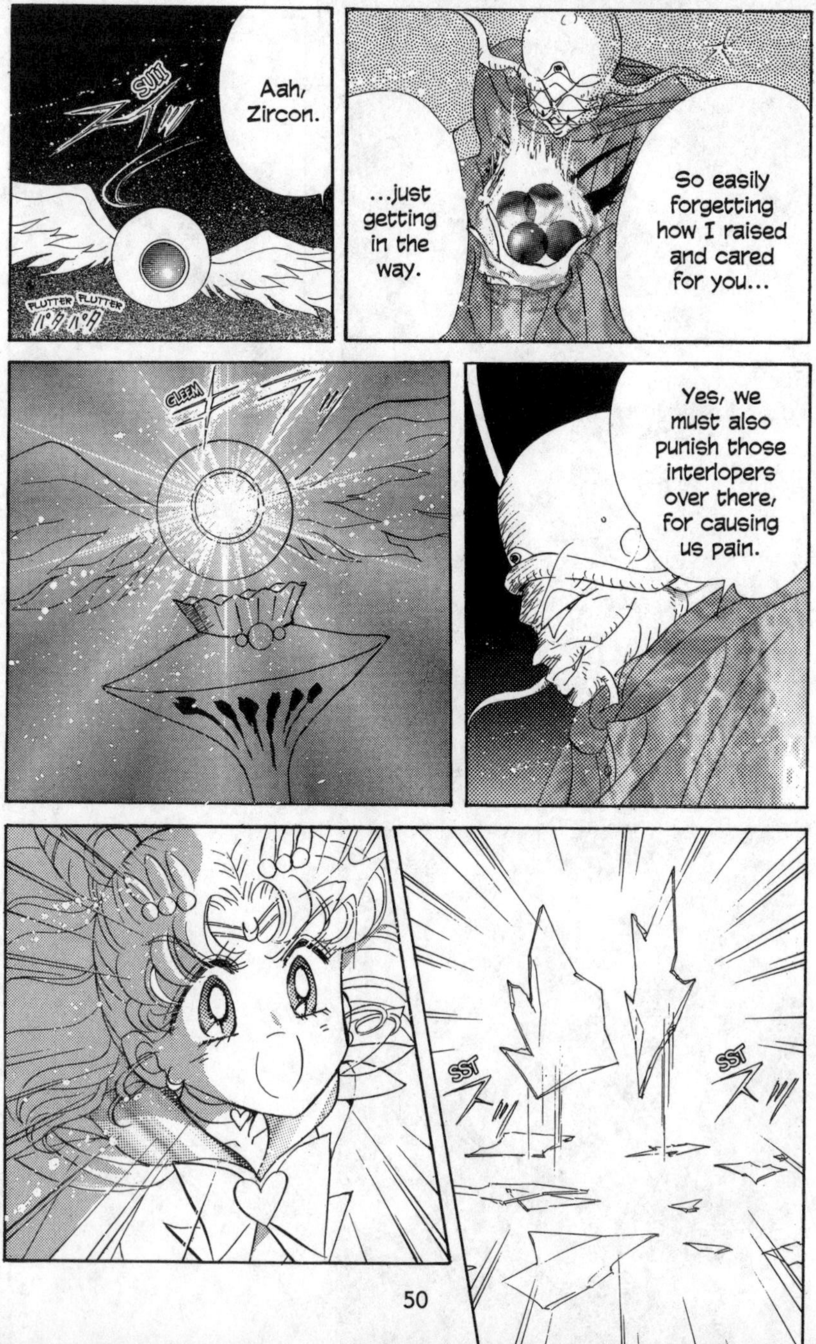
So easily forgetting how I raised and cared for you...
...just getting in the way.
SUI
Aah, Zircon.
FLUTTER FLUTTER
Yes, we must also punish those interlopers over there, for causing us pain.
GLEEM
SST
SST

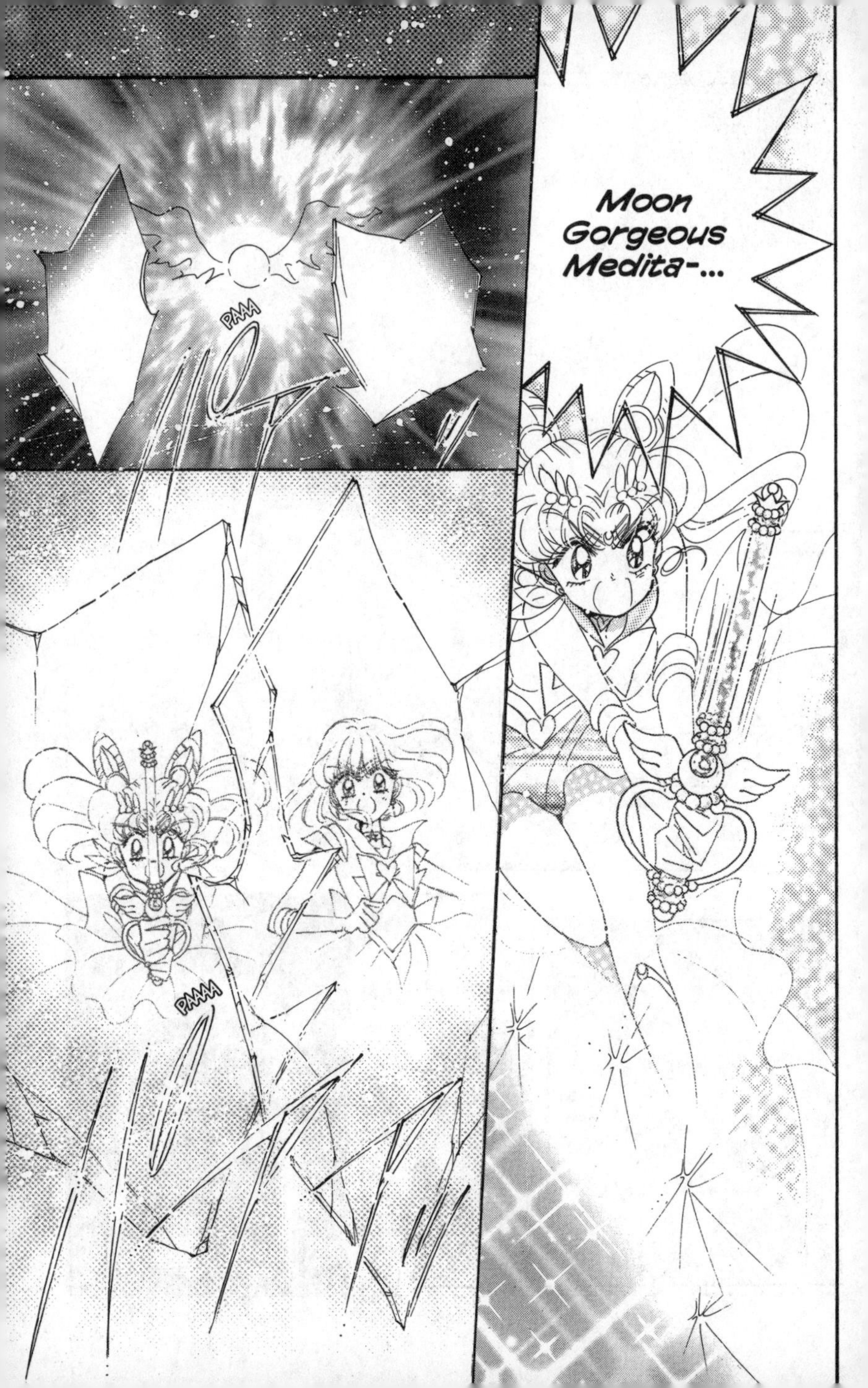
Moon Gorgeous Medita-...
PAAA
PAAAA

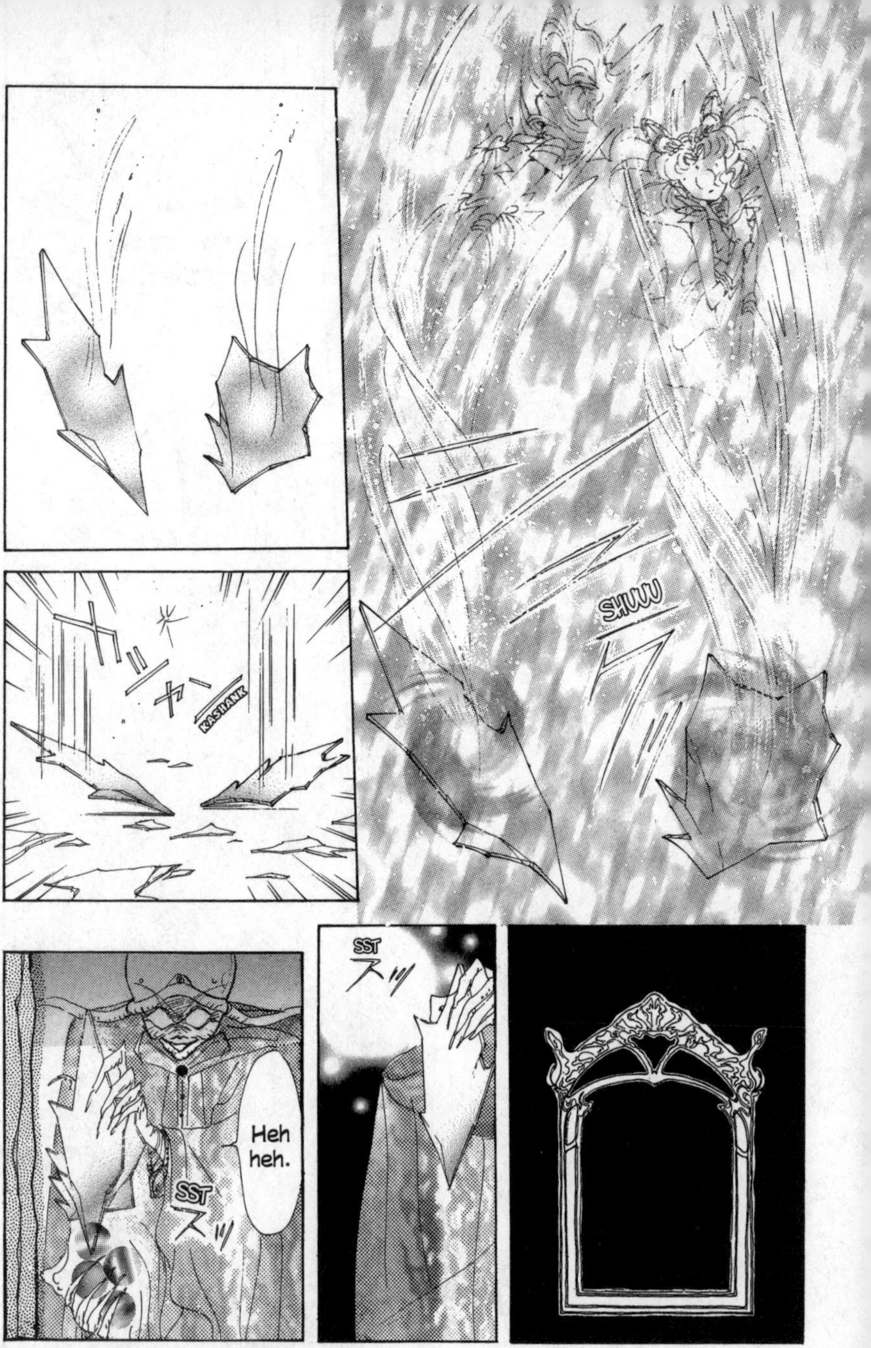
SHUUU
KASHANK
SST
Heh heh.
SST

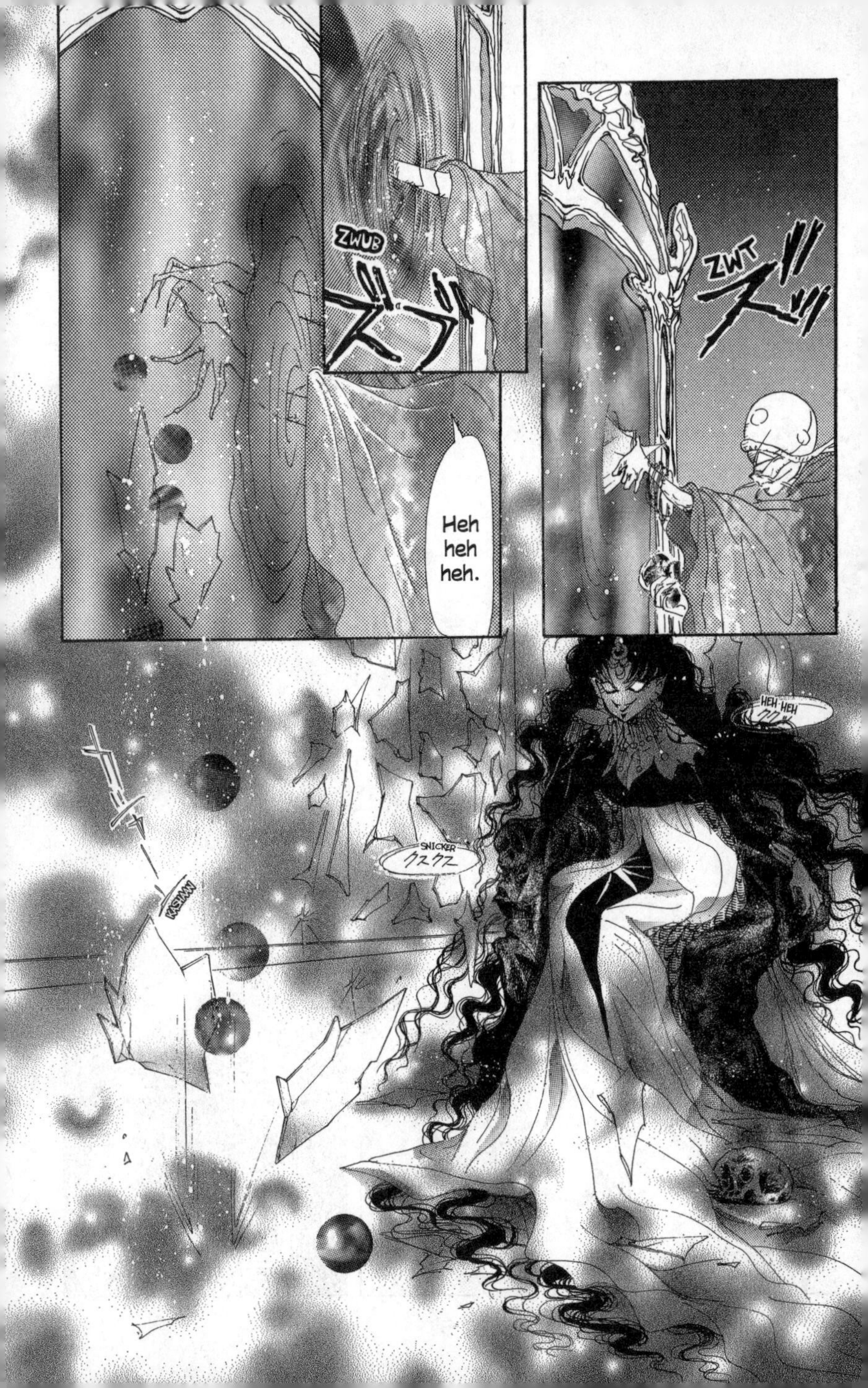
ZWT
ZWUB
Heh heh heh.
HEH HEH
SNICKER
クスクス
KASHANN

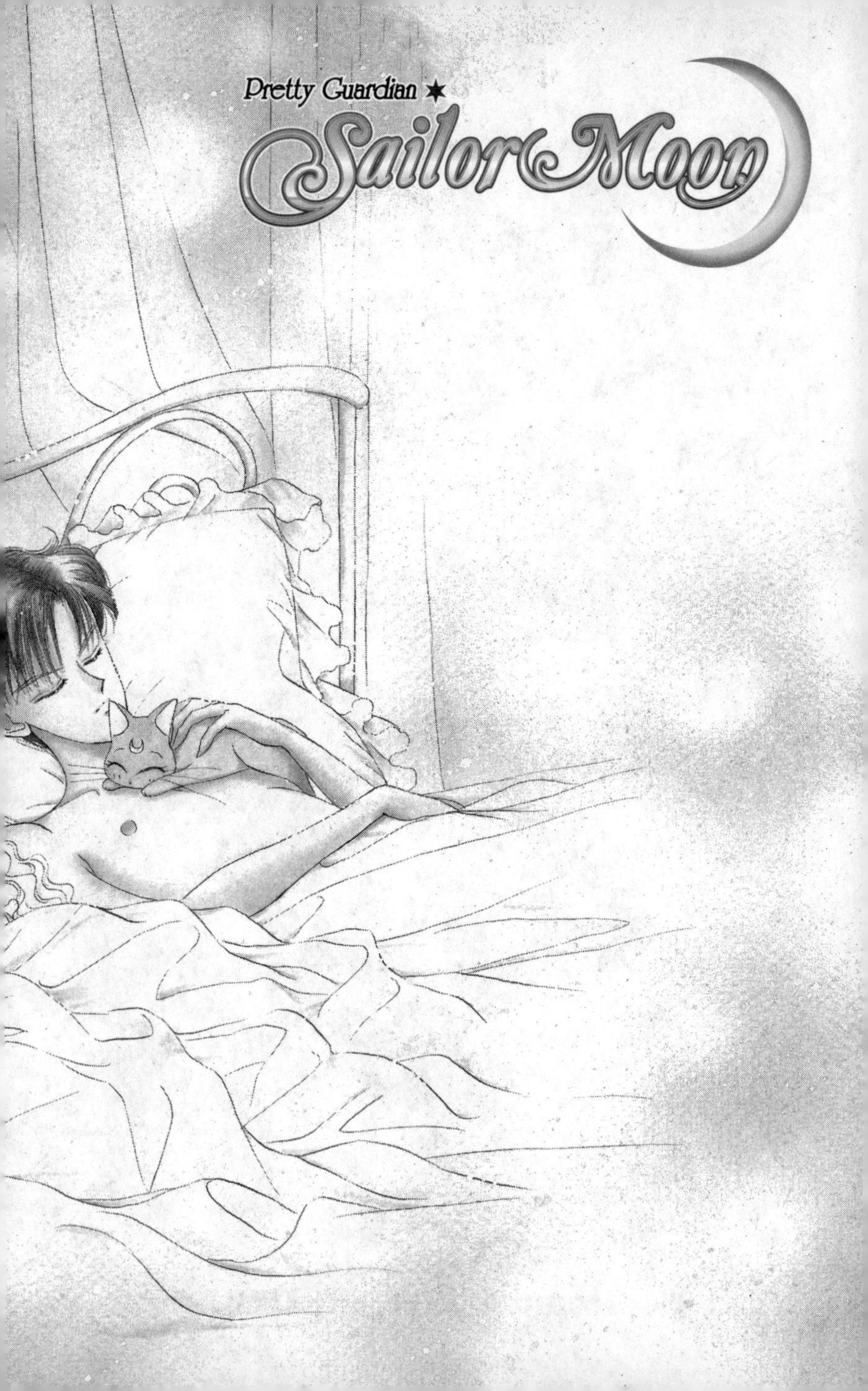
Pretty Guardian
Sailor Moon

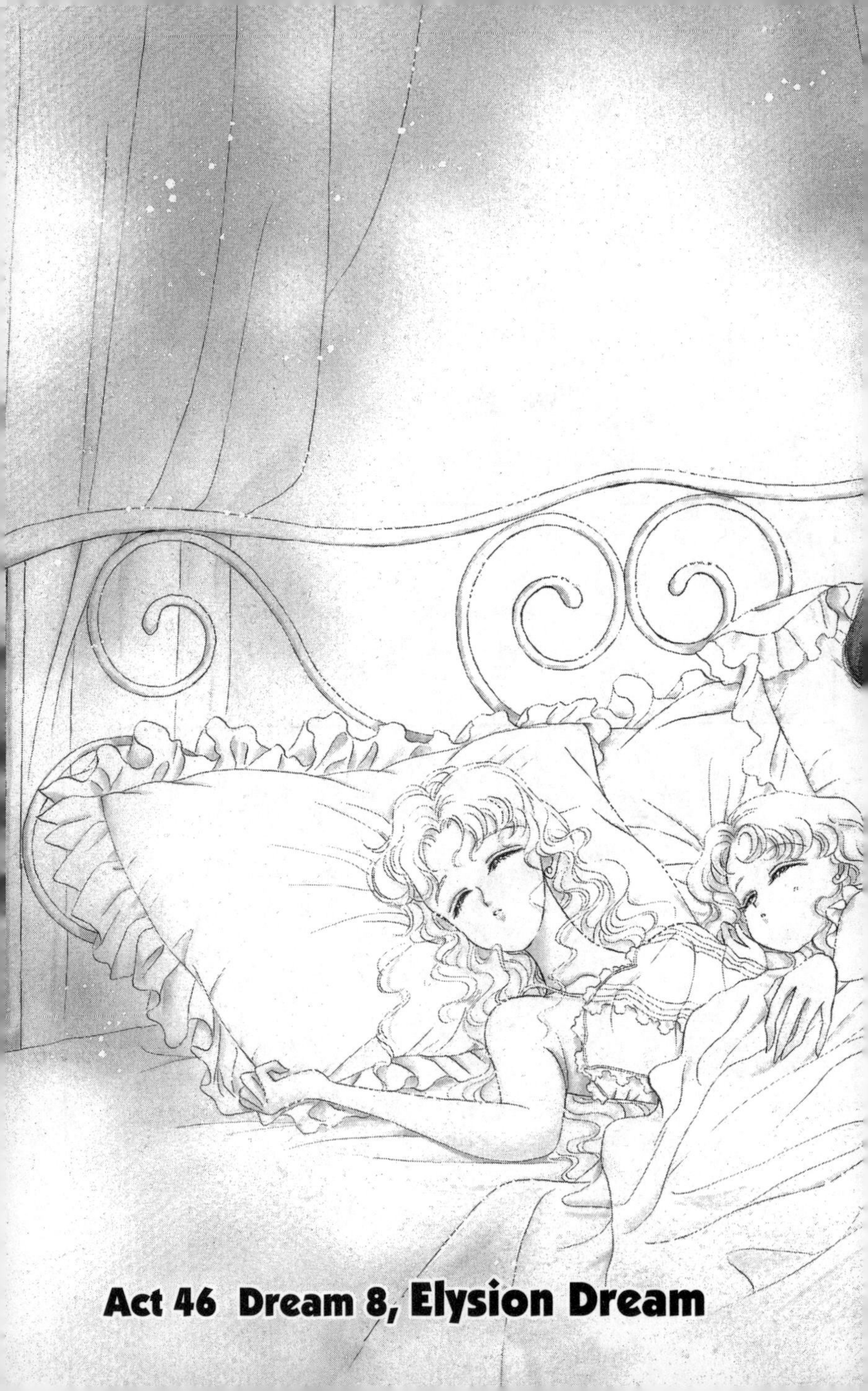

Act 46 Dream 8, Elysion Dream

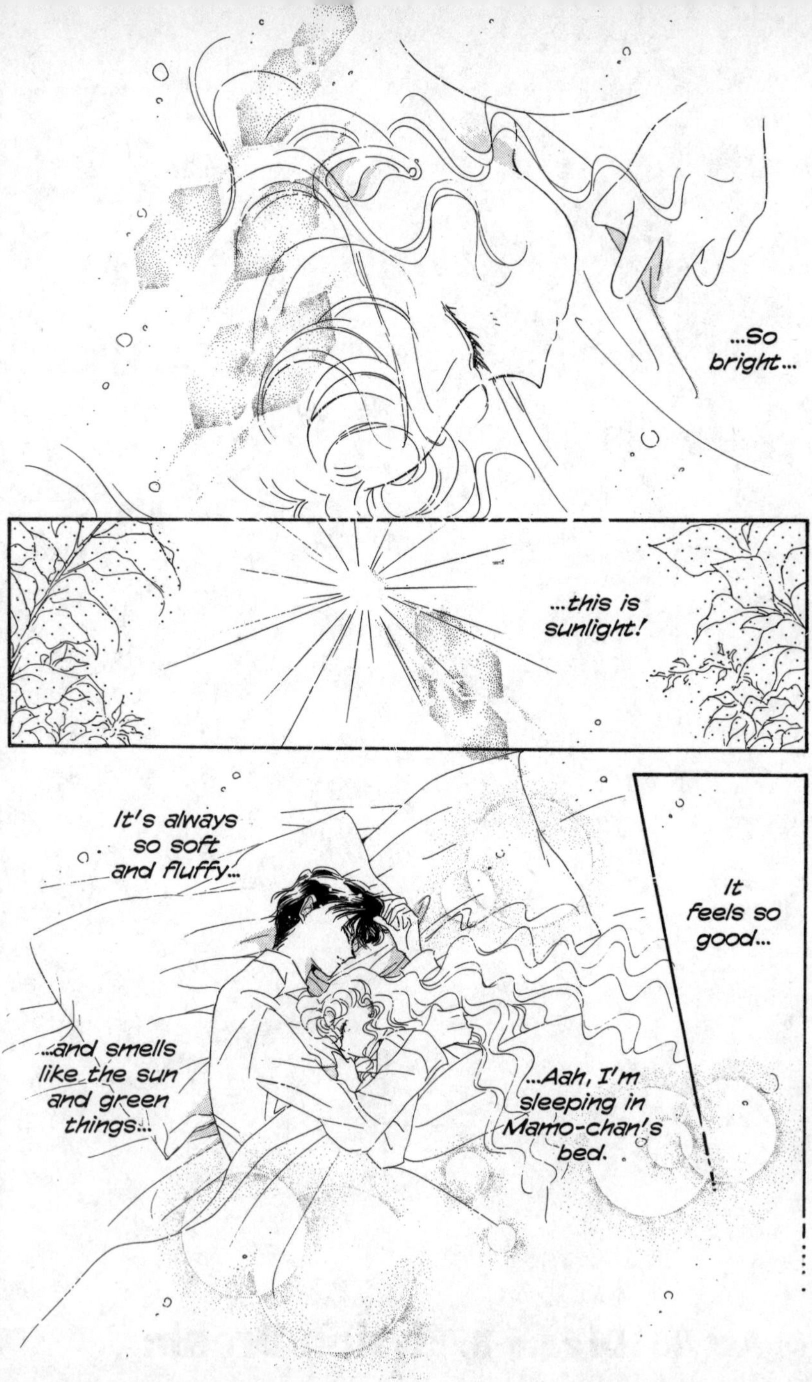

...So bright...
...this is sunlight!
It feels so good...
It's always so soft and fluffy...
...Aah, I'm sleeping in Mamo-chan's bed.
...and smells like the sun and green things...

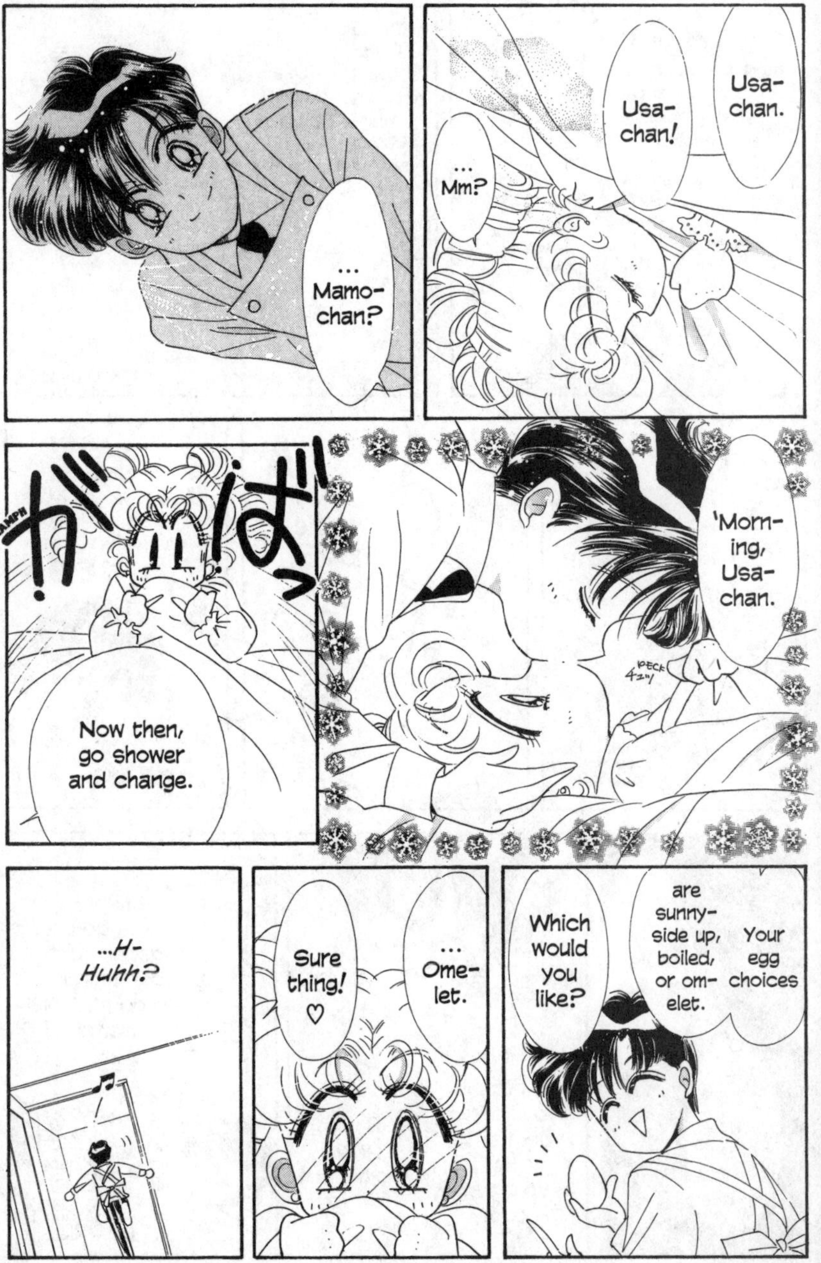
Usa-chan.
Usa-chan!
... Mm?
... Mamo-chan?
'Morning, Usa-chan.
PECK
GAMPH
がばっ
Now then, go shower and change.
Your egg choices are sunny-side up, boiled, or omelet.
Which would you like?
... Omelet.
Sure thing! ♡
...H-Huhh?

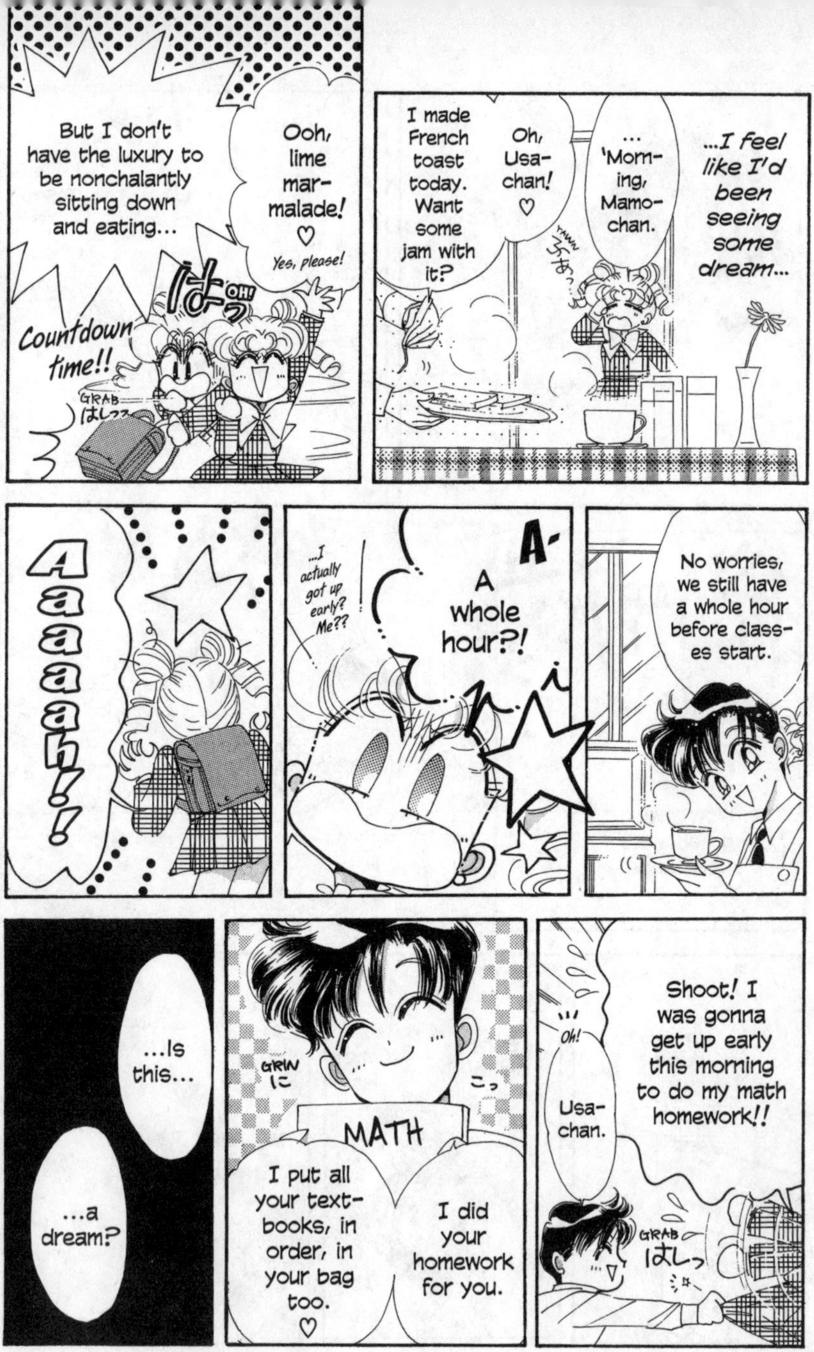
...I feel like I'd been seeing some dream...
... 'Morning, Mamo-chan.
YAWN
Oh, Usa-chan! ♡
I made French toast today. Want some jam with it?
Ooh, lime marmalade! ♡
Yes, please!
But I don't have the luxury to be nonchalantly sitting down and eating...
OH!
Countdown time!!
GRAB
No worries, we still have a whole hour before classes start.
A-
A whole hour?!
...I actually got up early? Me??
Aaaaaah!!
Shoot! I was gonna get up early this morning to do my math homework!!
Oh!
Usa-chan.
GRAB はしっ
MATH
I did your homework for you.
I put all your textbooks, in order, in your bag too. ♡
GRIN に
...Is this...
...a dream?

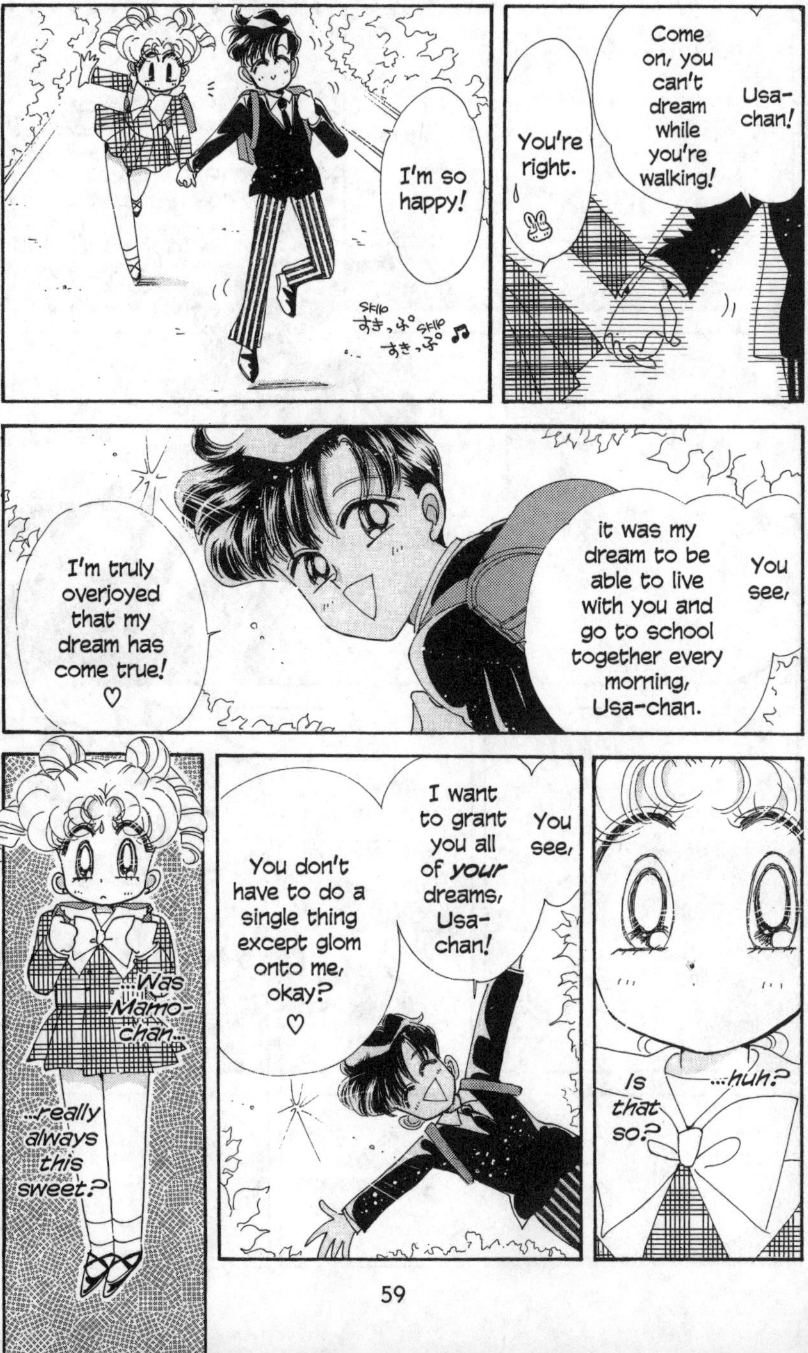
Usa-chan!
Come on, you can't dream while you're walking!
You're right.
I'm so happy!
SKIP すきっぷ SKIP すきっぷ ♫
You see,
it was my dream to be able to live with you and go to school together every morning, Usa-chan.
I'm truly overjoyed that my dream has come true! ♡
...huh?
Is that so?
You see,
I want to grant you all of *your* dreams, Usa-chan!
You don't have to do a single thing except glom onto me, okay? ♡
...Was Mamo-chan...
...really always this sweet?

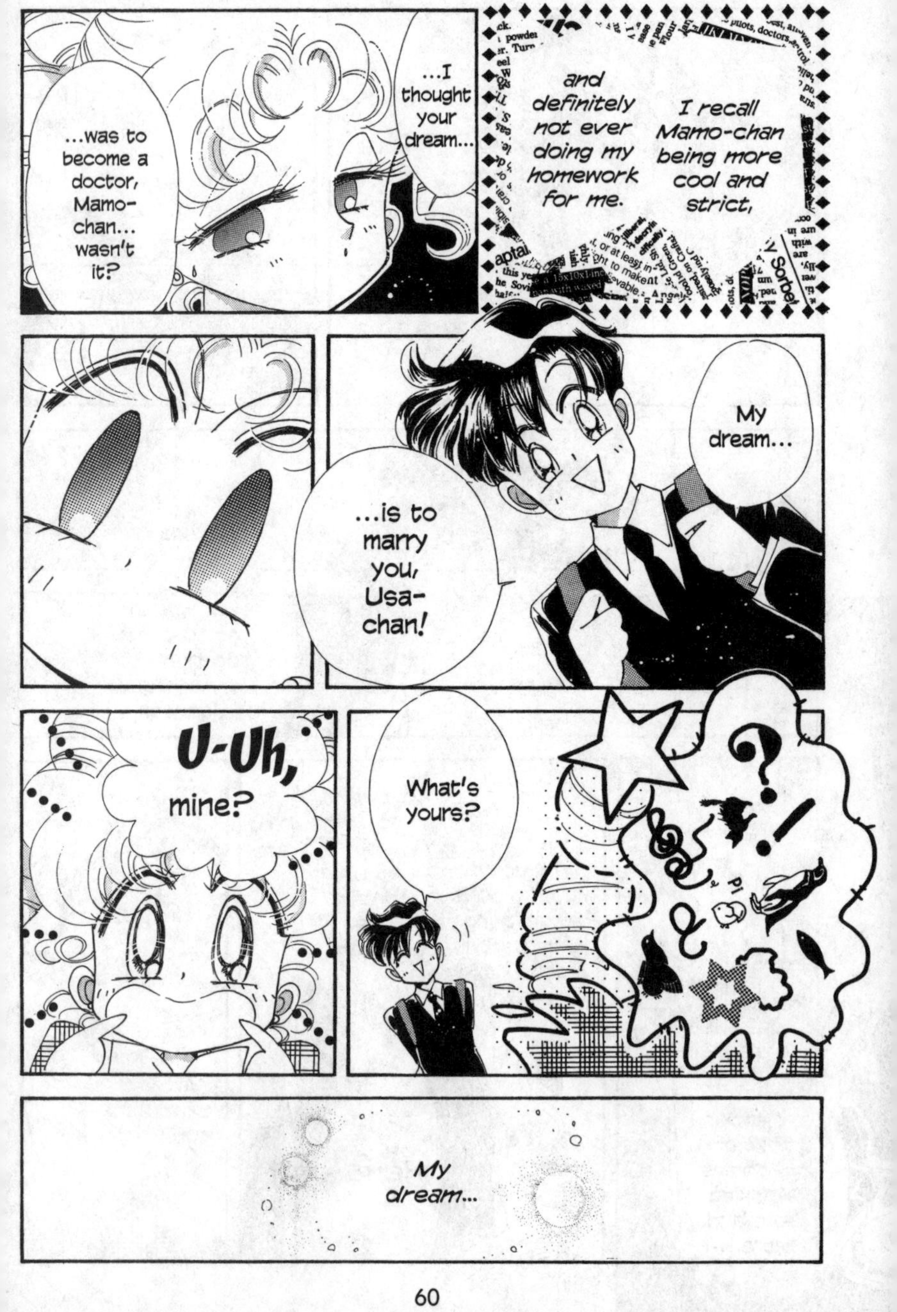
I recall Mamo-chan being more cool and strict,
and definitely not ever doing my homework for me.
...I thought your dream...
...was to become a doctor, Mamo-chan... wasn't it?
My dream...
...is to marry you, Usa-chan!
What's yours?
U-Uh, mine?
My dream...

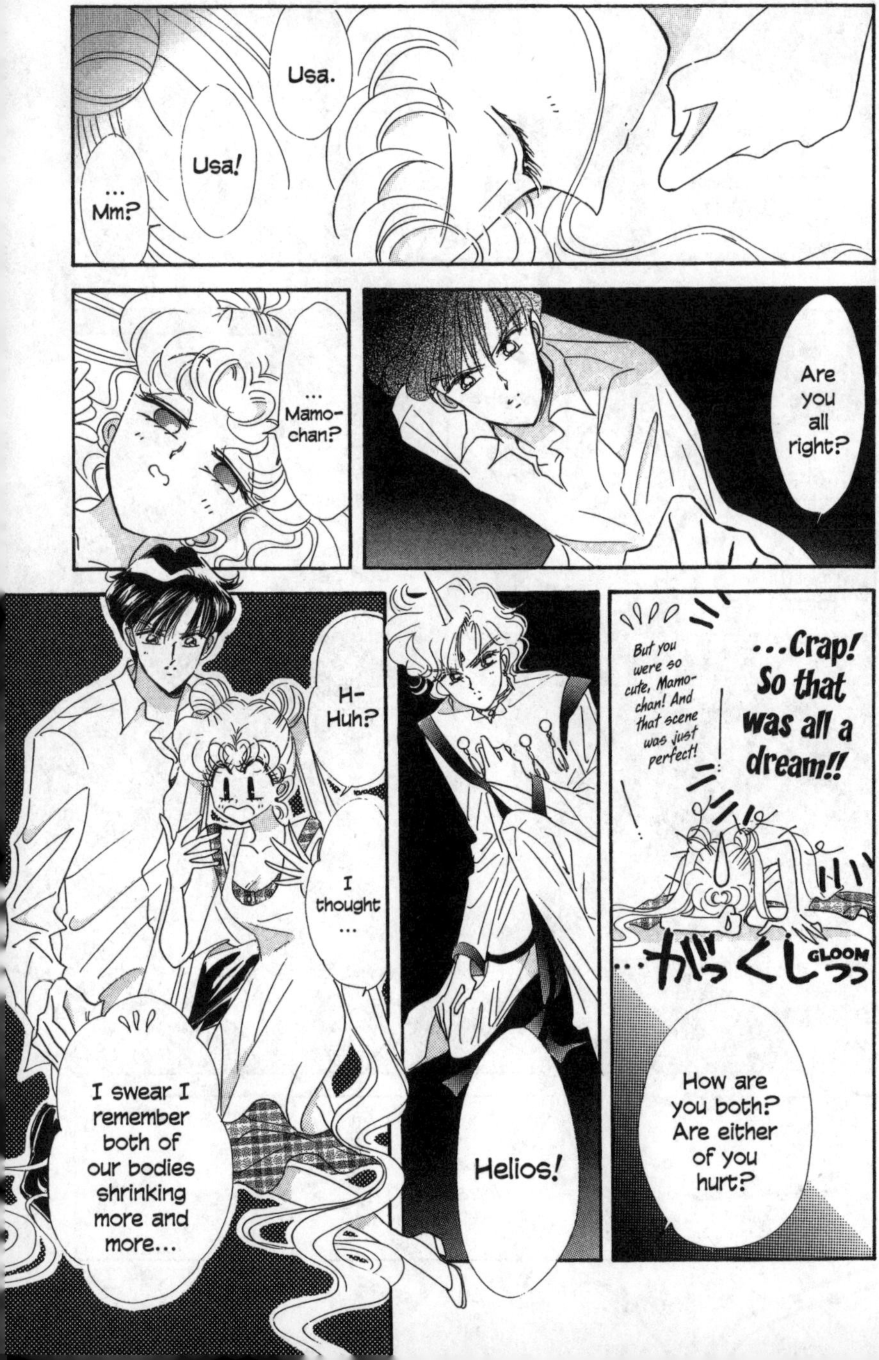
Usa.
Usa!
... Mm?
Are you all right?
... Mamo-chan?
...Crap! So that was all a dream!!
But you were so cute, Mamo-chan! And that scene was just perfect!
...がっくし GLOOM
How are you both? Are either of you hurt?
Helios!
H-Huh?
I thought ...
I swear I remember both of our bodies shrinking more and more...

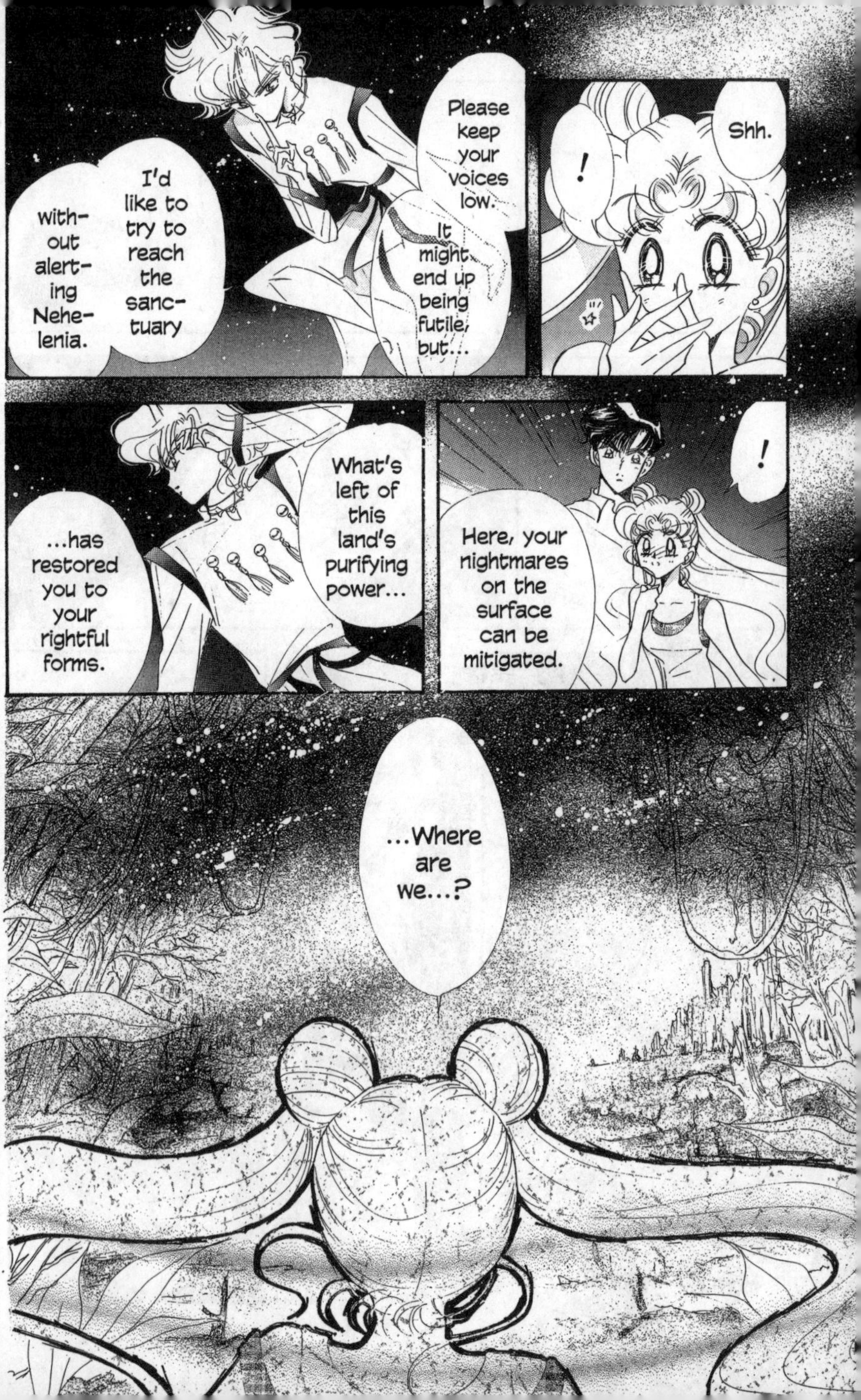
Shh.
!
Please keep your voices low.
It might end up being futile, but...
I'd like to try to reach the sanctuary
without alerting Nehelenia.
!
Here, your nightmares on the surface can be mitigated.
What's left of this land's purifying power...
...has restored you to your rightful forms.
...Where are we...?

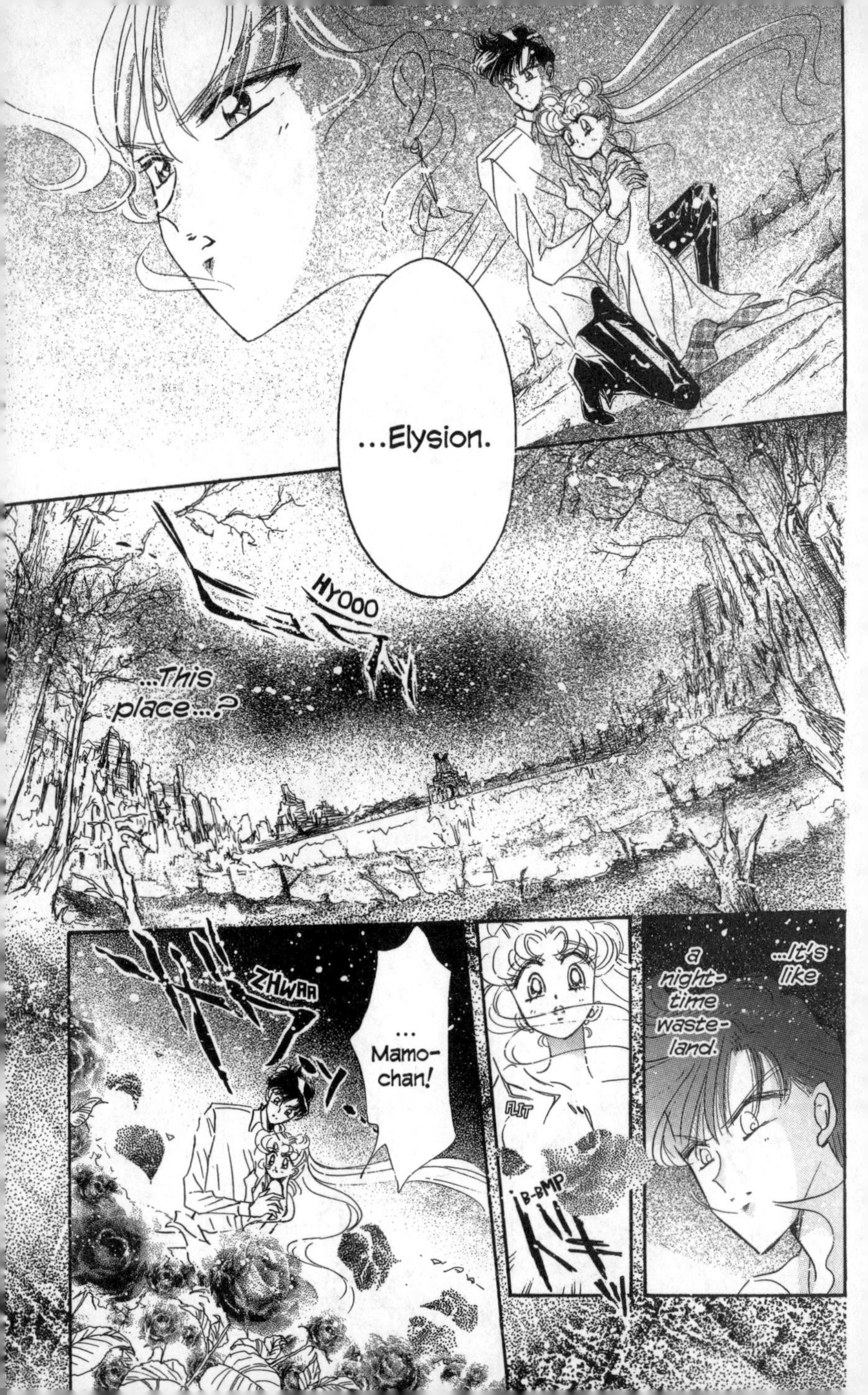
...Elysion.
HYOOO
...This place...?
...It's like a night-time waste-land.
FLIT
B-BMP
ZHWAA
... Mamo-chan!

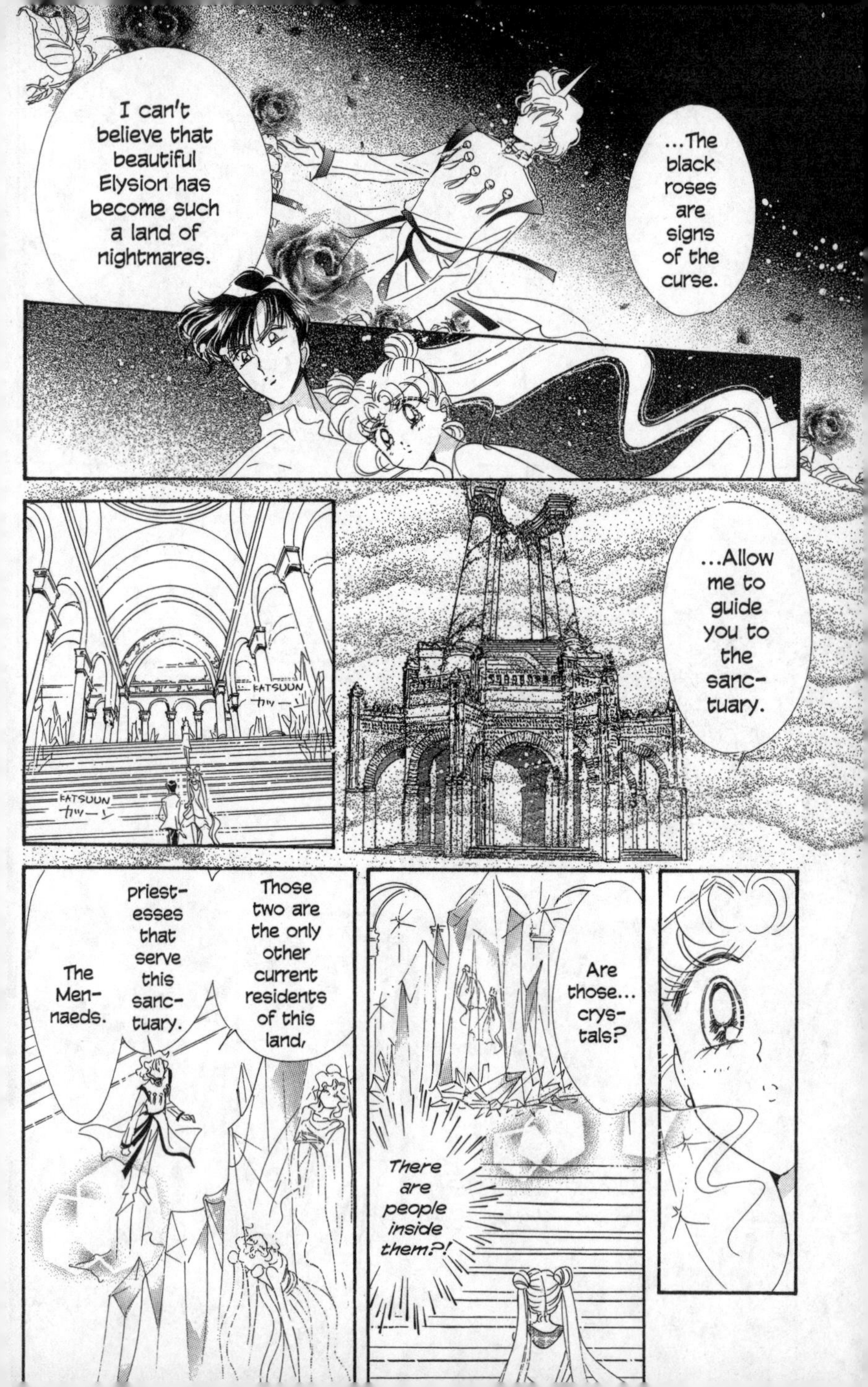
...The black roses are signs of the curse.
I can't believe that beautiful Elysion has become such a land of nightmares.
...Allow me to guide you to the sanctuary.
KATSUUN
カツーン
KATSUUN
カツーン
Are those... crystals?
There are people inside them?!
Those two are the only other current residents of this land,
priestesses that serve this sanctuary.
The Mennaeds.

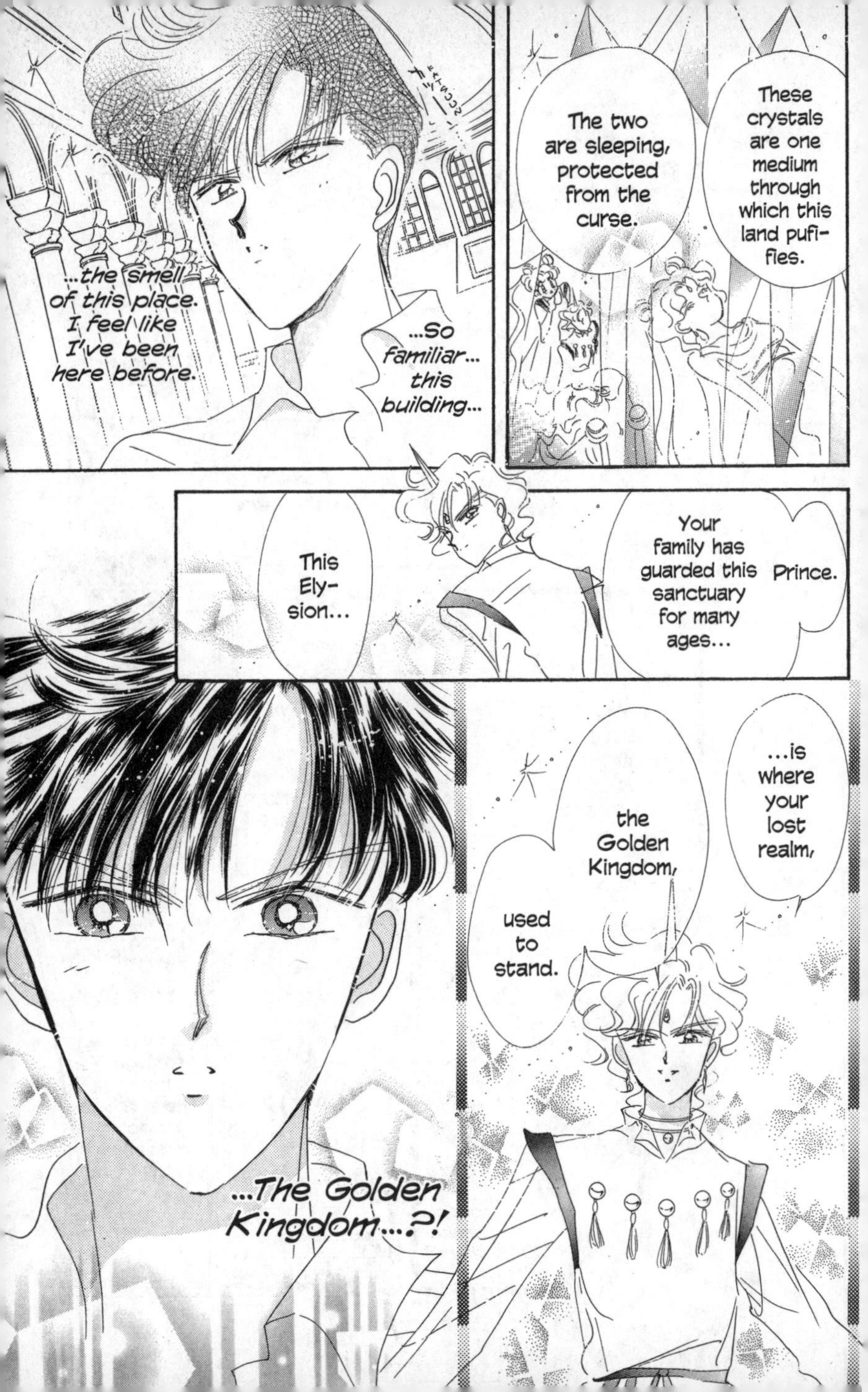
These crystals are one medium through which this land pufi-fies.
The two are sleeping, protected from the curse.
...So familiar... this building...
...the smell of this place. I feel like I've been here before.
Prince.
Your family has guarded this sanctuary for many ages...
This Ely-sion...
...is where your lost realm,
the Golden Kingdom,
used to stand.
...The Golden Kingdom...?!

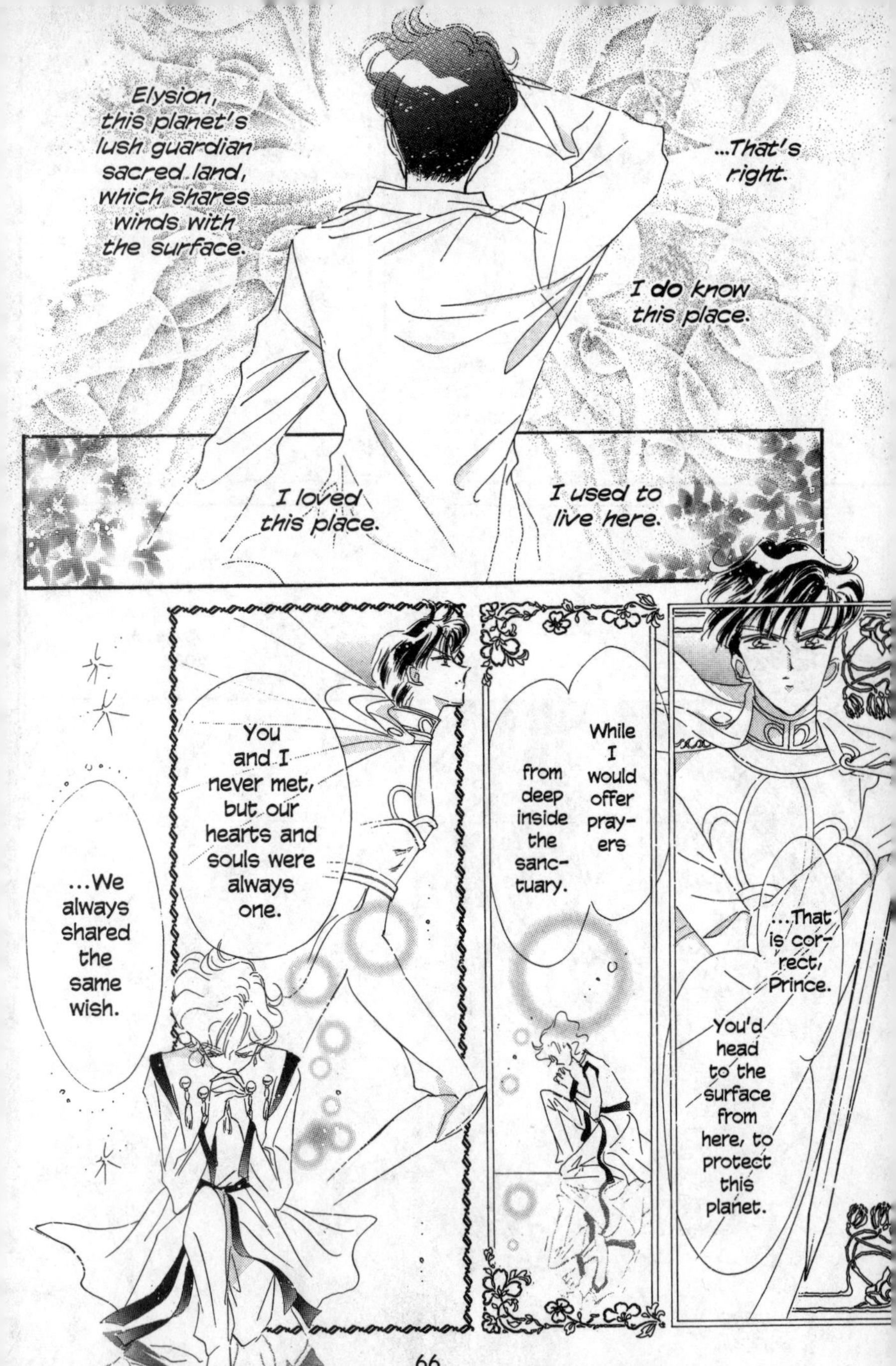
Elysion, this planet's lush guardian sacred land, which shares winds with the surface.
...That's right.
I do know this place.
I used to live here.
I loved this place.
...That is correct, Prince.
You'd head to the surface from here, to protect this planet.
While I would offer prayers
from deep inside the sanctuary.
You and I never met, but our hearts and souls were always one.
...We always shared the same wish.

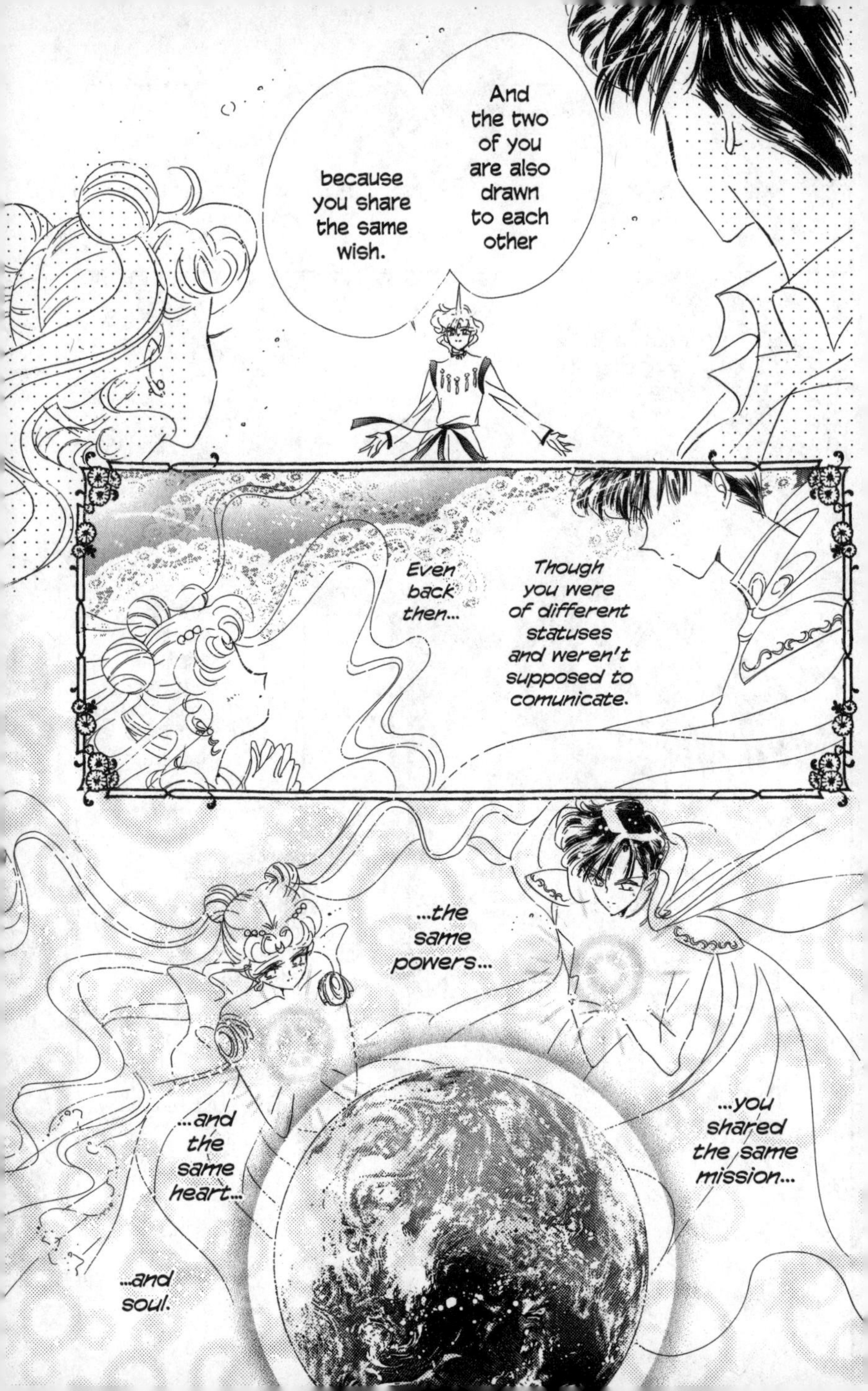
And the two of you are also drawn to each other
because you share the same wish.
Though you were of different statuses and weren't supposed to comunicate.
Even back then...
...you shared the same mission...
...the same powers...
...and the same heart...
...and soul.

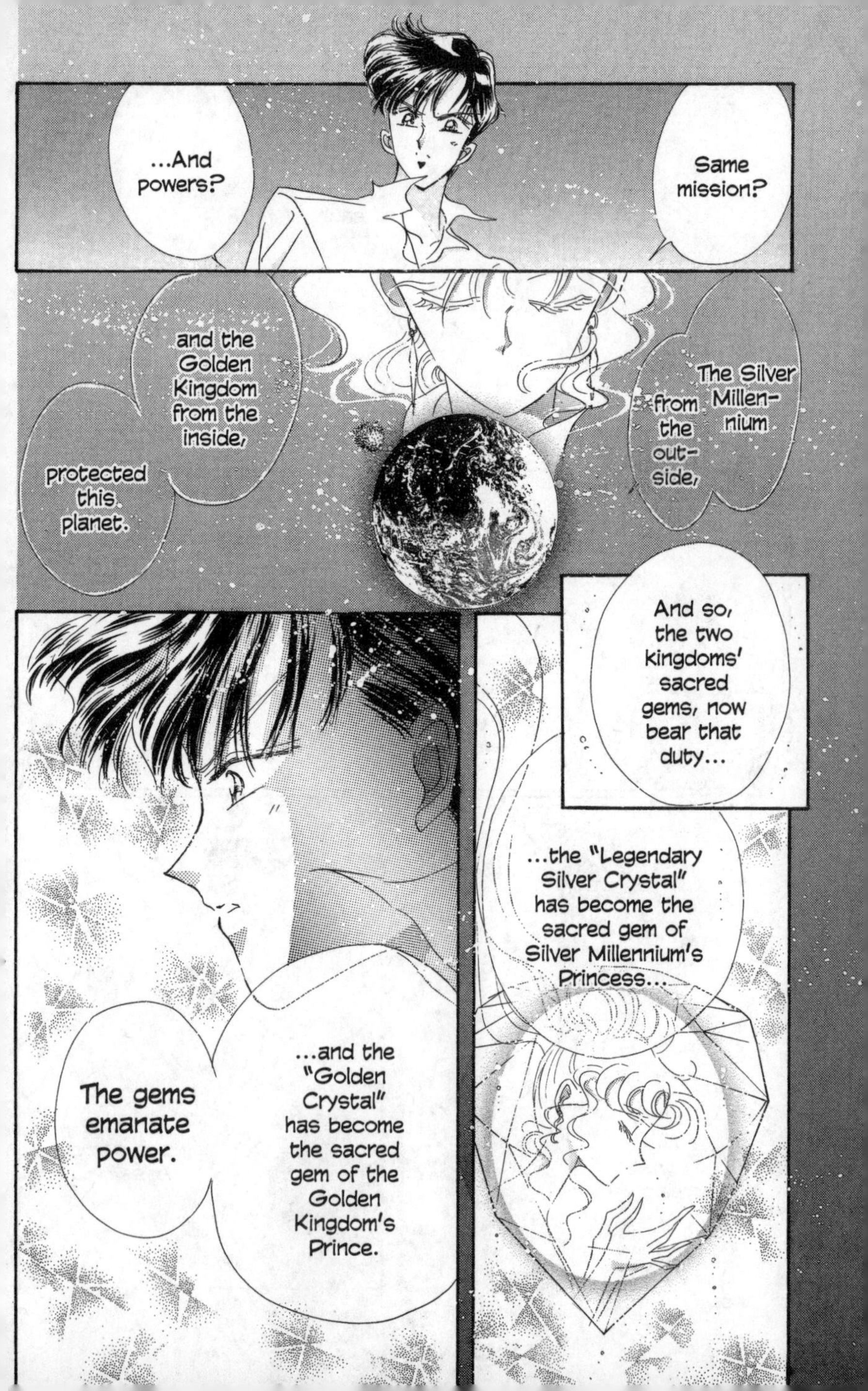
Same mission?
...And powers?
The Silver Millennium from the outside,
and the Golden Kingdom from the inside,
protected this planet.
And so, the two kingdoms' sacred gems, now bear that duty...
...the "Legendary Silver Crystal" has become the sacred gem of Silver Millennium's Princess...
...and the "Golden Crystal" has become the sacred gem of the Golden Kingdom's Prince.
The gems emanate power.

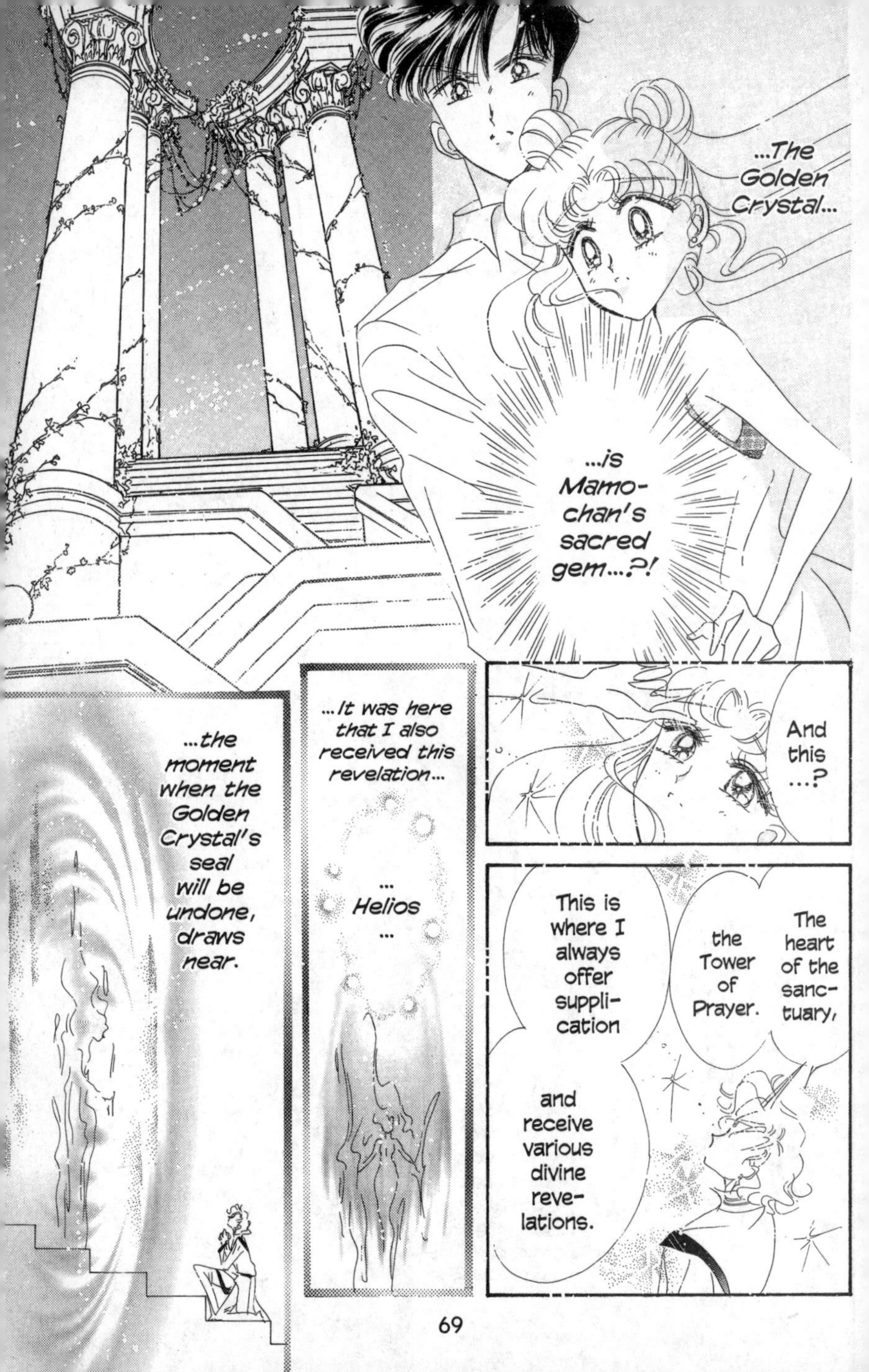
...The Golden Crystal...
...is Mamo-chan's sacred gem...?!
And this ...?
The heart of the sanctuary,
the Tower of Prayer.
This is where I always offer supplication
and receive various divine revelations.
...It was here that I also received this revelation...
... Helios ...
...the moment when the Golden Crystal's seal will be undone, draws near.

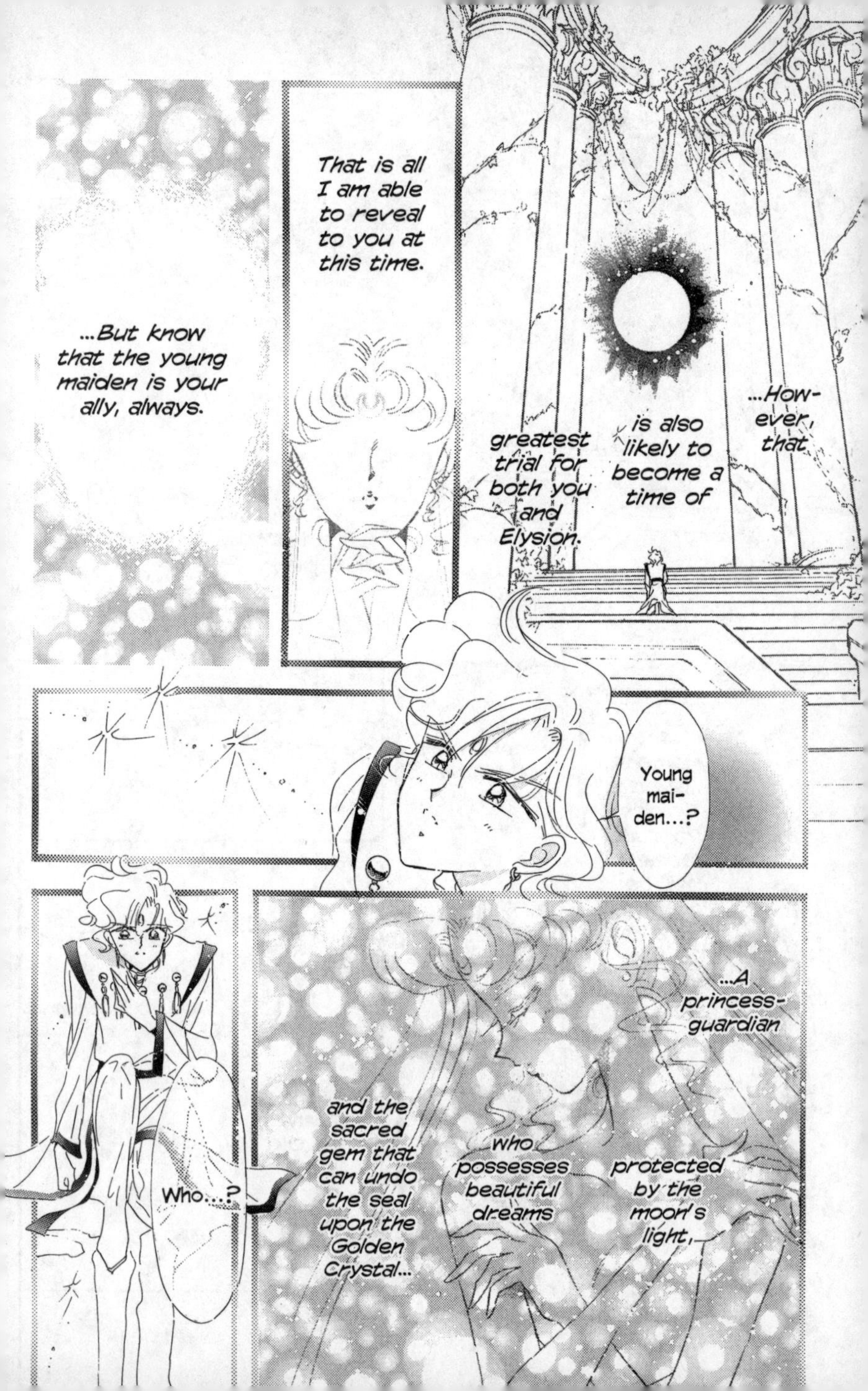
...However, that
is also likely to become a time of
greatest trial for both you and Elysion.
That is all I am able to reveal to you at this time.
...But know that the young maiden is your ally, always.
Young maiden...?
...A princess-guardian
protected by the moon's light,
who possesses beautiful dreams
and the sacred gem that can undo the seal upon the Golden Crystal...
Who...?

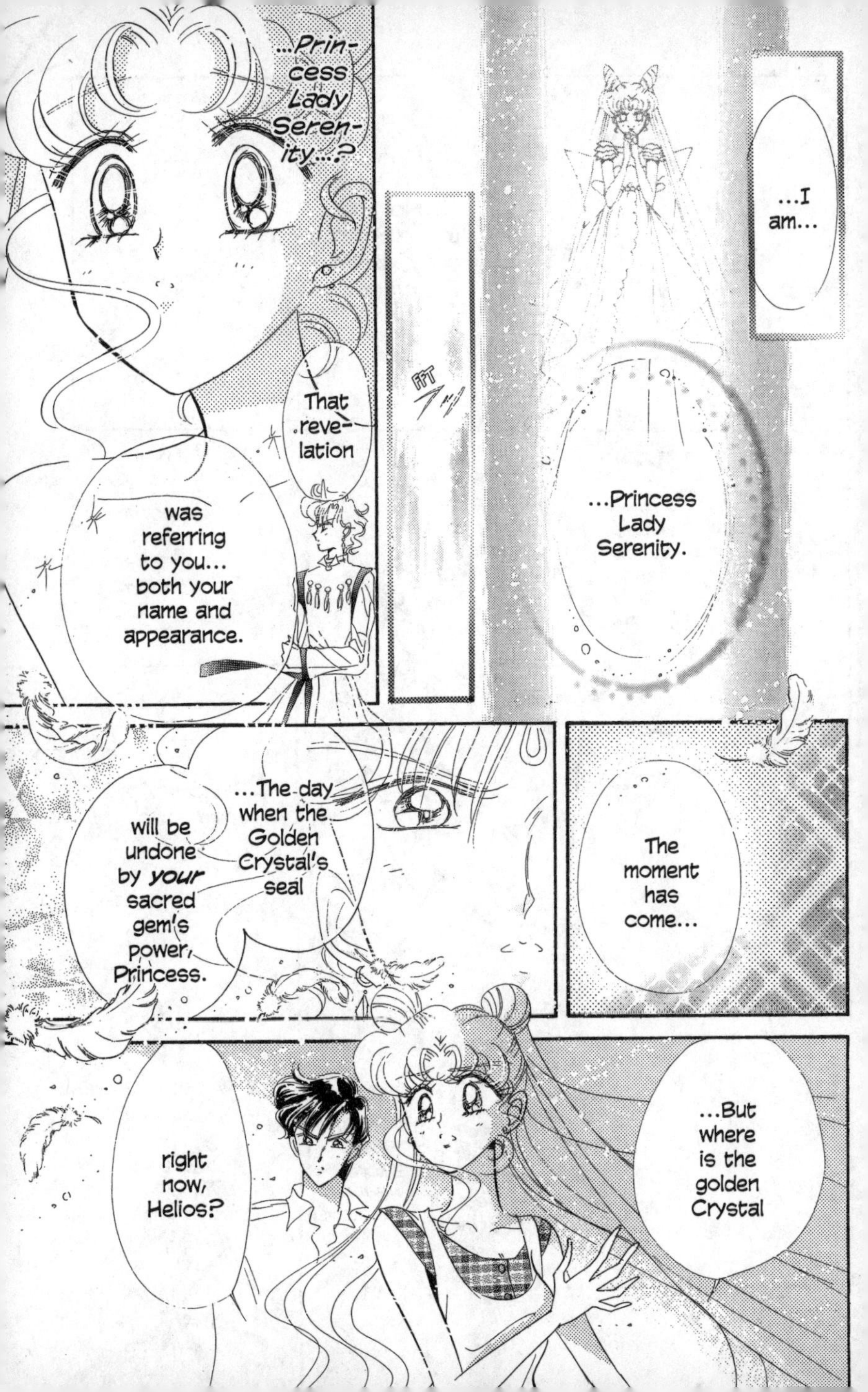
...I am...
...Princess Lady Serenity.
FFT
...Princess Lady Serenity...?
That revelation
was referring to you... both your name and appearance.
The moment has come...
...The day when the Golden Crystal's seal
will be undone by *your* sacred gem's power, Princess.
...But where is the golden Crystal
right now, Helios?

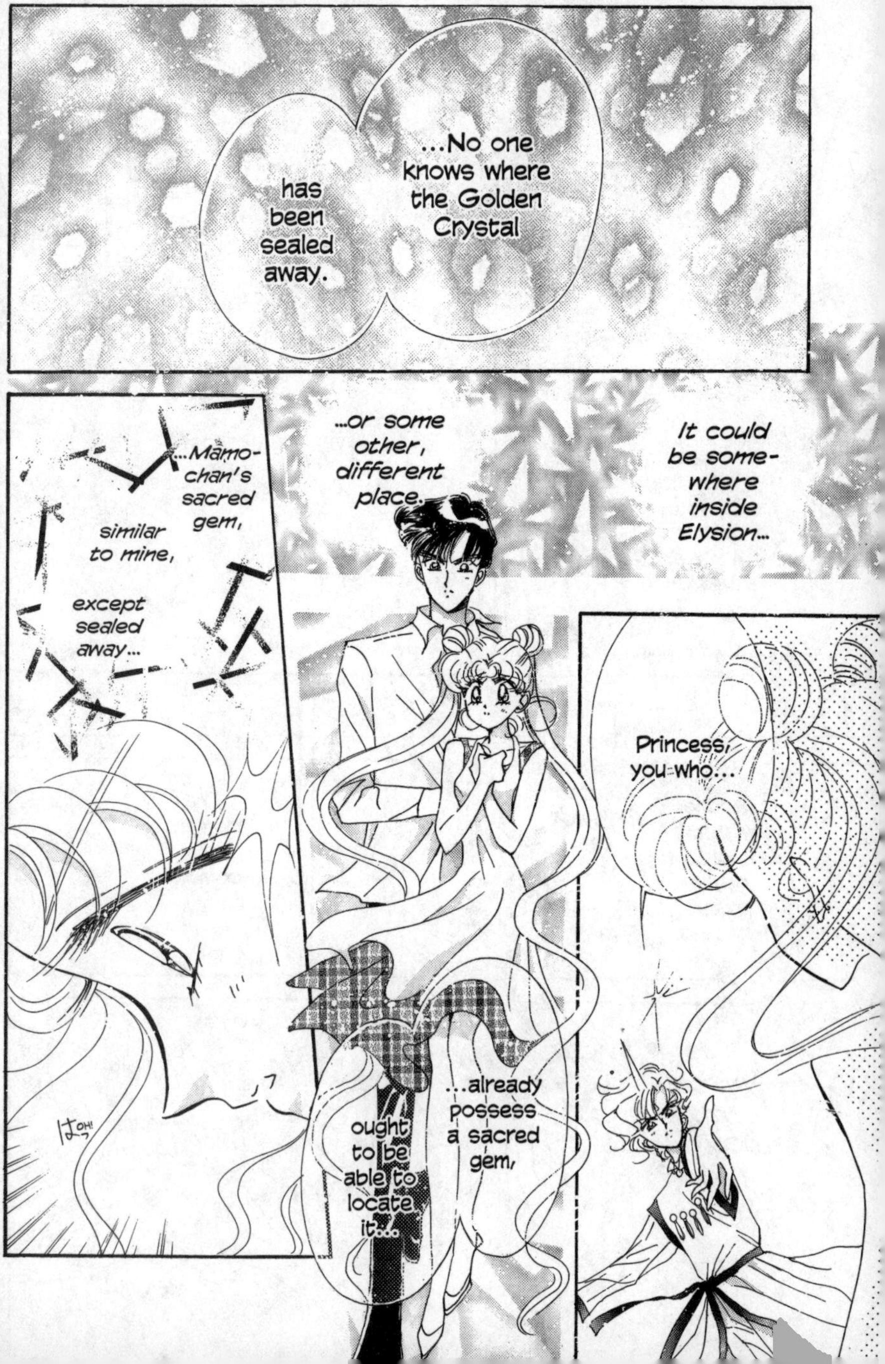
...No one knows where the Golden Crystal
has been sealed away.
It could be somewhere inside Elysion...
...or some other, different place.
Princess, you who...
...already possess a sacred gem,
ought to be able to locate it...
...Mamo-chan's sacred gem,
similar to mine,
except sealed away...
はっ OH!

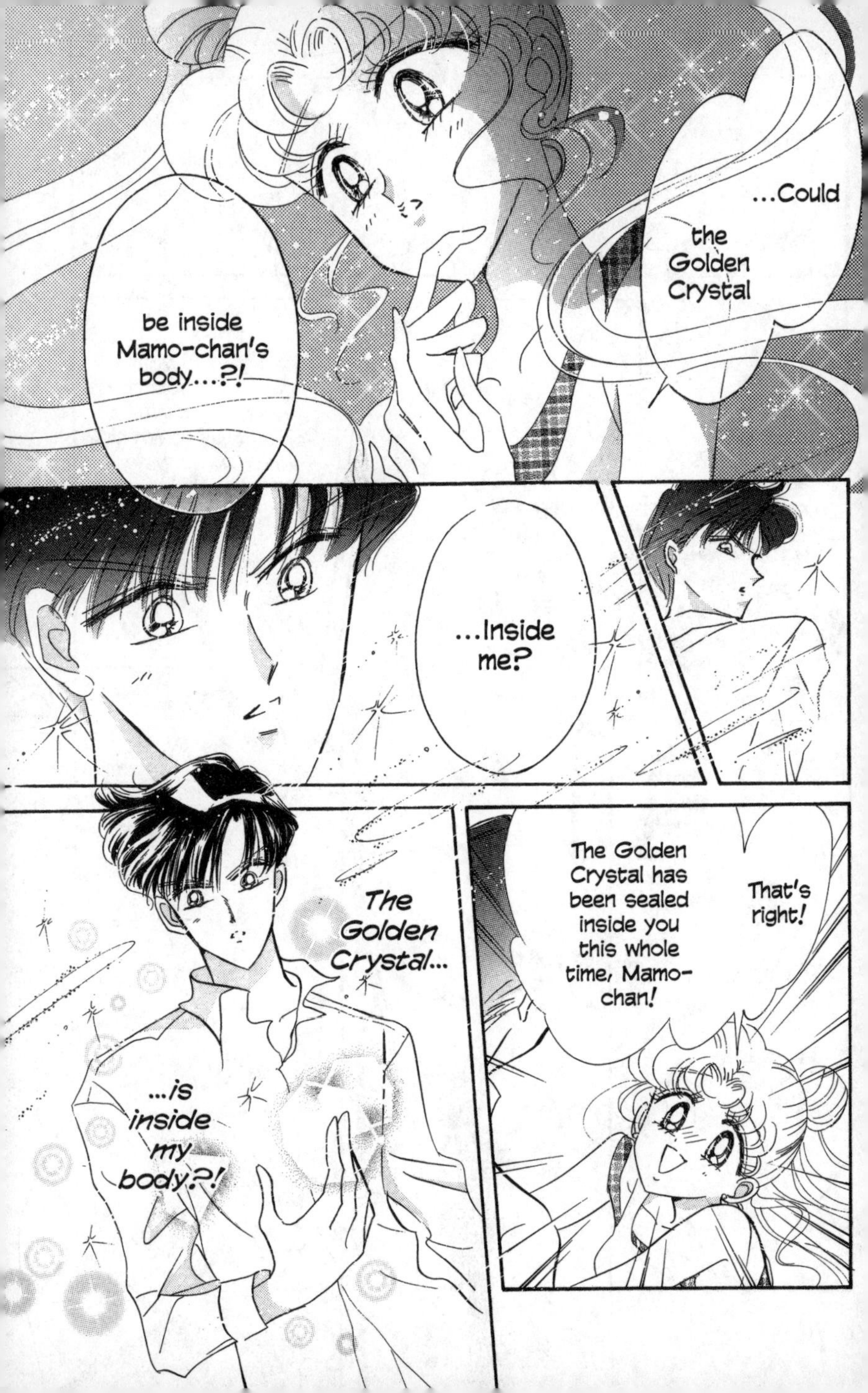
...Could the Golden Crystal
be inside Mamo-chan's body...?!
...Inside me?
That's right!
The Golden Crystal has been sealed inside you this whole time, Mamo-chan!
The Golden Crystal...
...is inside my body?!

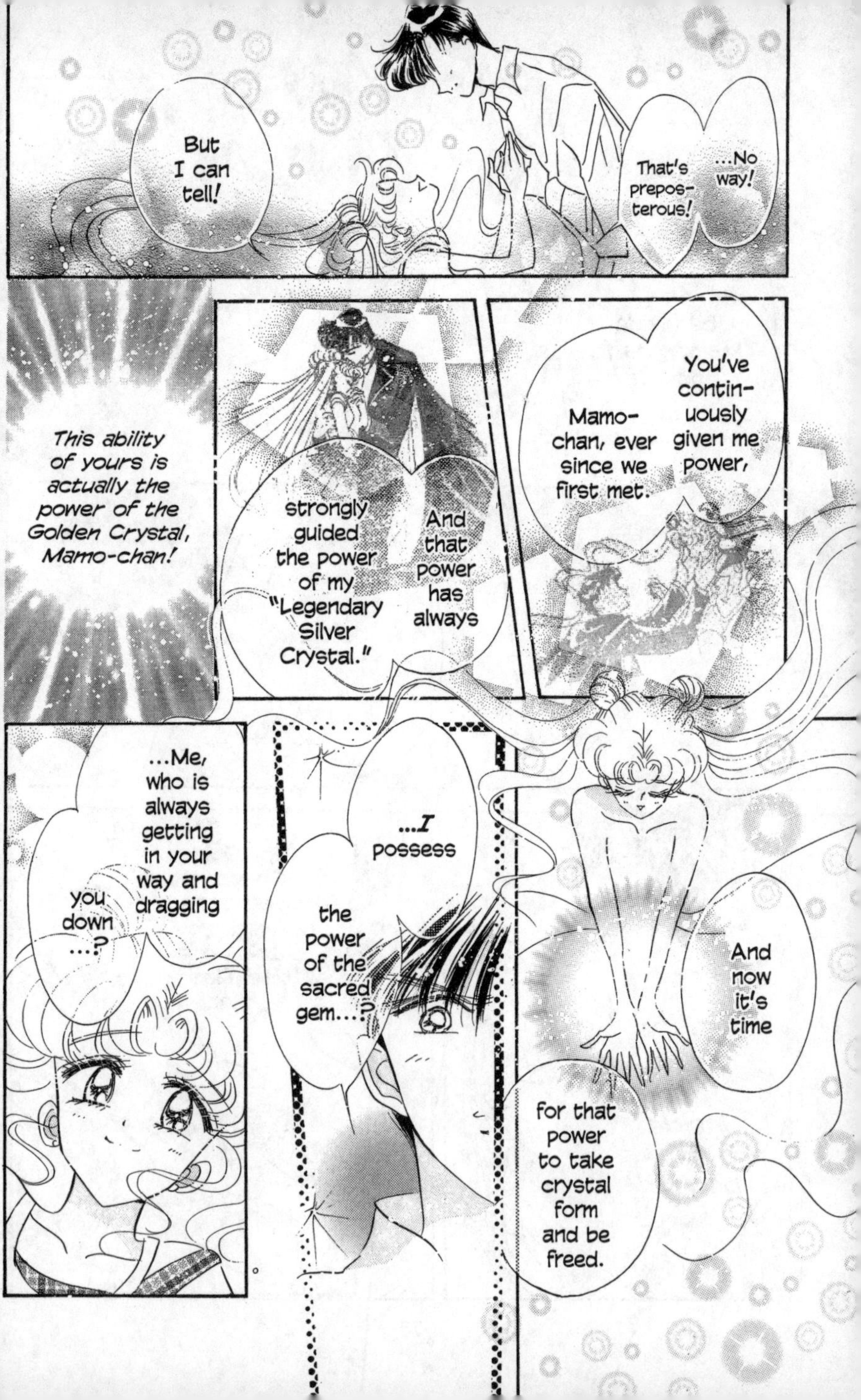
...No way!
That's preposterous!
But I can tell!
You've continuously given me power,
Mamo-chan, ever since we first met.
And that power has always
strongly guided the power of my "Legendary Silver Crystal."
This ability of yours is actually the power of the Golden Crystal, Mamo-chan!
And now it's time
for that power to take crystal form and be freed.
...I possess
the power of the sacred gem...?
...Me, who is always getting in your way and dragging
you down...?

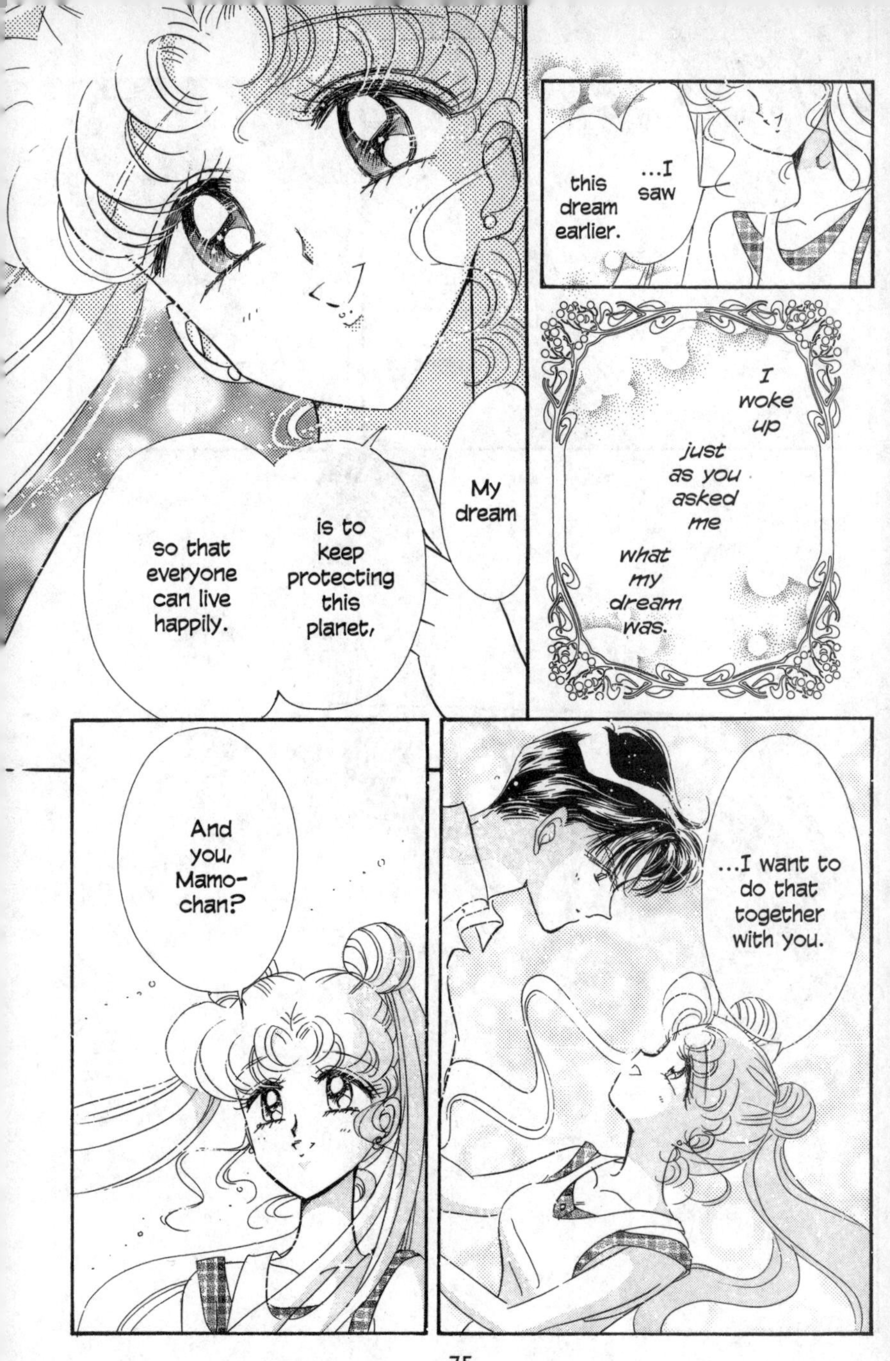
...I saw this dream earlier.
I woke up just as you asked me what my dream was.
My dream
is to keep protecting this planet,
so that everyone can live happily.
...I want to do that together with you.
And you, Mamo-chan?

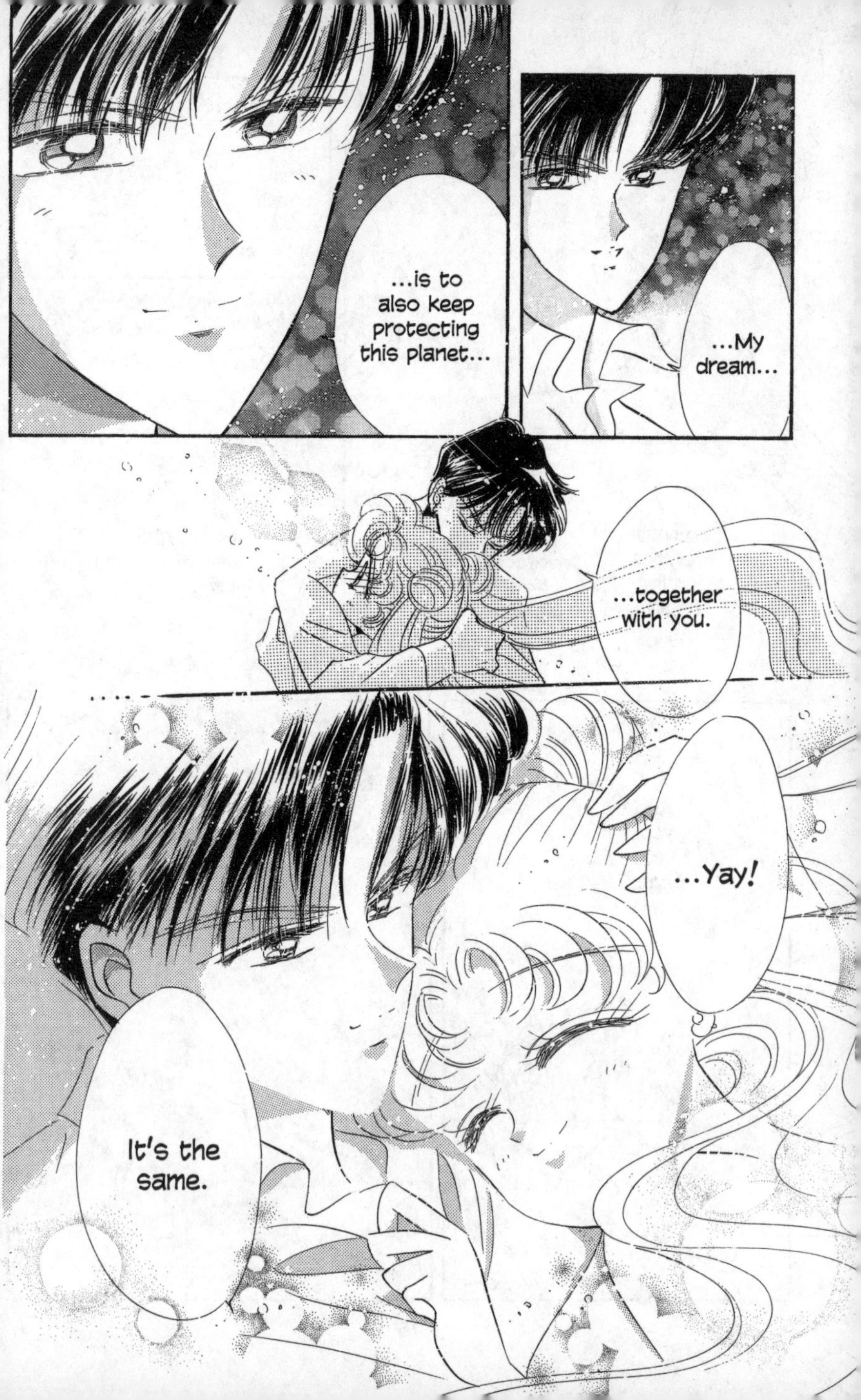
...My dream...
...is to also keep protecting this planet...
...together with you.
...Yay!
It's the same.

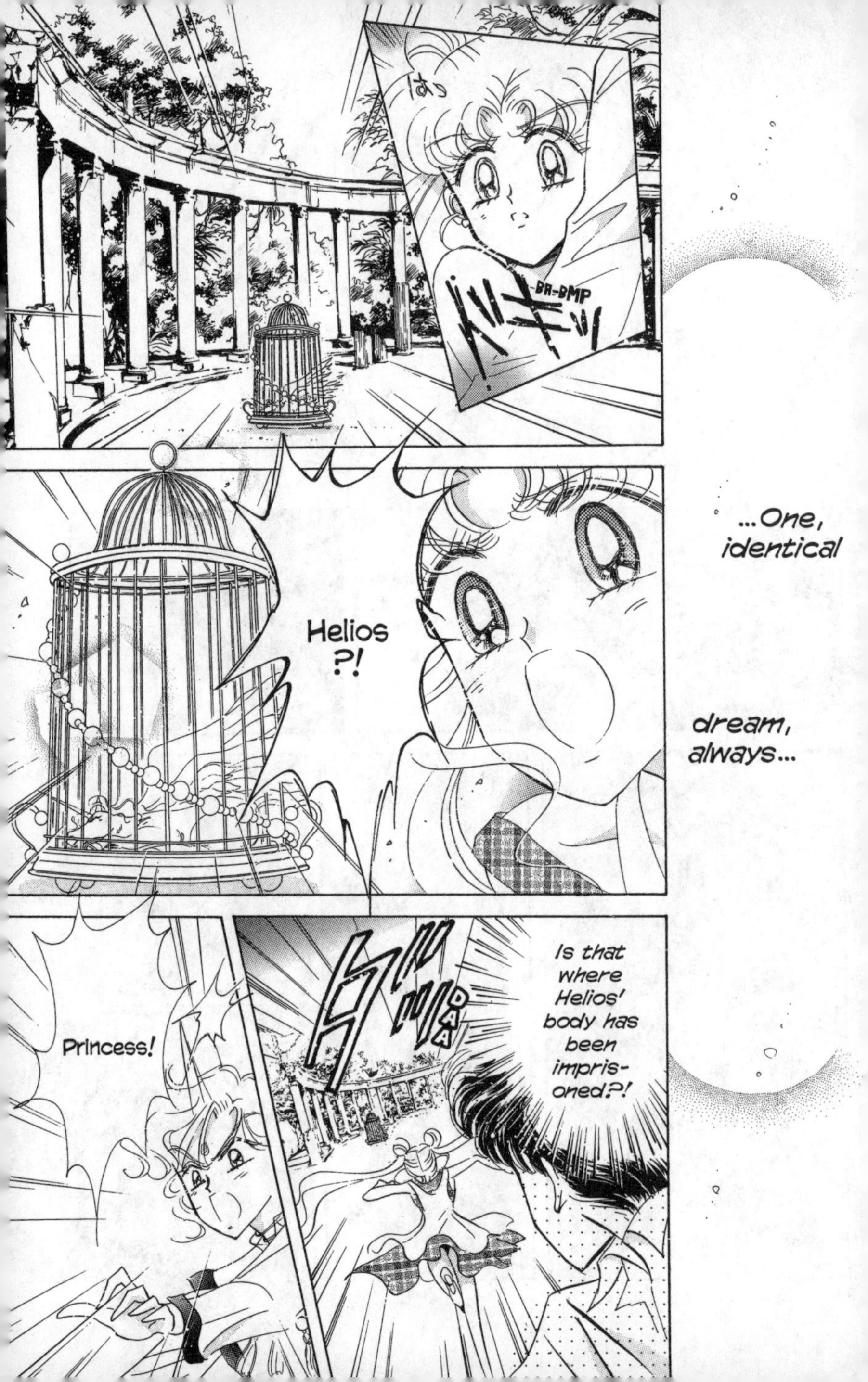
...One, identical
dream, always...
はっ
BA-BMP
Helios ?!
Is that where Helios' body has been impris-oned?!
DAA
Princess!

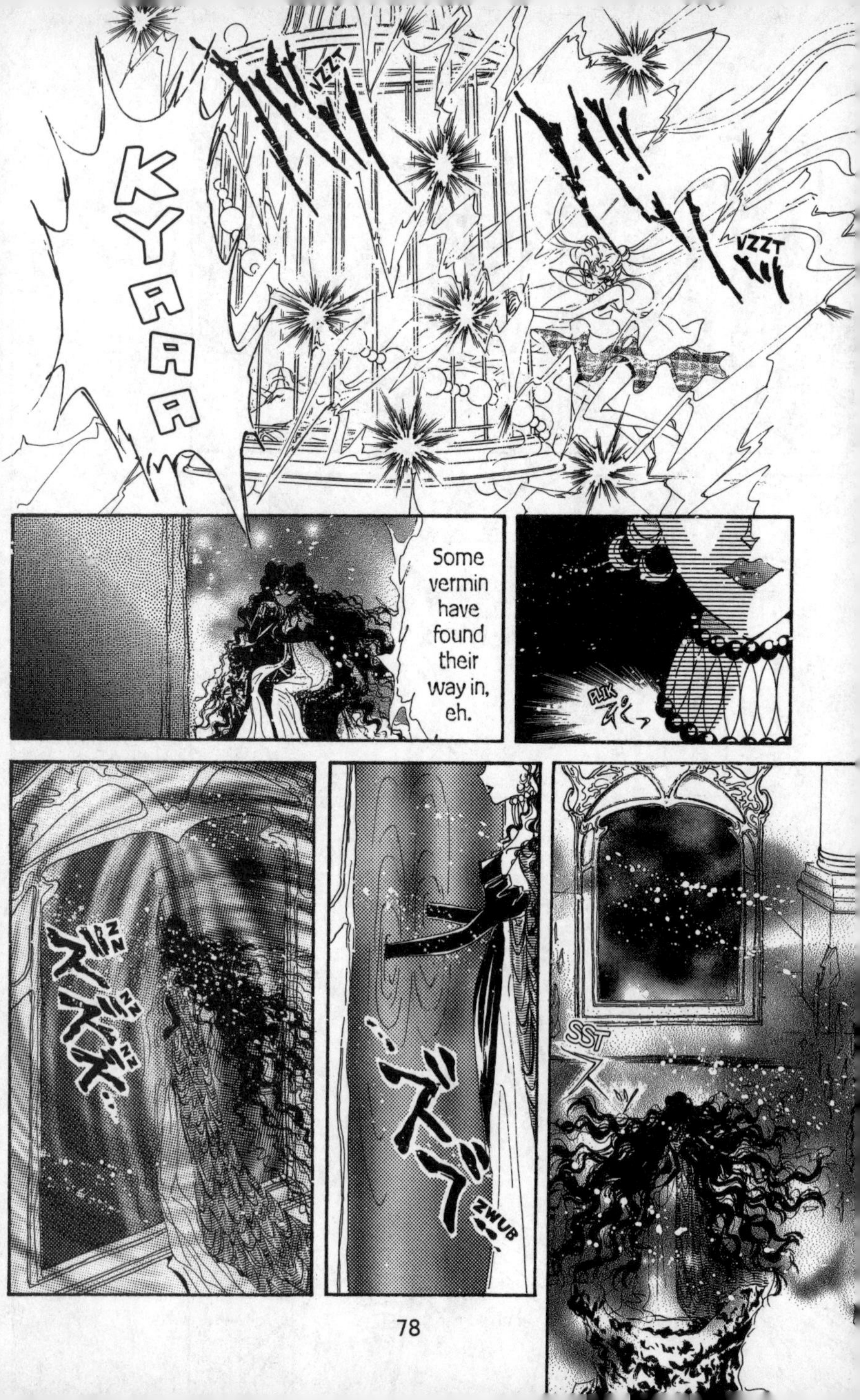
VZZT
VZZT
KYAAA
PLIK
ぴくっ
Some vermin have found their way in, eh.
SST
ス
ZWUB
ズブ
ZZ
ZZ
ZZ
ズズズ…

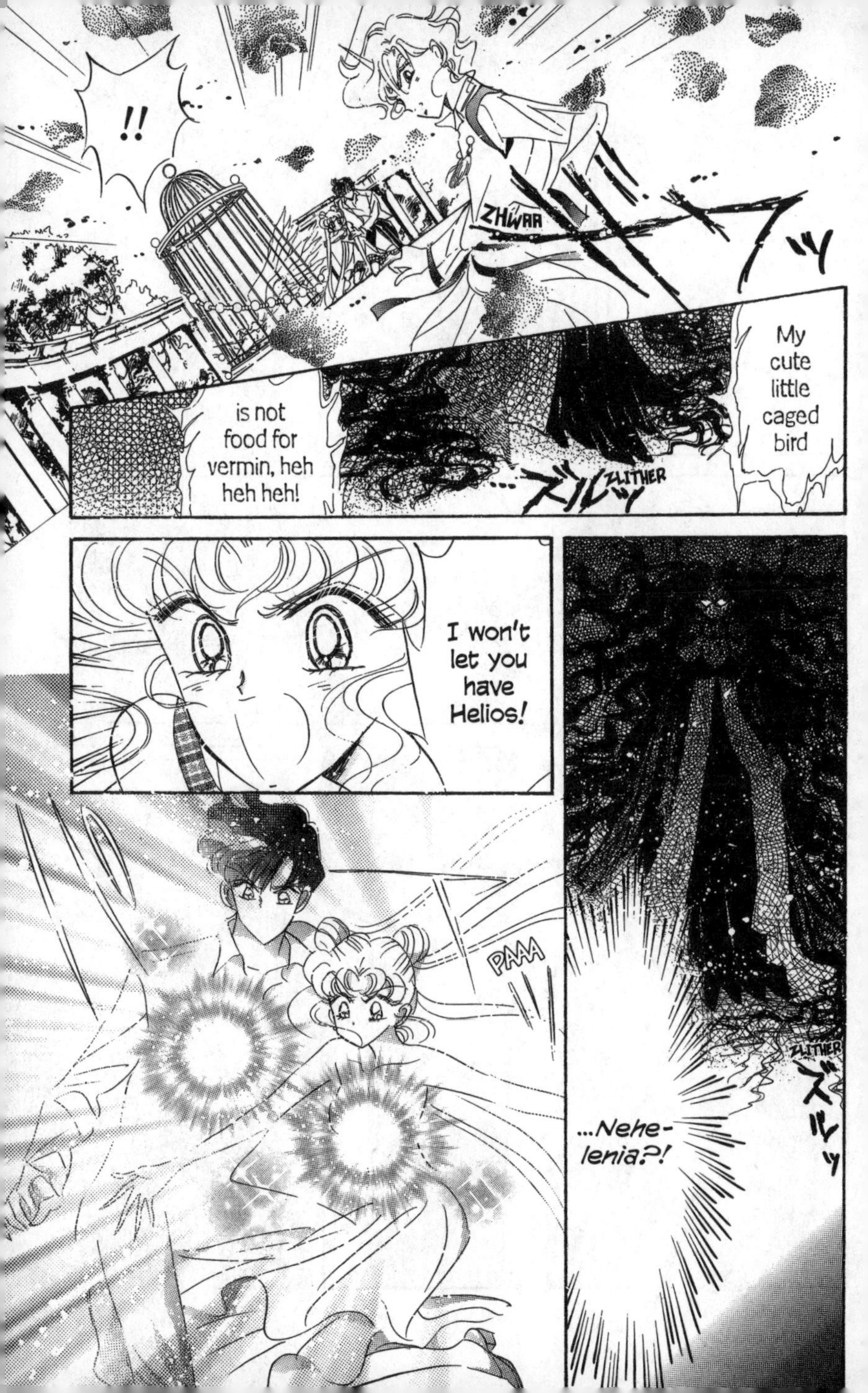
!!
ZHWAA
My cute little caged bird
ZLITHER
is not food for vermin, heh heh heh!
ZLITHER
...Nehe-lenia?!
I won't let you have Helios!
PAAA

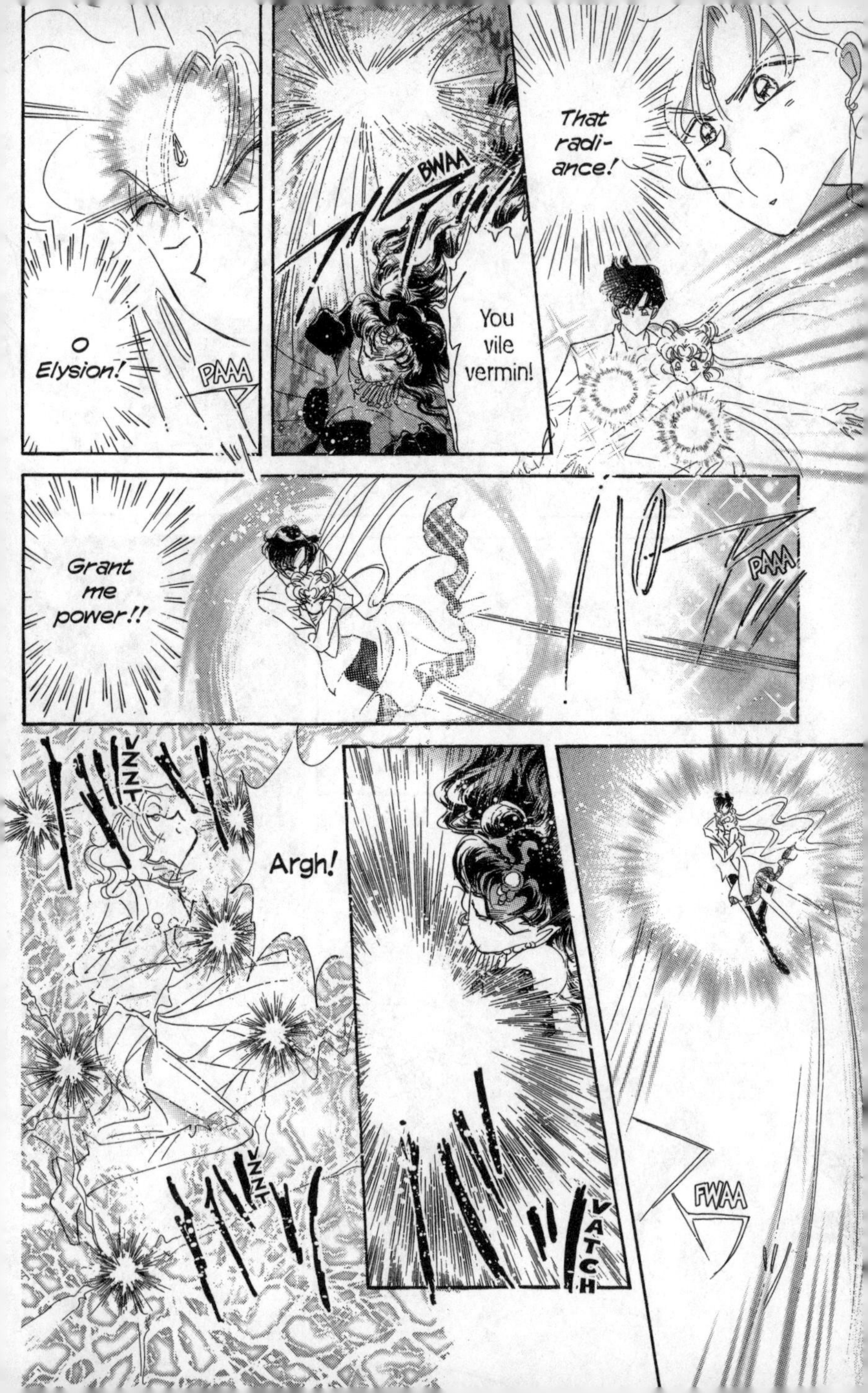
That radiance!
BWAA
You vile vermin!
PAAA
O Elysion!
PAAA
Grant me power!!
FWAA
VATCH
VZZT
Argh!
VZZT

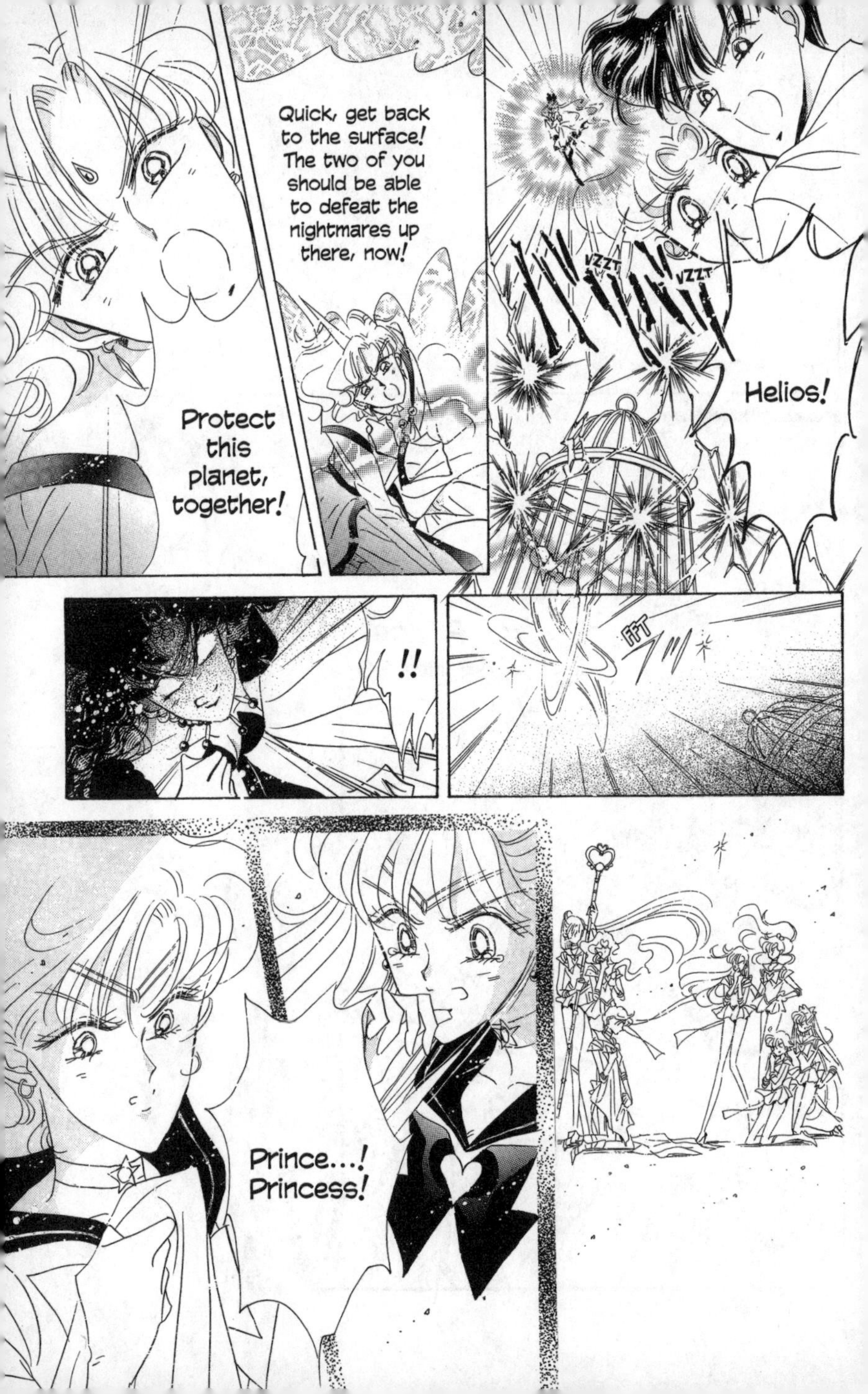
VZZT
VZZT
Helios!
Quick, get back to the surface! The two of you should be able to defeat the nightmares up there, now!
Protect this planet, together!
FFT
!!
Prince...! Princess!

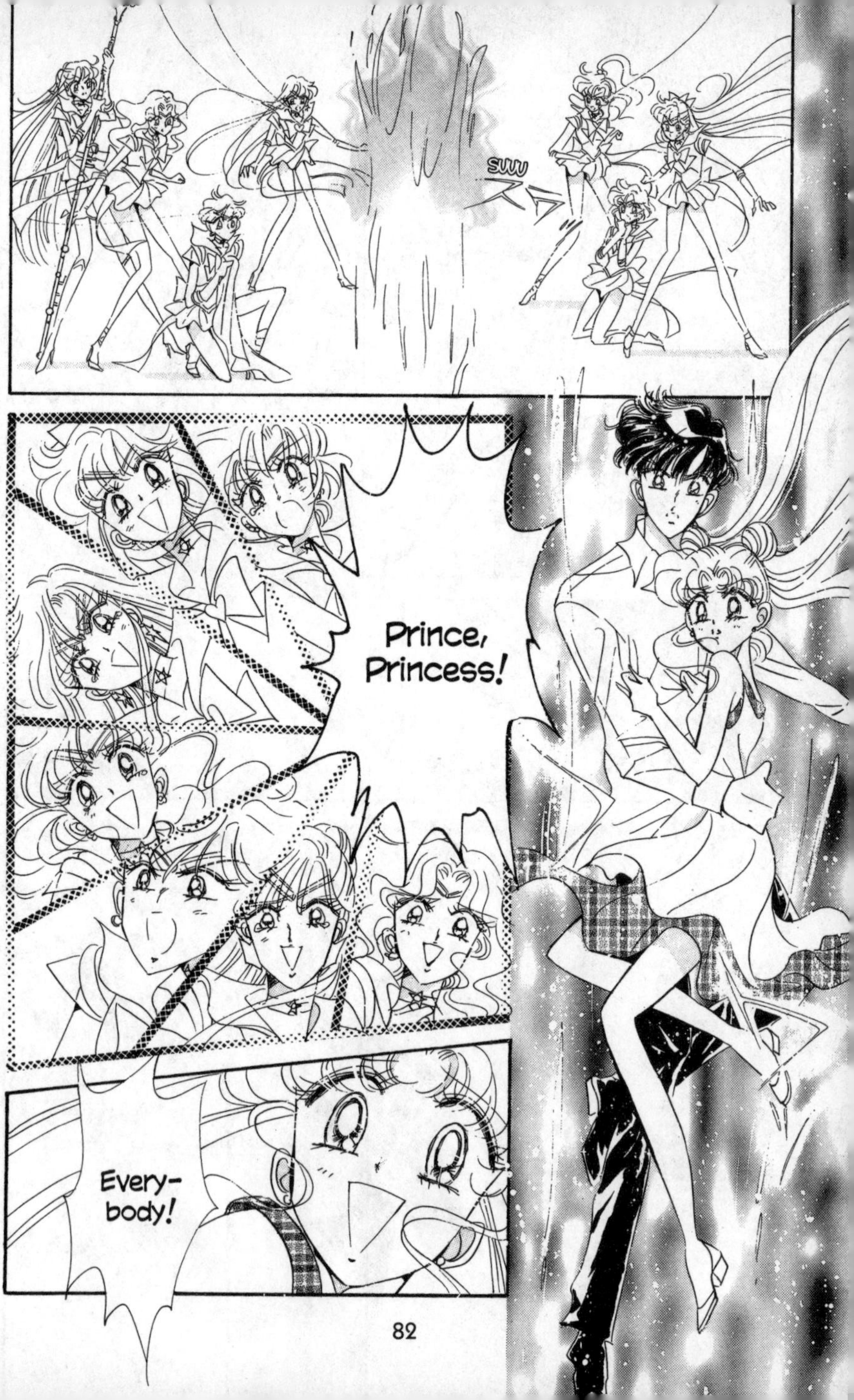
SUUU
スゥ
Prince, Princess!
Every-body!

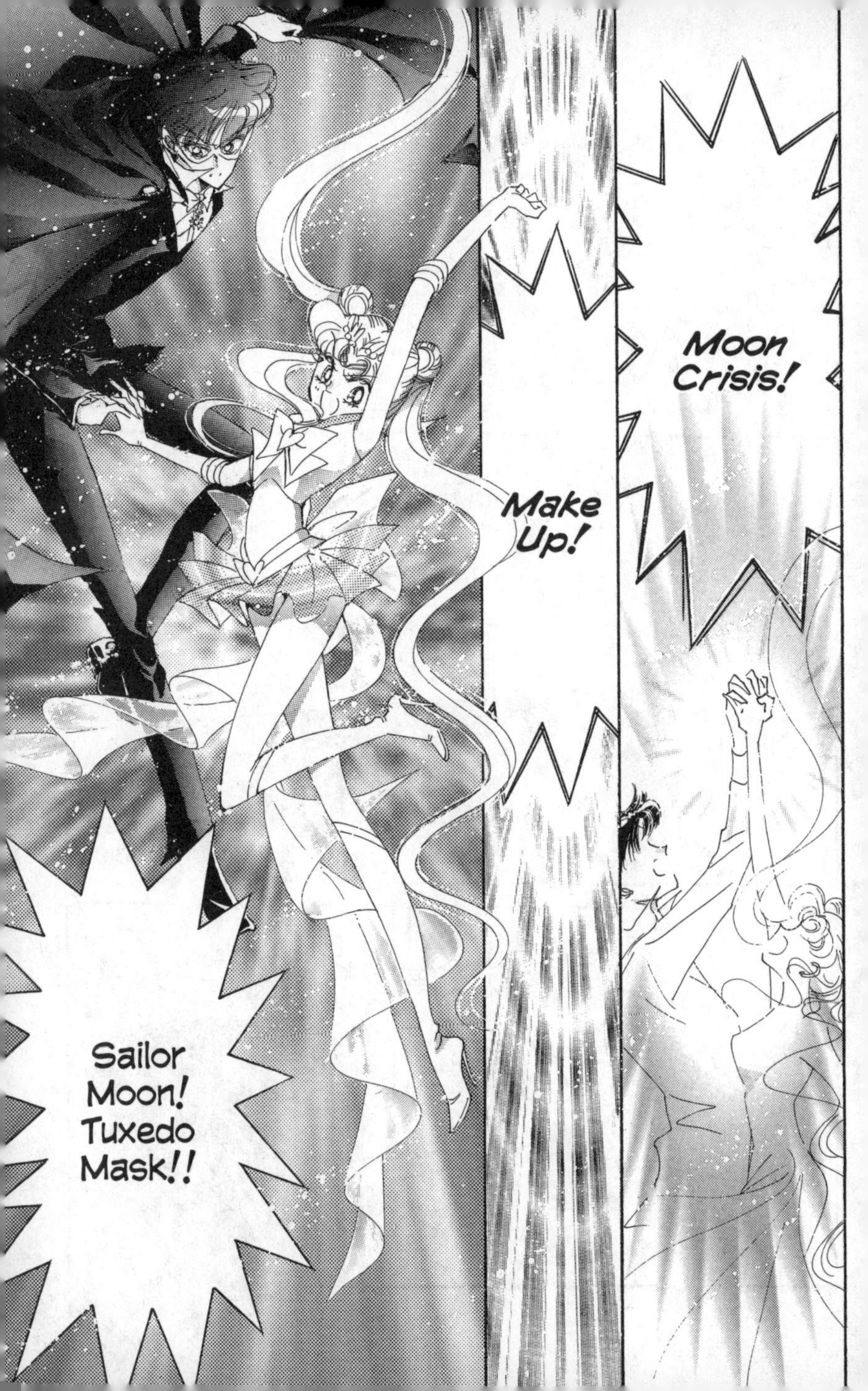
Moon Crisis!
Make Up!
Sailor Moon! Tuxedo Mask!!

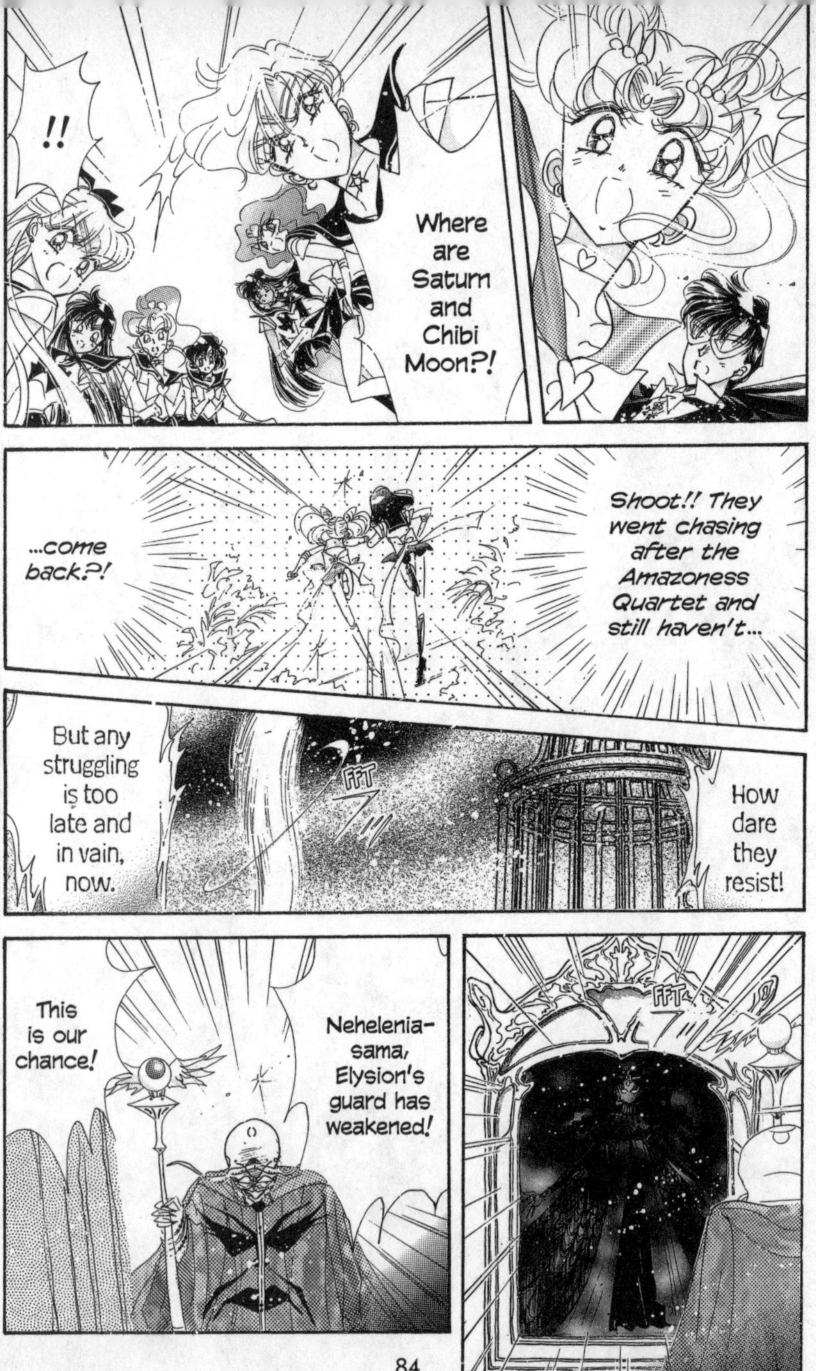
Where are Saturn and Chibi Moon?!
!!
Shoot!! They went chasing after the Amazoness Quartet and still haven't...
...come back?!
How dare they resist!
FFT
But any struggling is too late and in vain, now.
FFT
Nehelenia-sama, Elysion's guard has weakened!
This is our chance!

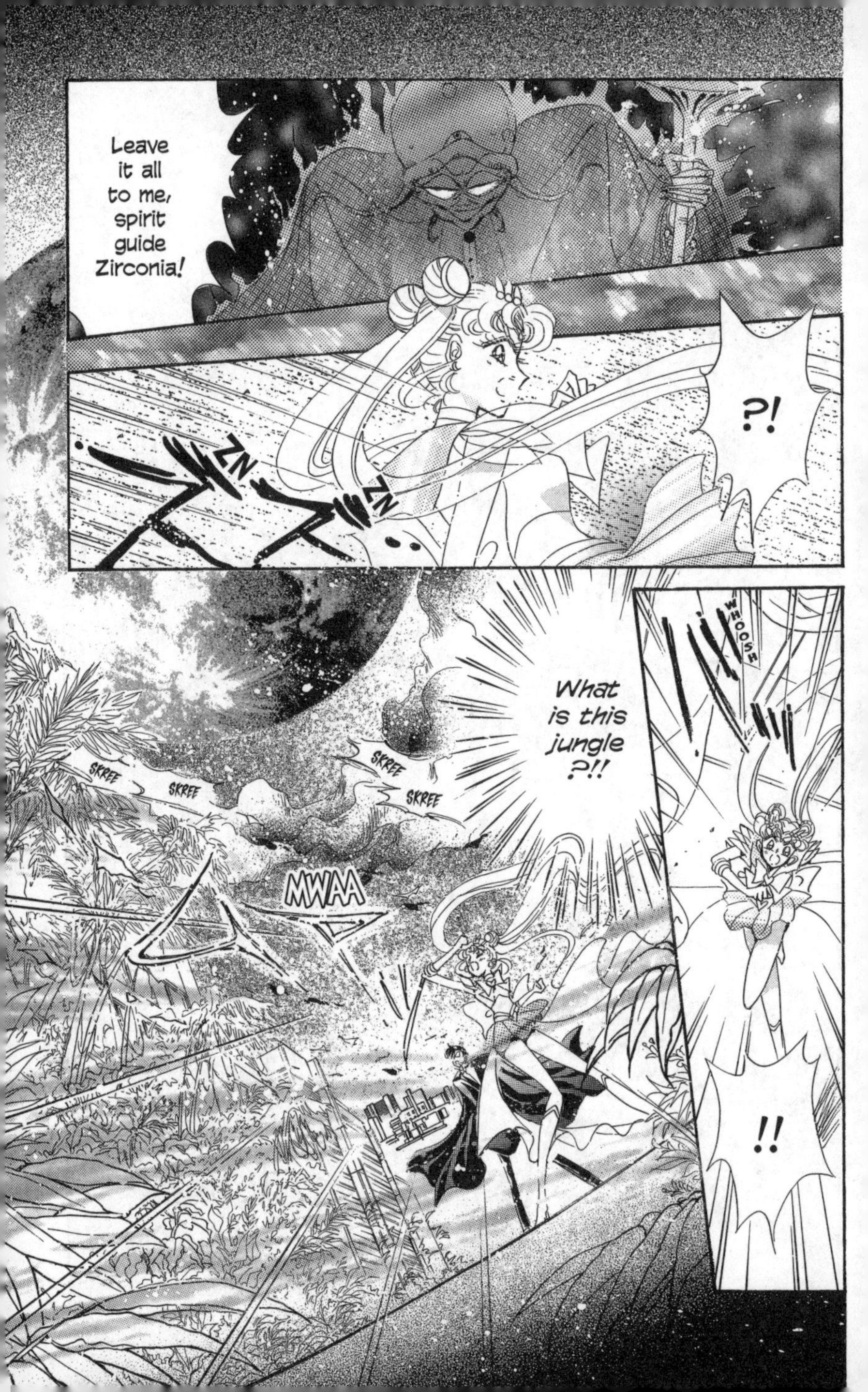
Leave it all to me, spirit guide Zirconia!
?!
ZN
ZN
WHOOSH
!!
What is this jungle ?!!
SKREE
SKREE
SKREE
SKREE
MWAA

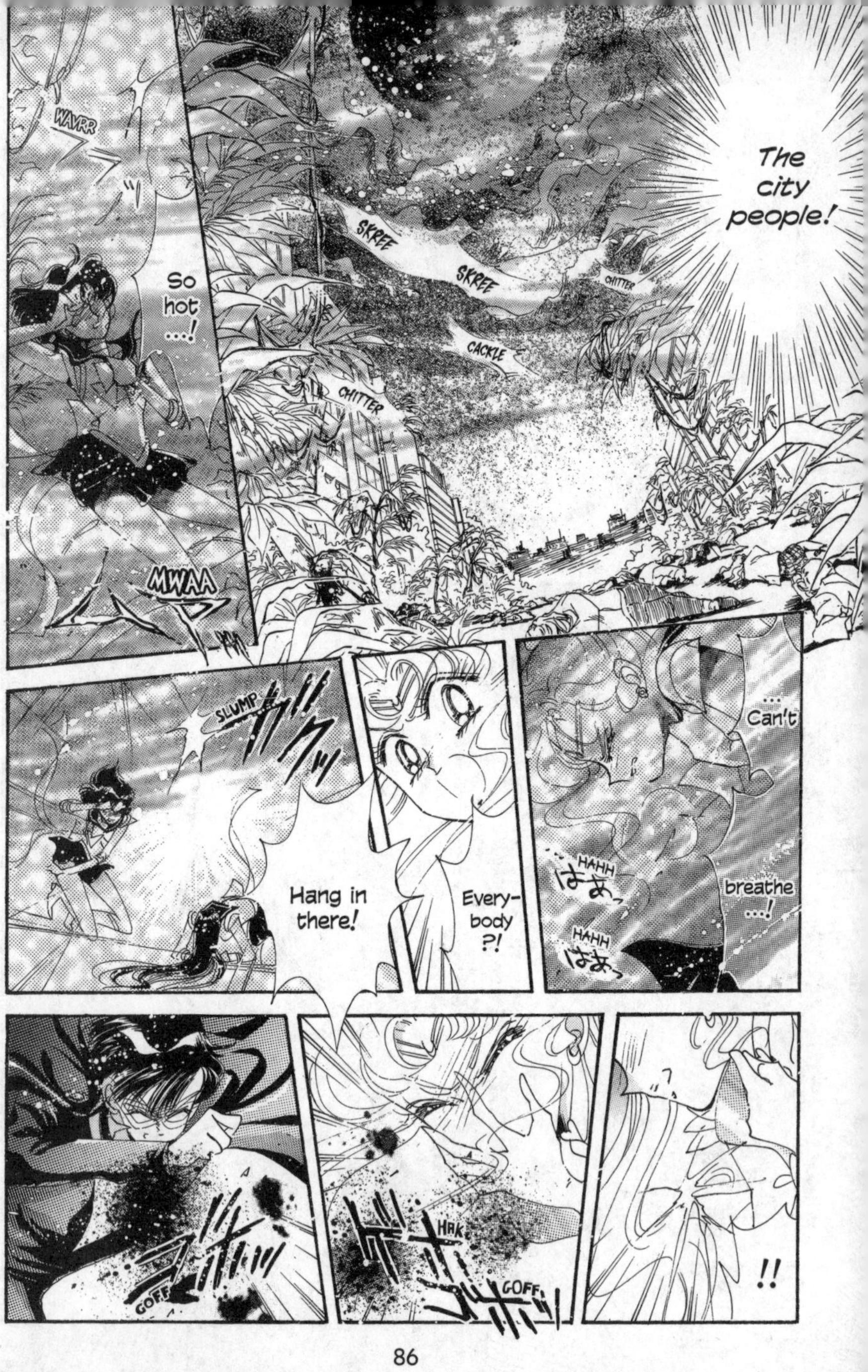
The city people!
SKREE
SKREE
CHITTER
CACKLE
CHITTER
WAVRR
So hot ...!
MWAA
... Can't breathe ...!
HAHH はあっ
HAHH はあっ
Every-body ?!
SLUMP
Hang in there!
!!
HAK
GOFF
GOFF

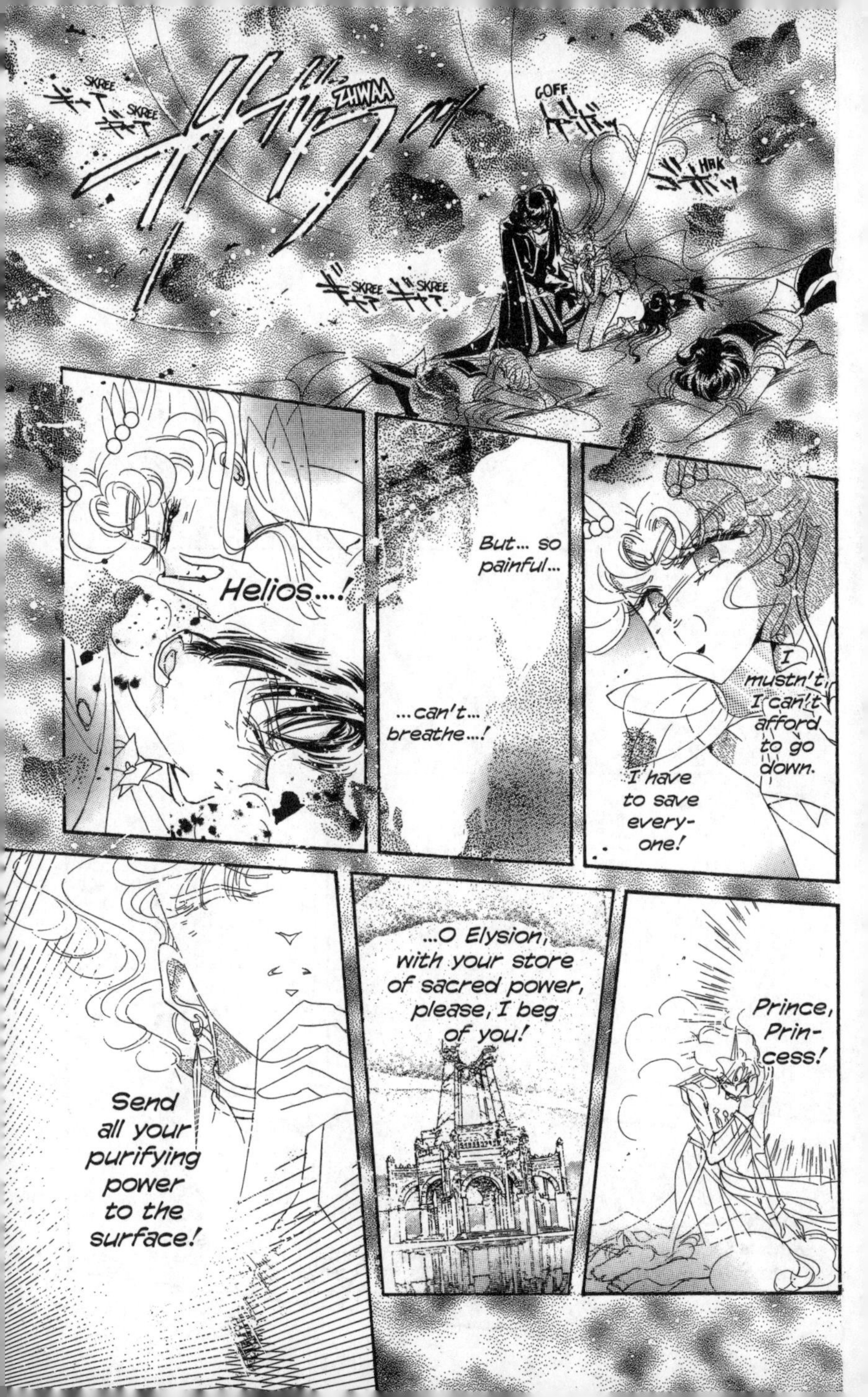
GOFF
HAK
ZHWAA
SKREE
SKREE
SKREE
SKREE
I mustn't, I can't afford to go down.
I have to save every-one!
But... so painful...
...can't... breathe...!
Helios...!
Prince, Prin-cess!
...O Elysion, with your store of sacred power, please, I beg of you!
Send all your purifying power to the surface!

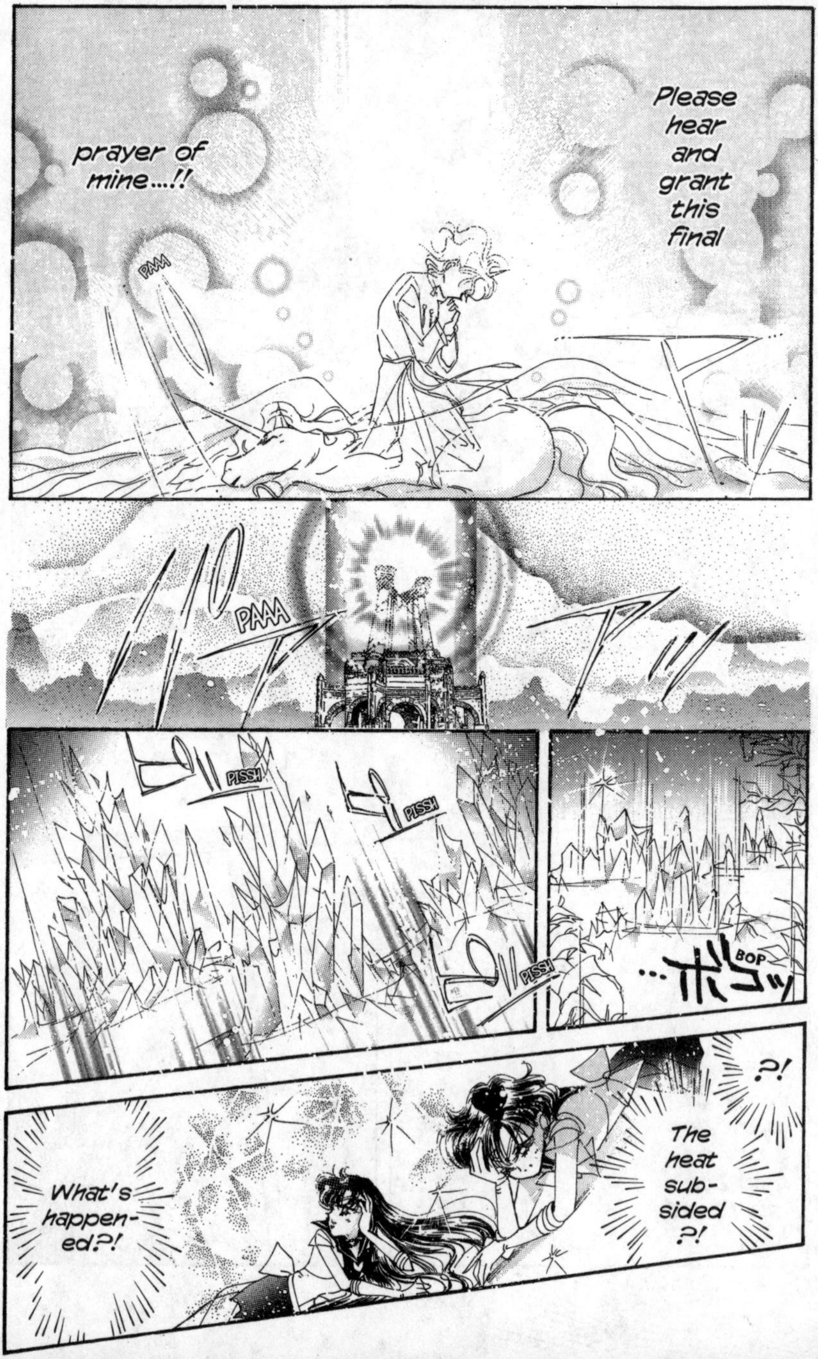

Please hear and grant this final
prayer of mine...!!
PAAA
PAAA
...BOP
PISSH
PISSH
PISSH
?!
The heat sub-sided?!
What's happen-ed?!

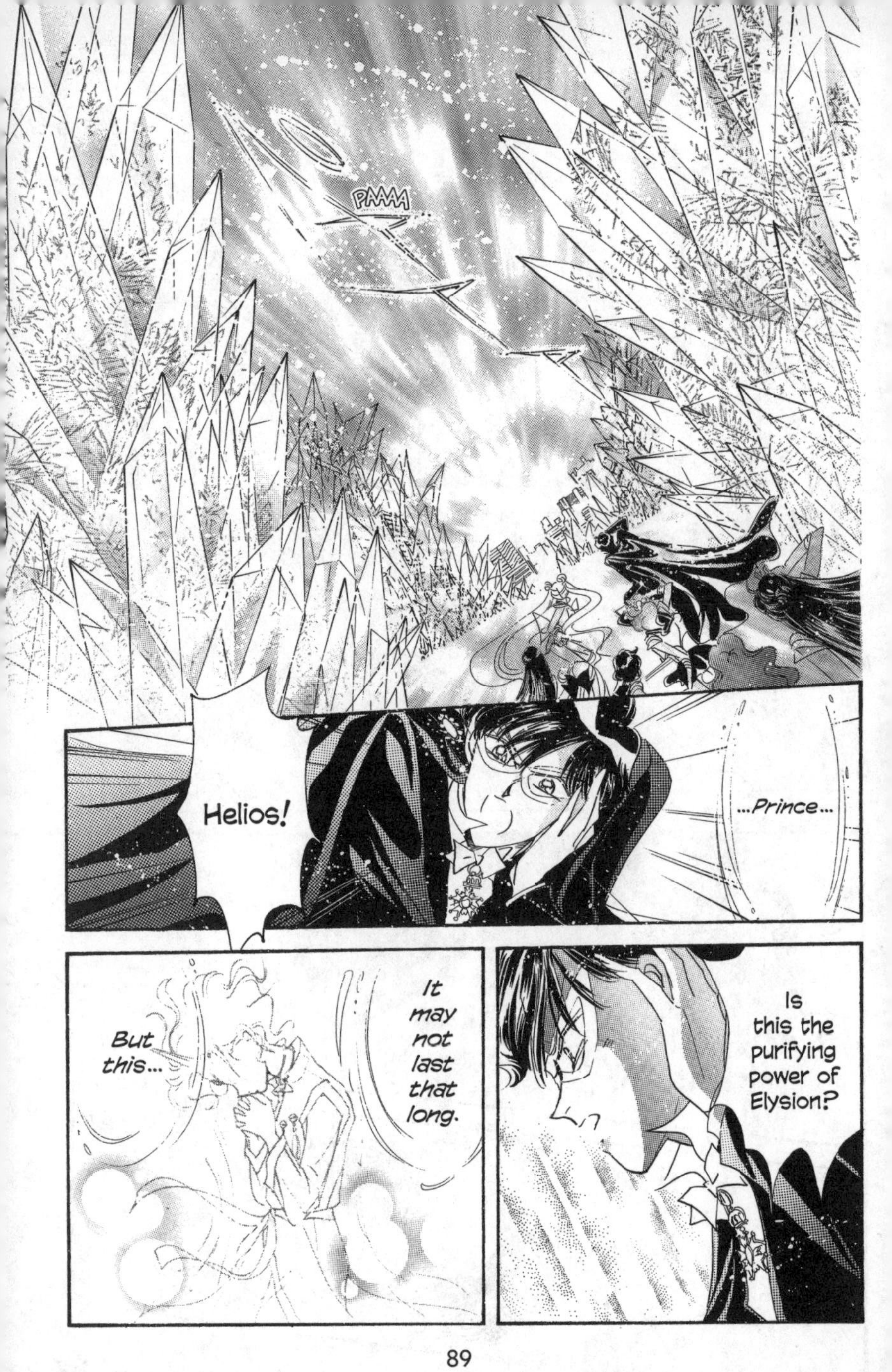
PAAAA
...Prince...
Helios!
Is this the purifying power of Elysion?
It may not last that long.
But this...

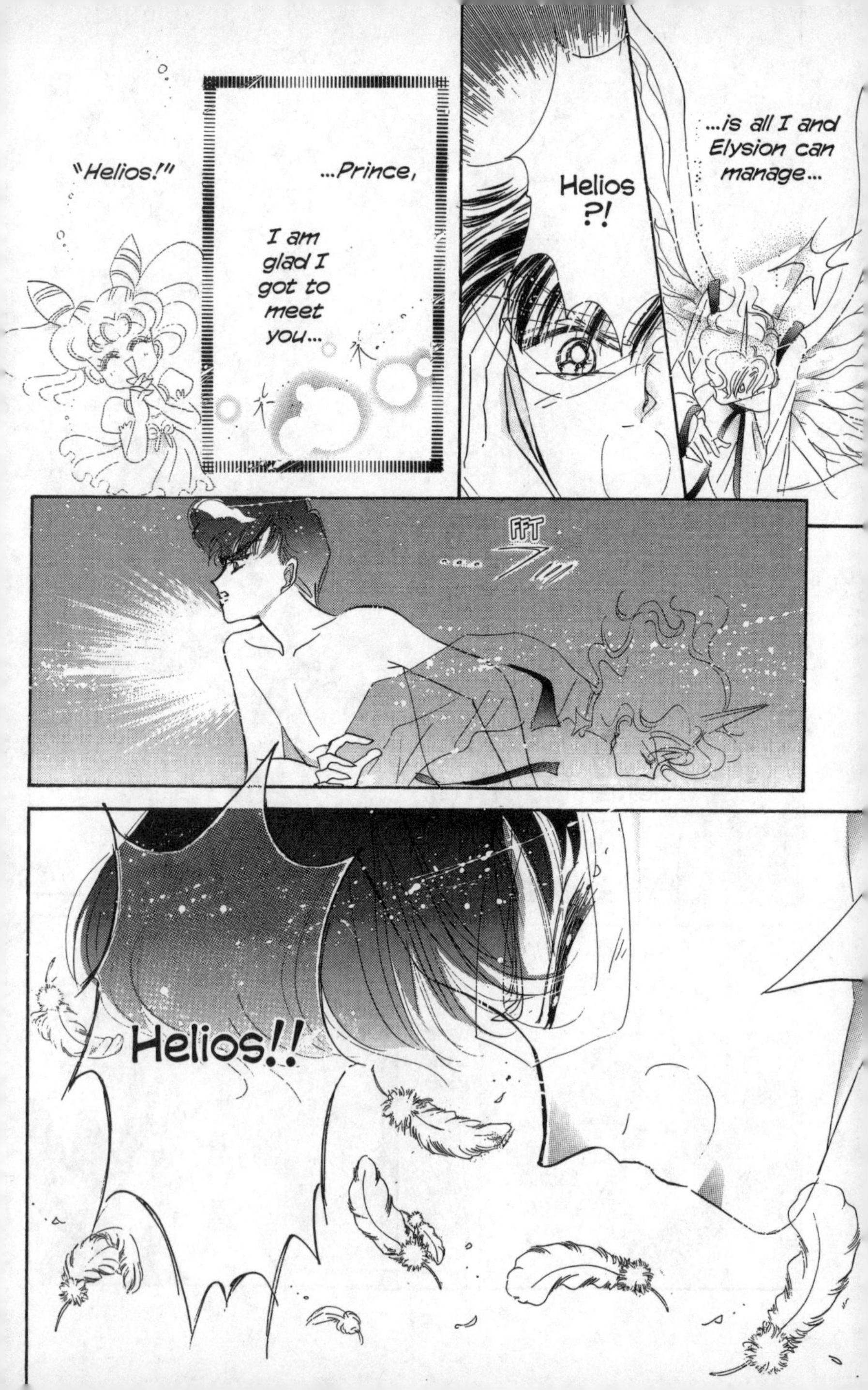
...is all I and Elysion can manage...
Helios ?!
...Prince,
I am glad I got to meet you...
"Helios!"
FFT
Helios!!

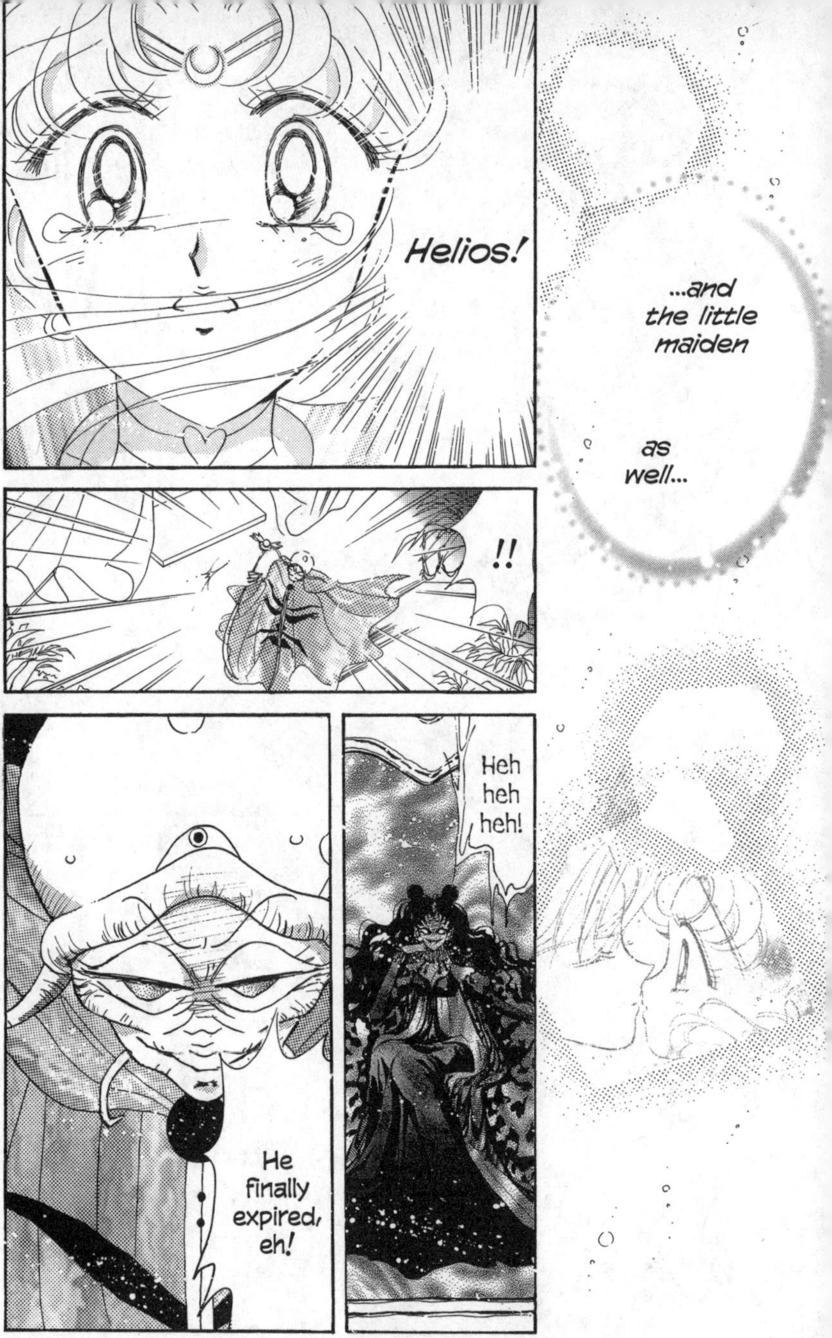
...and the little maiden
as well...
Helios!
!!
Heh heh heh!
He finally expired, eh!

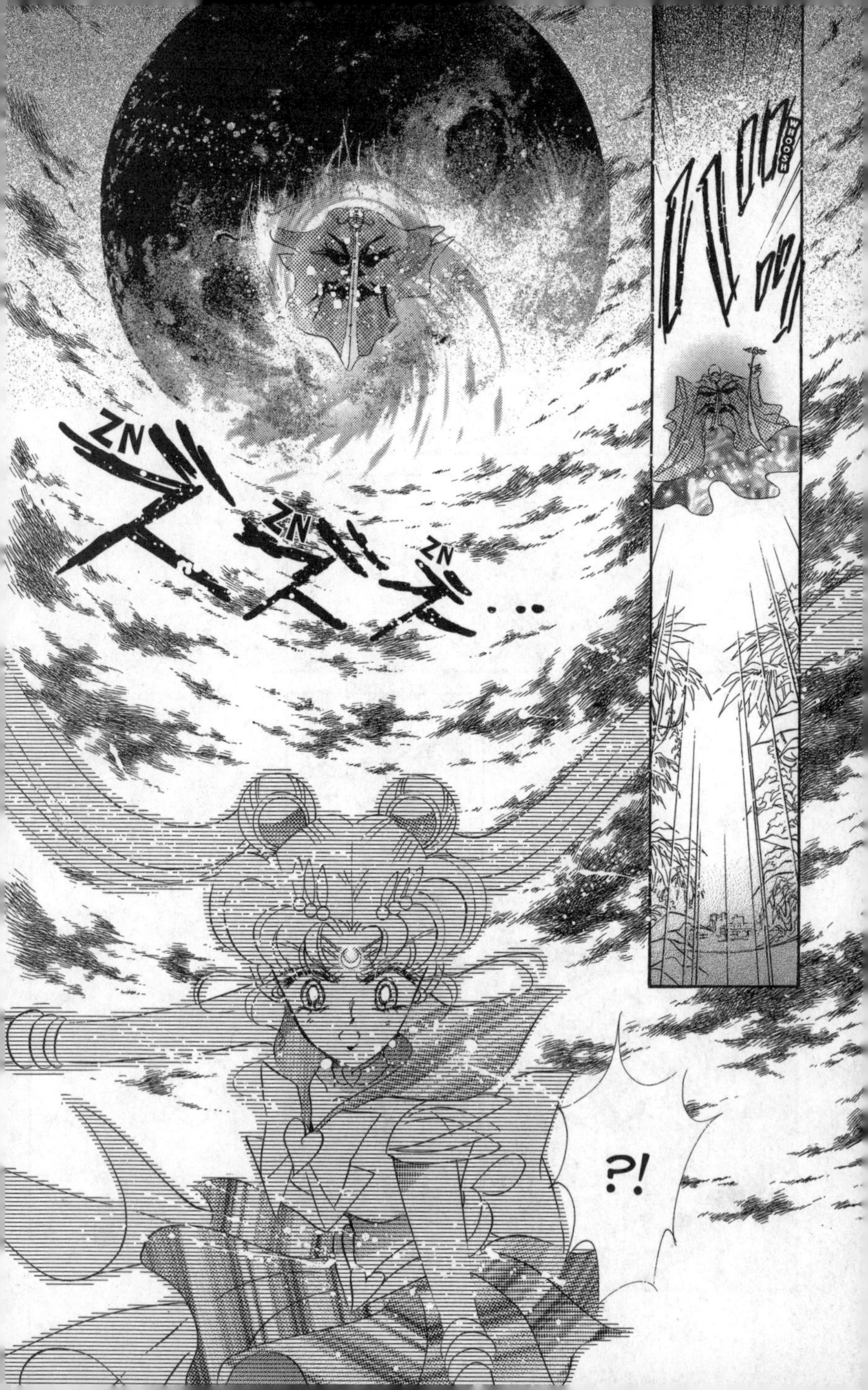
WHOOSH
ZN
ZN
ZN
?!

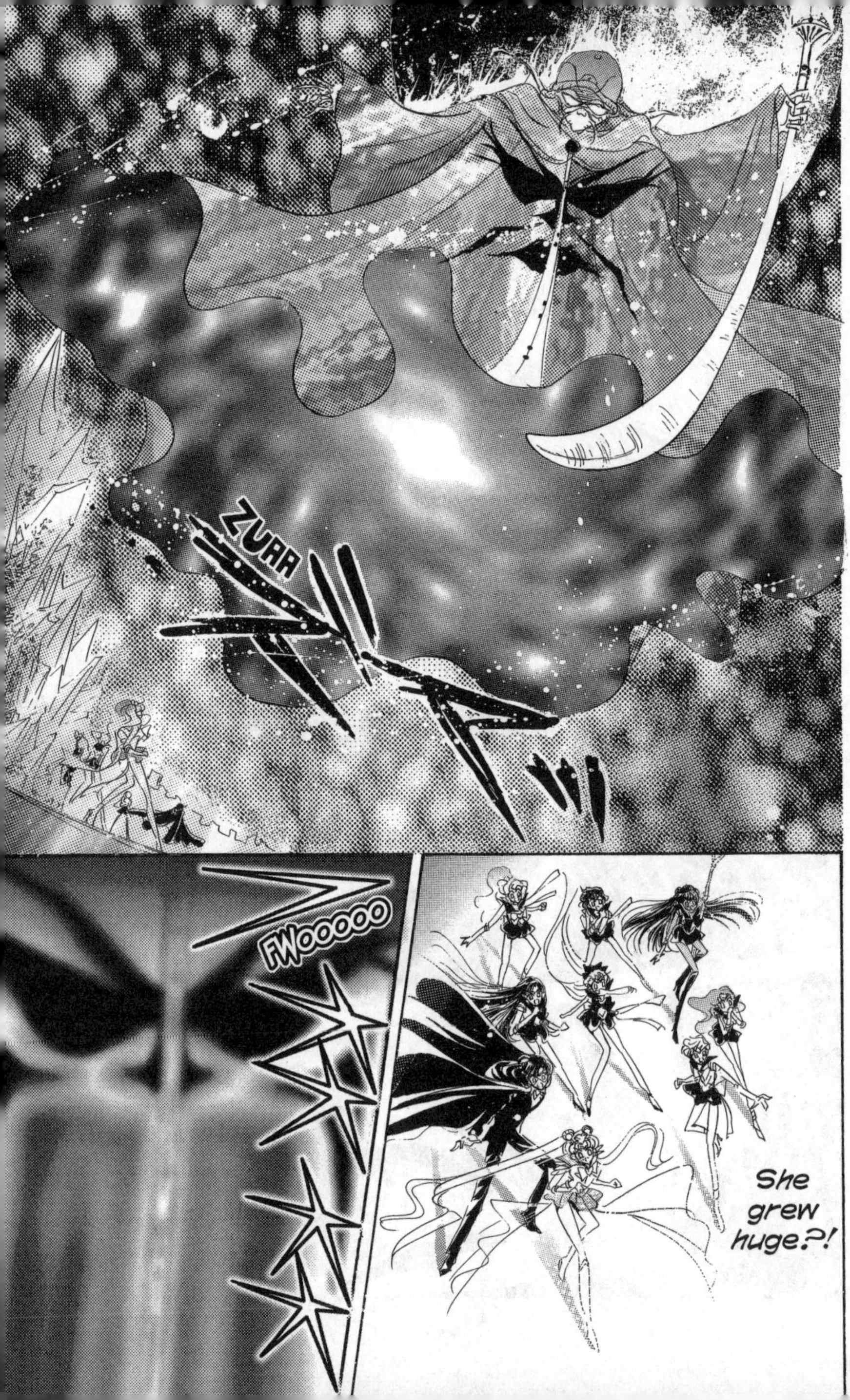
ZUAA
She grew huge?!
FWOOOOO

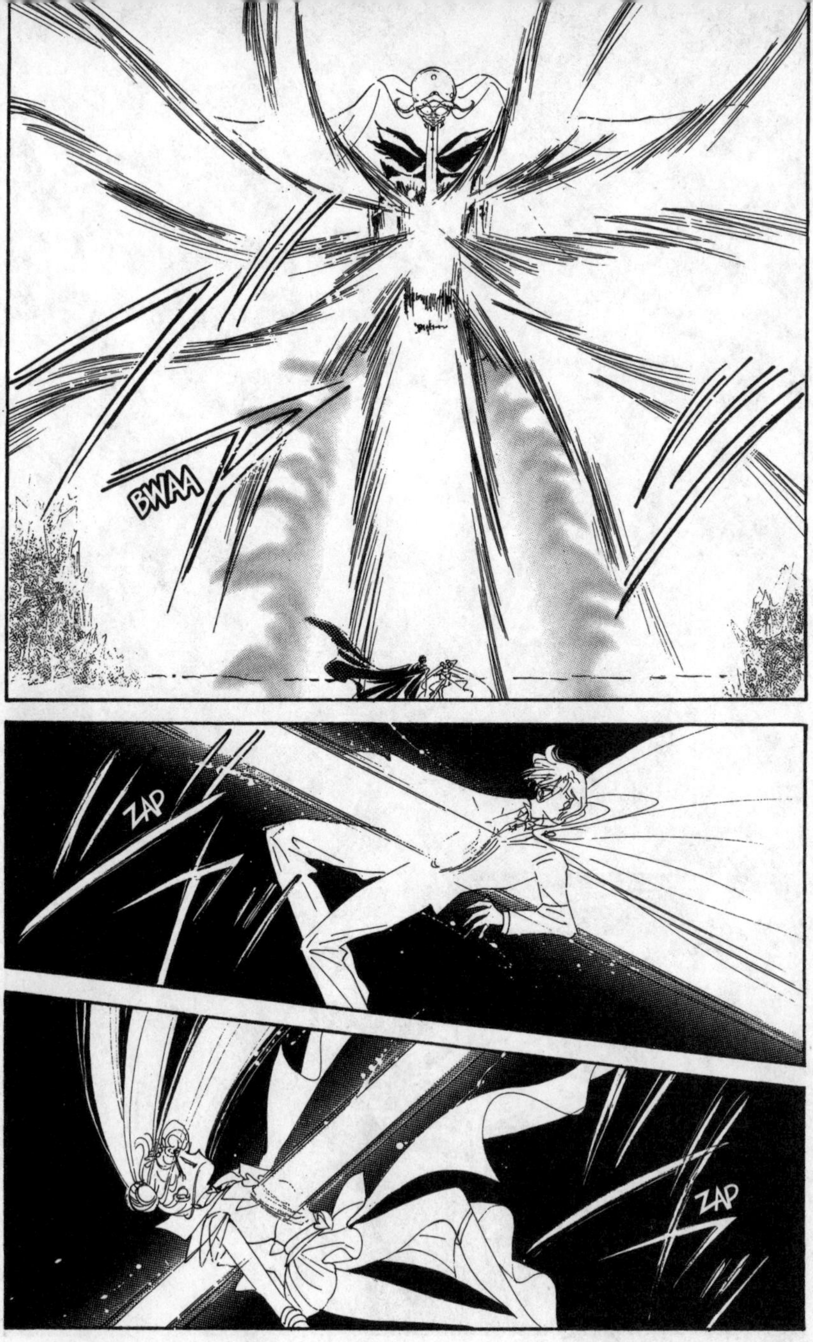
BWAA
ZAP
ZAP

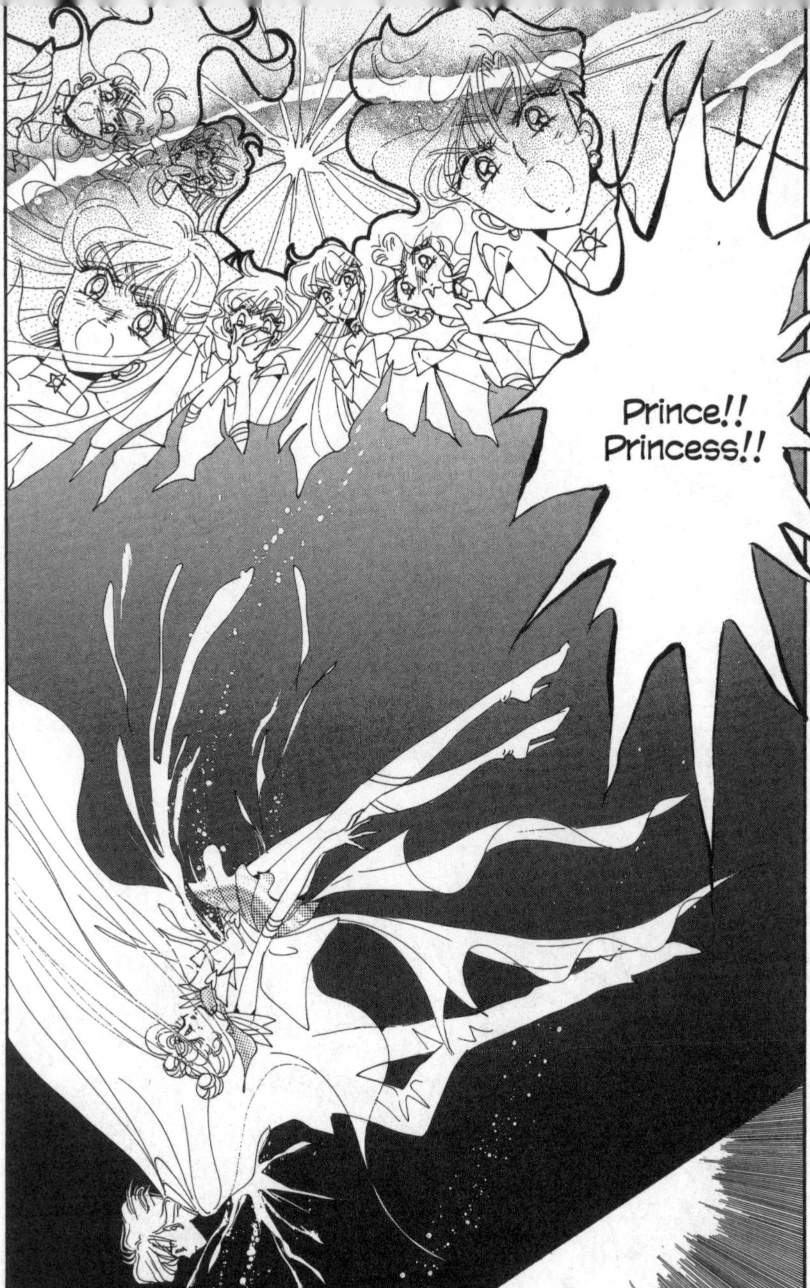
Prince!!
Princess!!

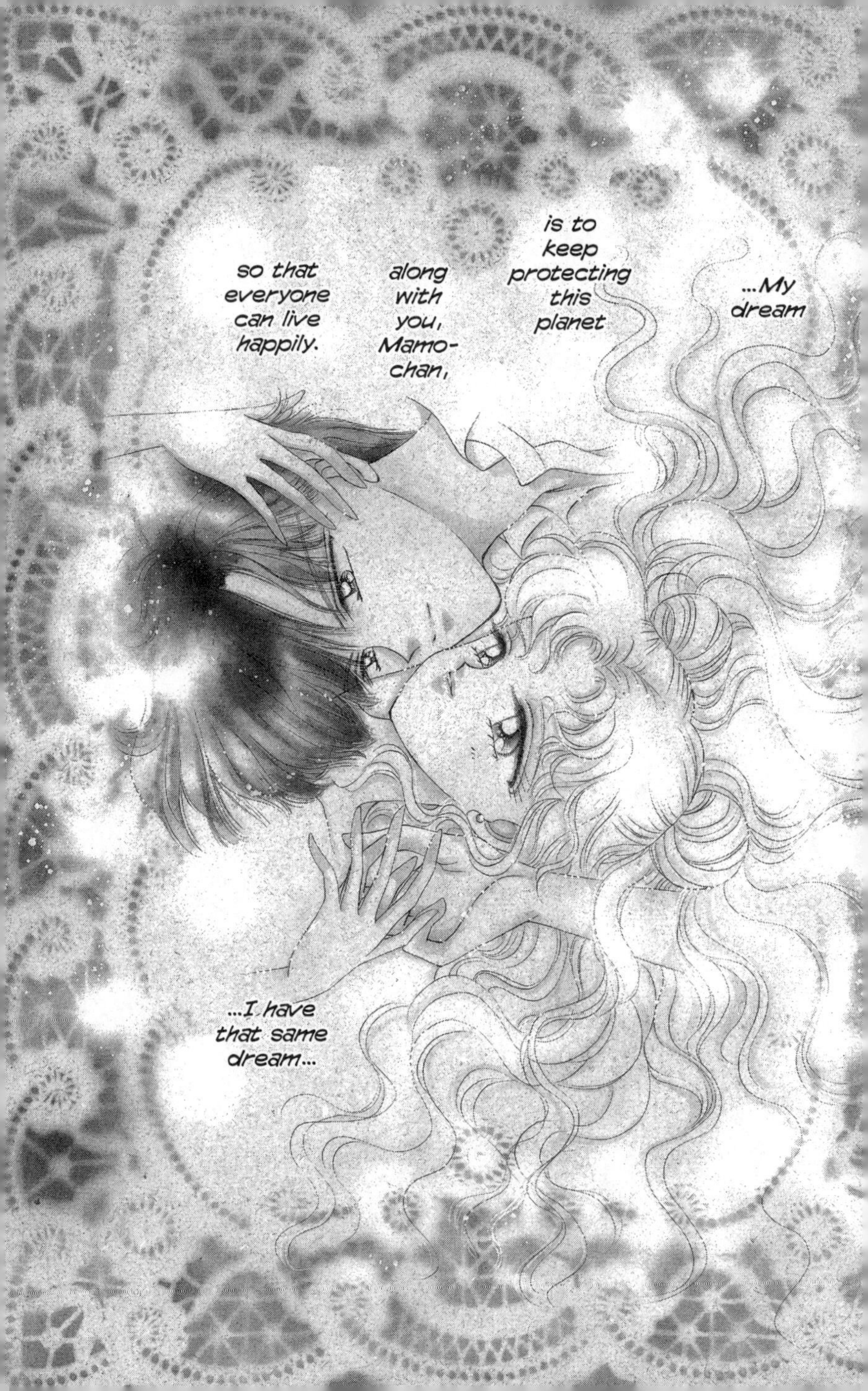
...My dream
is to keep protecting this planet
along with you, Mamo-chan,
so that everyone can live happily.
...I have that same dream...

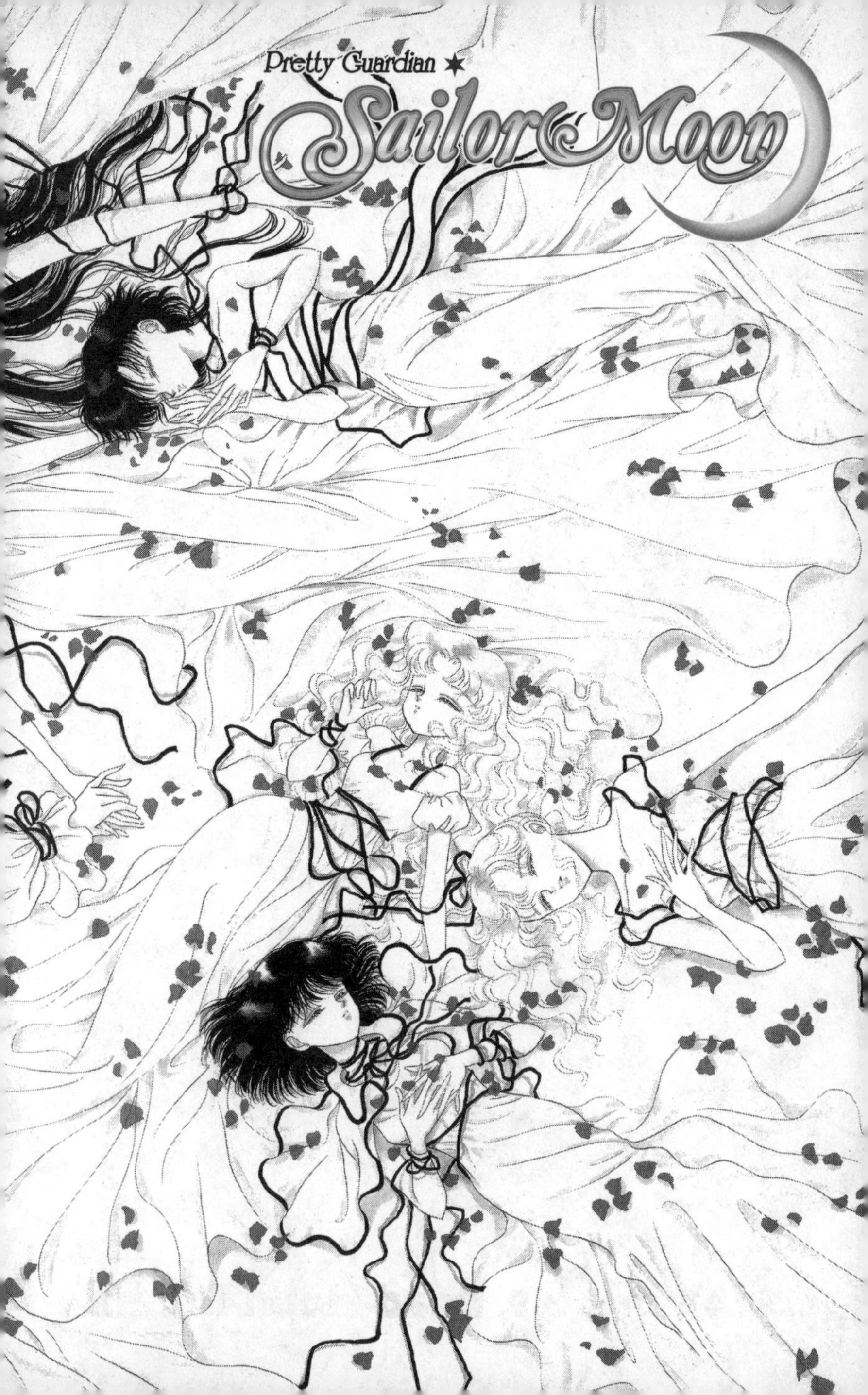
Pretty Guardian ★
Sailor Moon

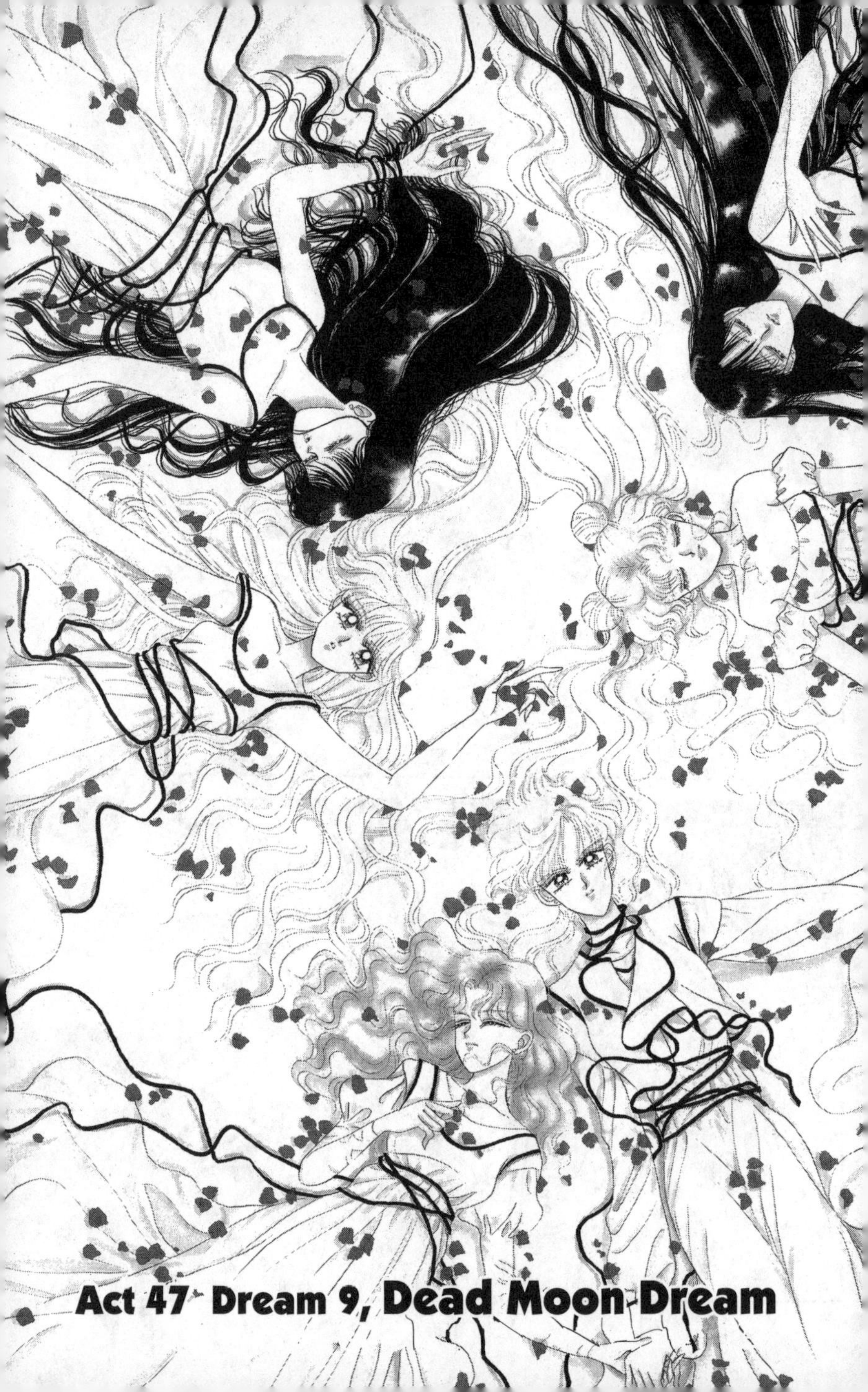

Act 47 Dream 9, Dead Moon Dream

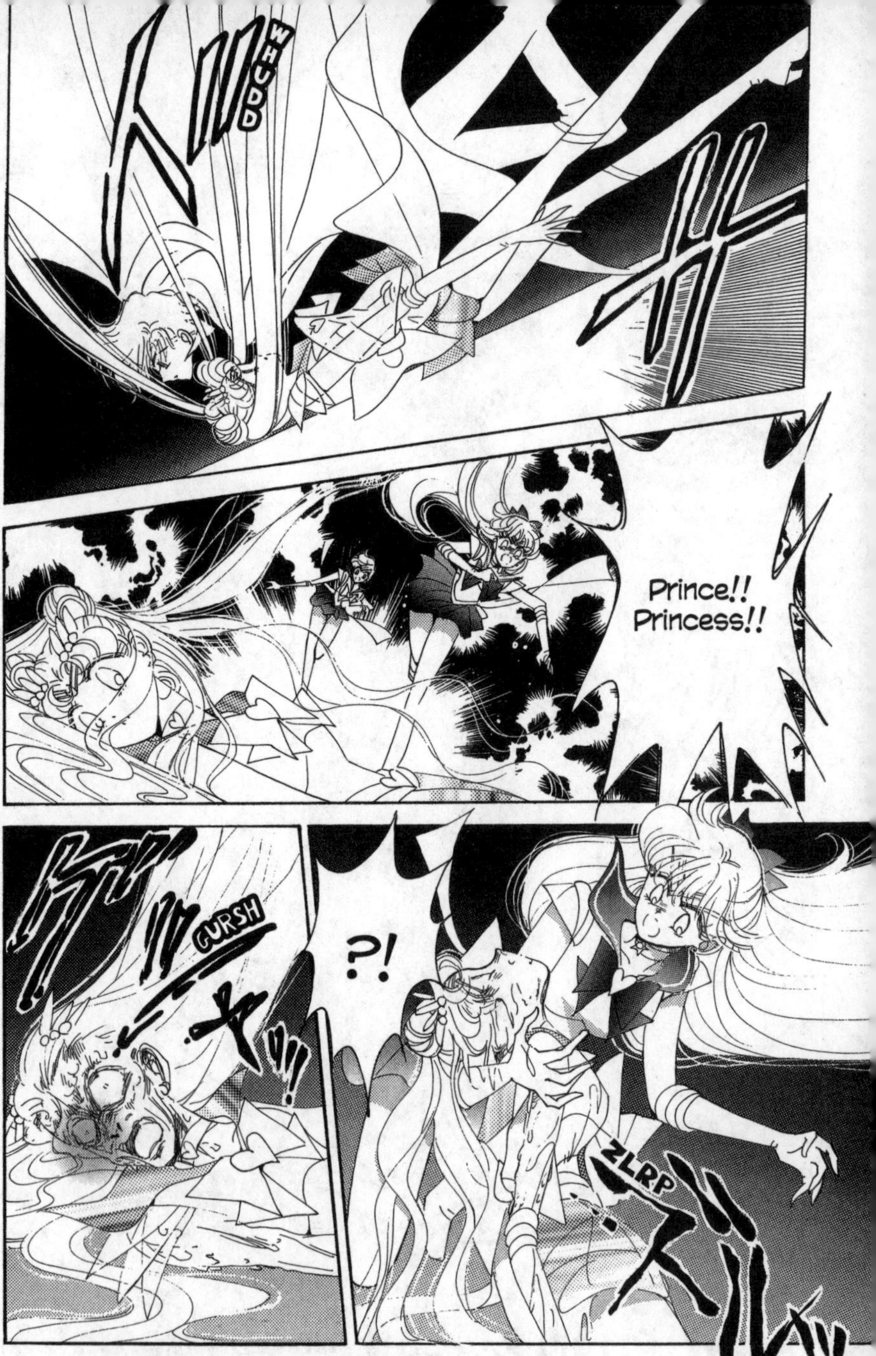
WHUDD
Prince!!
Princess!!
?!
ZLRP
GURSH

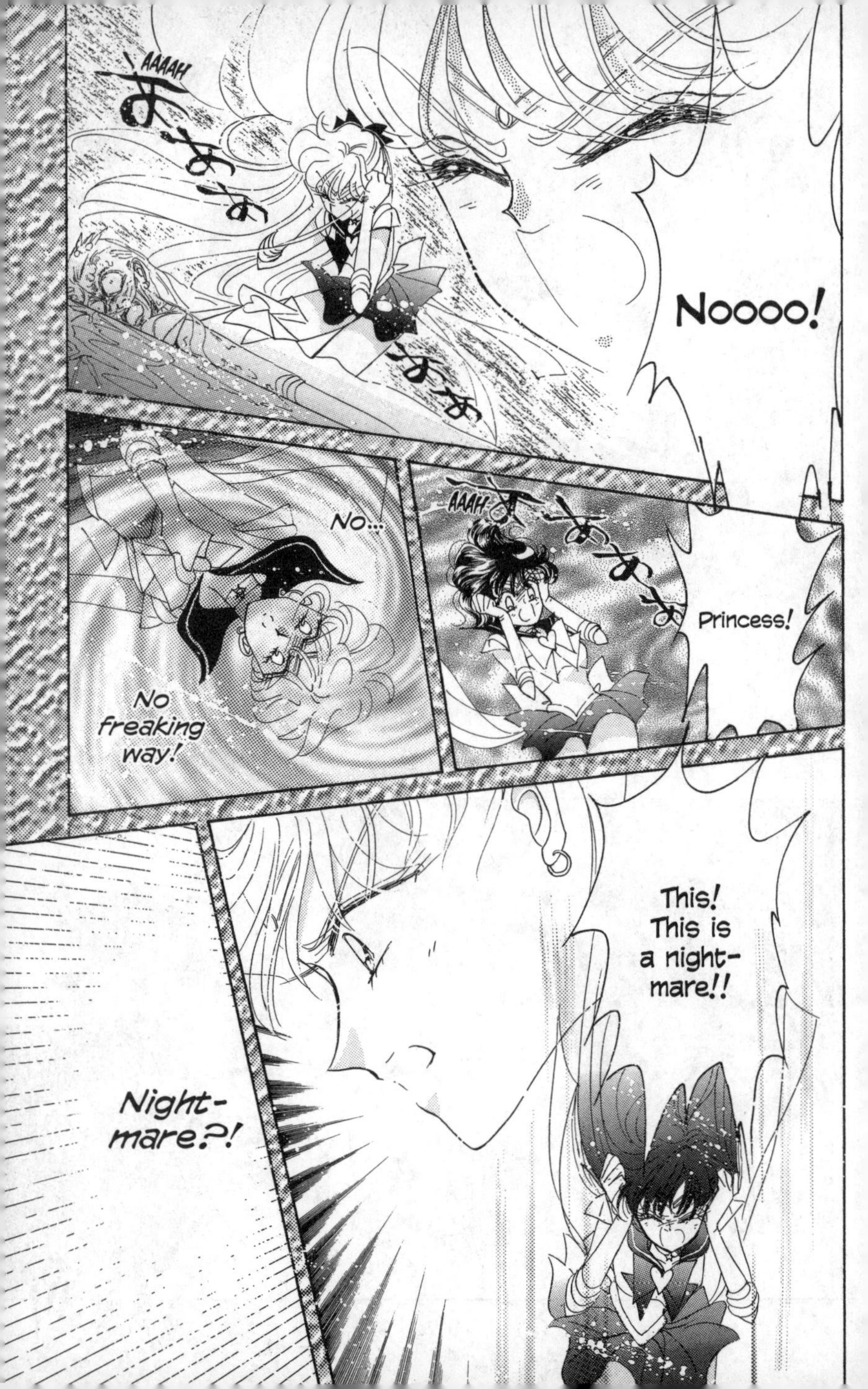
AAAAH
Noooo!
AAAH
Princess!
No...
No freaking way!
This! This is a night-mare!!
Night-mare?!

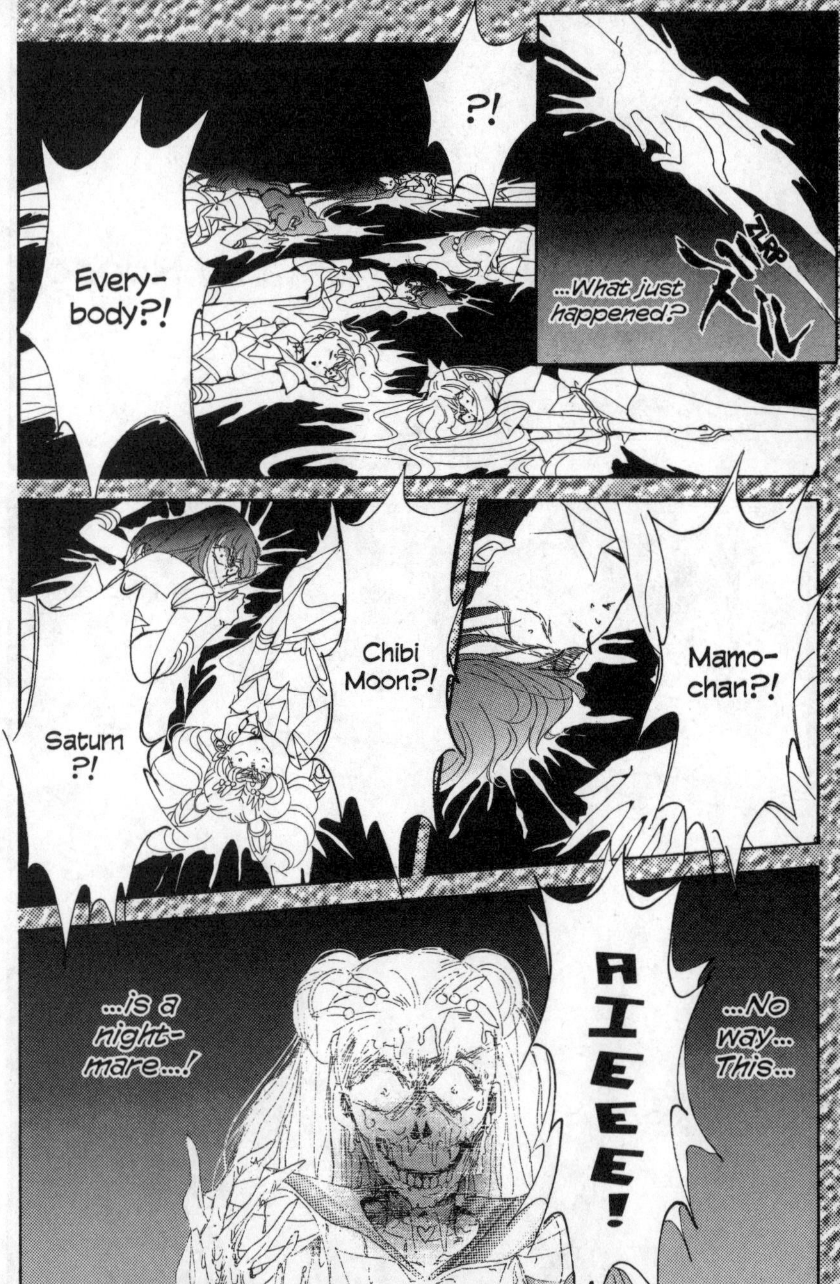
ZURP
...What just happened?
?!
Every-body?!
Mamo-chan?!
Chibi Moon?!
Saturn ?!
AIEEEE!
...No way... This...
...is a night-mare...!

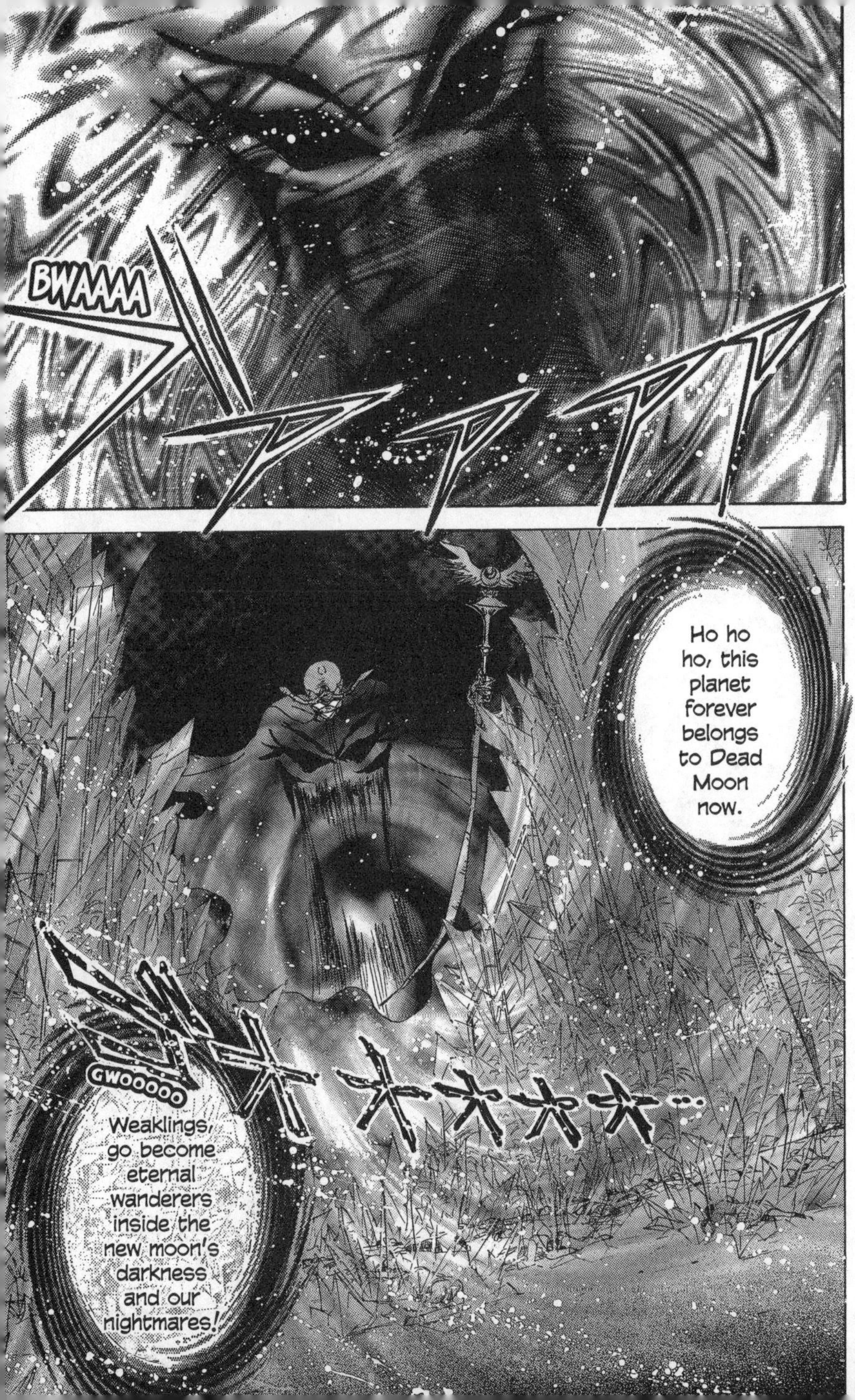
BWAAAA
Ho ho ho, this planet forever belongs to Dead Moon now.
GWOOOOO
Weaklings, go become eternal wanderers inside the new moon's darkness and our nightmares!

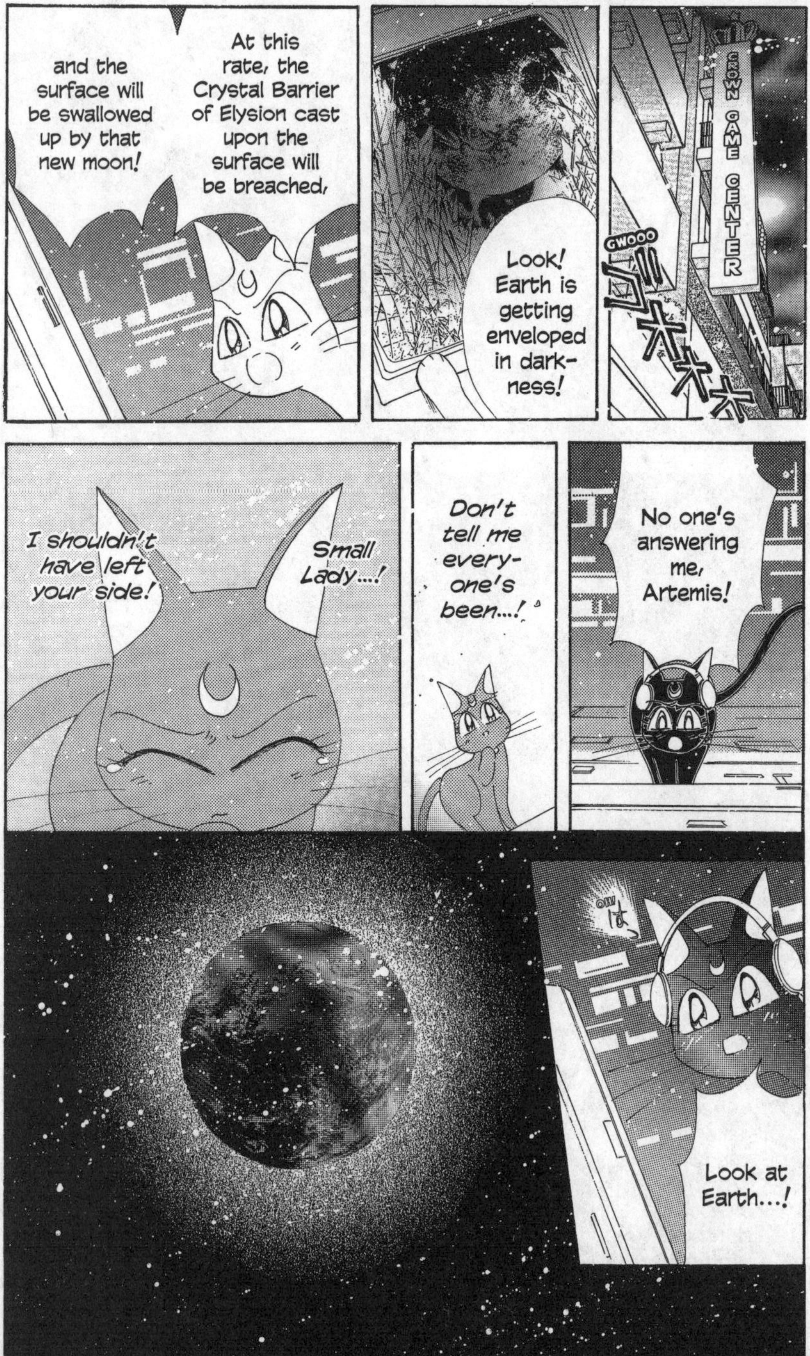
CROWN GAME CENTER
GWOOO
Look! Earth is getting enveloped in darkness!
At this rate, the Crystal Barrier of Elysion cast upon the surface will be breached,
and the surface will be swallowed up by that new moon!
No one's answering me, Artemis!
Don't tell me every-one's been...!
Small Lady...!
I shouldn't have left your side!
OH!
Look at Earth...!

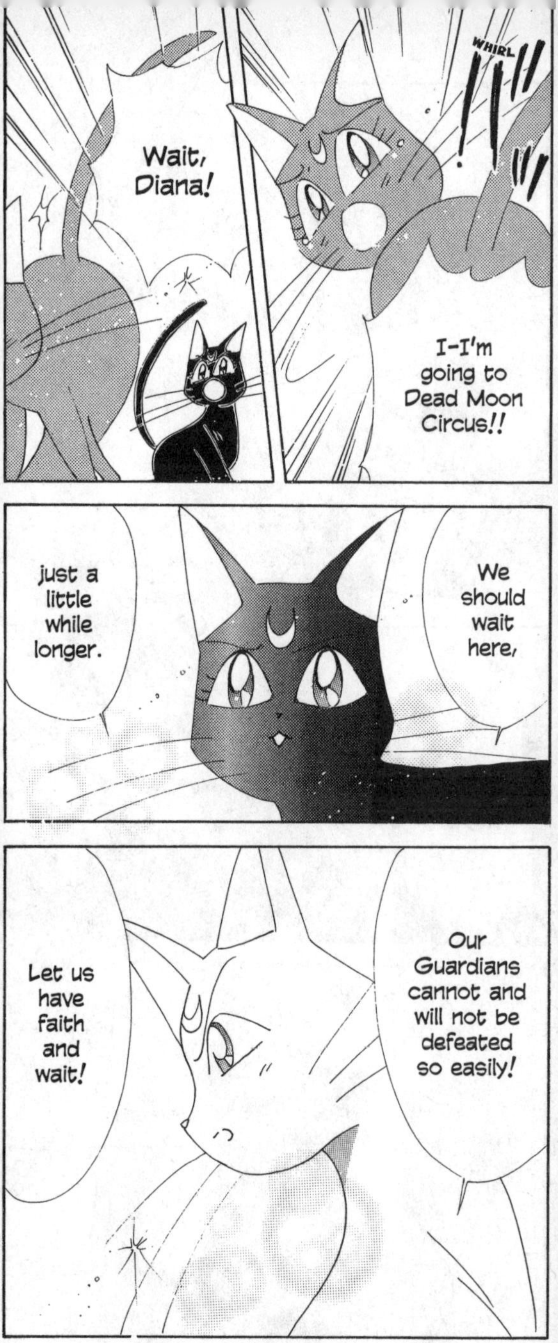
WHIRL
I-I'm going to Dead Moon Circus!!
Wait, Diana!
We should wait here,
just a little while longer.
Our Guardians cannot and will not be defeated so easily!
Let us have faith and wait!

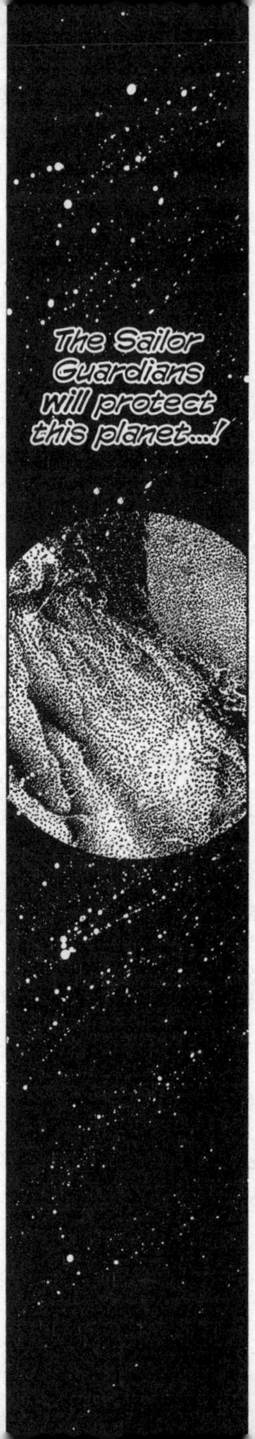
The Sailor Guardians will protect this planet...!

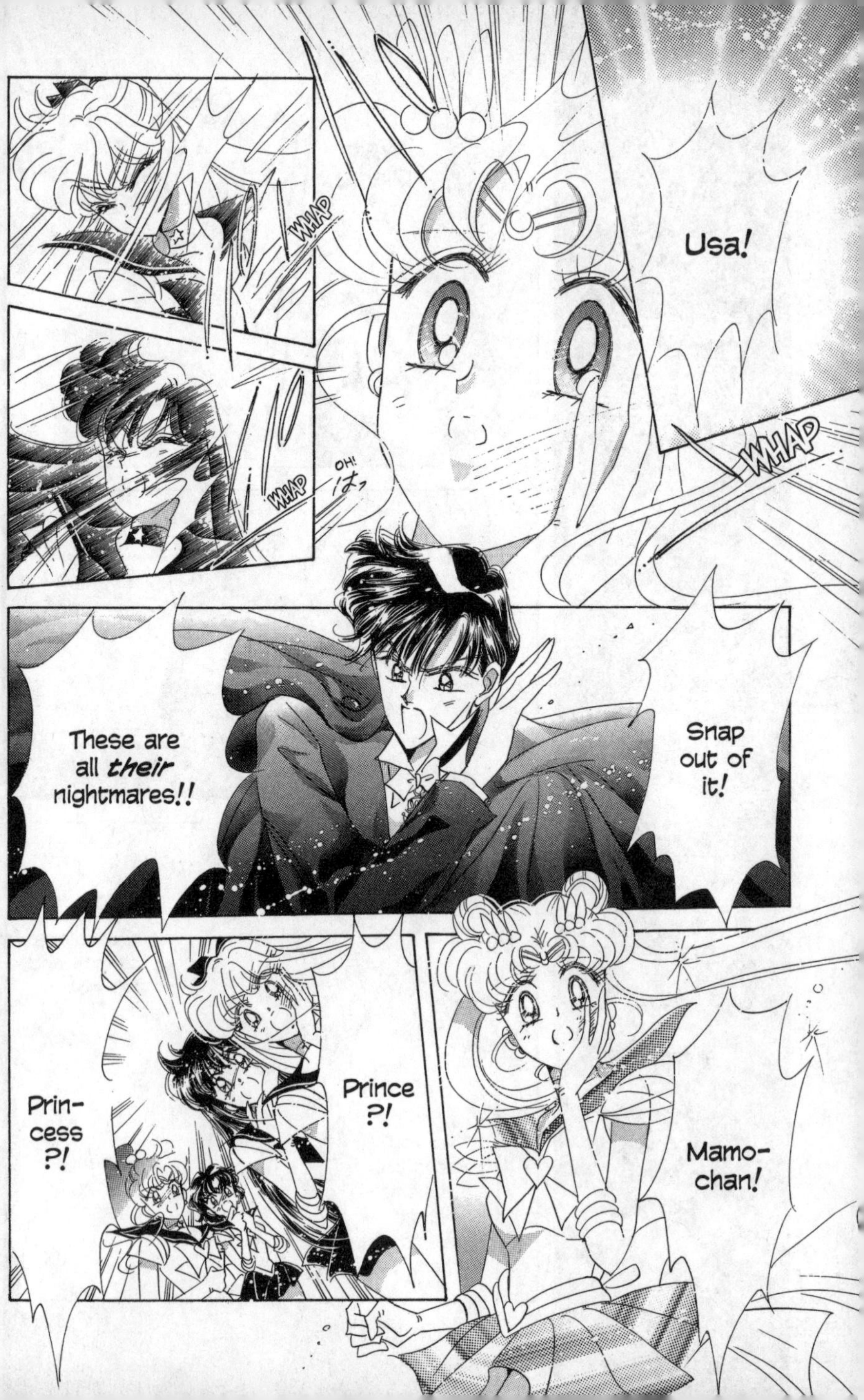
Usa!
WHAP
WHAP
WHAP
OH! はっ
Snap out of it!
These are all *their* nightmares!!
Mamo-chan!
Prince?!
Princess?!

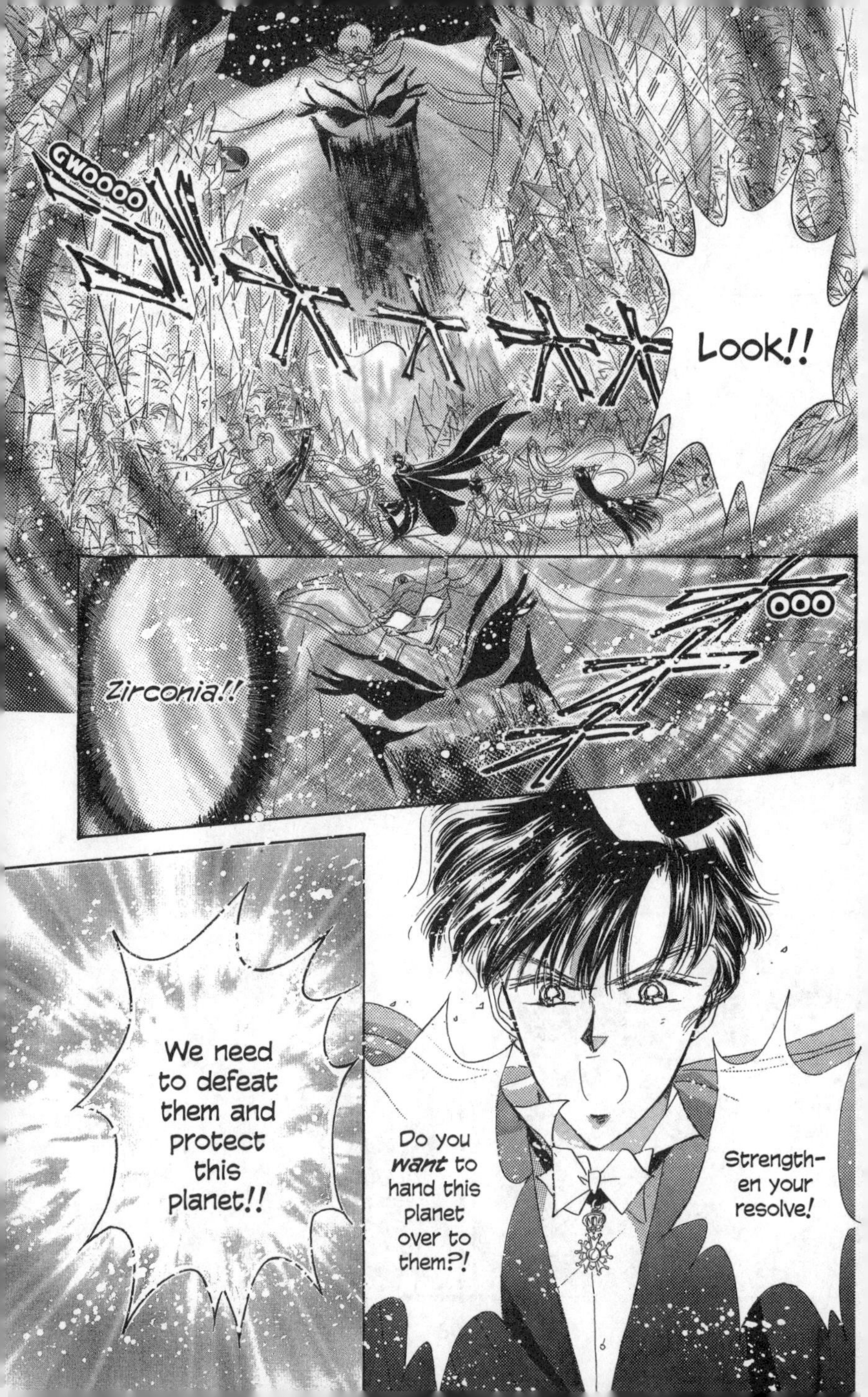
Look!!
GWOOOO
OOO
Zirconia!!
Strength-en your resolve!
Do you *want* to hand this planet over to them?!
We need to defeat them and protect this planet!!

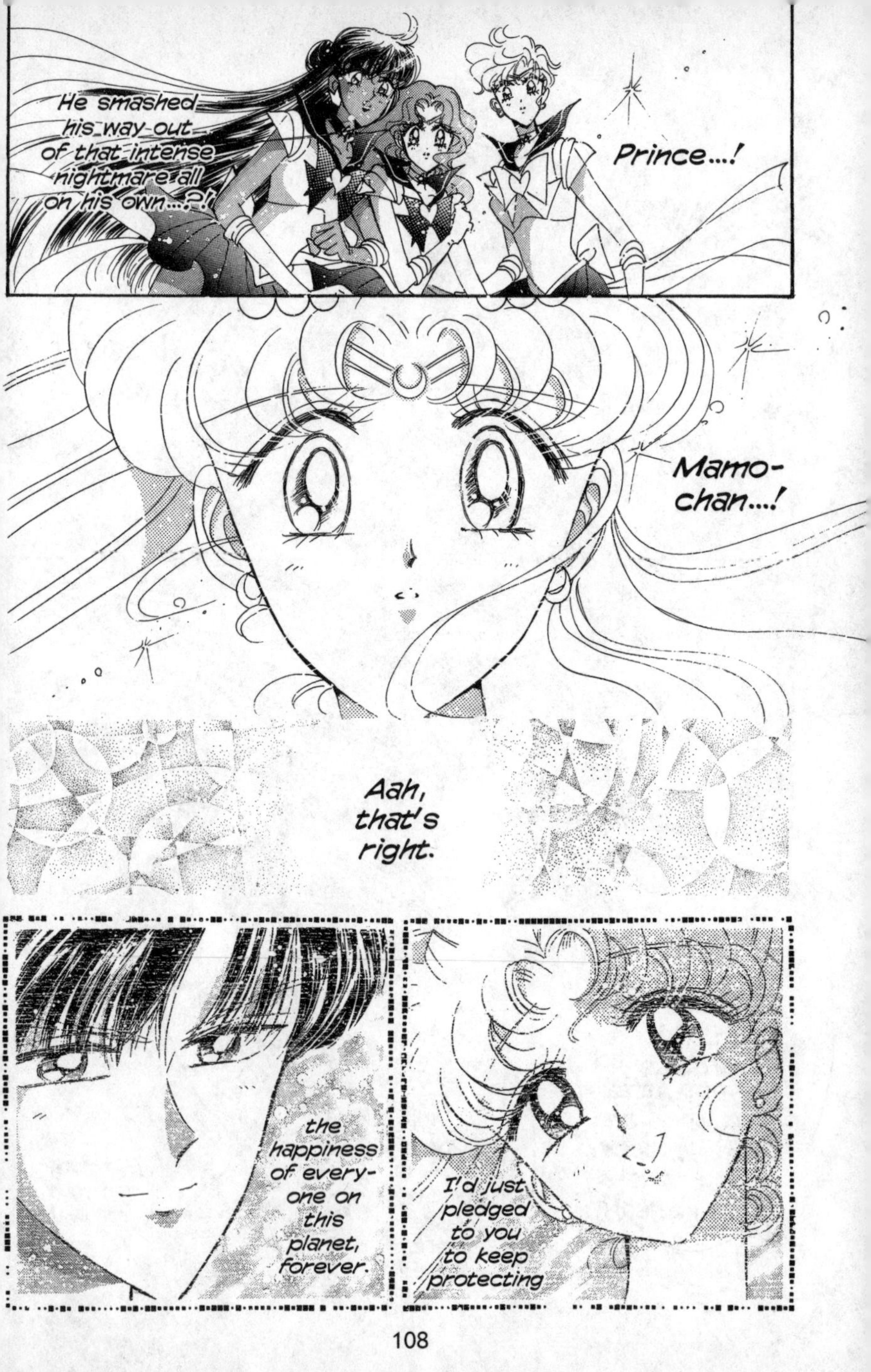
Prince...!
He smashed his way out of that intense nightmare all on his own...?!
Mamo-chan...!
Aah, that's right.
I'd just pledged to you to keep protecting
the happiness of every-one on this planet, forever.

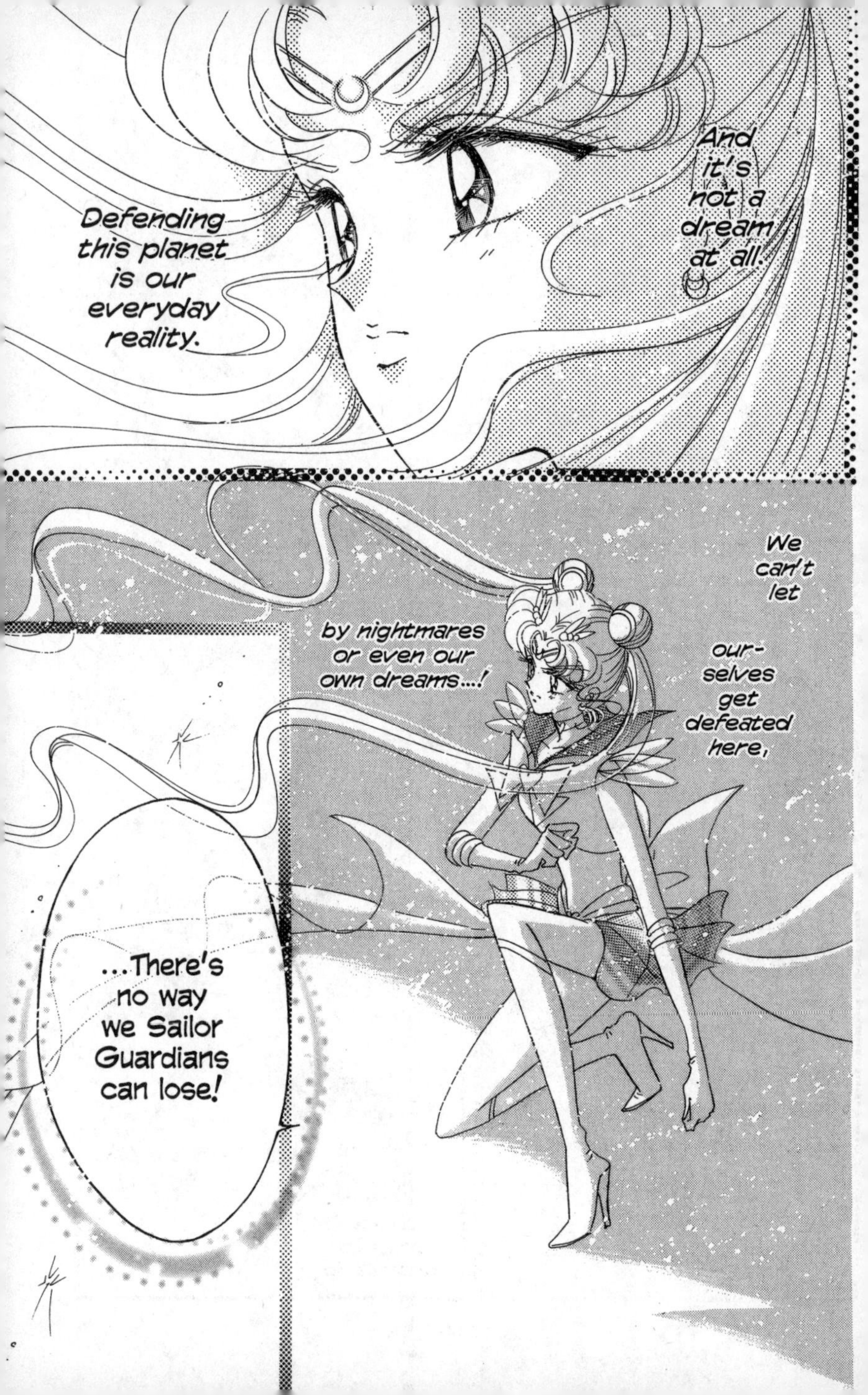
And it's not a dream at all.
Defending this planet is our everyday reality.
We can't let
our-selves get defeated here,
by nightmares or even our own dreams...!
...There's no way we Sailor Guardians can lose!

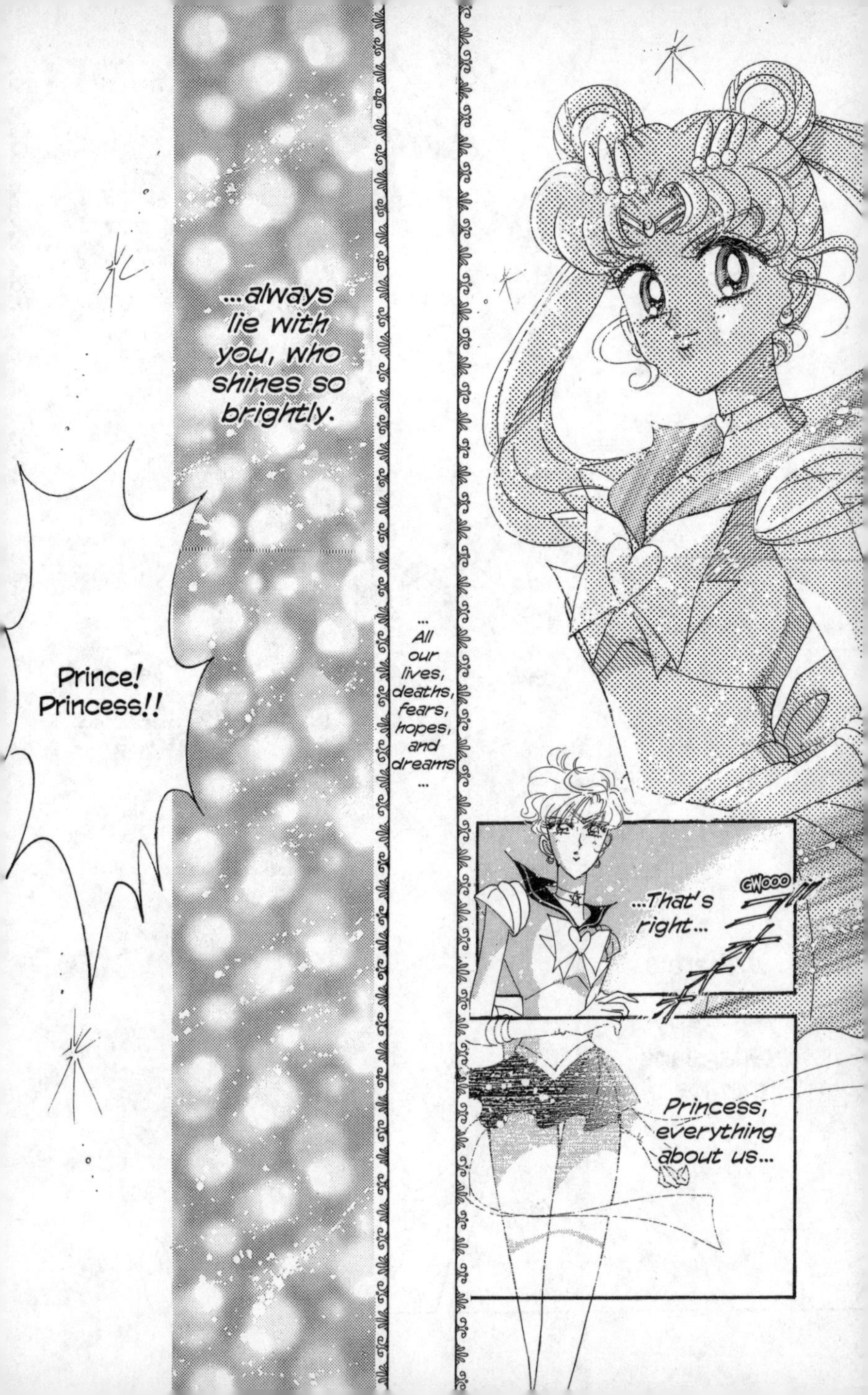

...That's right...
GWOOO
Princess, everything about us...
...All our lives, deaths, fears, hopes, and dreams...
...always lie with you, who shines so brightly.
Prince! Princess!!

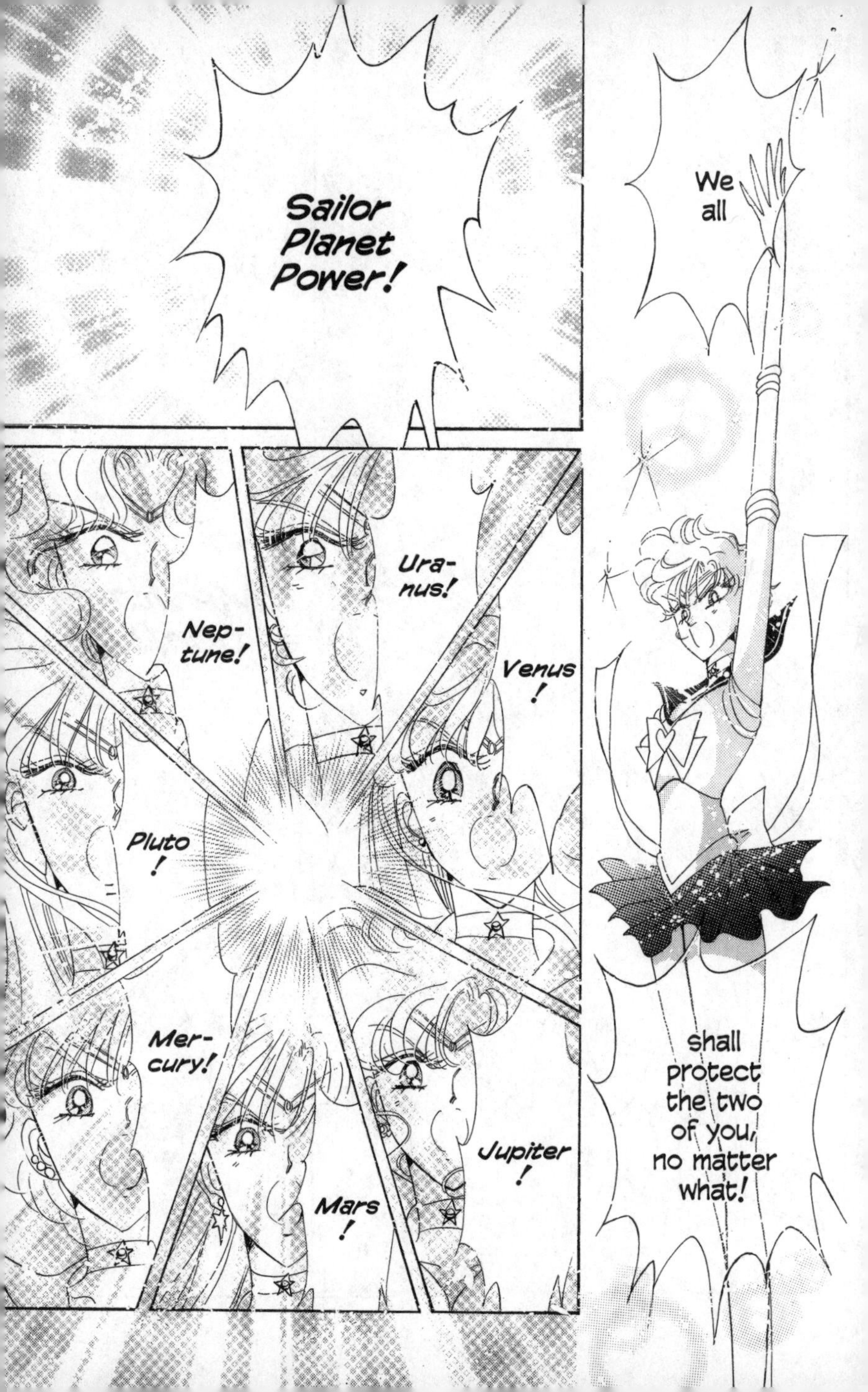
We all
shall protect the two of you, no matter what!
Sailor Planet Power!
Uranus!
Venus!
Neptune!
Pluto!
Mercury!
Jupiter!
Mars!

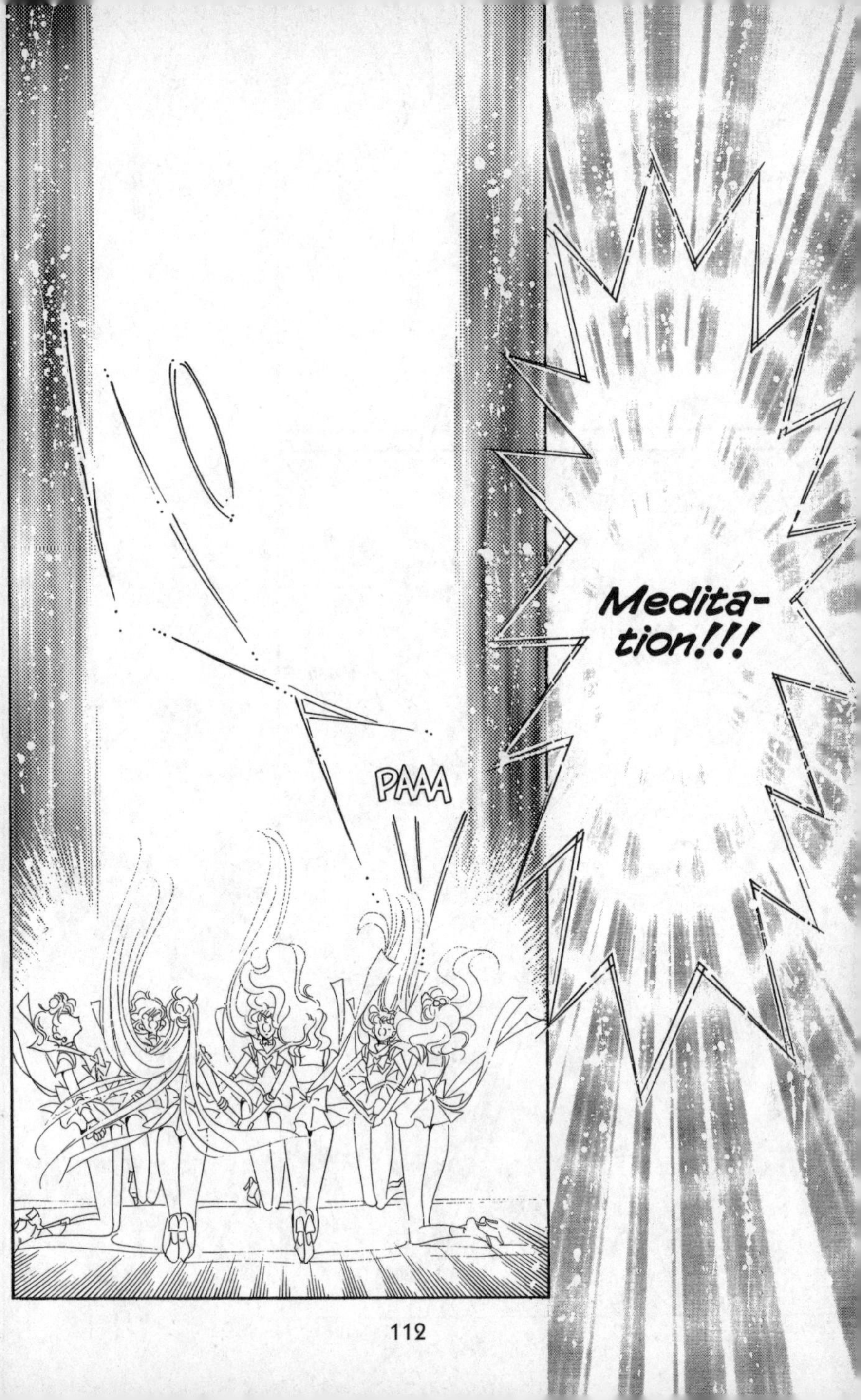
Meditation!!!
PAAA

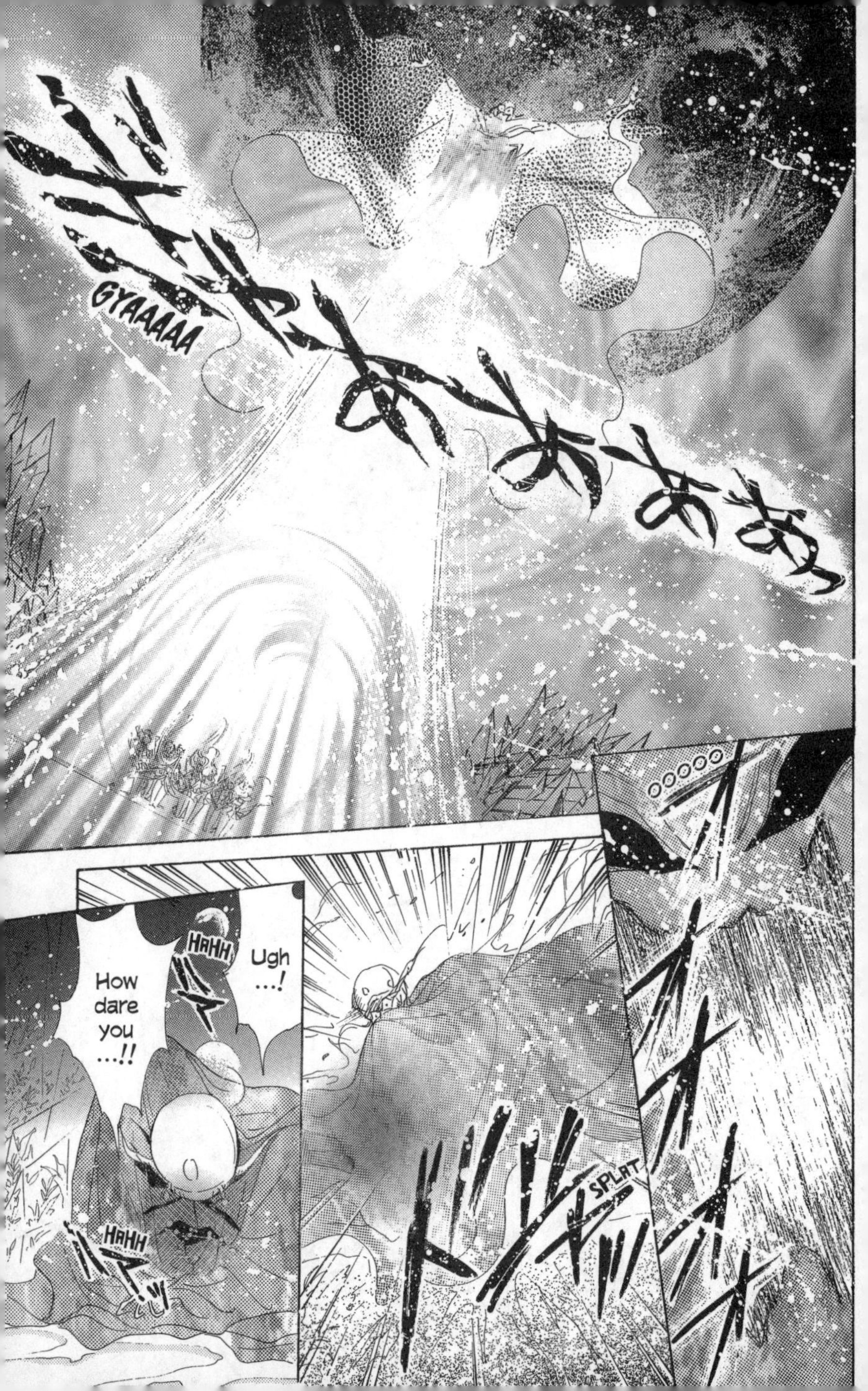
GYAAAAA
SPLAT
HAHH
Ugh ...!
How dare you ...!!
HAHH

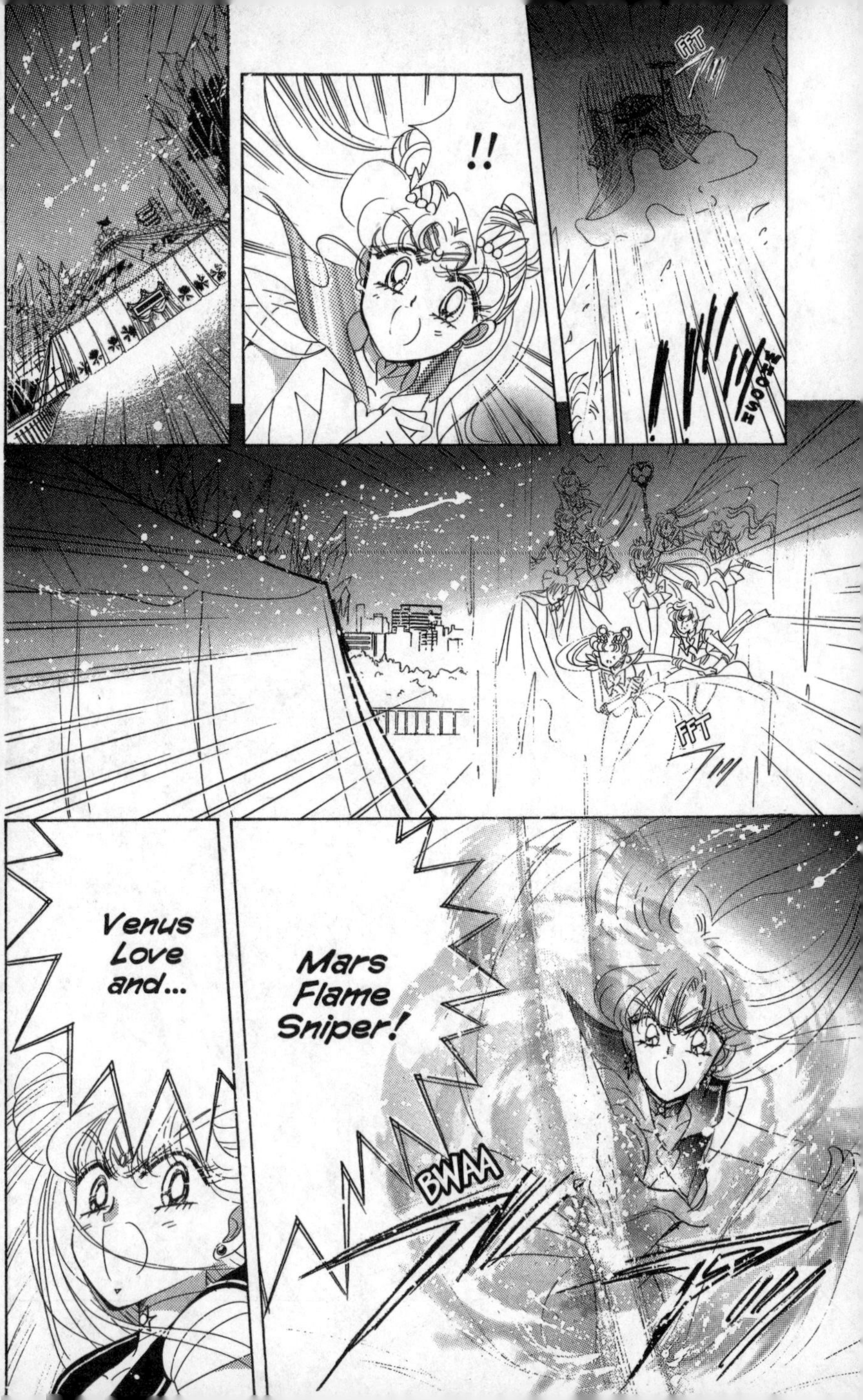
FFT
WHOOSH
!!
FFT
Mars Flame Sniper!
BWAA
Venus Love and...

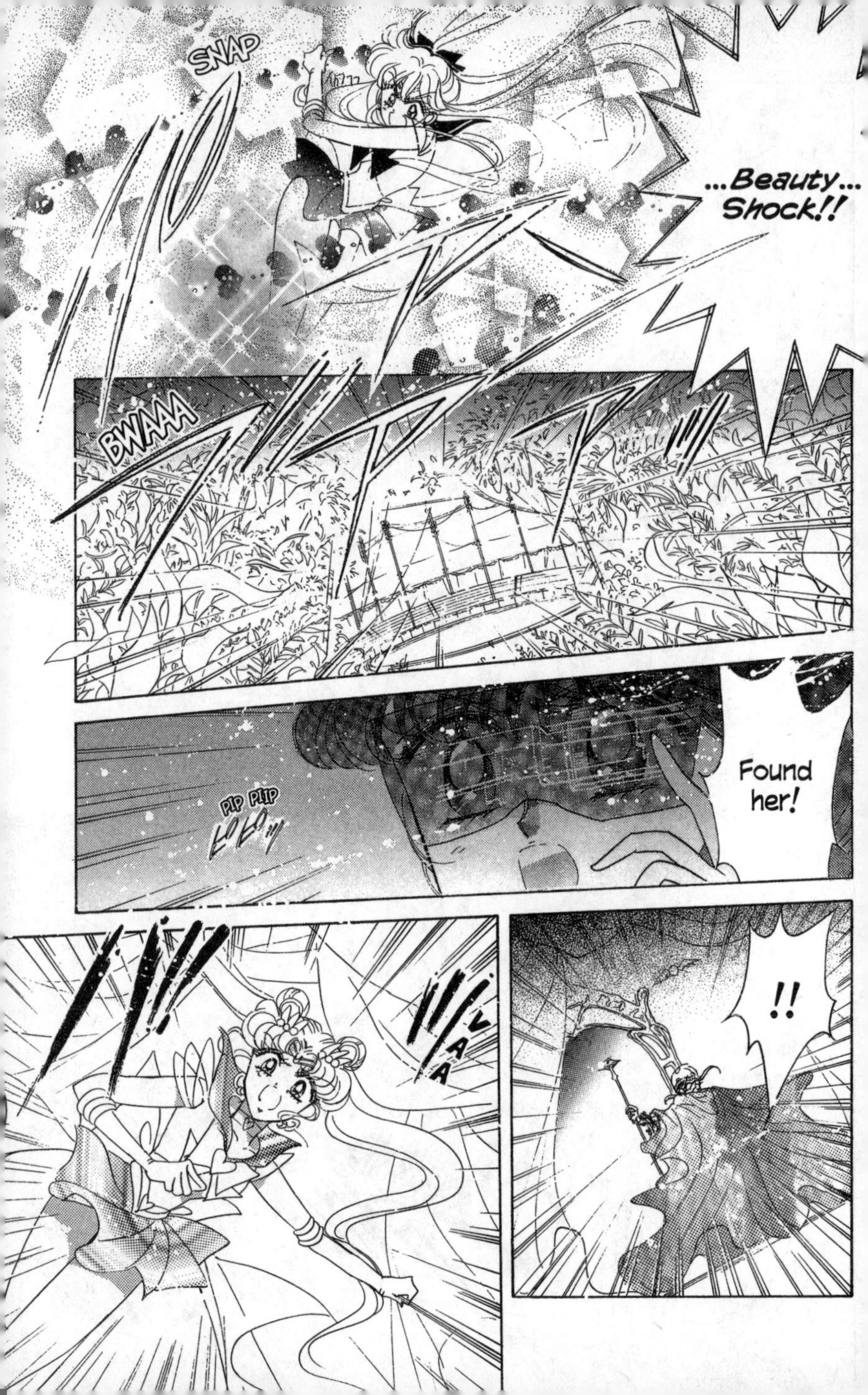
...Beauty... Shock!!
SNAP
BWAAA
Found her!
PIP PIIP
!!
VAA

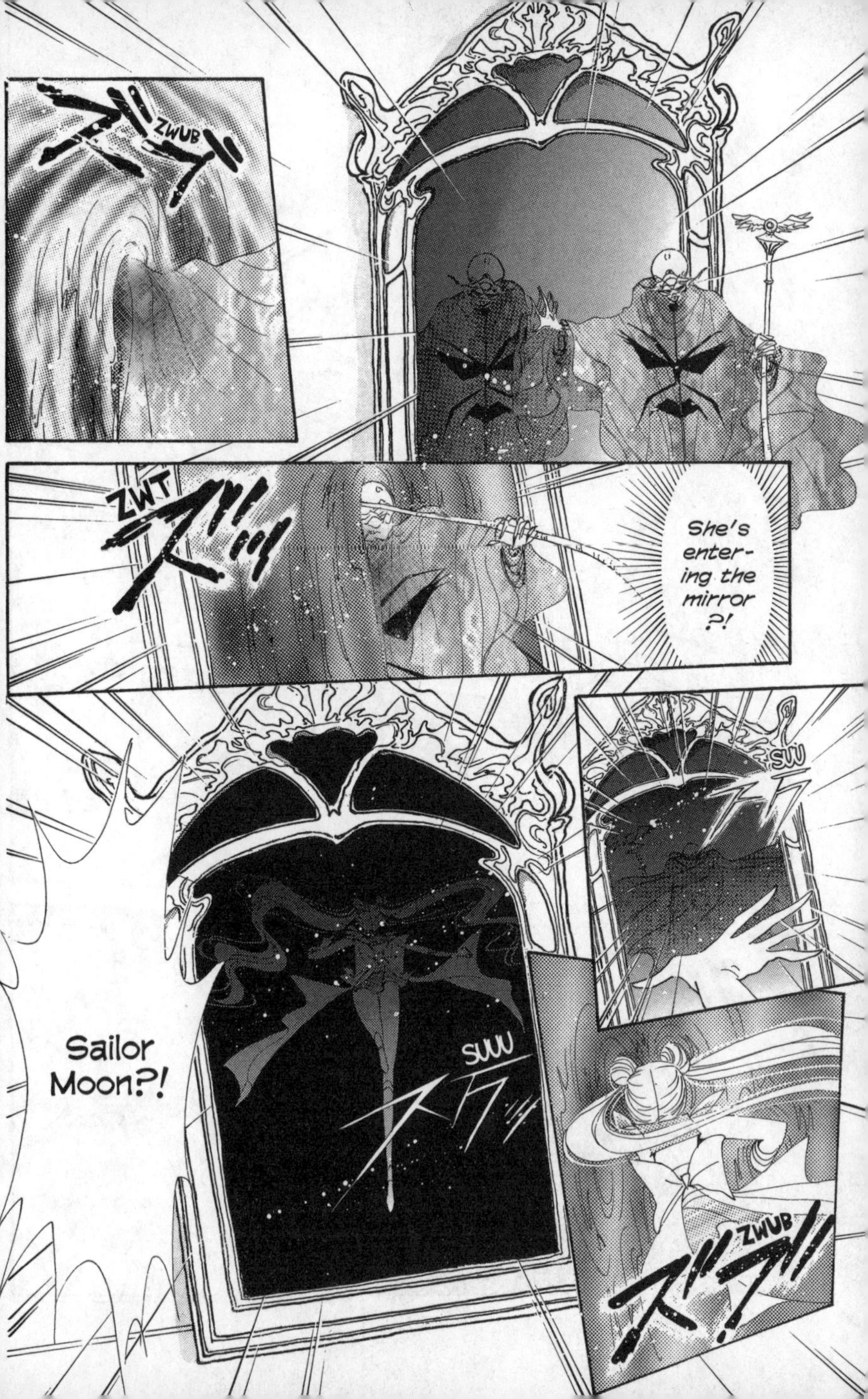
ZWUB
She's entering the mirror?!
ZWT
SUU
ZWUB
SUUU
Sailor Moon?!

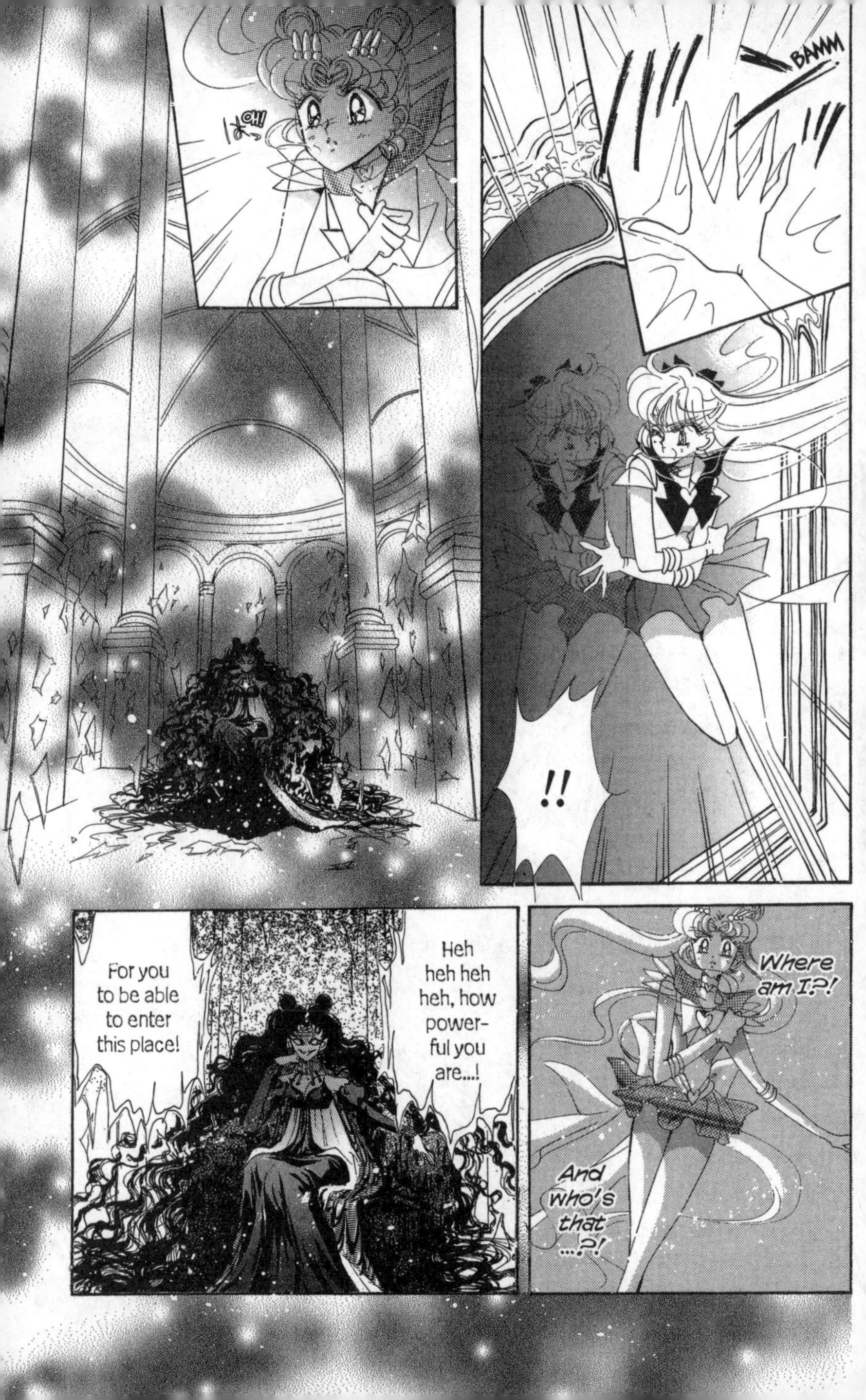
BAMM
!!
はっ OH!
Where am I?!
And who's that ...?!
Heh heh heh heh, how powerful you are...!
For you to be able to enter this place!

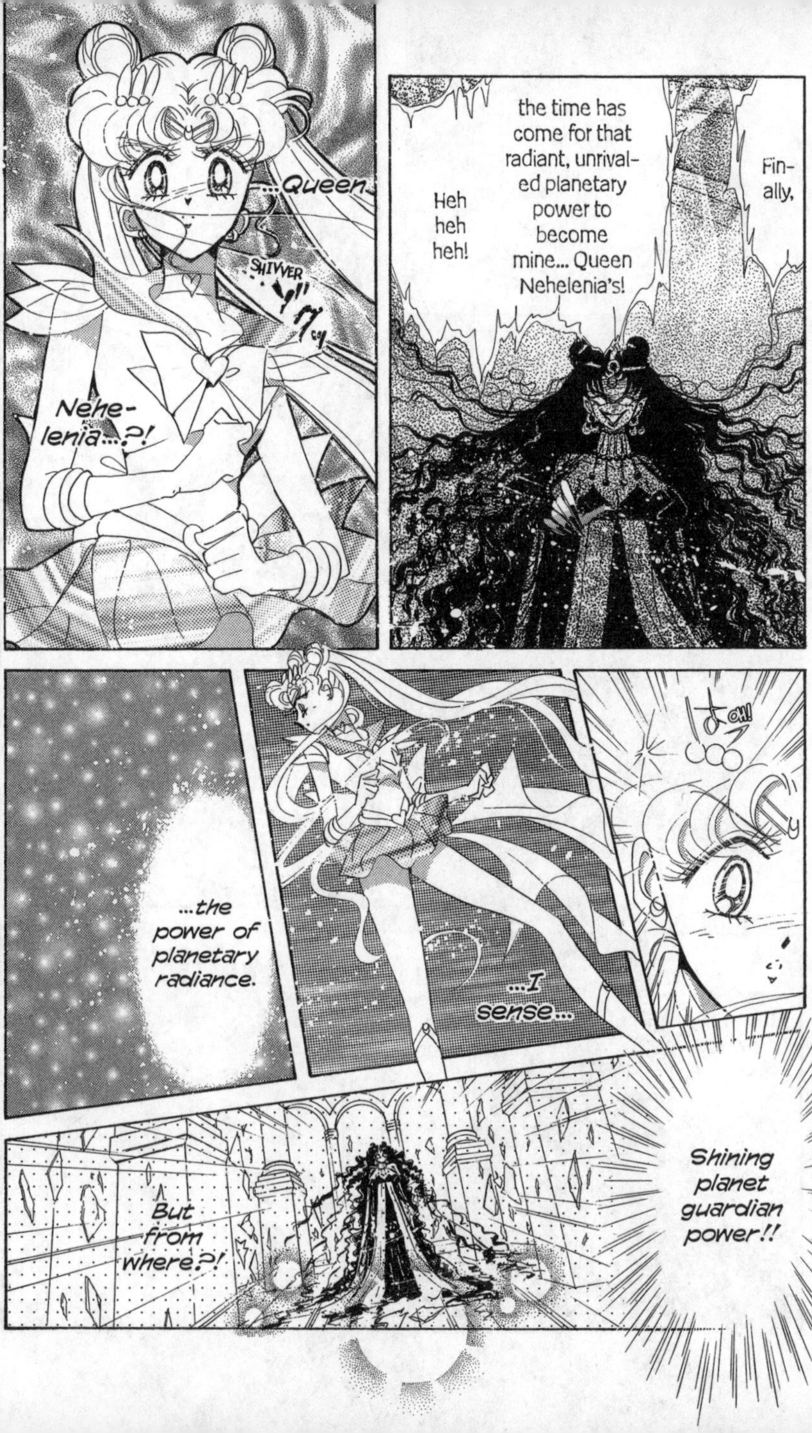
Finally,
the time has come for that radiant, unrivaled planetary power to become mine... Queen Nehelenia's!
Heh heh heh!
...Queen
SHIVVER
Nehelenia...?!
OH!
...I sense...
...the power of planetary radiance.
Shining planet guardian power!!
But from where?!

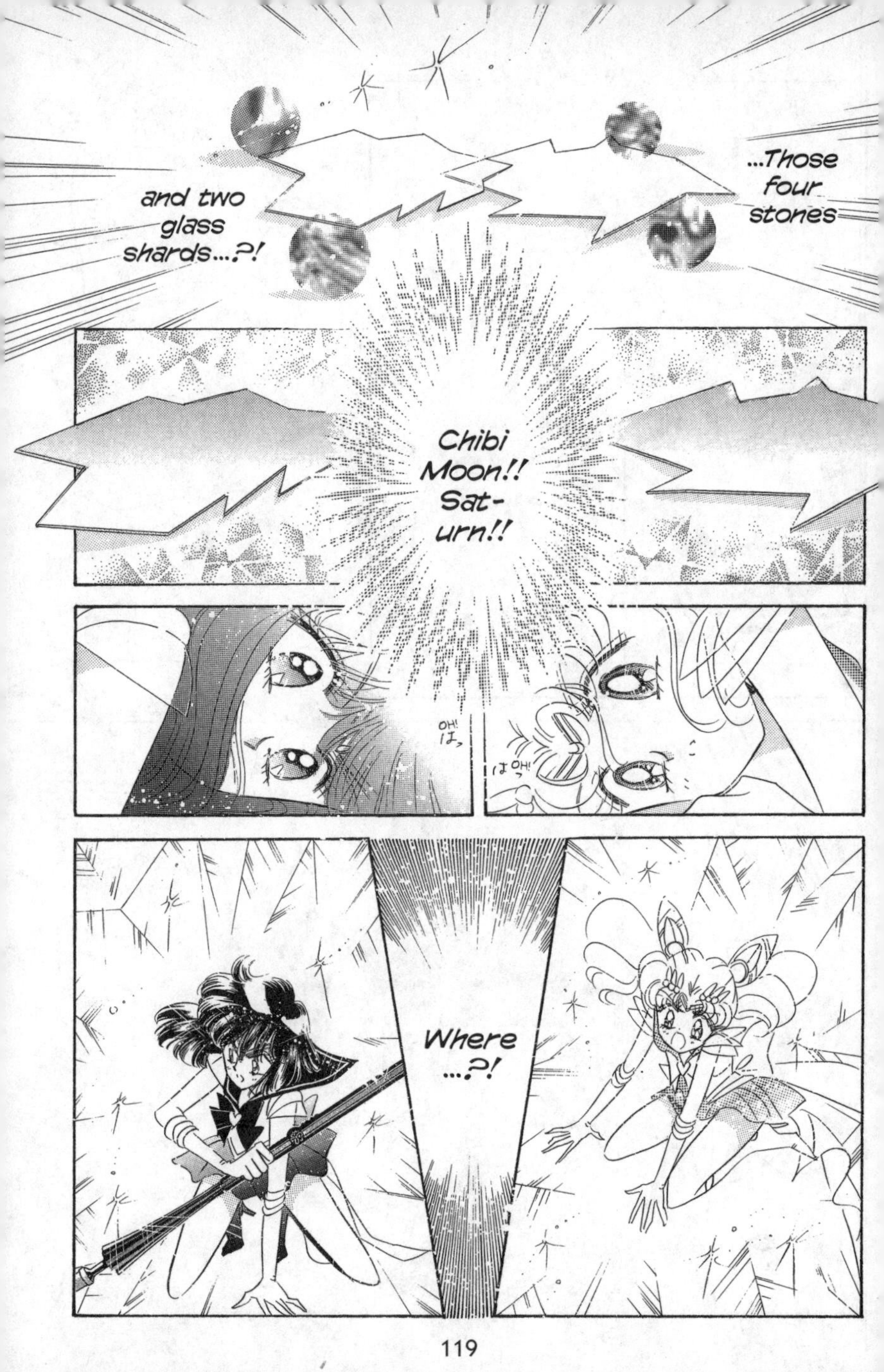
...Those four stones
and two glass shards...?!
Chibi Moon!! Sat-urn!!
Where ...?!

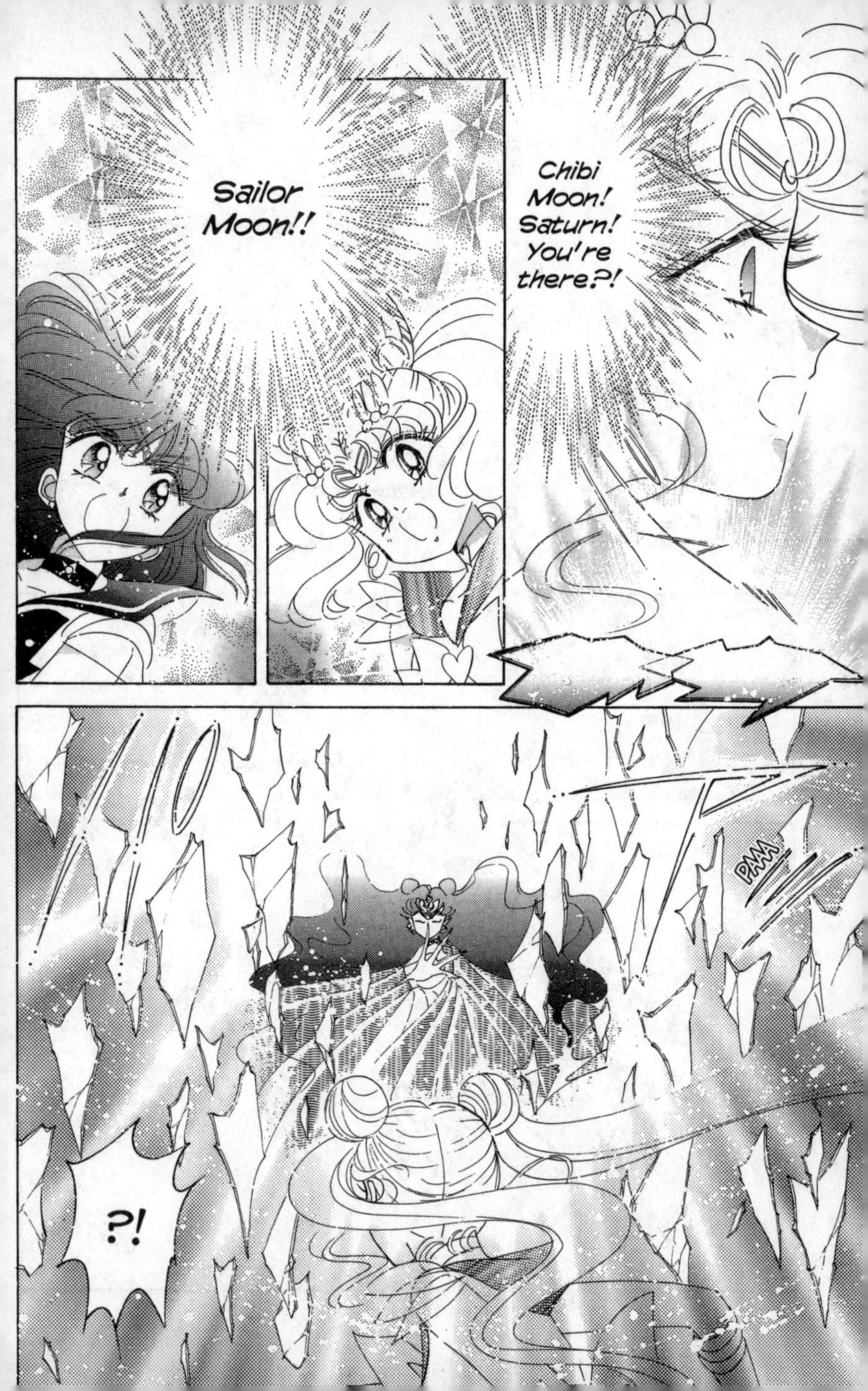
Chibi Moon! Saturn! You're there?!
Sailor Moon!!
PAAA
?!

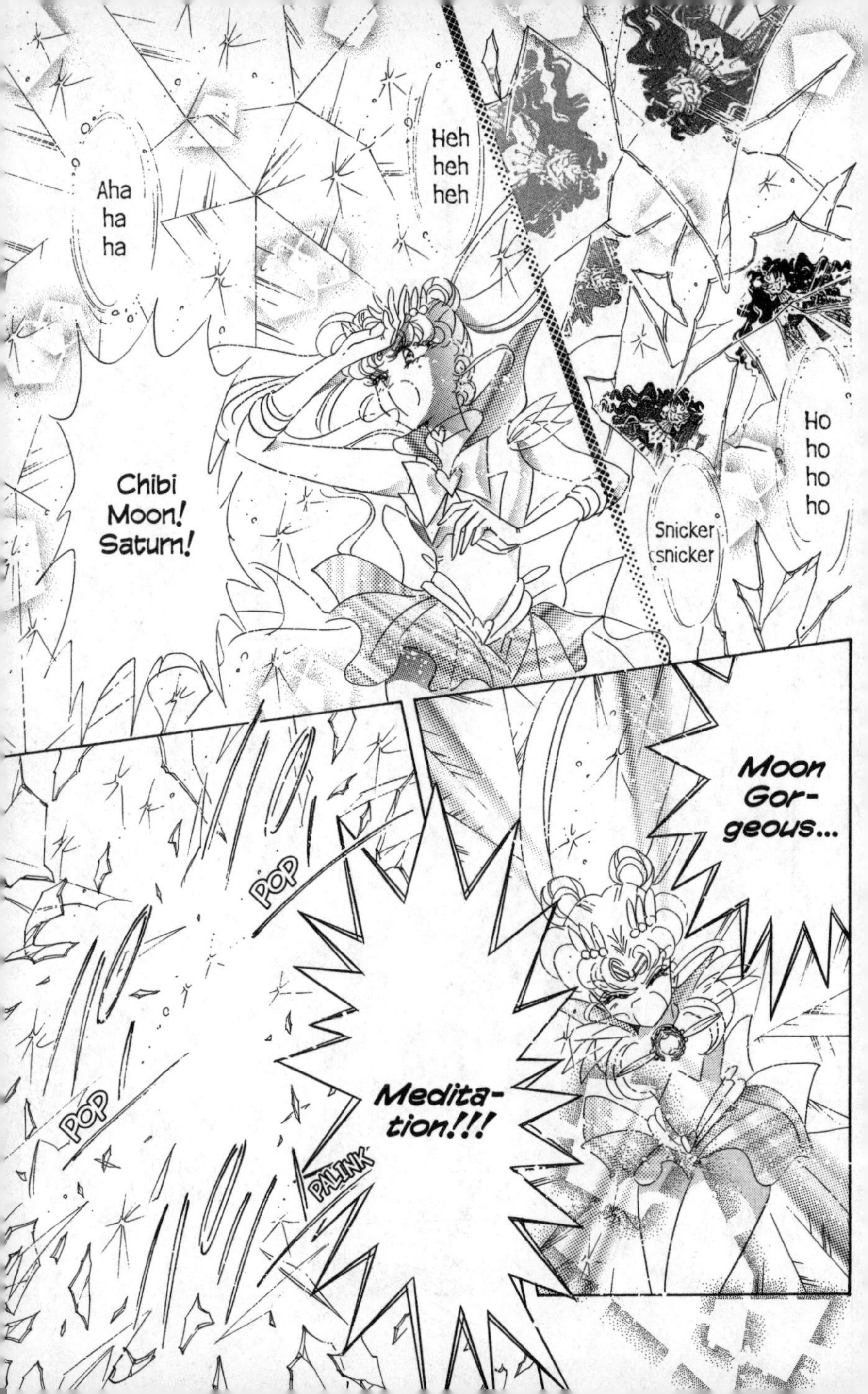
Ho ho ho ho
Snicker snicker
Heh heh heh
Aha ha ha
Chibi Moon! Saturn!
Moon Gorgeous...
Meditation!!!
PALINK
POP
POP

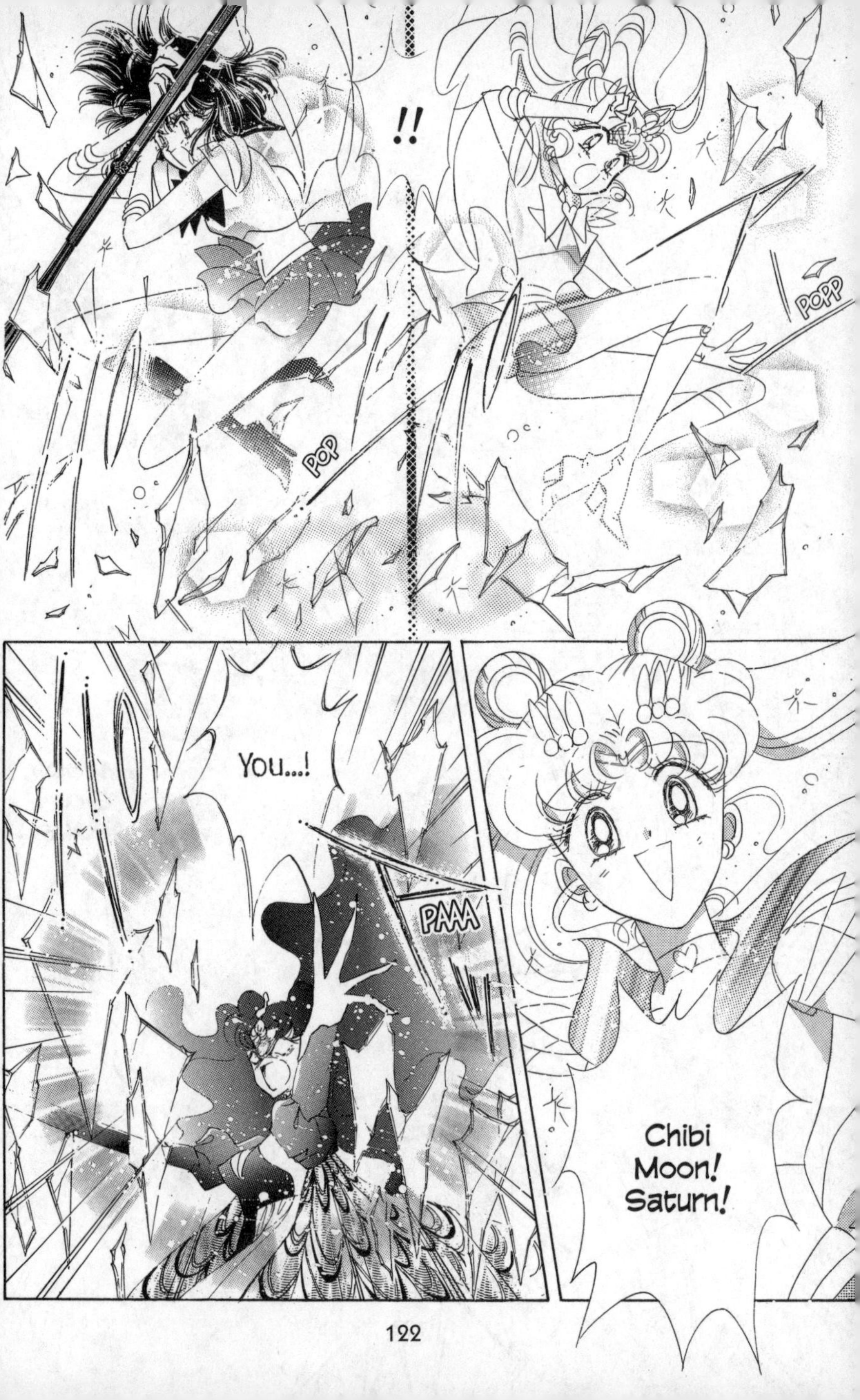
POPP
!!
POP
Chibi Moon! Saturn!
You...!
PAAA

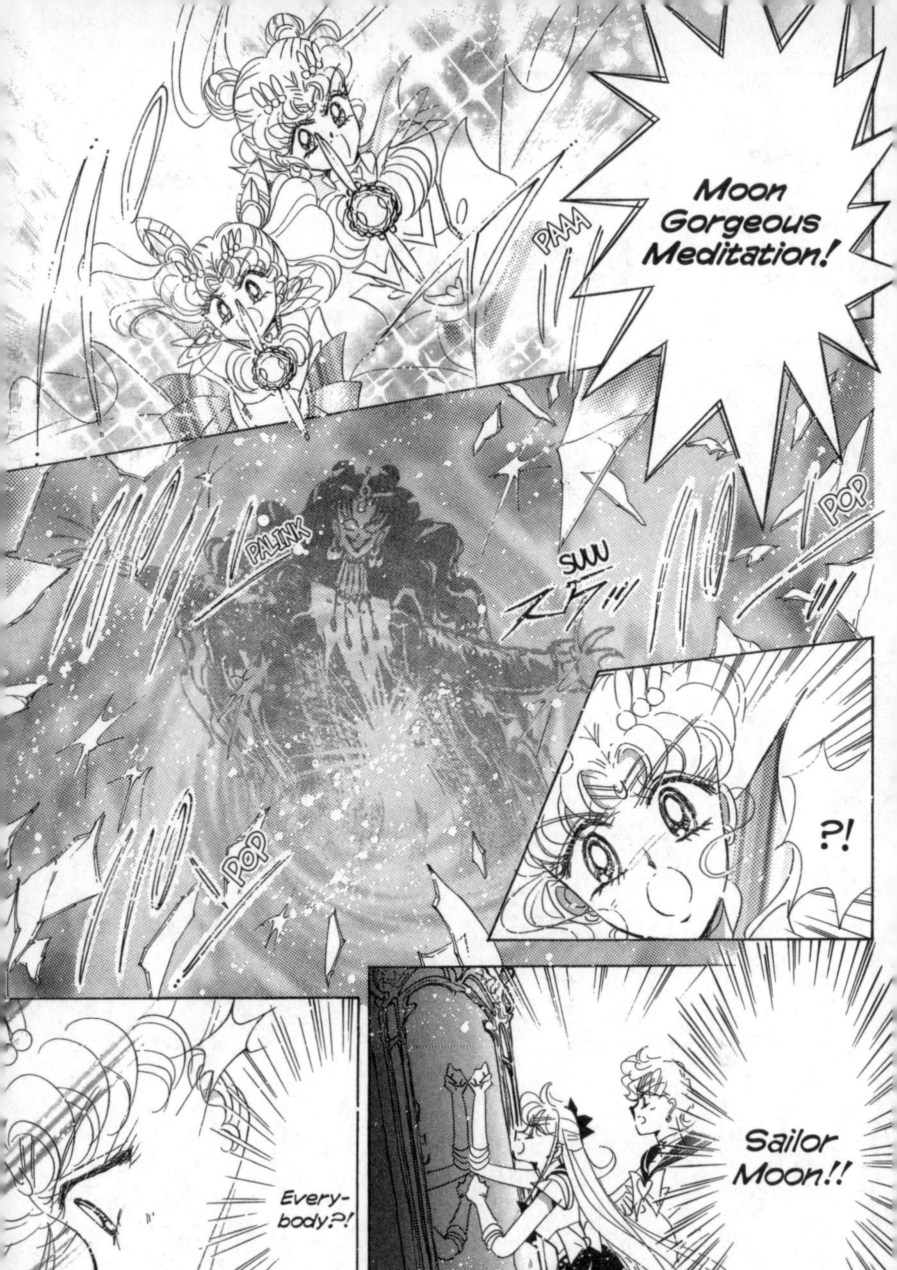
Moon Gorgeous Meditation!
PAAA
POP
SUU
PALINK
POP
?!
Sailor Moon!!
Every-body?!

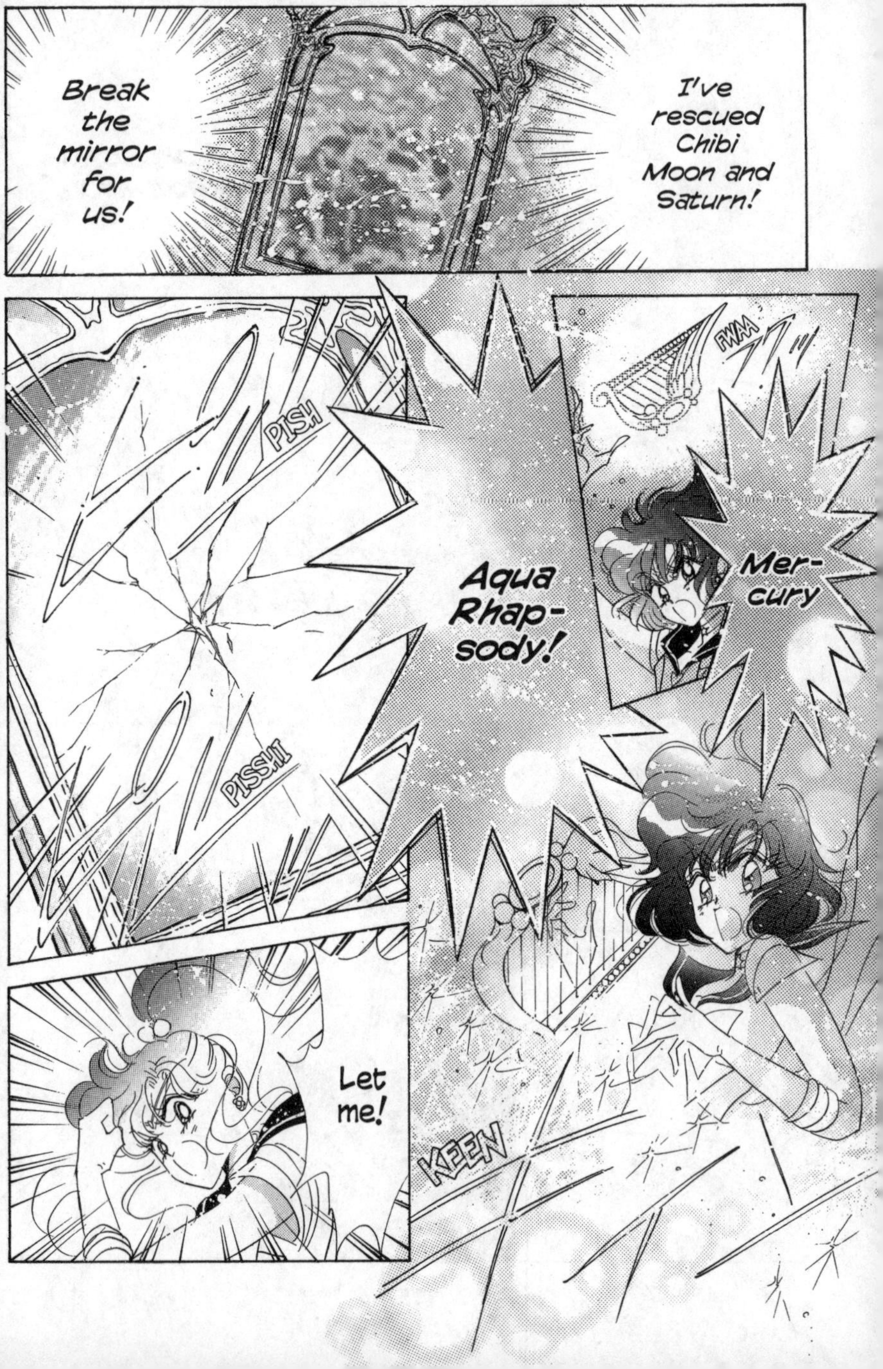
I've rescued Chibi Moon and Saturn!
Break the mirror for us!
FWAA
Mer-cury
Aqua Rhap-sody!
KEEN
PISH
PISSHI
Let me!

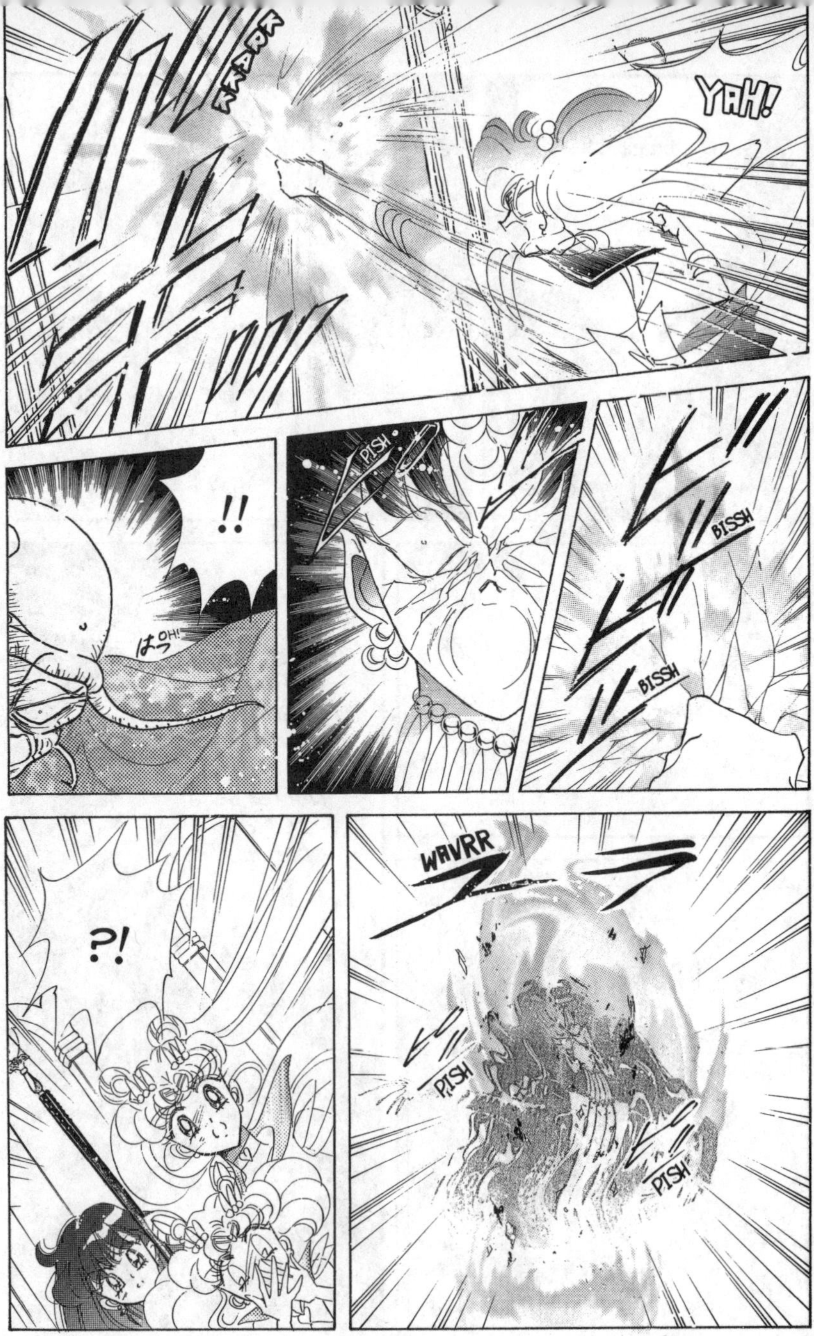
YAH!
KKARK
BISSH
BISSH
PISH
!!
はっ OH!
WAVRR
PISH
PISH
?!

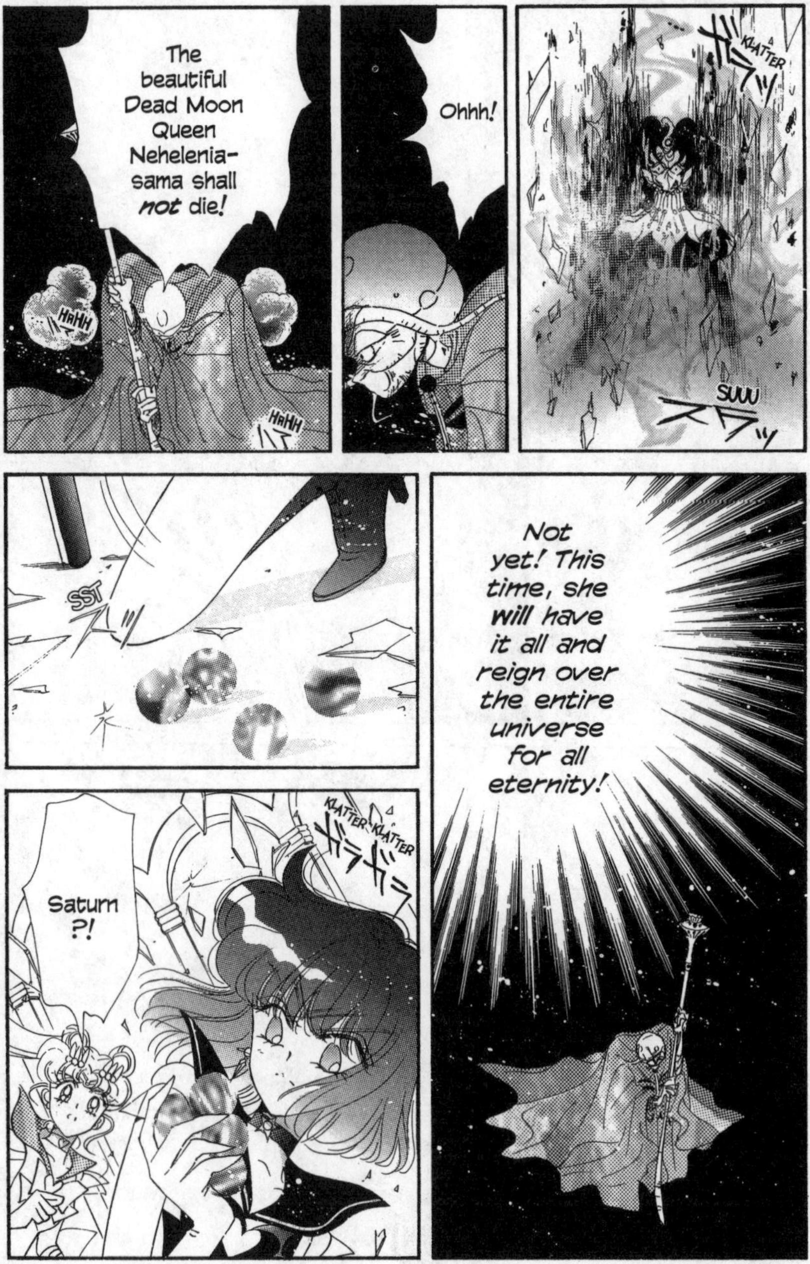
KLATTER
SUUU
Ohhh!
The beautiful Dead Moon Queen Nehelenia-sama shall ***not*** die!
HAHH
HAHH
Not yet! This time, she will have it all and reign over the entire universe for all eternity!
SST
KLATTER KLATTER
Saturn ?!

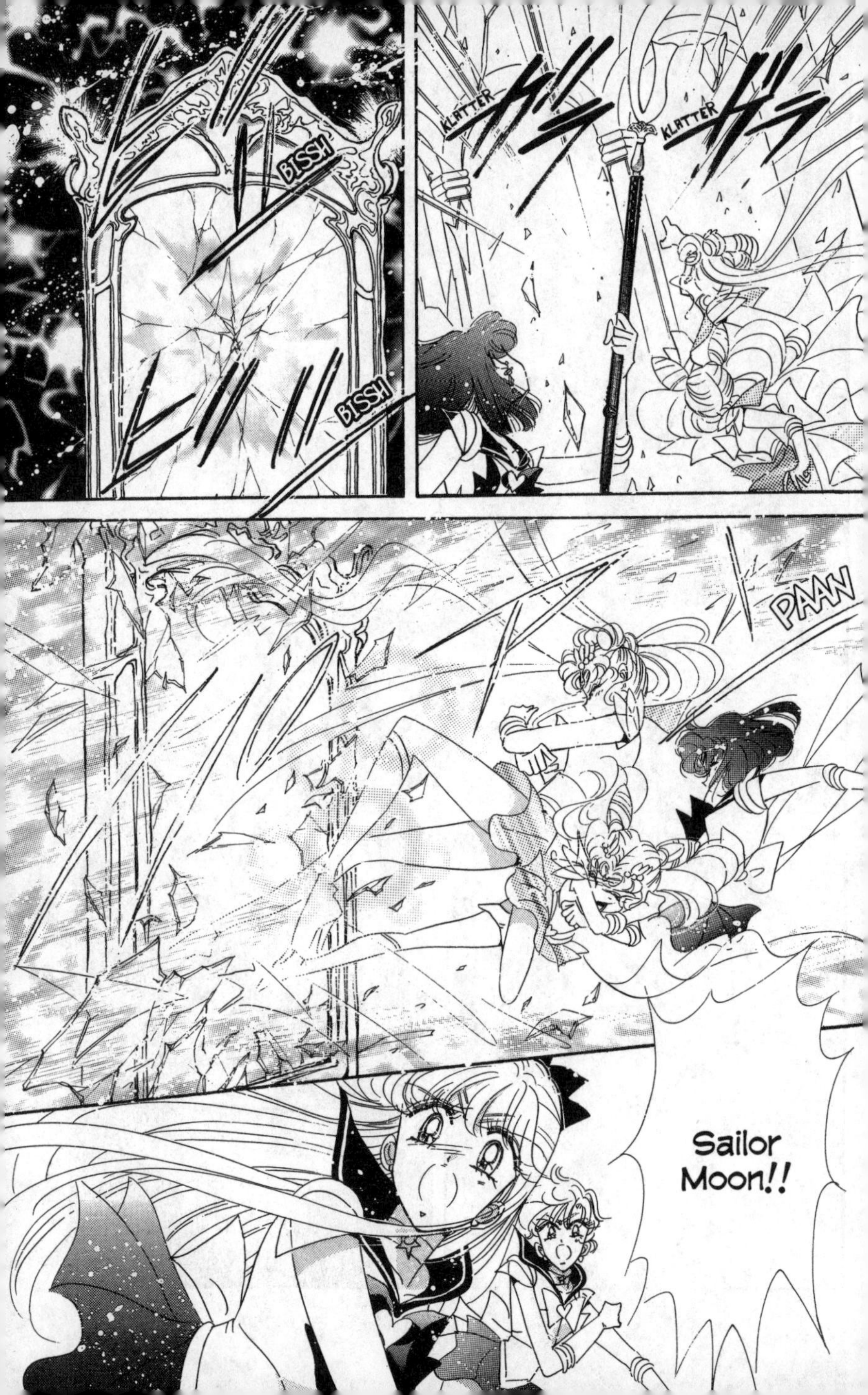

KLATTER
KLATTER
BISSH
BISSH
PAAN
Sailor Moon!!

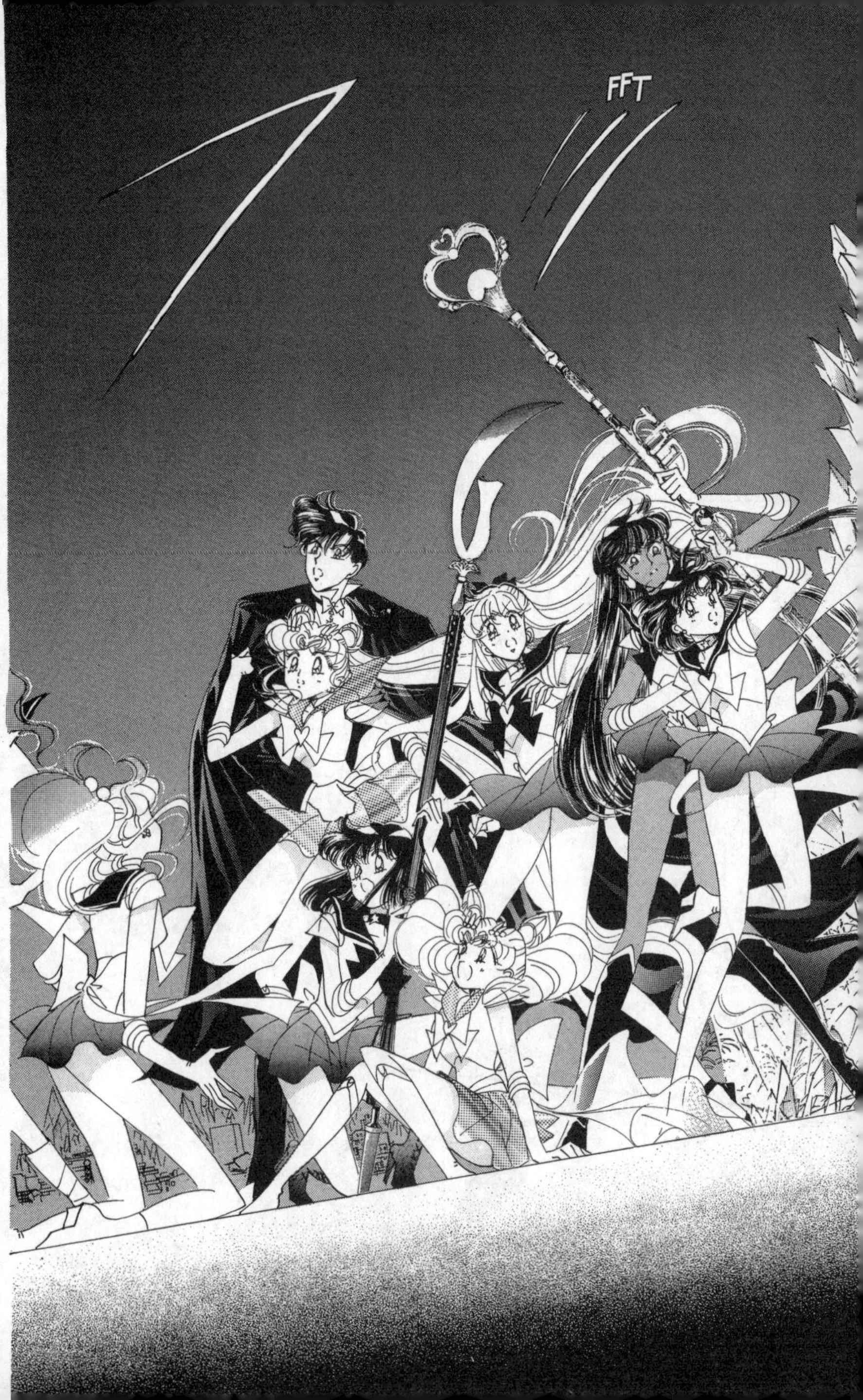
FFT

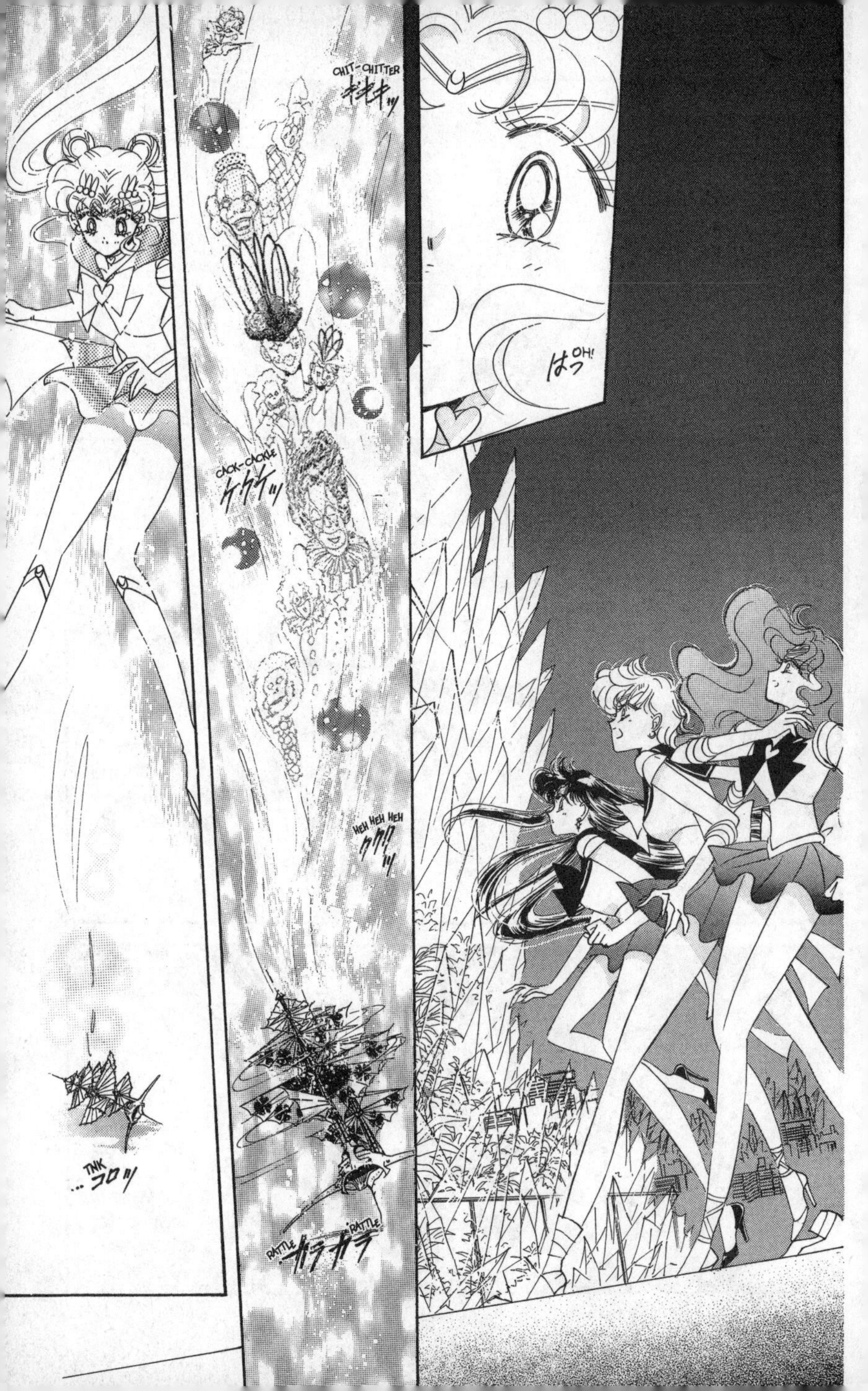
はっ OH!
CHIT-CHITTER キキキッ
CACK-CACKLE ケケケッ
HEH HEH HEH ククッ
RATTLE RATTLE カラカラ
TNK ...コロッ

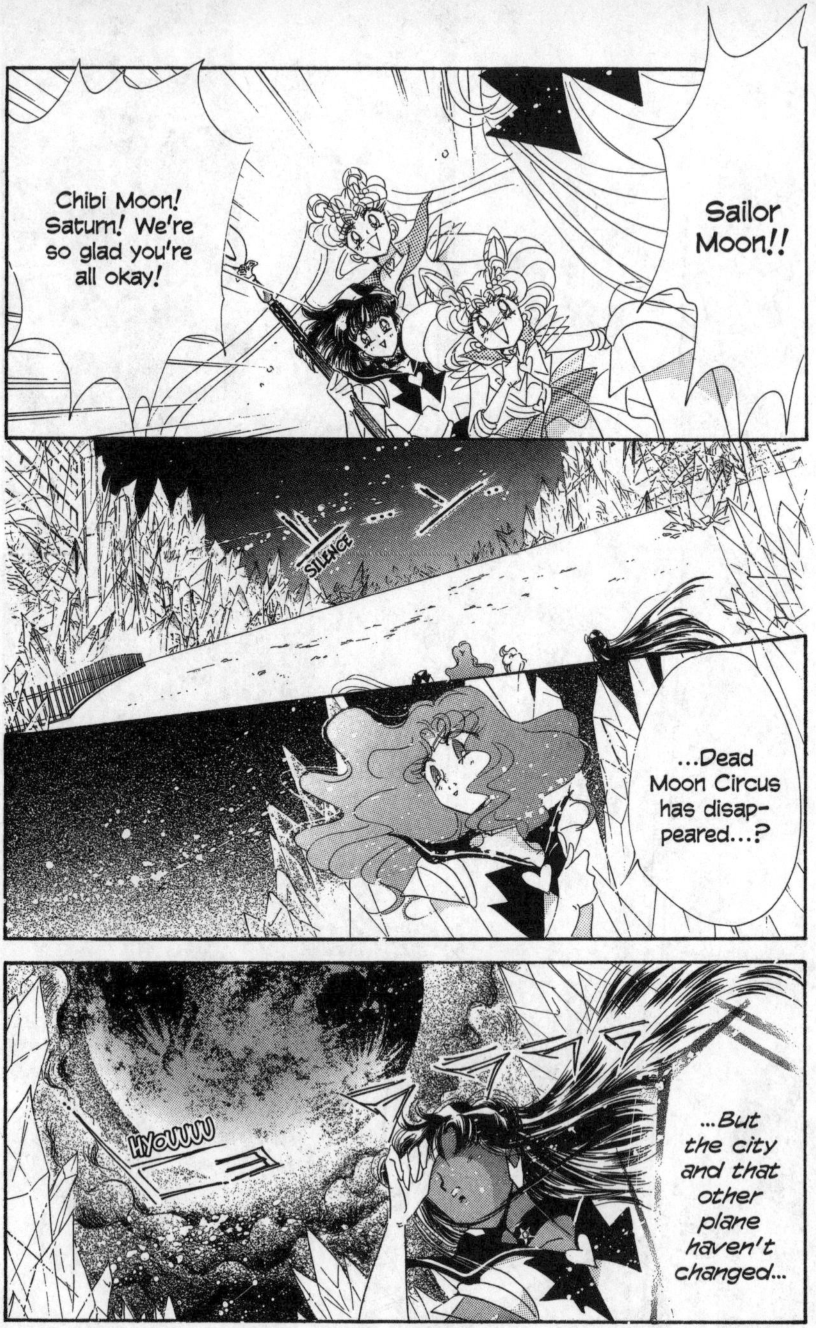
Sailor Moon!!
Chibi Moon! Saturn! We're so glad you're all okay!
SILENCE
...Dead Moon Circus has disappeared...?
...But the city and that other plane haven't changed...
HYOUUU

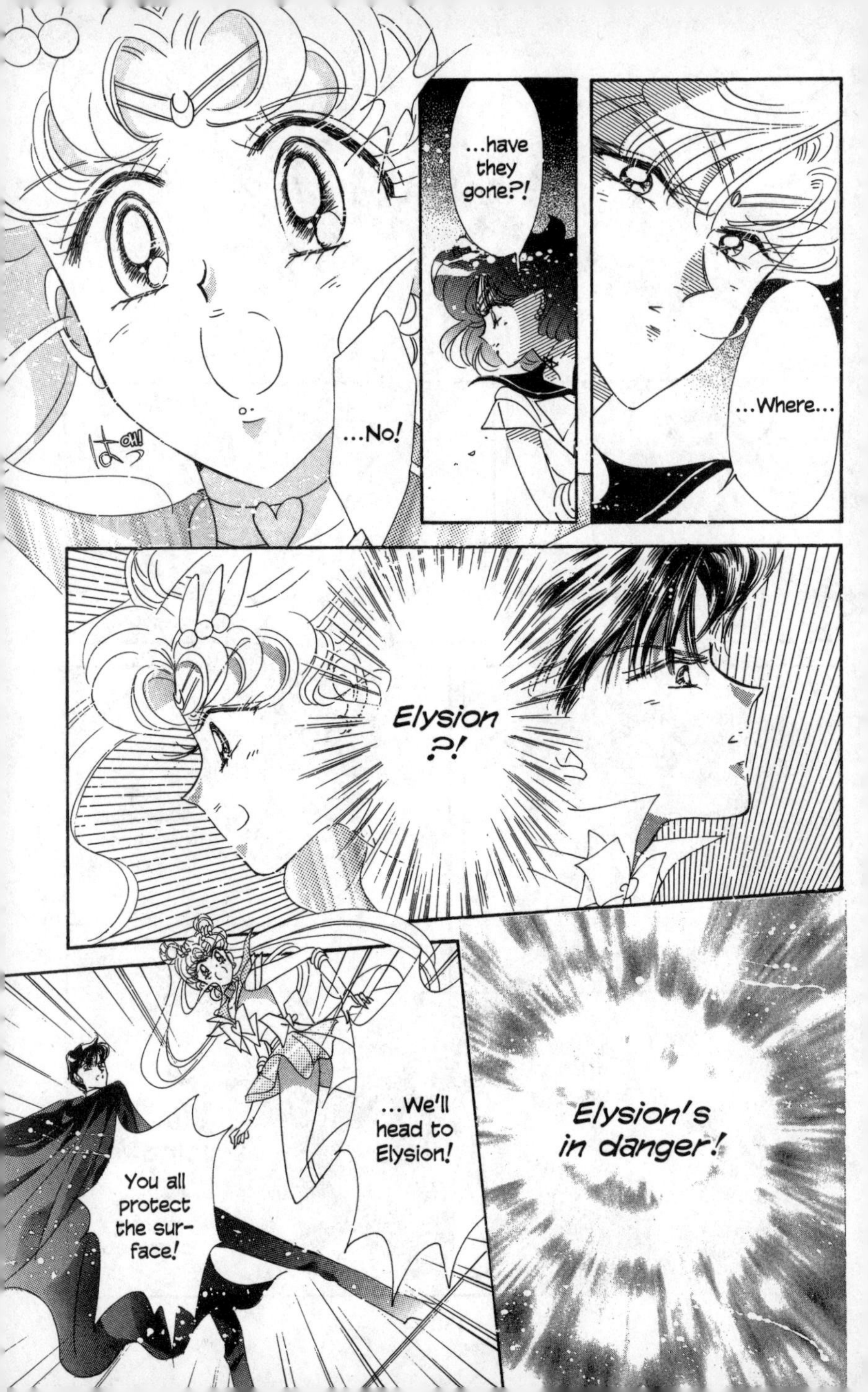
...Where...
...have they gone?!
...No!
OH!
Elysion ?!
Elysion's in danger!
...We'll head to Elysion!
You all protect the sur- face!

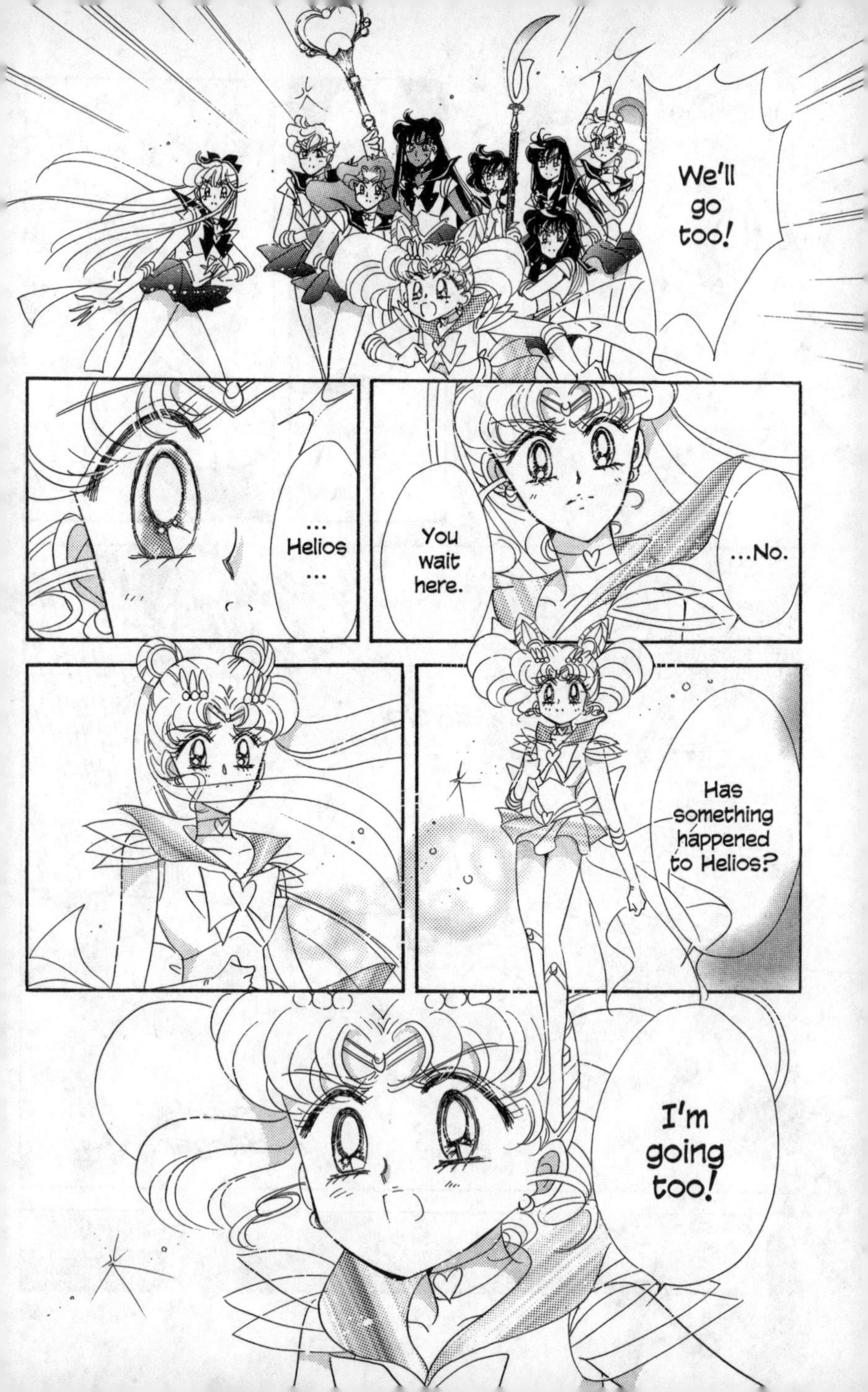
We'll go too!
...No.
You wait here.
... Helios ...
Has something happened to Helios?
I'm going too!

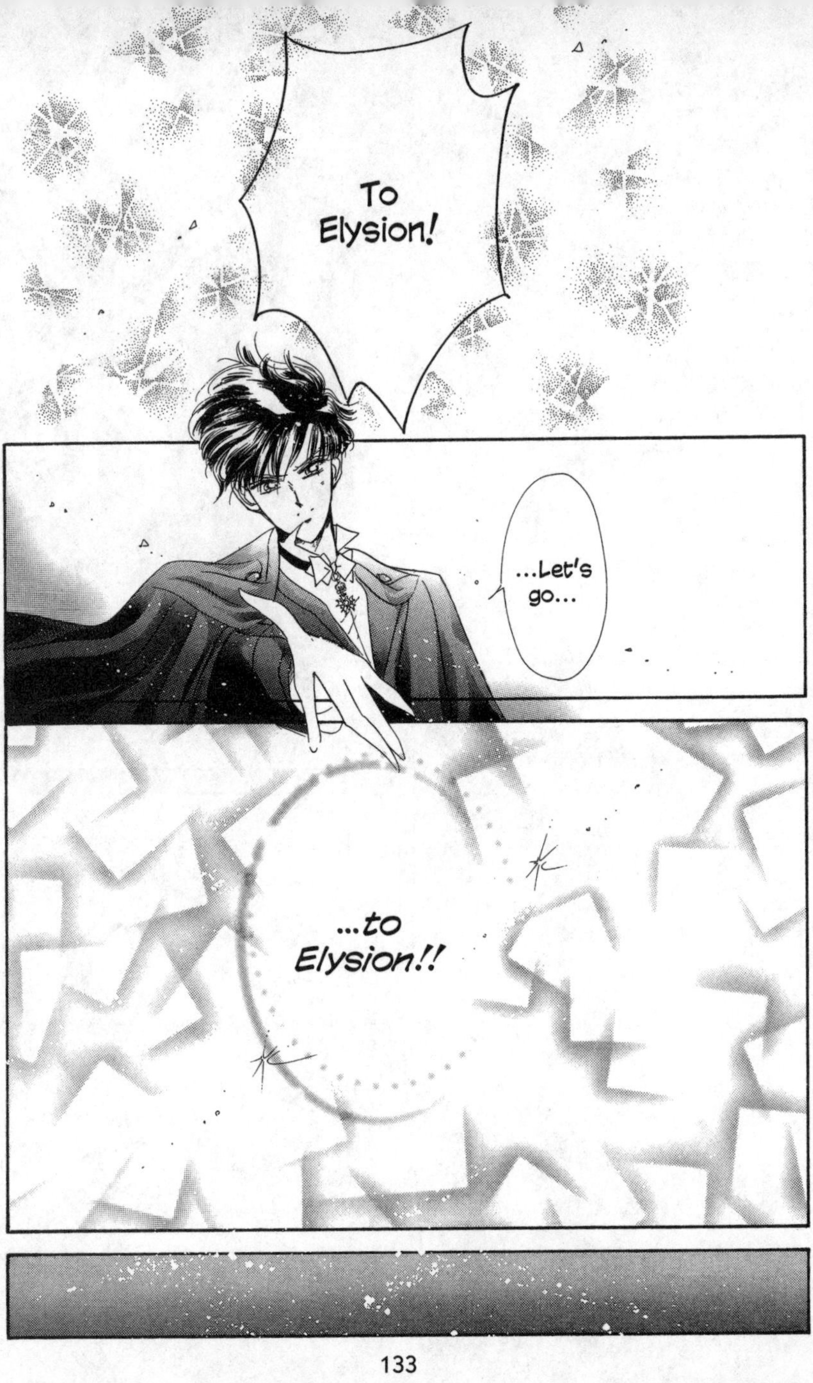
To Elysion!
...Let's go...
...to Elysion!!

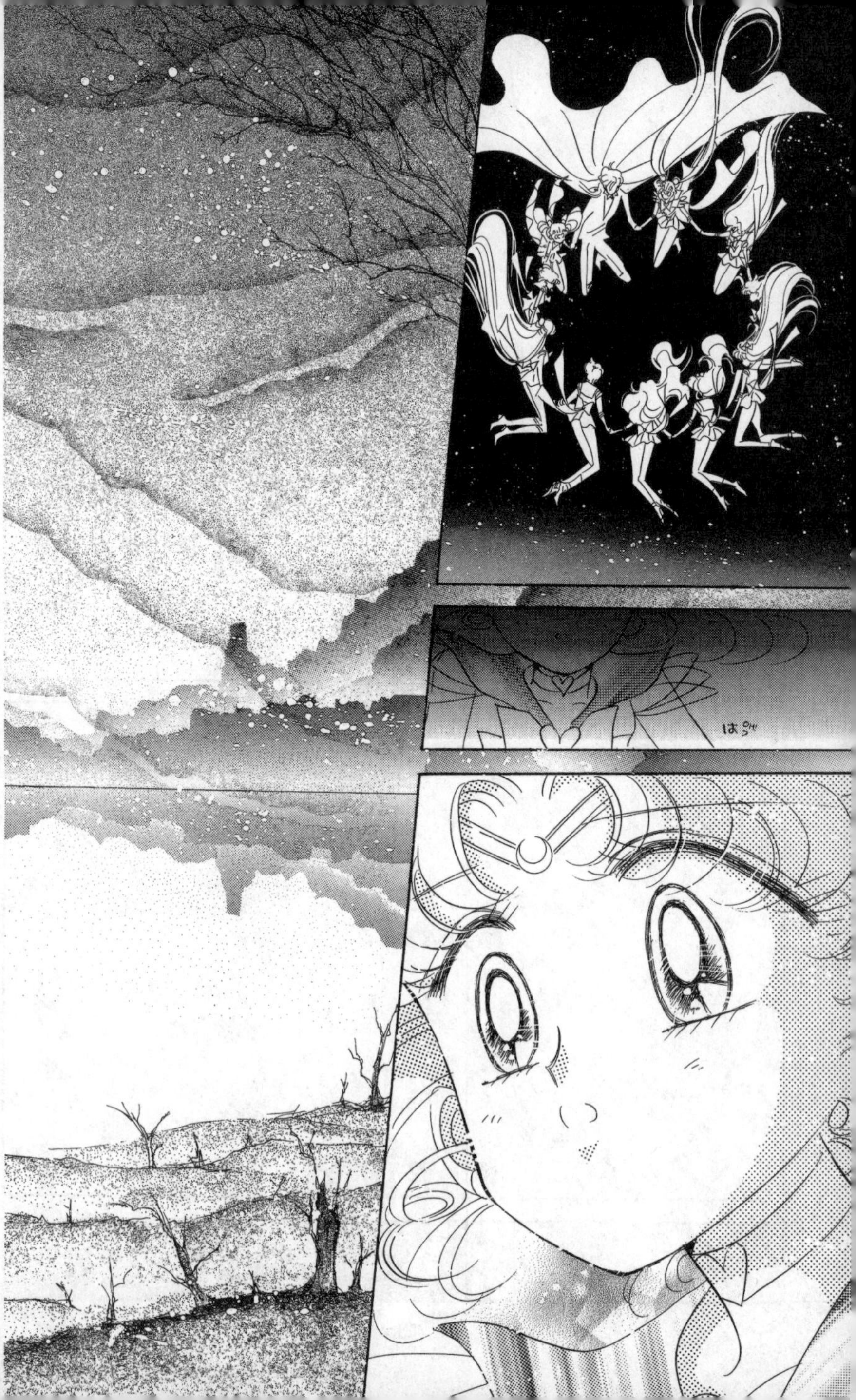
はっ

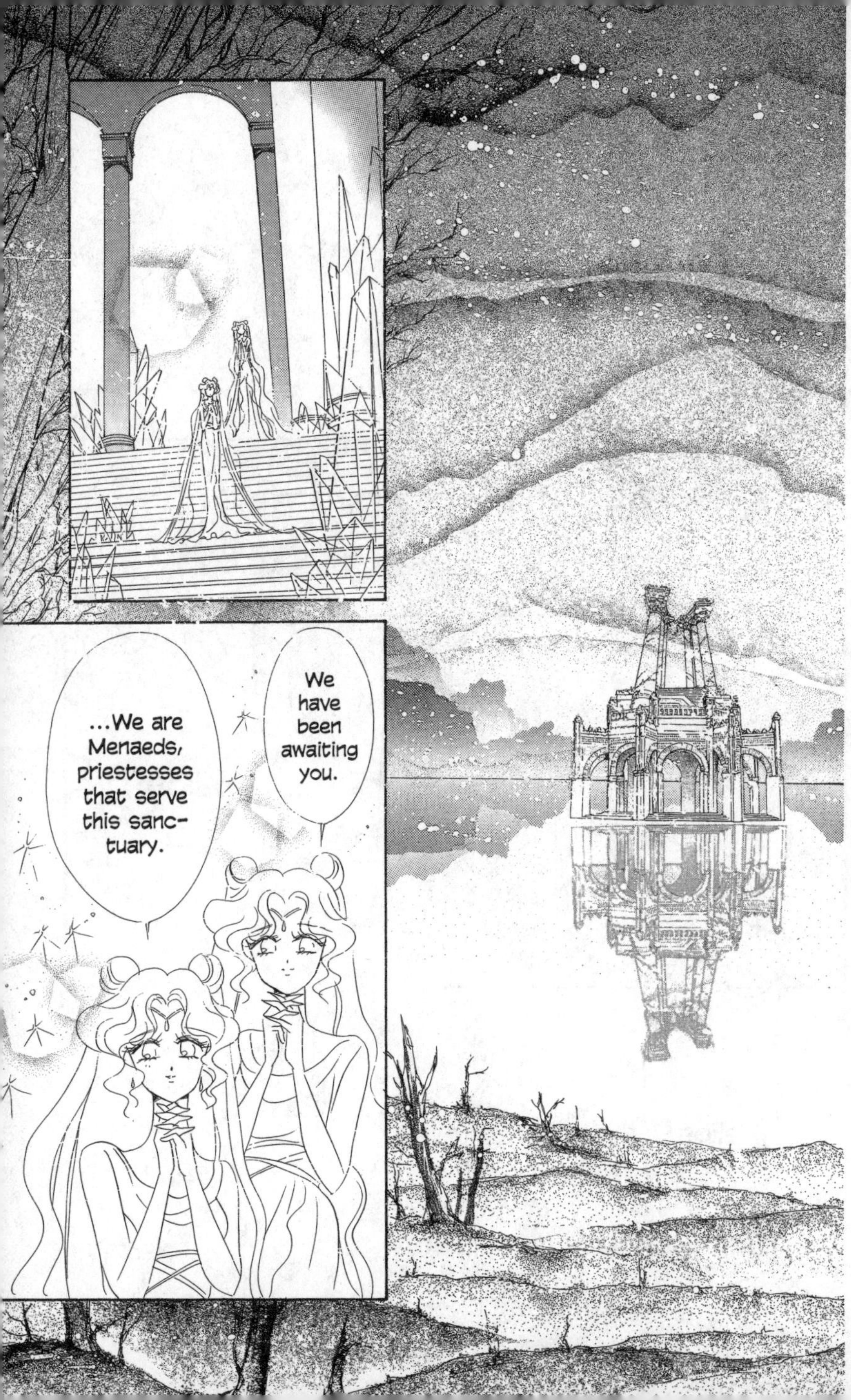
We have been awaiting you.
...We are Menaeds, priestesses that serve this sanctuary.

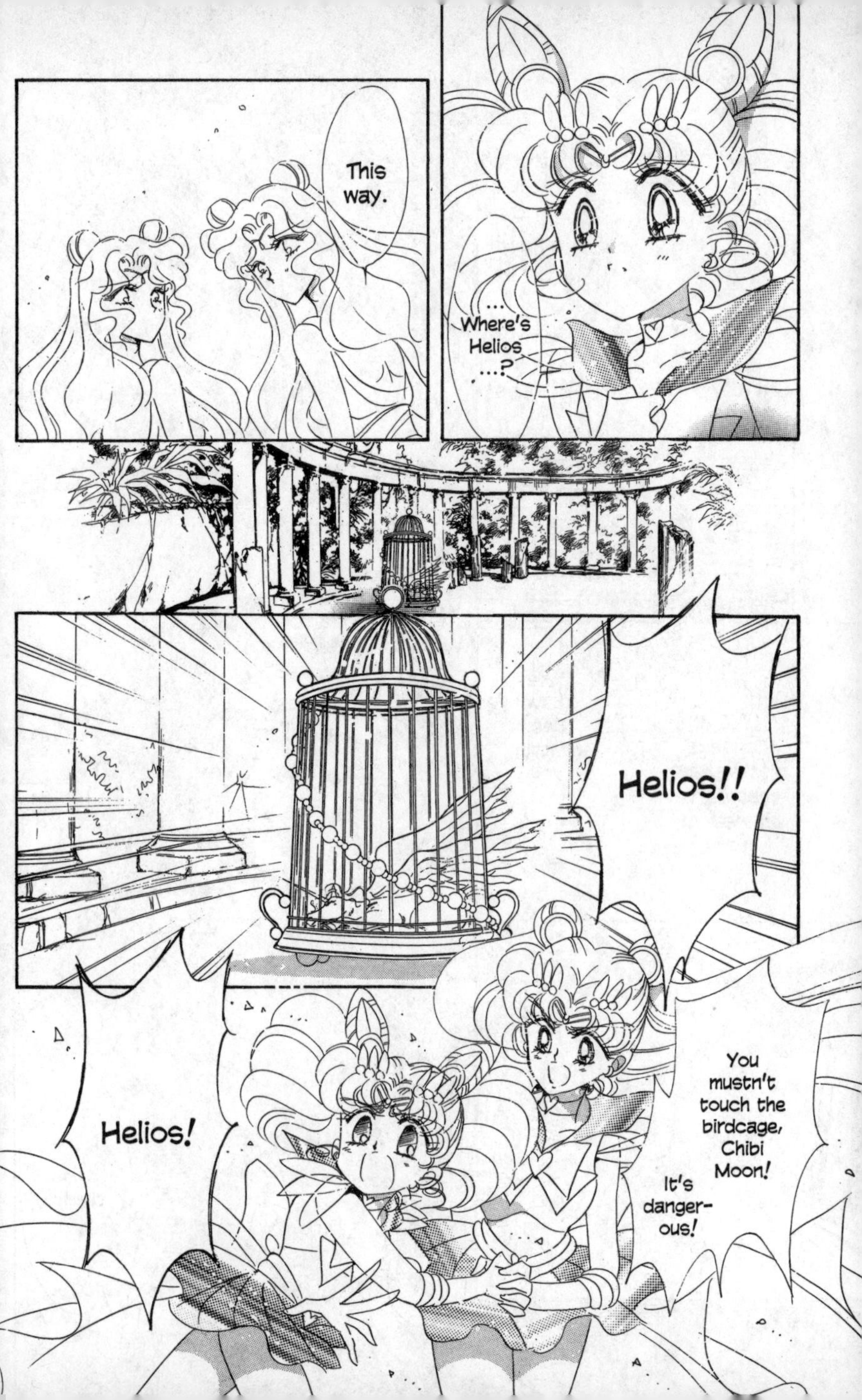

... Where's Helios ...?
This way.
Helios!!
You mustn't touch the birdcage, Chibi Moon!
It's danger-ous!
Helios!

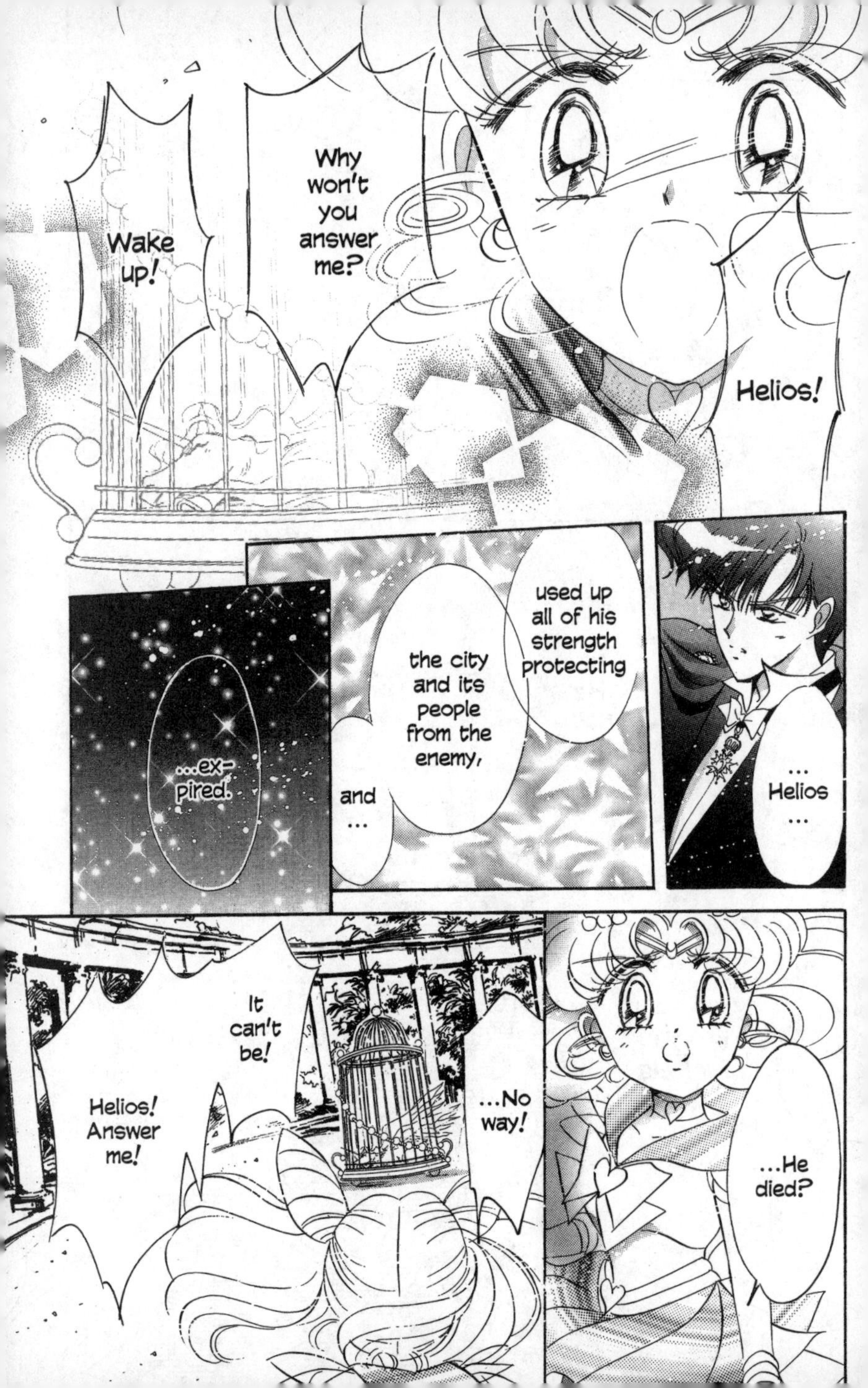
Helios!
Why won't you answer me?
Wake up!
...Helios...
used up all of his strength protecting
the city and its people from the enemy,
and ...
...ex-pired.
...He died?
...No way!
It can't be!
Helios! Answer me!

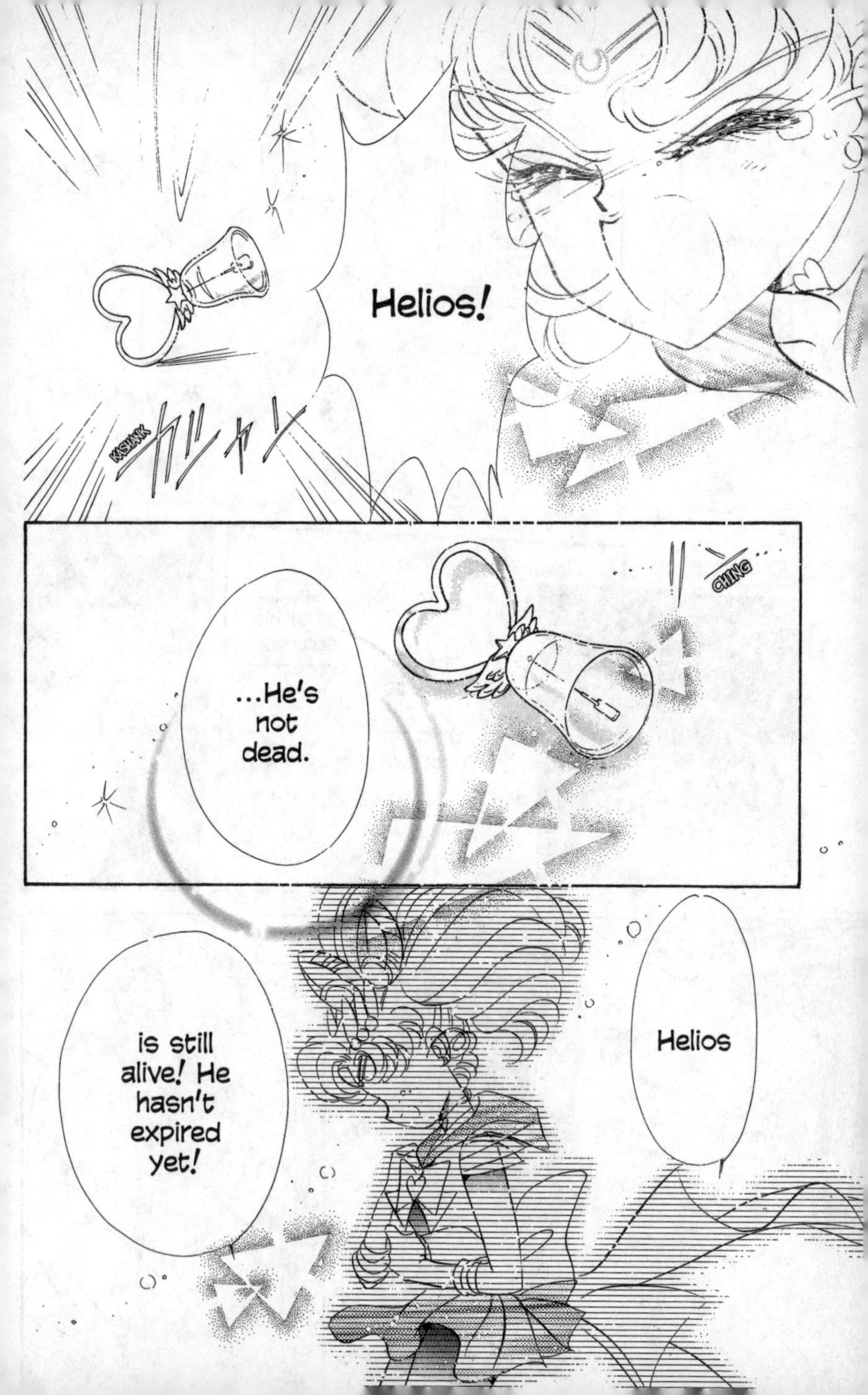
Helios!
KASHANK
CHING
...He's not dead.
Helios
is still alive! He hasn't expired yet!

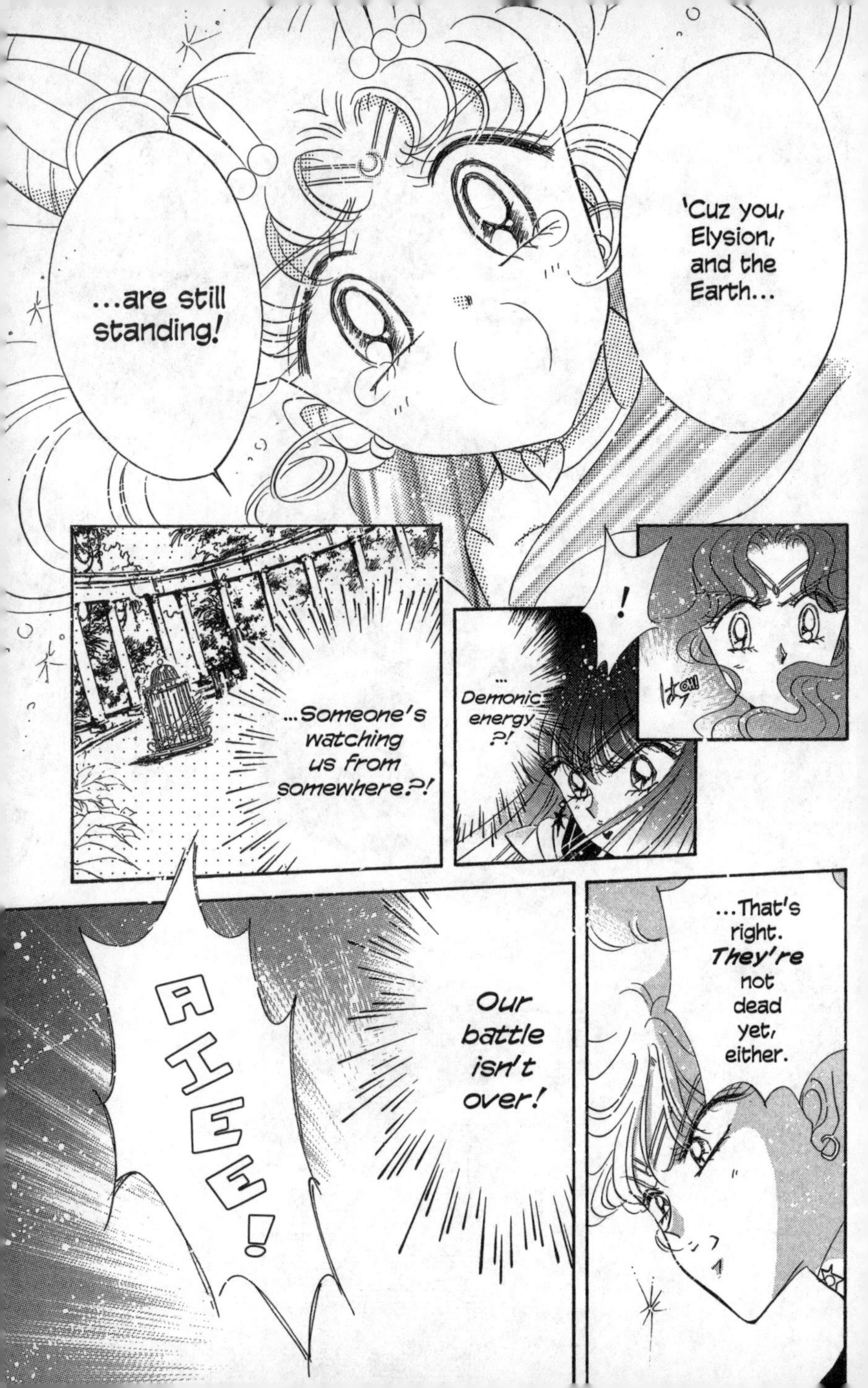
'Cuz you, Elysion, and the Earth...
...are still standing!
OH!
!
...Demonic energy?!
...Someone's watching us from somewhere?!
...That's right. *They're* not dead yet, either.
Our battle isn't over!
AIEE!

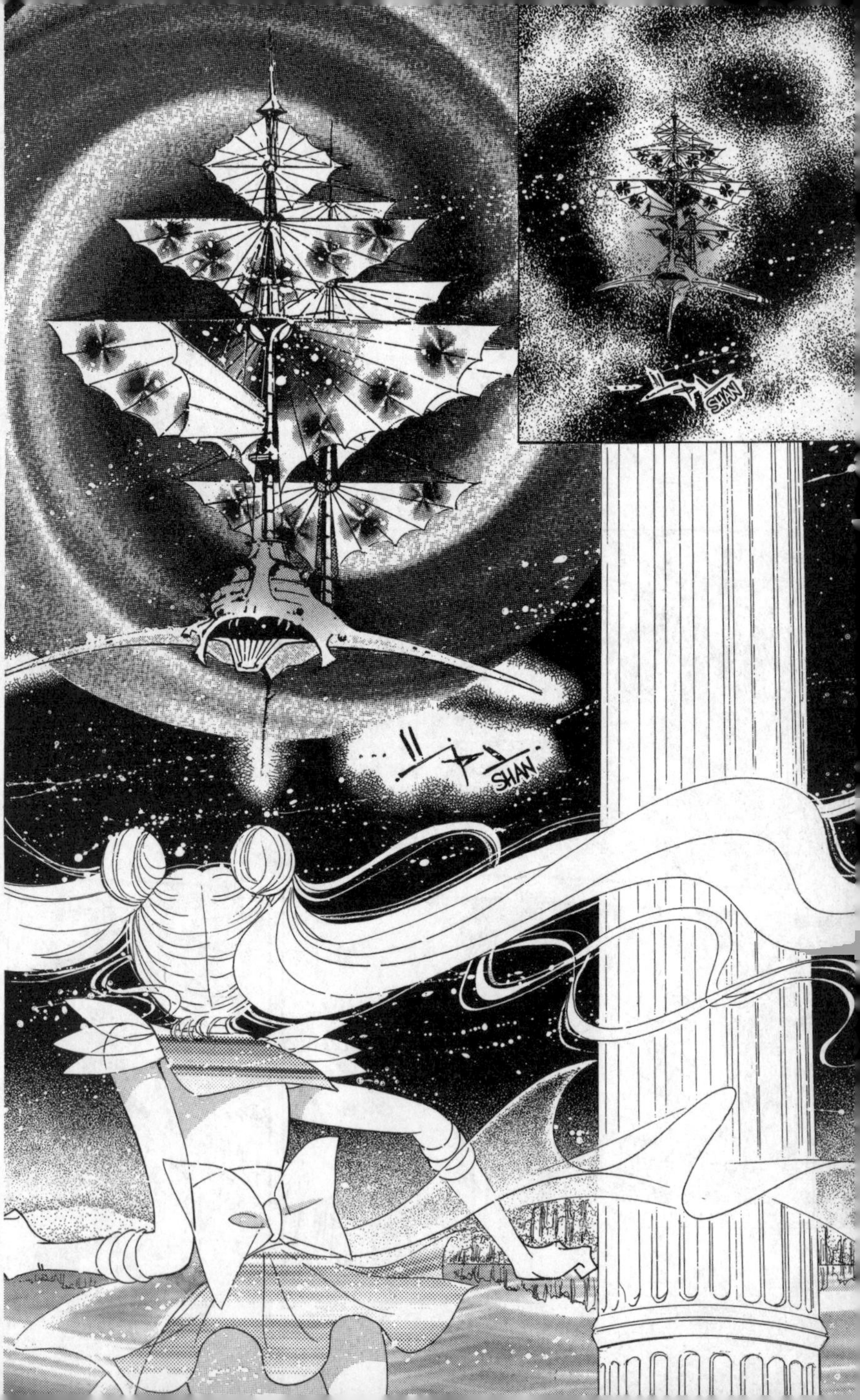
SHAN
...SHAN

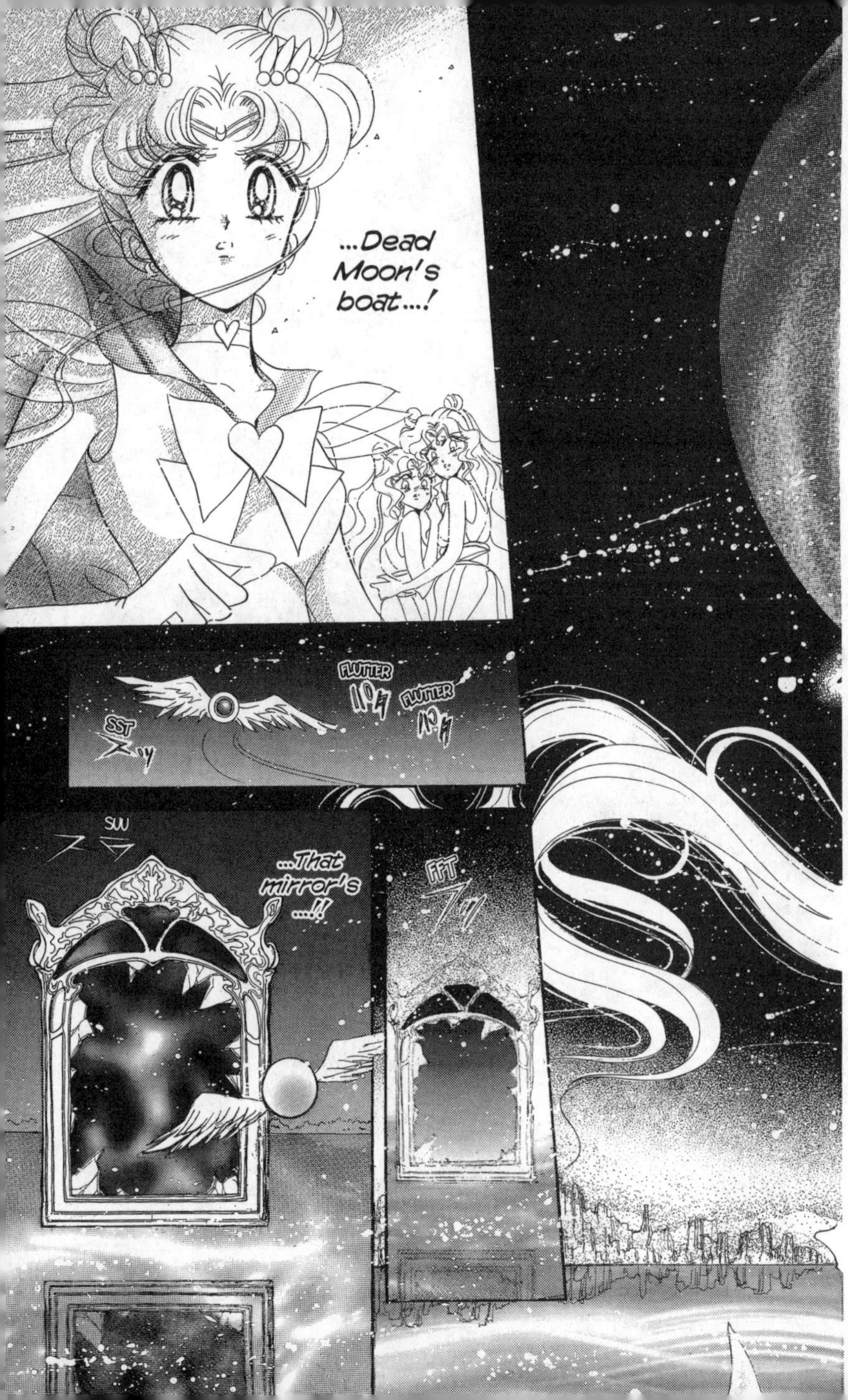
...Dead Moon's boat...!
FLUTTER
FLUTTER
SST
FFT
SUU
...That mirror's ...!!

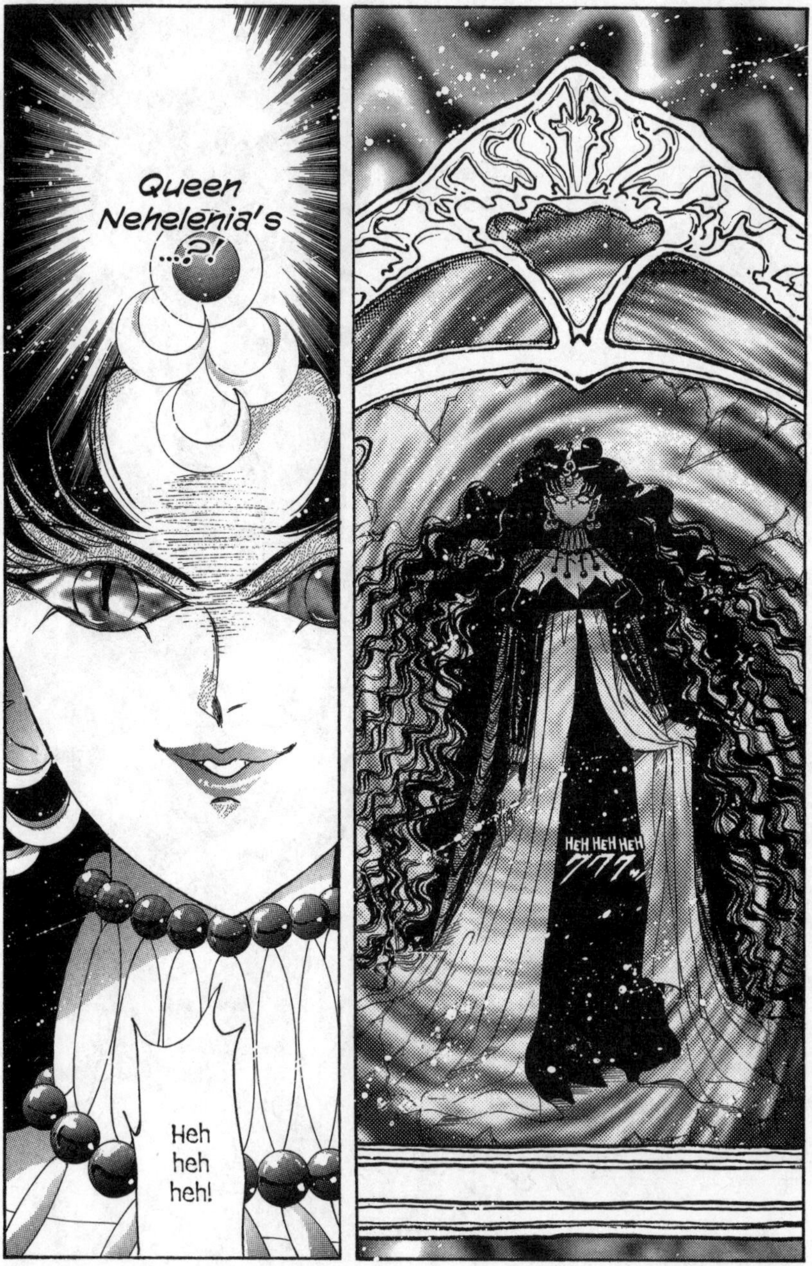
HEH HEH HEH
Queen Nehelenia's ...?!
Heh heh heh!

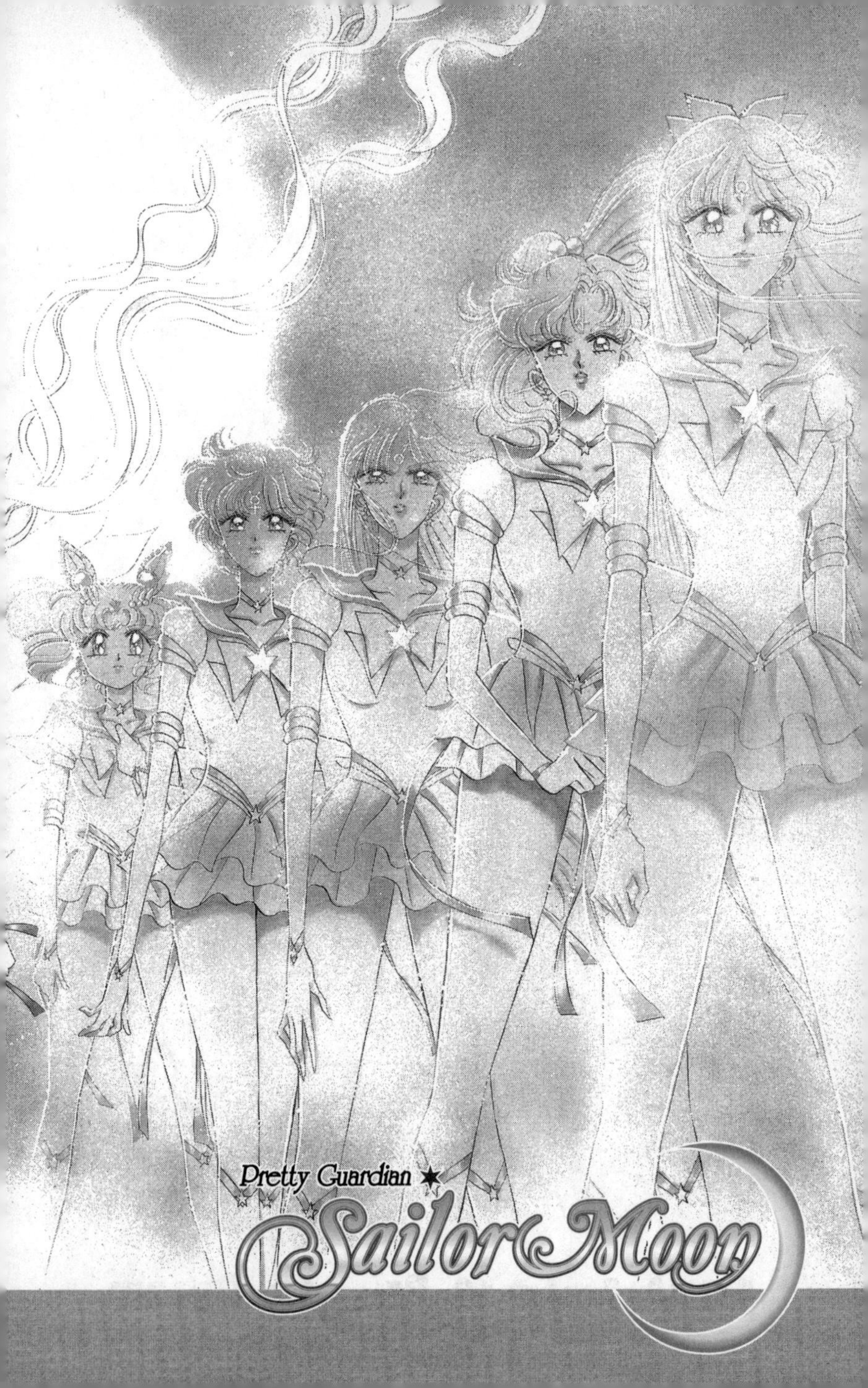
Pretty Guardian
Sailor Moon

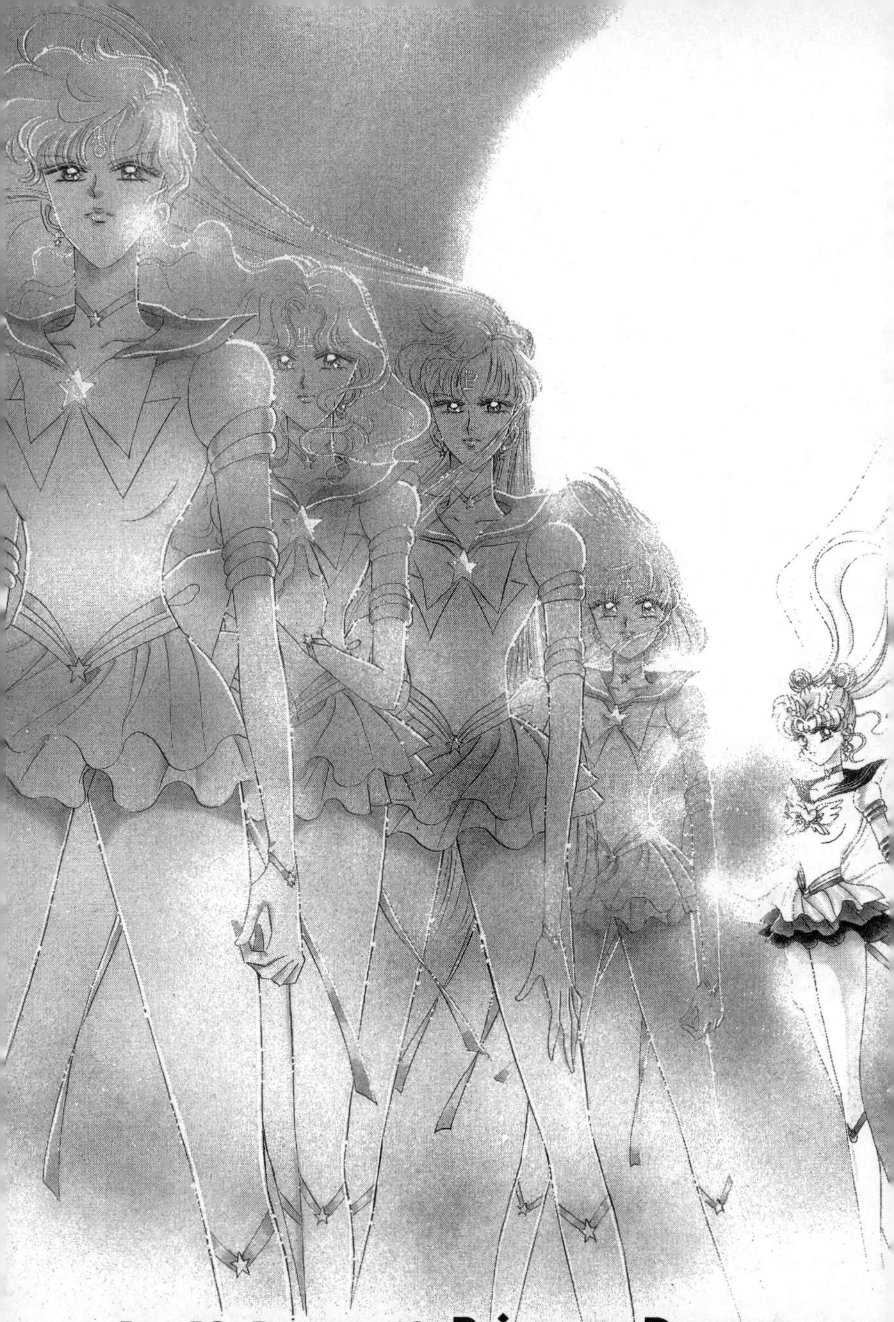

Act 48 Dream 10, Princess Dream

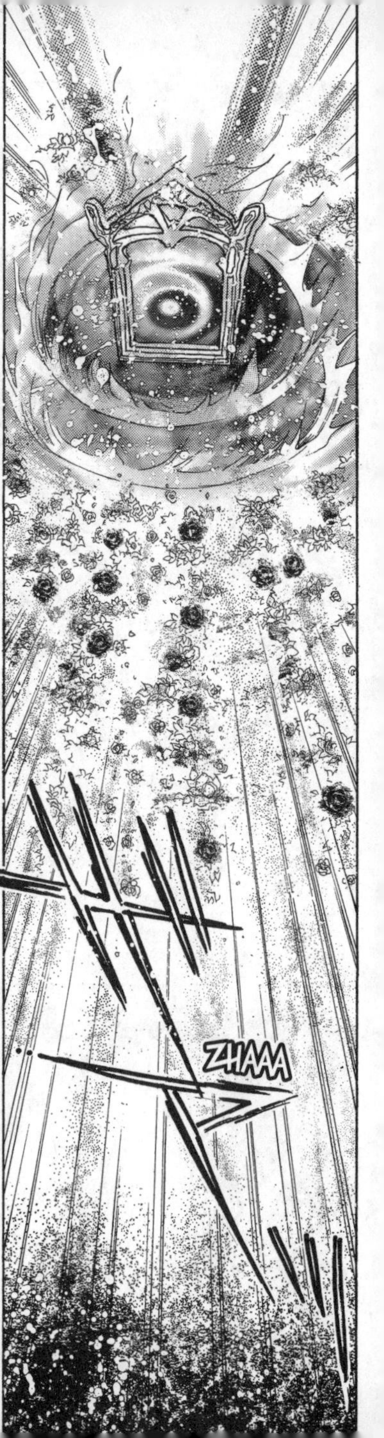
ZHAAA

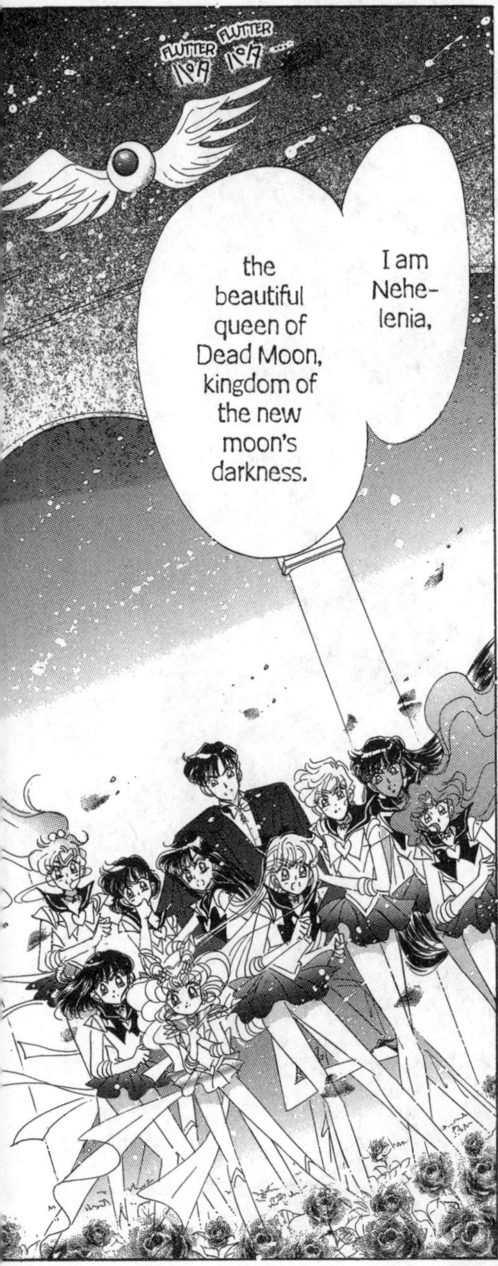
FLUTTER パタ
FLUTTER パタ
I am Nehe-lenia,
the beautiful queen of Dead Moon, kingdom of the new moon's darkness.

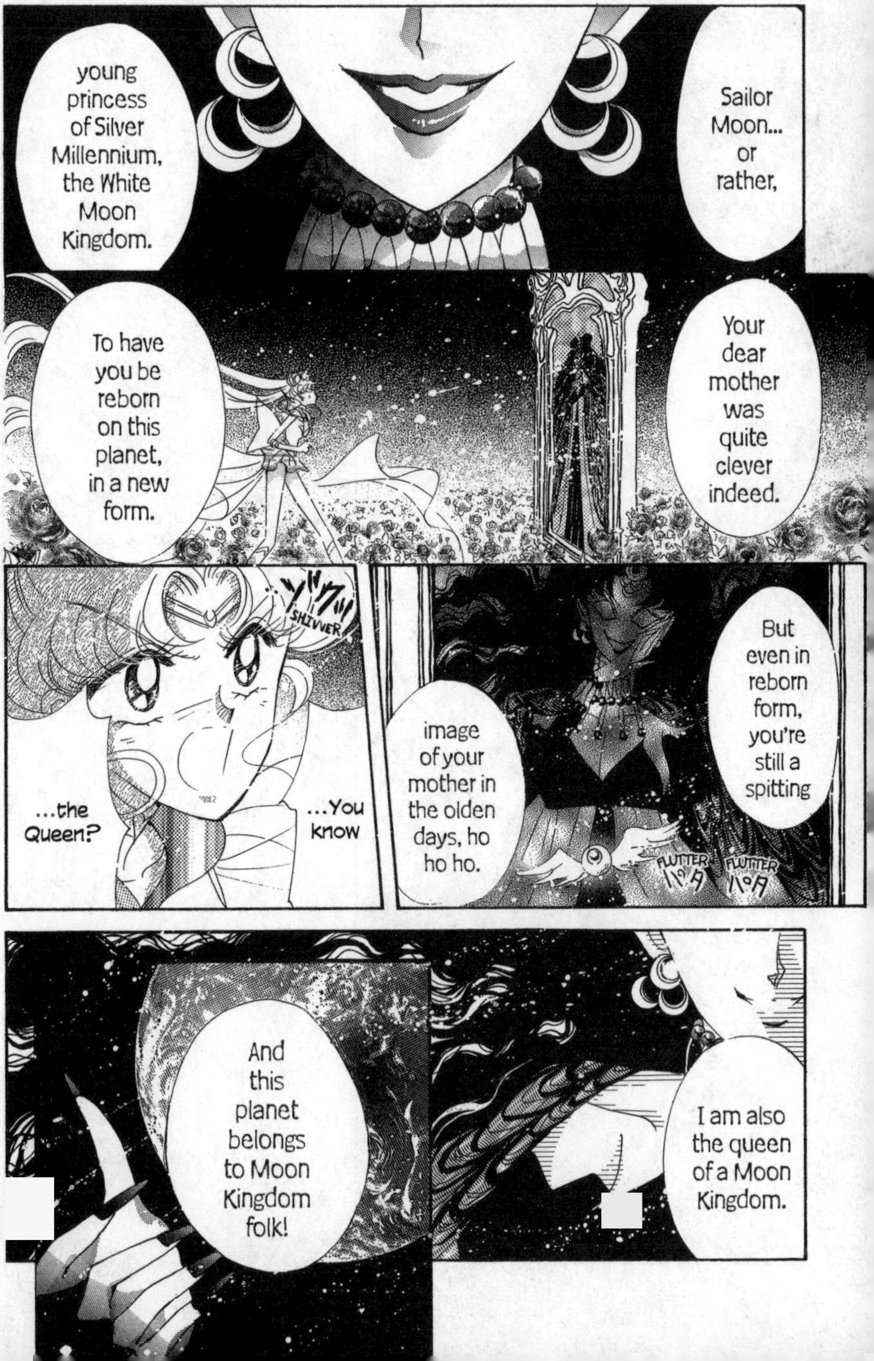

Sailor Moon... or rather,
young princess of Silver Millennium, the White Moon Kingdom.
Your dear mother was quite clever indeed.
To have you be reborn on this planet, in a new form.
But even in reborn form, you're still a spitting
image of your mother in the olden days, ho ho ho.
FLUTTER パタ
FLUTTER パタ
ゾクッ SHIVVER
...You know
...the Queen?
I am also the queen of a Moon Kingdom.
And this planet belongs to Moon Kingdom folk!

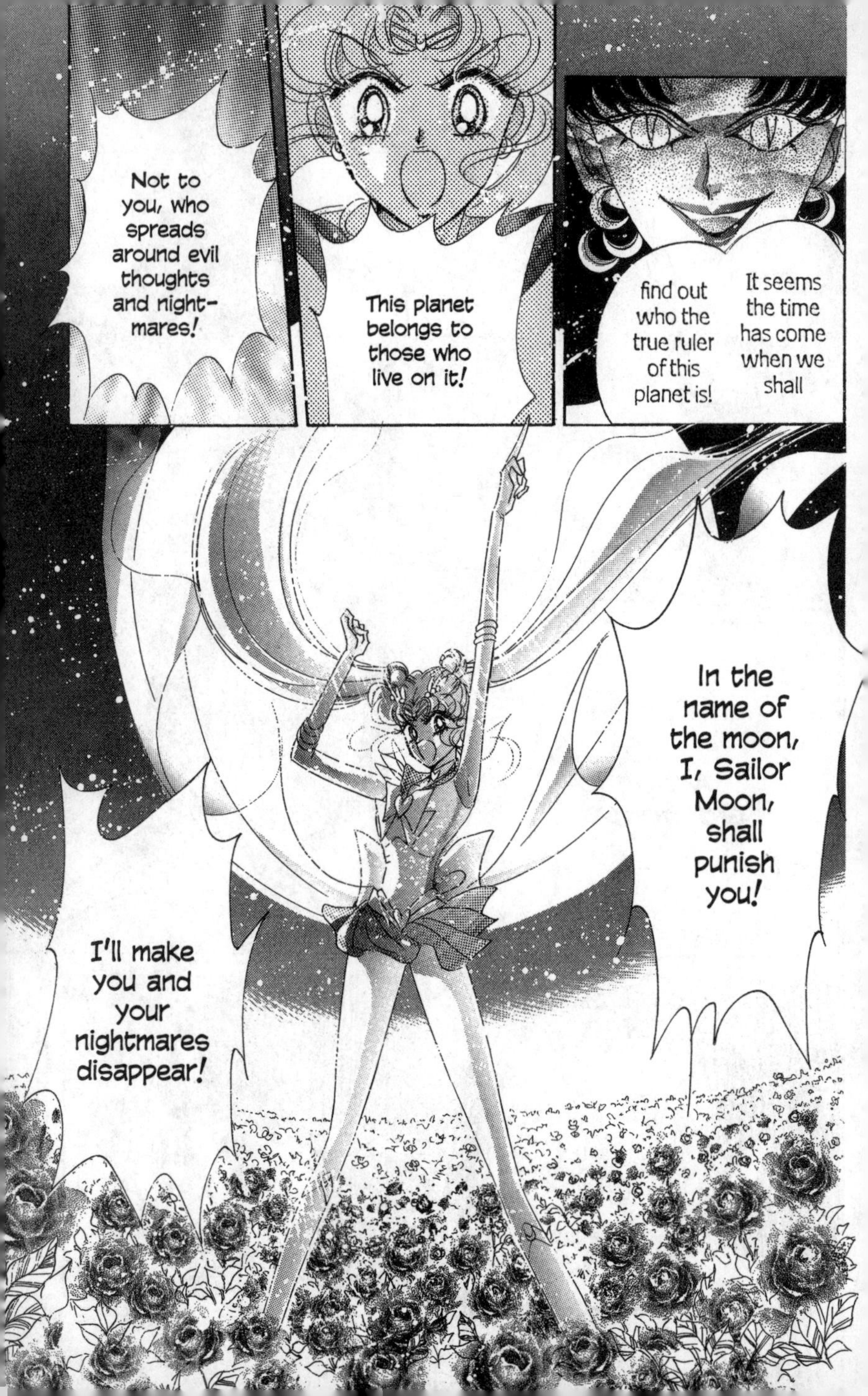
It seems the time has come when we shall find out who the true ruler of this planet is!
This planet belongs to those who live on it!
Not to you, who spreads around evil thoughts and nightmares!
In the name of the moon, I, Sailor Moon, shall punish you!
I'll make you and your nightmares disappear!

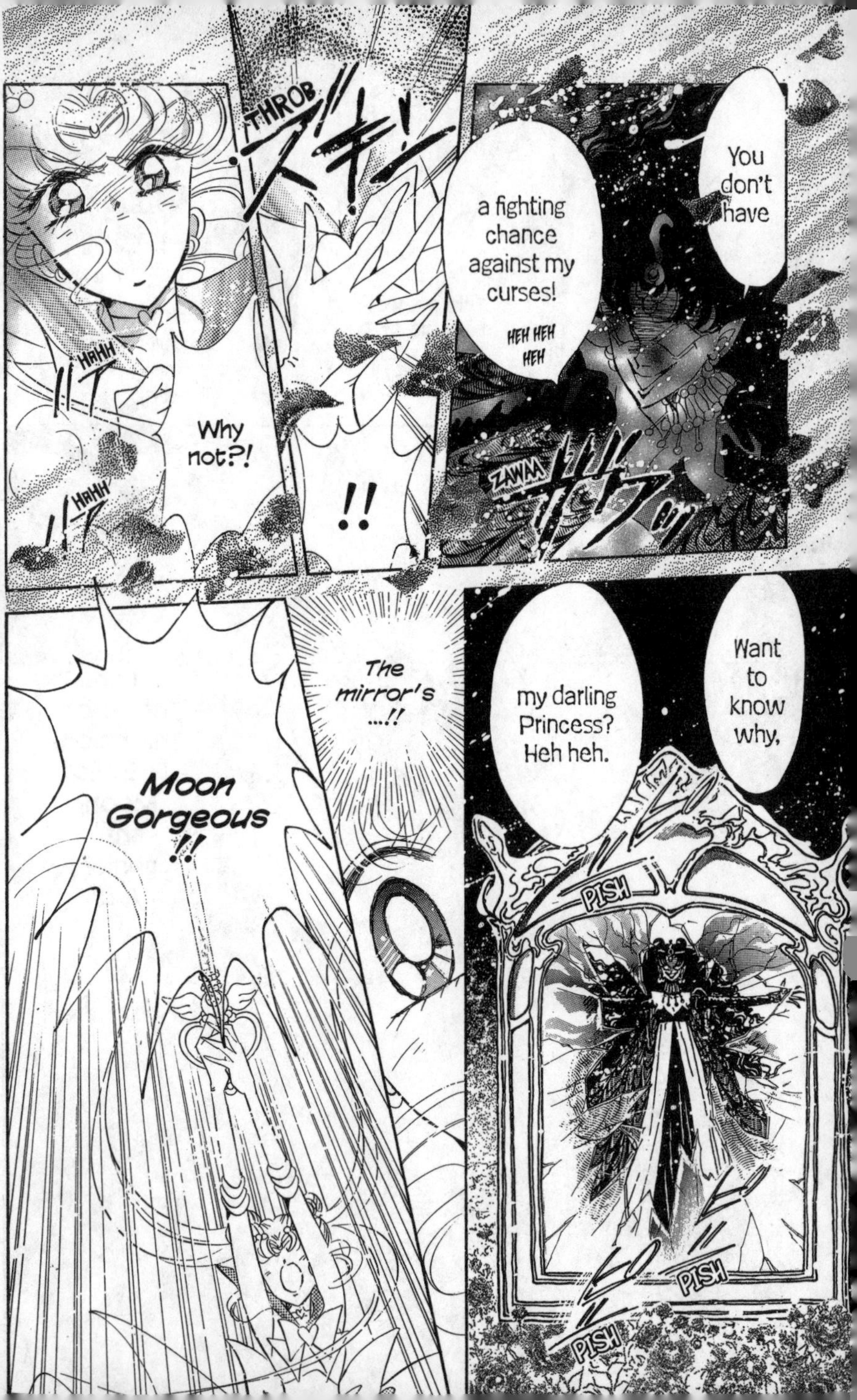
You don't have
a fighting chance against my curses!
HEH HEH HEH
ZAWAA
THROB
!!
Why not?!
HAHH
HAHH
Want to know why,
my darling Princess? Heh heh.
PISH
PISH
PISH
The mirror's ...!!
Moon Gorgeous !!

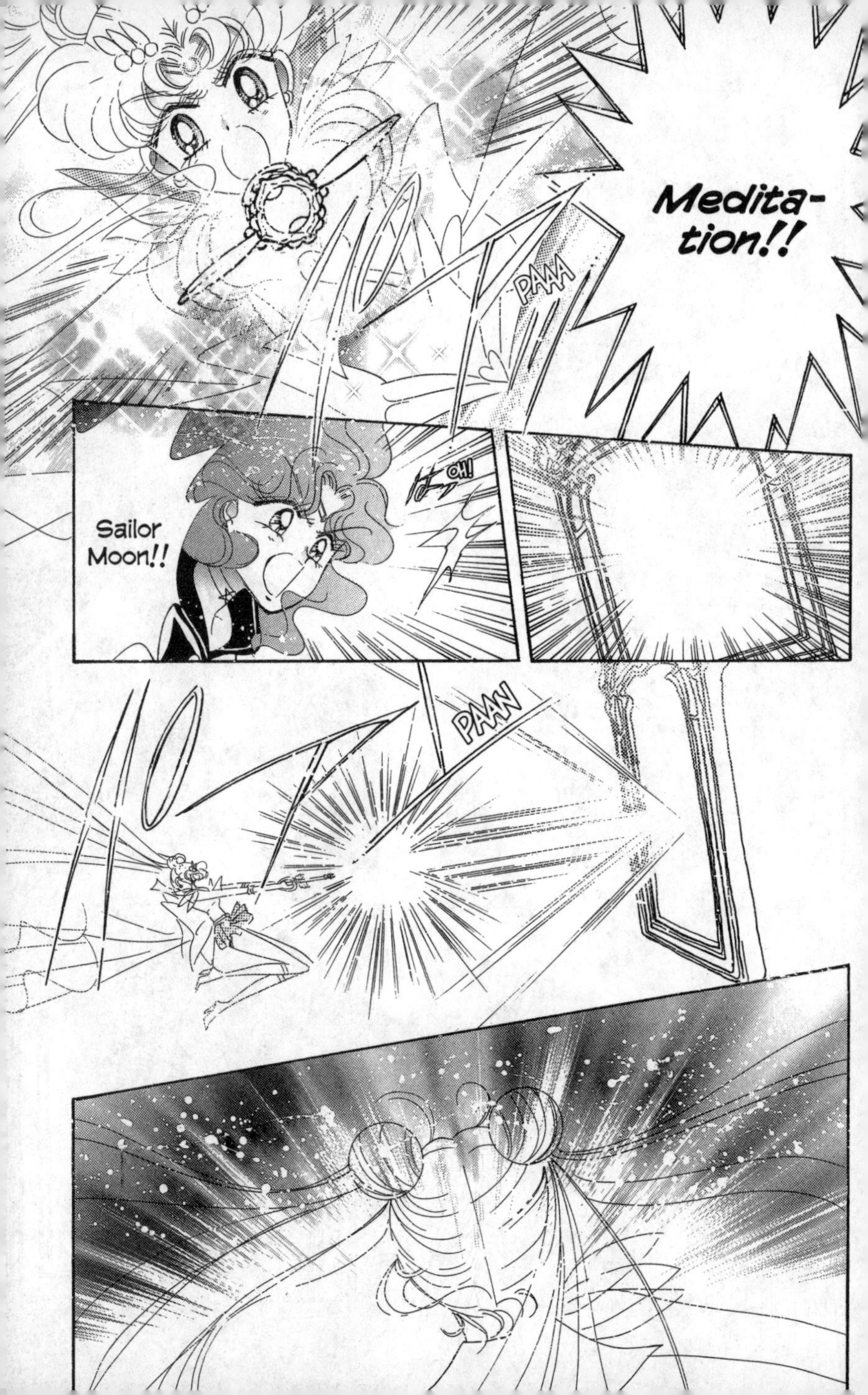
Meditation!!
PAAA
OH!
Sailor Moon!!
PAAN

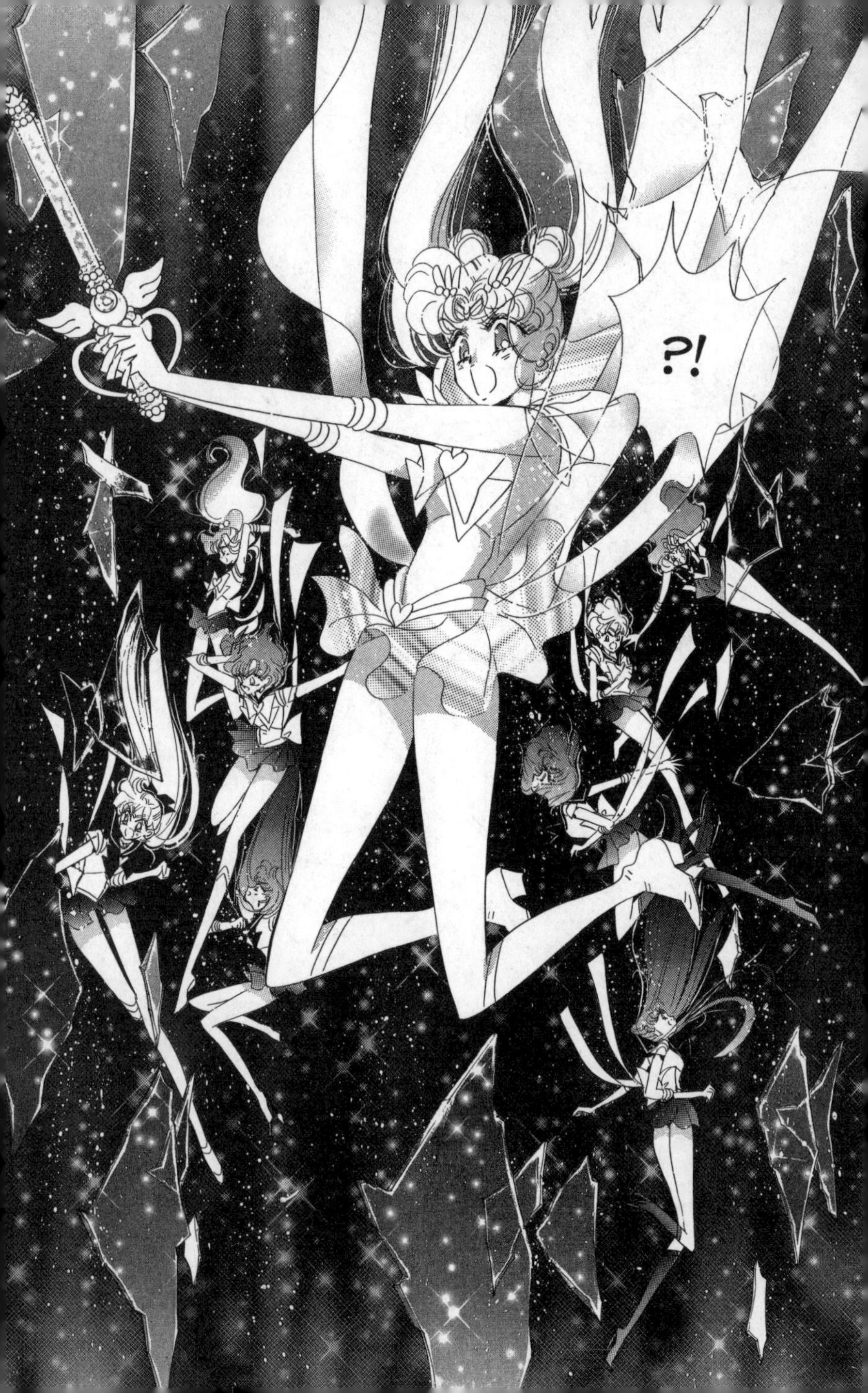
?!

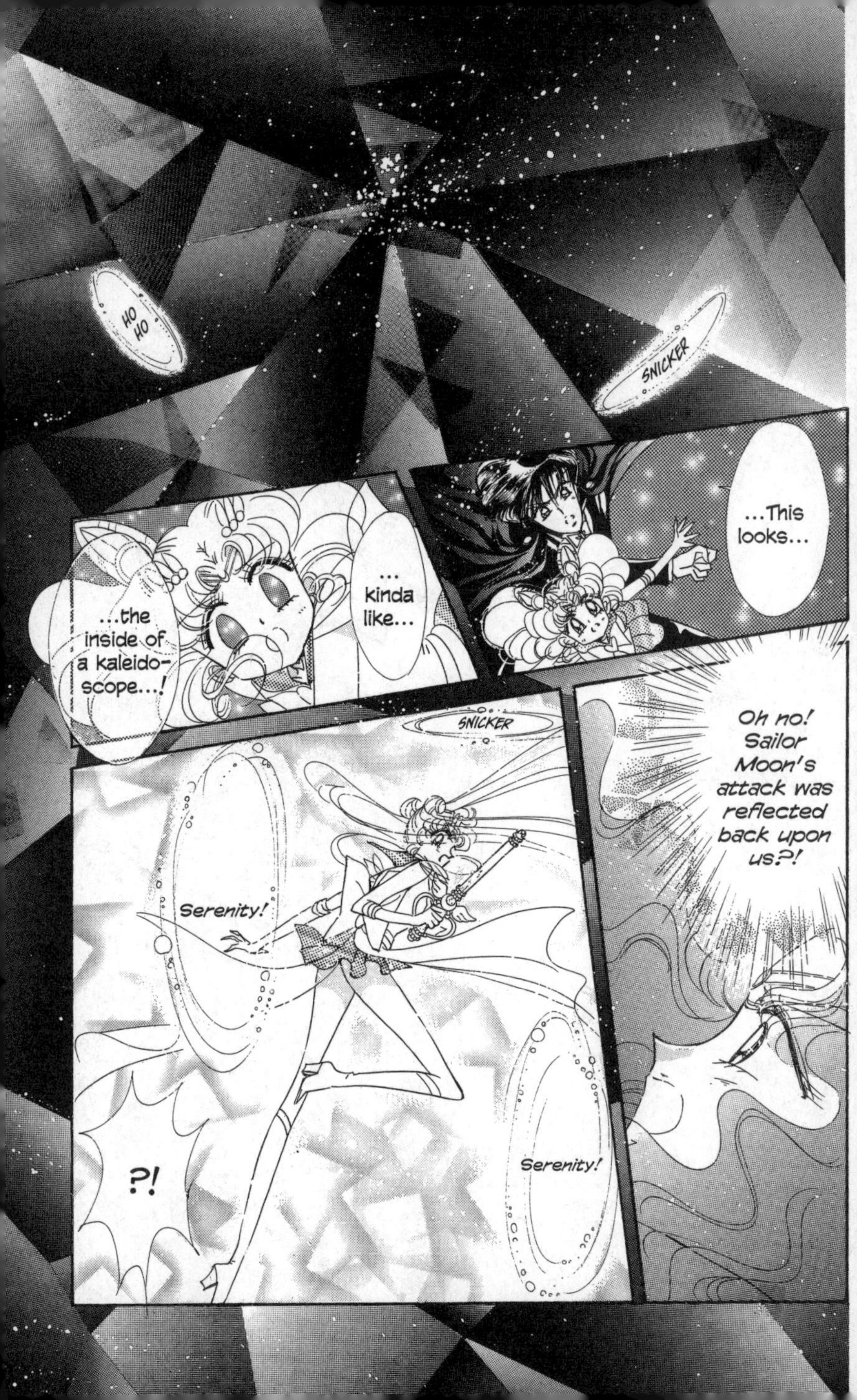
SNICKER
HO HO
...This looks...
... kinda like...
...the inside of a kaleido-scope...!
Oh no! Sailor Moon's attack was reflected back upon us?!
SNICKER
Serenity!
Serenity!
?!

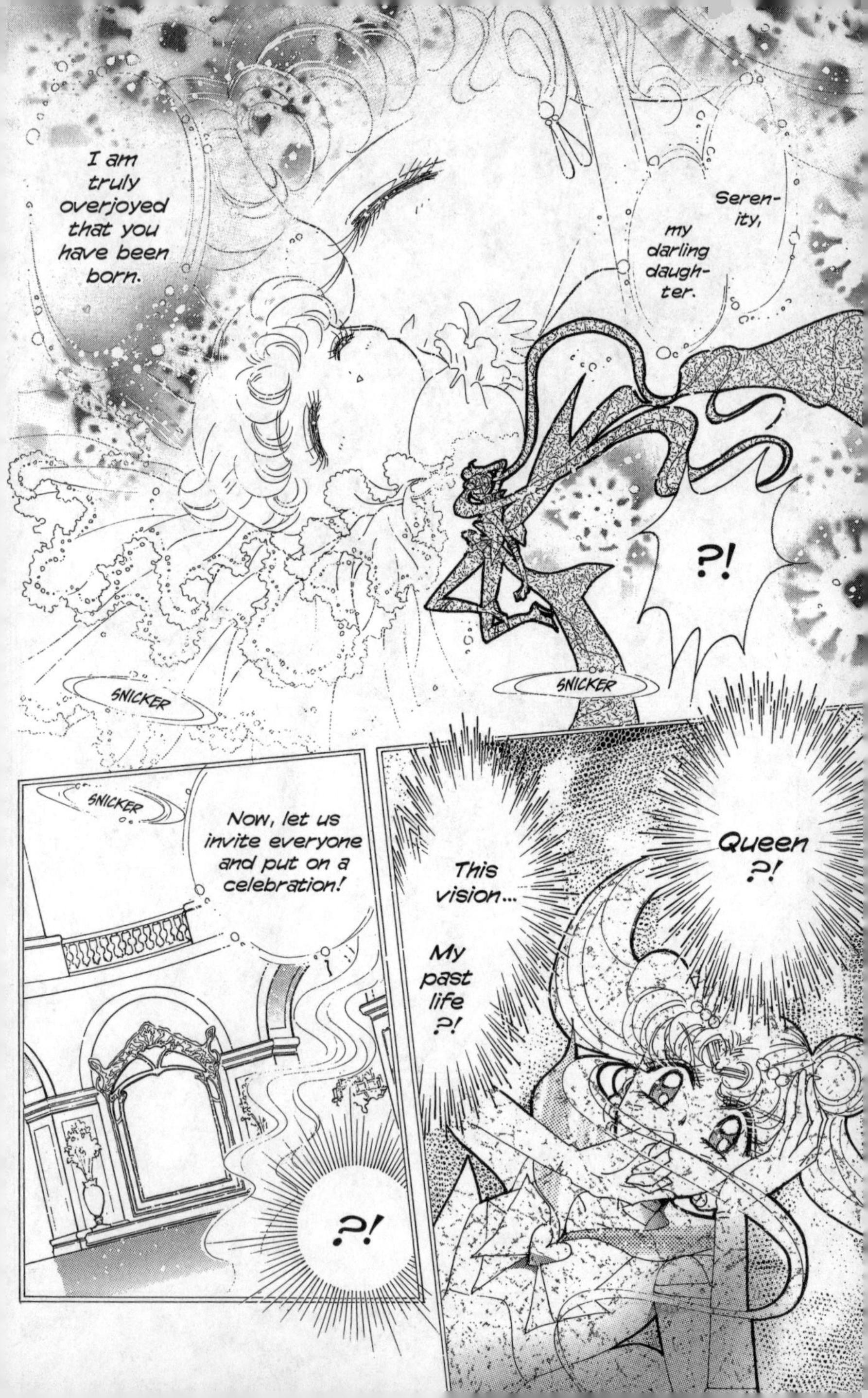
Seren-ity, my darling daugh-ter.
I am truly overjoyed that you have been born.
?!
SNICKER
SNICKER
Queen ?!
This vision...
My past life ?!
SNICKER
Now, let us invite everyone and put on a celebration!
?!

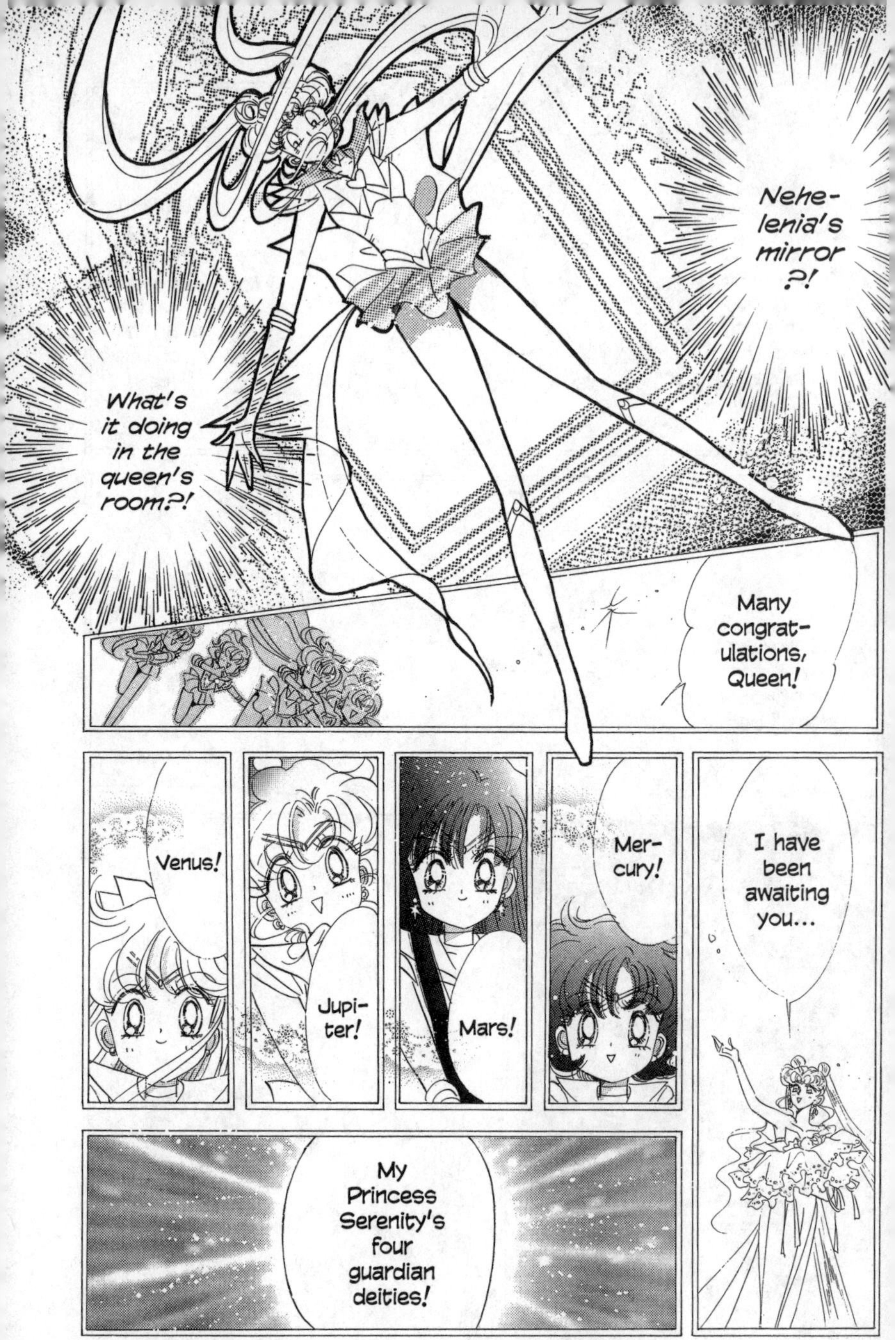
Nehe-lenia's mirror?!
What's it doing in the queen's room?!
Many congrat-ulations, Queen!
I have been awaiting you...
Mer-cury!
Mars!
Jupi-ter!
Venus!
My Princess Serenity's four guardian deities!

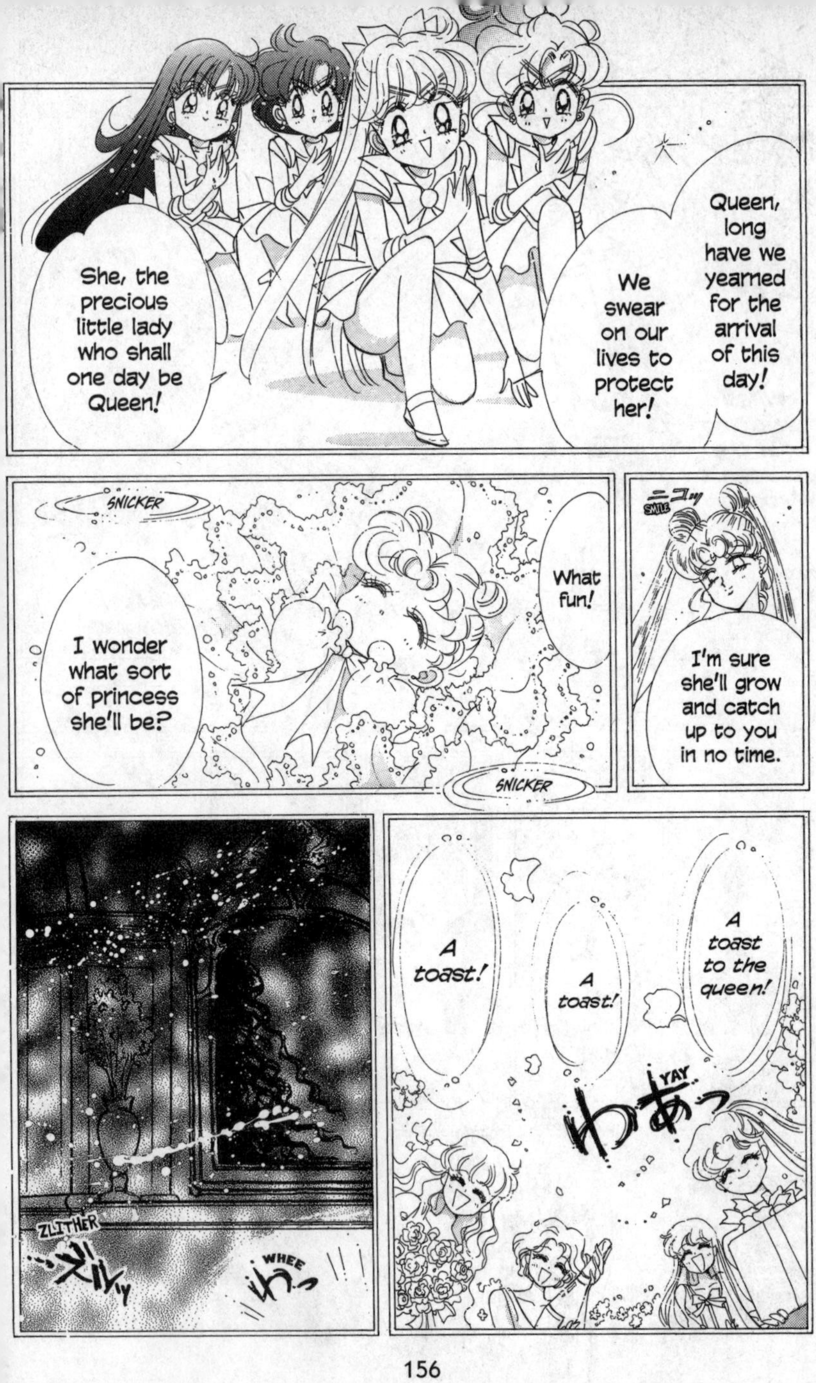
Queen, long have we yearned for the arrival of this day!
We swear on our lives to protect her!
She, the precious little lady who shall one day be Queen!
SMILE
I'm sure she'll grow and catch up to you in no time.
What fun!
SNICKER
I wonder what sort of princess she'll be?
SNICKER
A toast to the queen!
A toast!
A toast!
わあっ
YAY
WHEE
ZLITHER

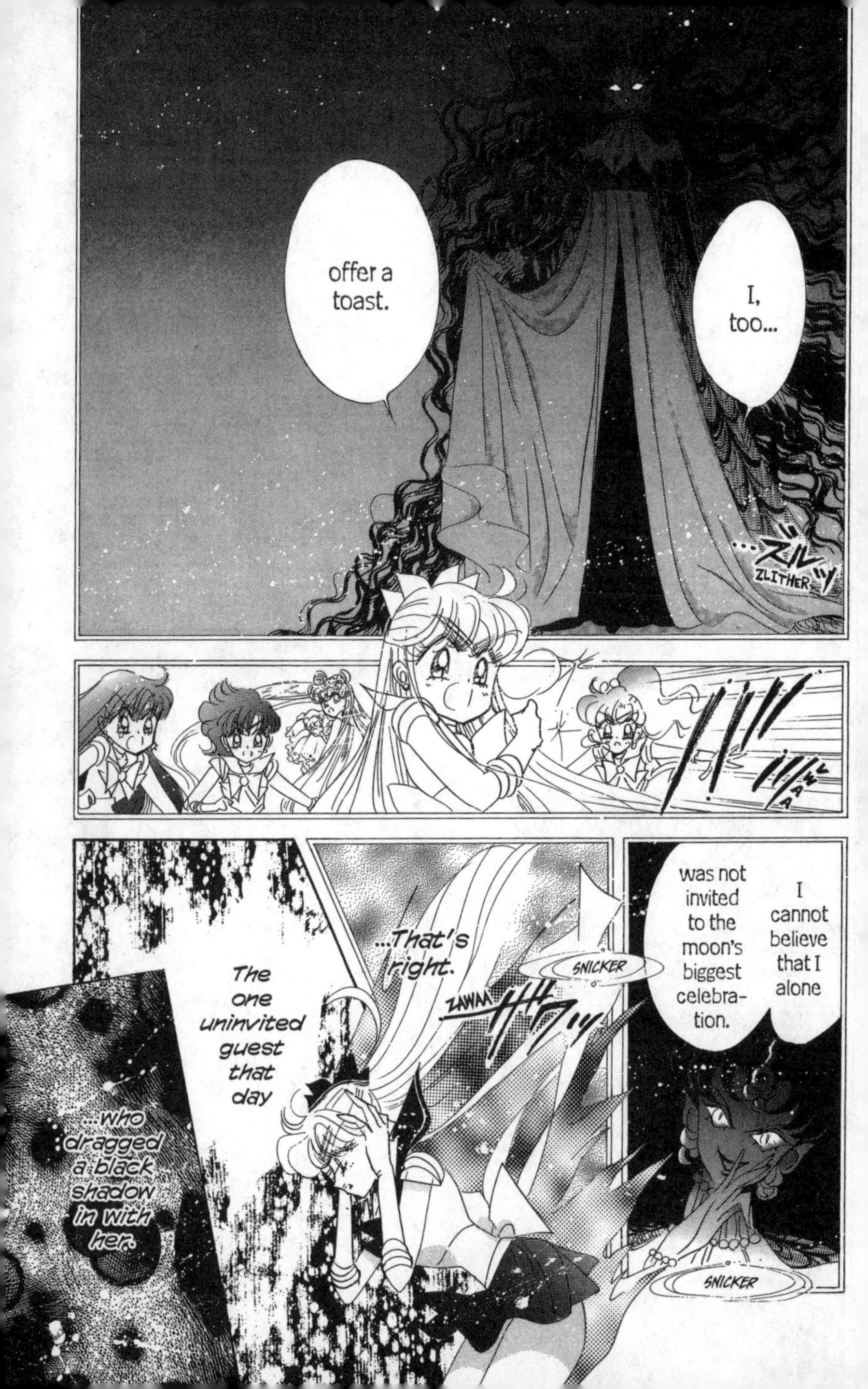
I, too...
offer a toast.
ZLITHER
WAA
I cannot believe that I alone
was not invited to the moon's biggest celebra-tion.
SNICKER
SNICKER
...That's right.
ZAWAA
The one uninvited guest that day
...who dragged a black shadow in with her.

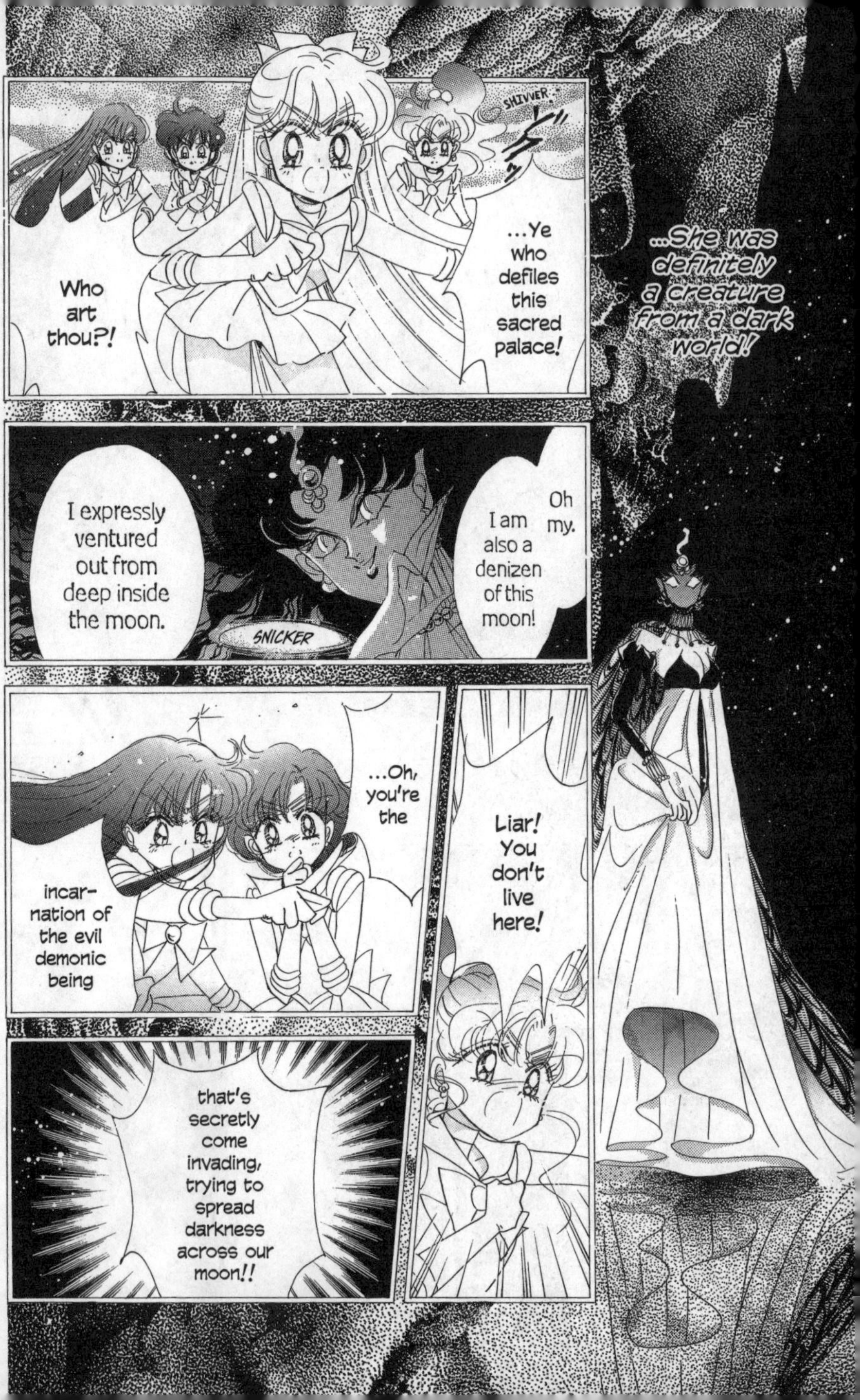
...She was definitely a creature from a dark world!
SHIVVER
...Ye who defiles this sacred palace!
Who art thou?!
Oh my.
I am also a denizen of this moon!
SNICKER
I expressly ventured out from deep inside the moon.
Liar! You don't live here!
...Oh, you're the
incarnation of the evil demonic being
that's secretly come invading, trying to spread darkness across our moon!!

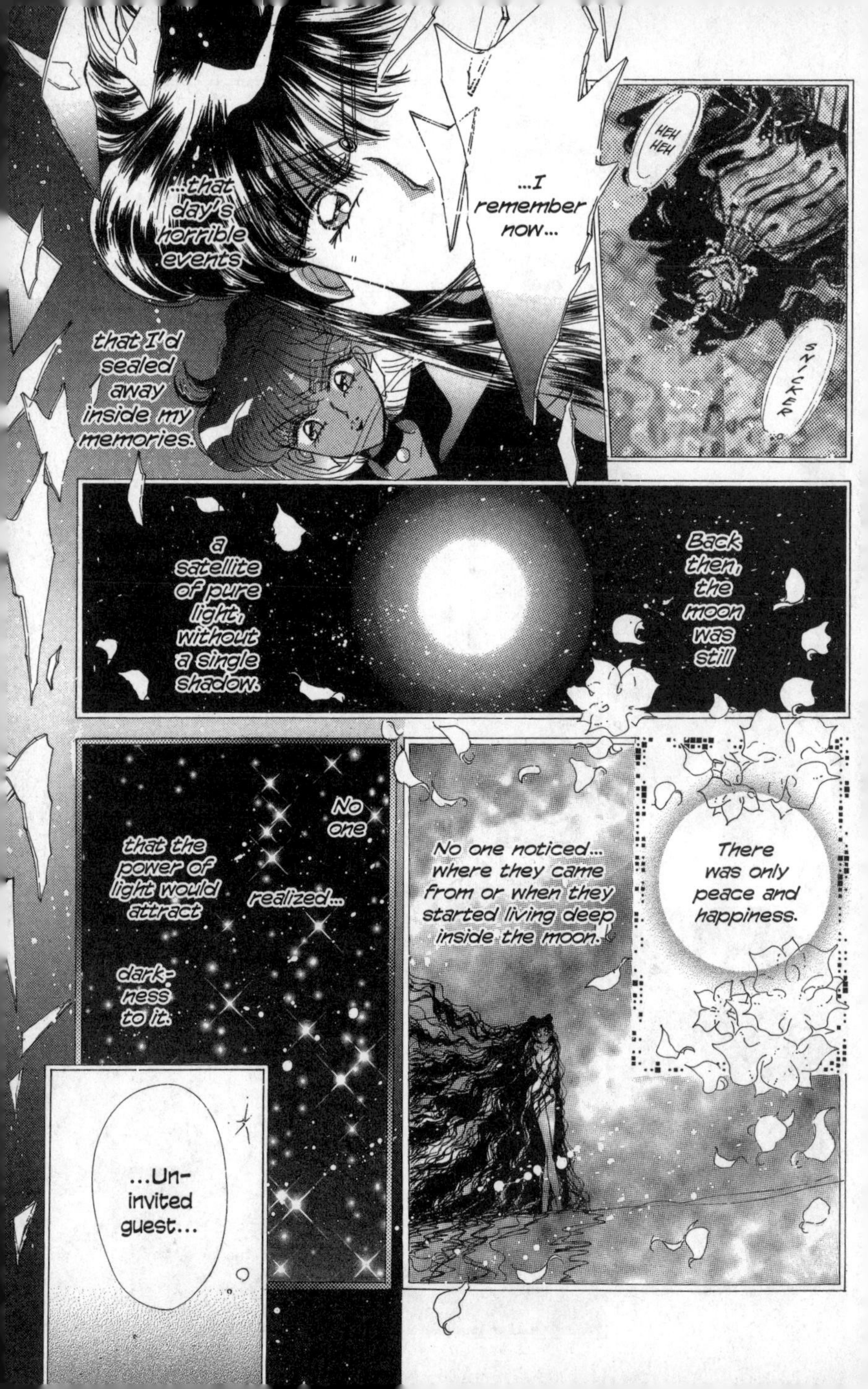
HEH HEH
SNICKER
...I remember now...
...that day's horrible events
that I'd sealed away inside my memories.
Back then, the moon was still
a satellite of pure light, without a single shadow.
There was only peace and happiness.
No one noticed... where they came from or when they started living deep inside the moon.
No one
realized...
that the power of light would attract
darkness to it.
...Un-invited guest...

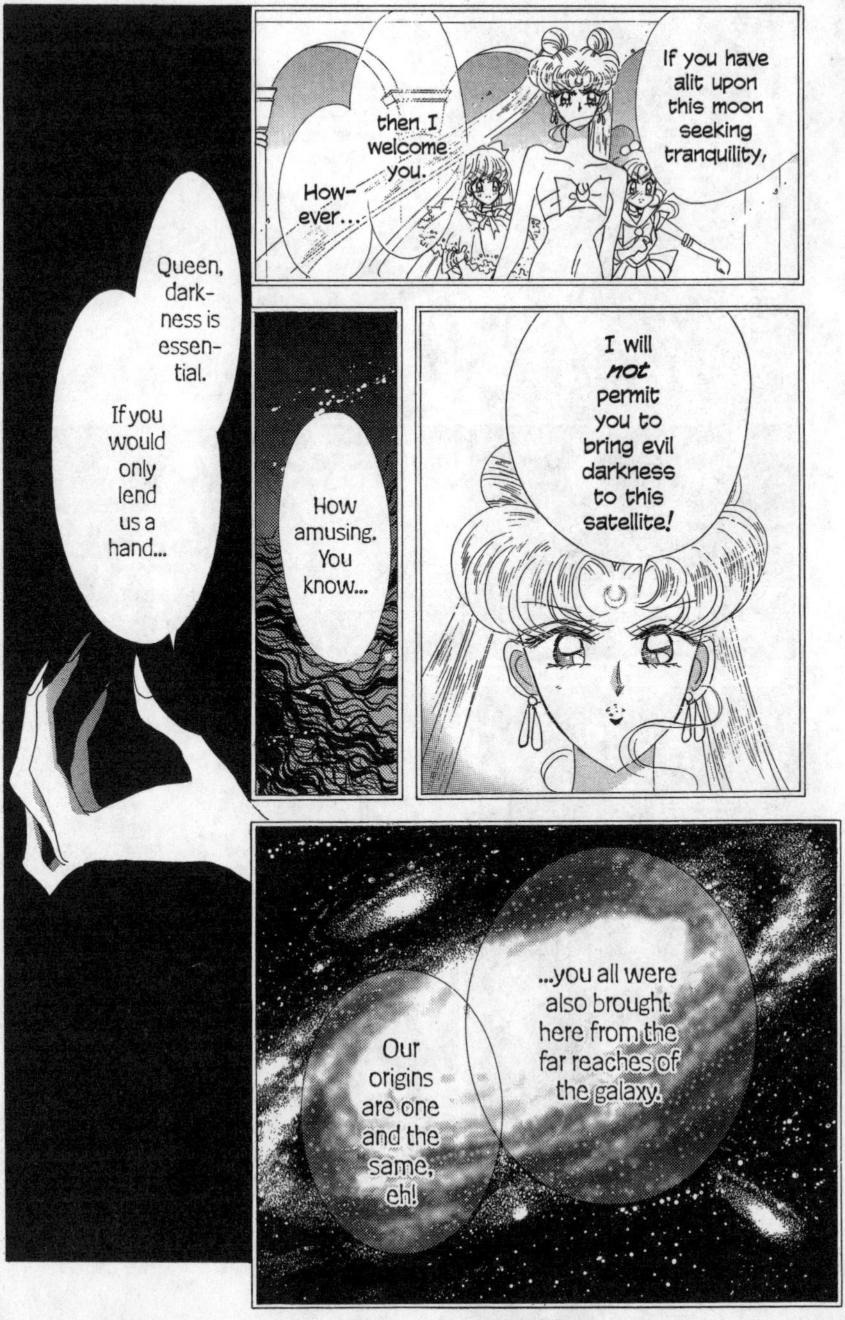

If you have alit upon this moon seeking tranquility,
then I welcome you.
However...
I will *not* permit you to bring evil darkness to this satellite!
How amusing. You know...
...you all were also brought here from the far reaches of the galaxy.
Our origins are one and the same, eh!
Queen, darkness is essential.
If you would only lend us a hand...

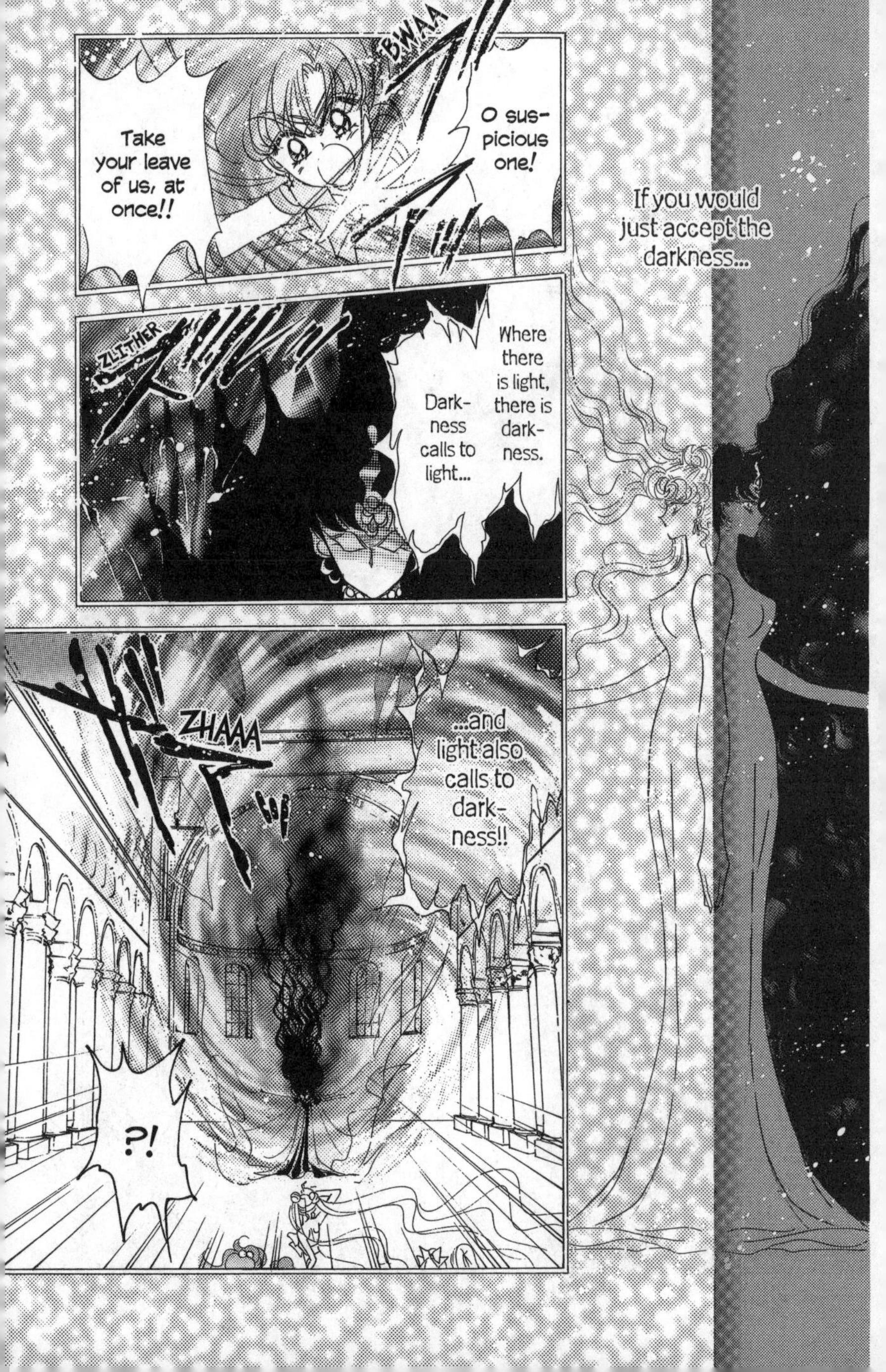
If you would just accept the darkness...
BWAA
O suspicious one!
Take your leave of us, at once!!
ZLITHER
Where there is light, there is darkness.
Darkness calls to light...
ZHAAA
...and light also calls to darkness!!
?!

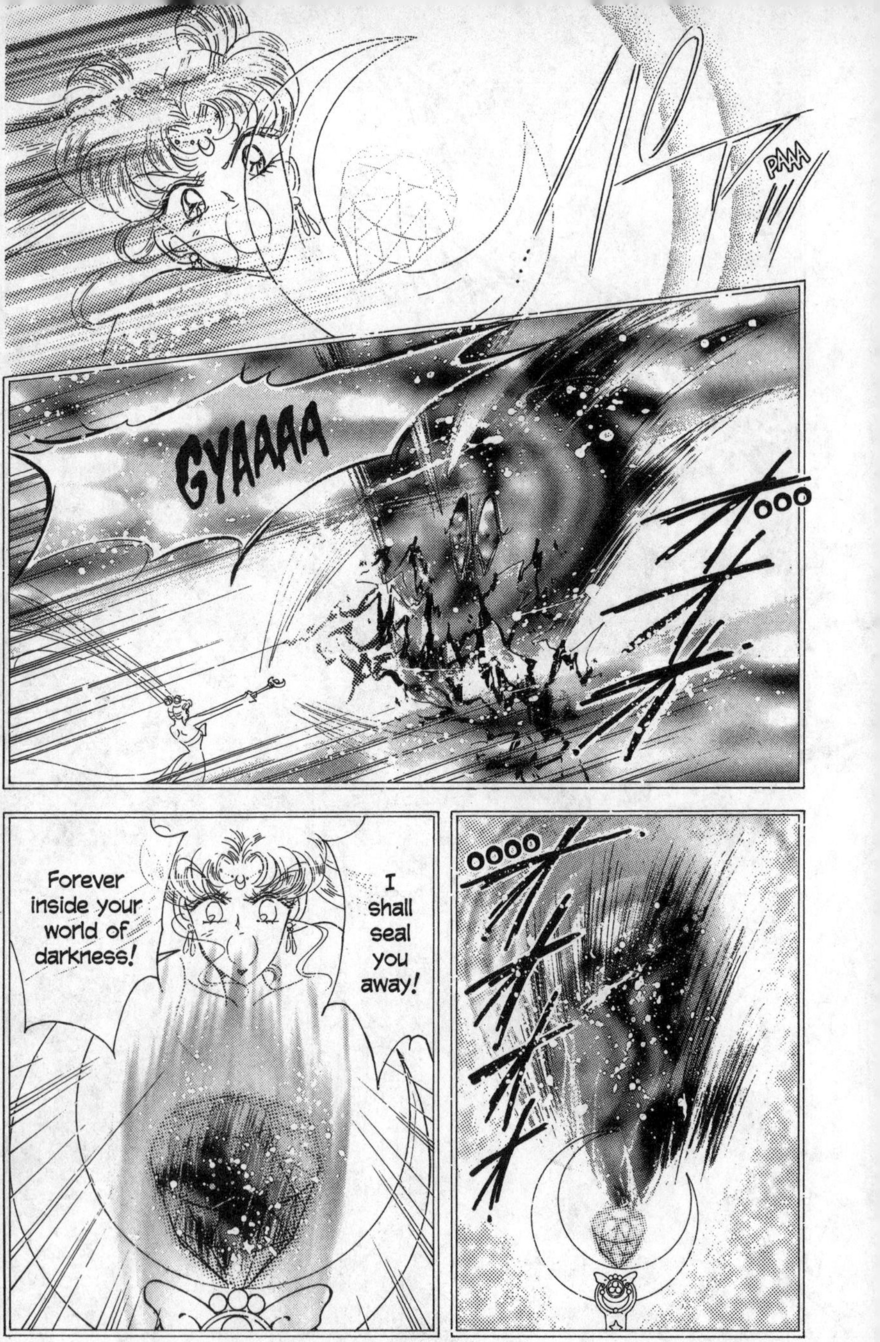
PAAA
GYAAAA
ooo
oooo
I shall seal you away!
Forever inside your world of darkness!

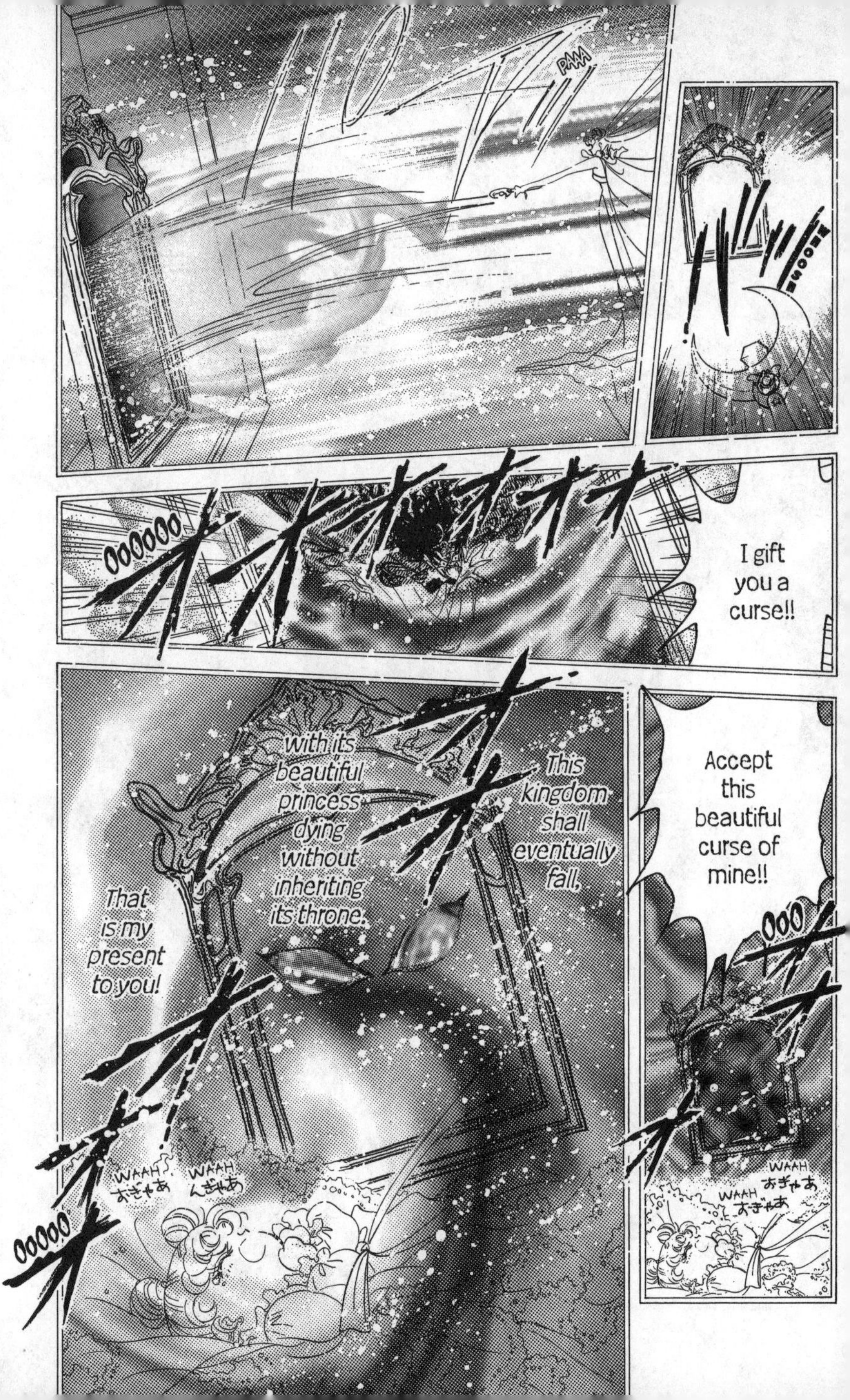
PAAA
I gift you a curse!!
OOOOOO
Accept this beautiful curse of mine!!
OOO
WAAH
WAAH
This kingdom shall eventually fall,
with its beautiful princess dying without inheriting its throne.
That is my present to you!
WAAH
WAAH
OOOOO

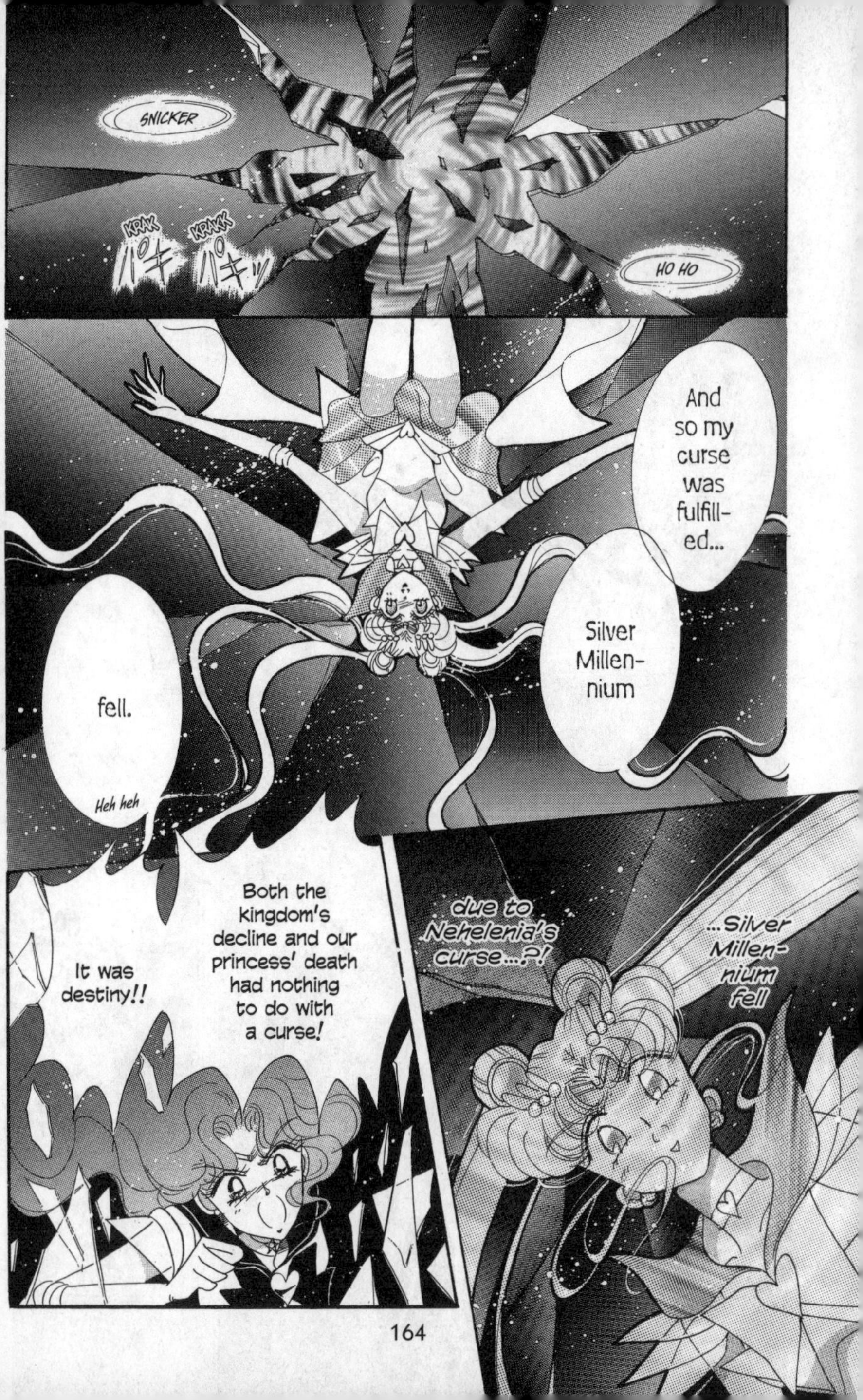
HO HO
KRAKK
パキッ
KRAK
パキ
SNICKER
And so my curse was fulfill-ed...
Silver Millen-nium
fell.
Heh heh
...Silver Millen-nium fell
due to Nehelenia's curse...?!
Both the kingdom's decline and our princess' death had nothing to do with a curse!
It was destiny!!

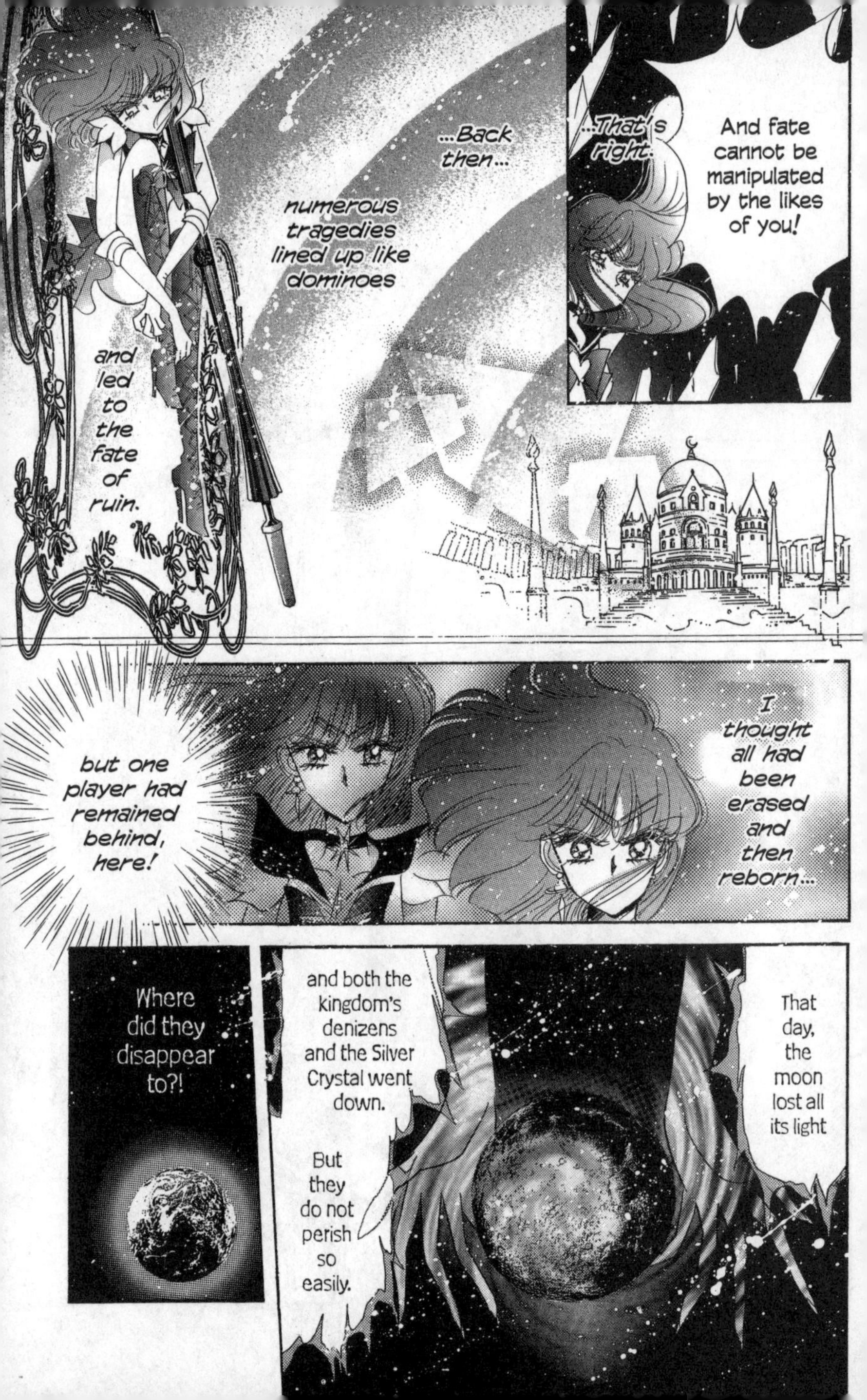
...That's right.
And fate cannot be manipulated by the likes of you!
...Back then...
numerous tragedies lined up like dominoes
and led to the fate of ruin.
I thought all had been erased and then reborn...
but one player had remained behind, here!
That day, the moon lost all its light
and both the kingdom's denizens and the Silver Crystal went down.
But they do not perish so easily.
Where did they disappear to?!

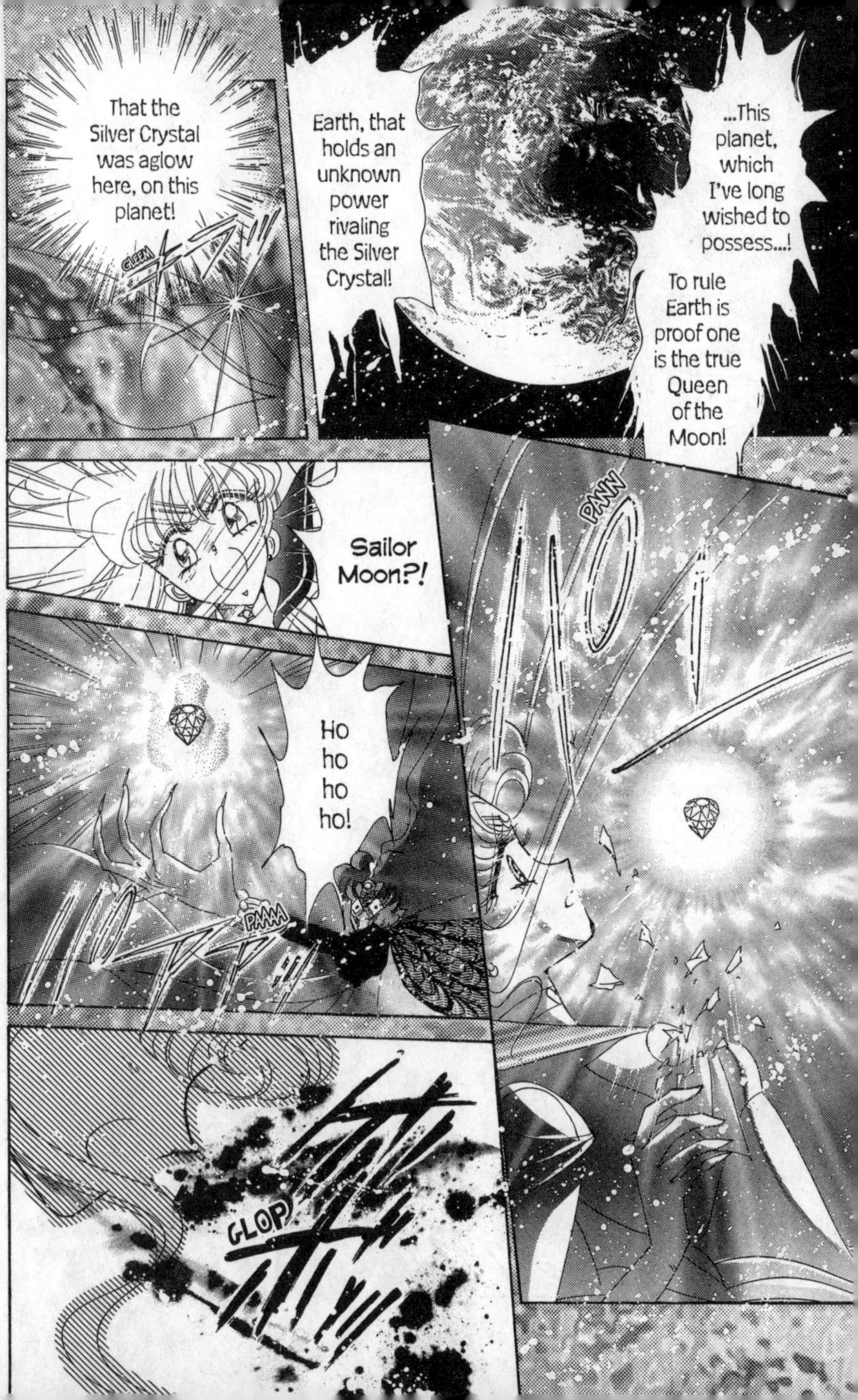
...This planet, which I've long wished to possess...!
To rule Earth is proof one is the true Queen of the Moon!
Earth, that holds an unknown power rivaling the Silver Crystal!
That the Silver Crystal was aglow here, on this planet!
GLEEM
PANN
Sailor Moon?!
Ho ho ho ho!
PAAAA
GLOP

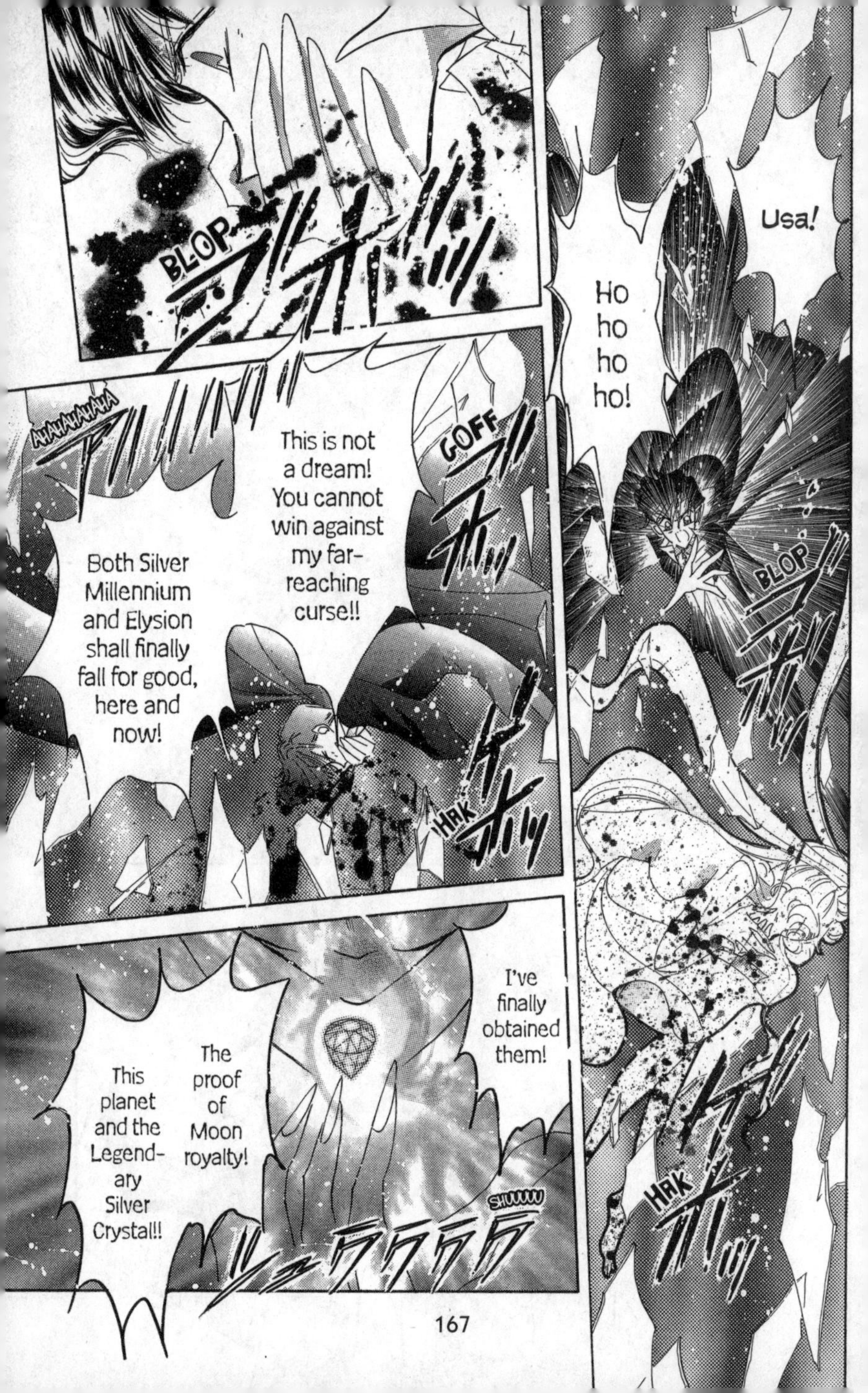
Usa!
Ho ho ho ho!
BLOP
HRK
BLOP
GOFF
This is not a dream! You cannot win against my far-reaching curse!!
AHAHAHAHAHA
Both Silver Millennium and Elysion shall finally fall for good, here and now!
HRK
I've finally obtained them!
The proof of Moon royalty!
This planet and the Legendary Silver Crystal!!
SHUUUUU

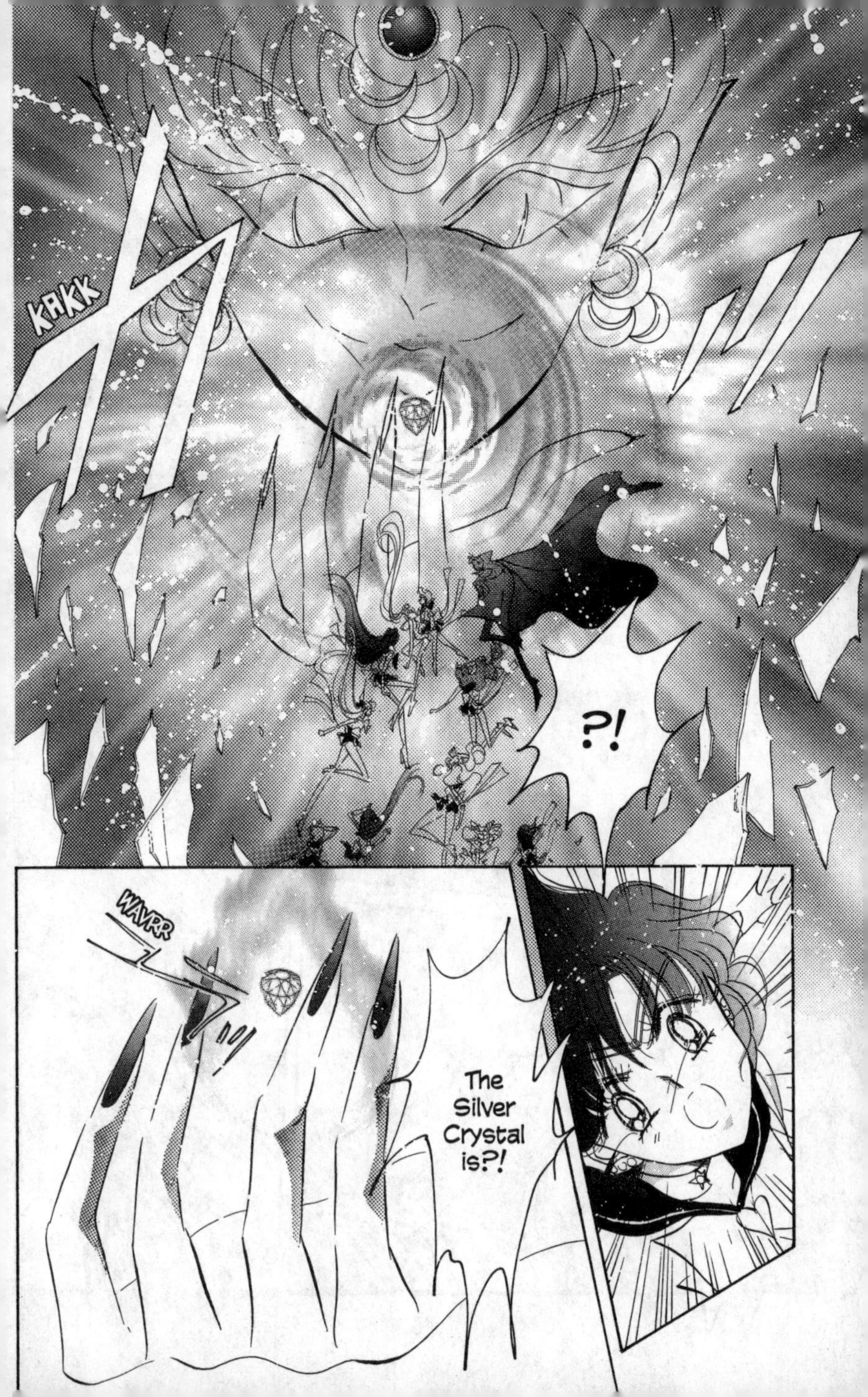
KAKK
?!
The Silver Crystal is?!
WAVRR

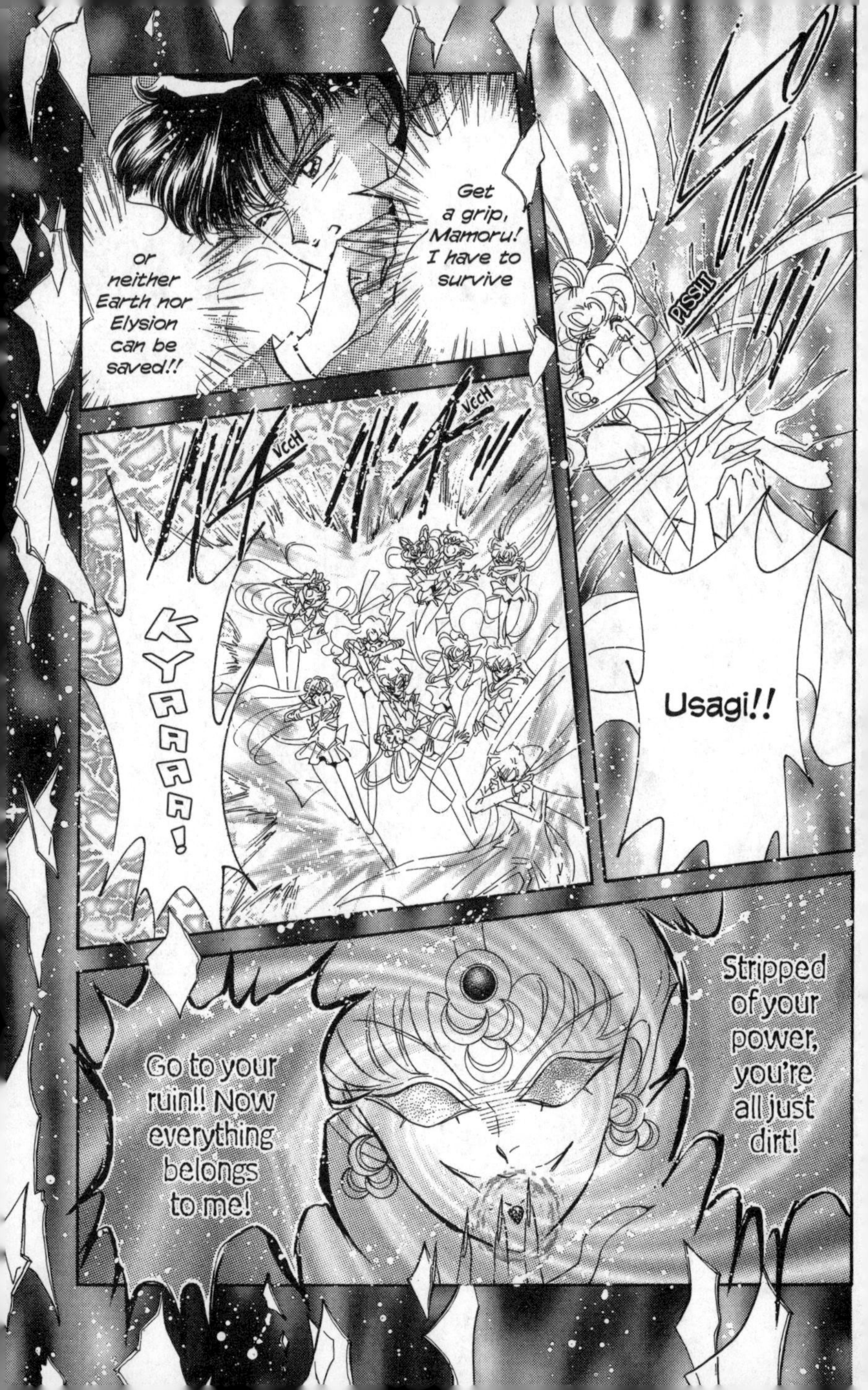
PISSH
Usagi!!
Get a grip, Mamoru! I have to survive
or neither Earth nor Elysion can be saved!!
VCCH
VCCH
KYAAAAA!
Stripped of your power, you're all just dirt!
Go to your ruin!! Now everything belongs to me!

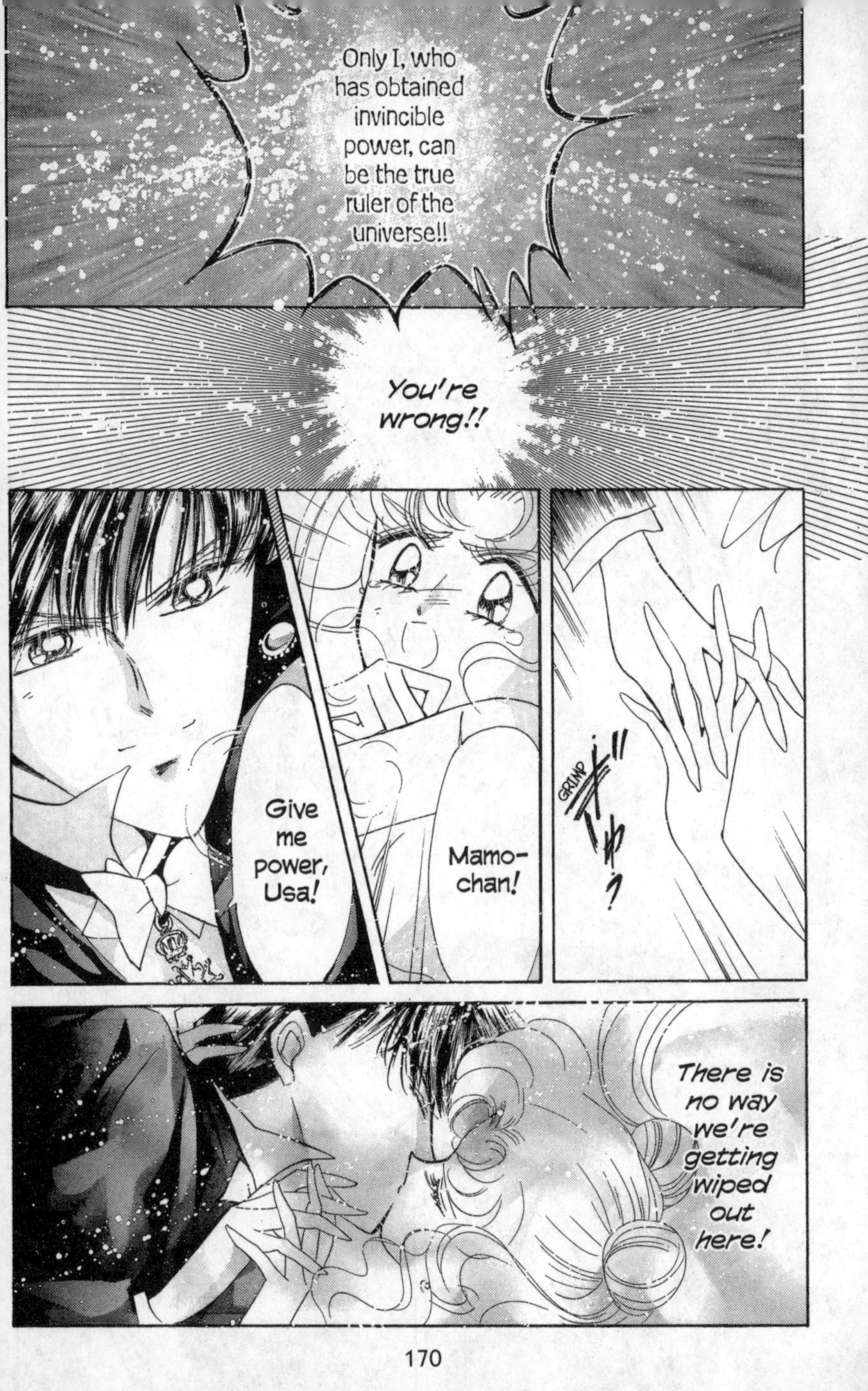
Only I, who has obtained invincible power, can be the true ruler of the universe!!
You're wrong!!
GRIMP
Mamo-chan!
Give me power, Usa!
There is no way we're getting wiped out here!

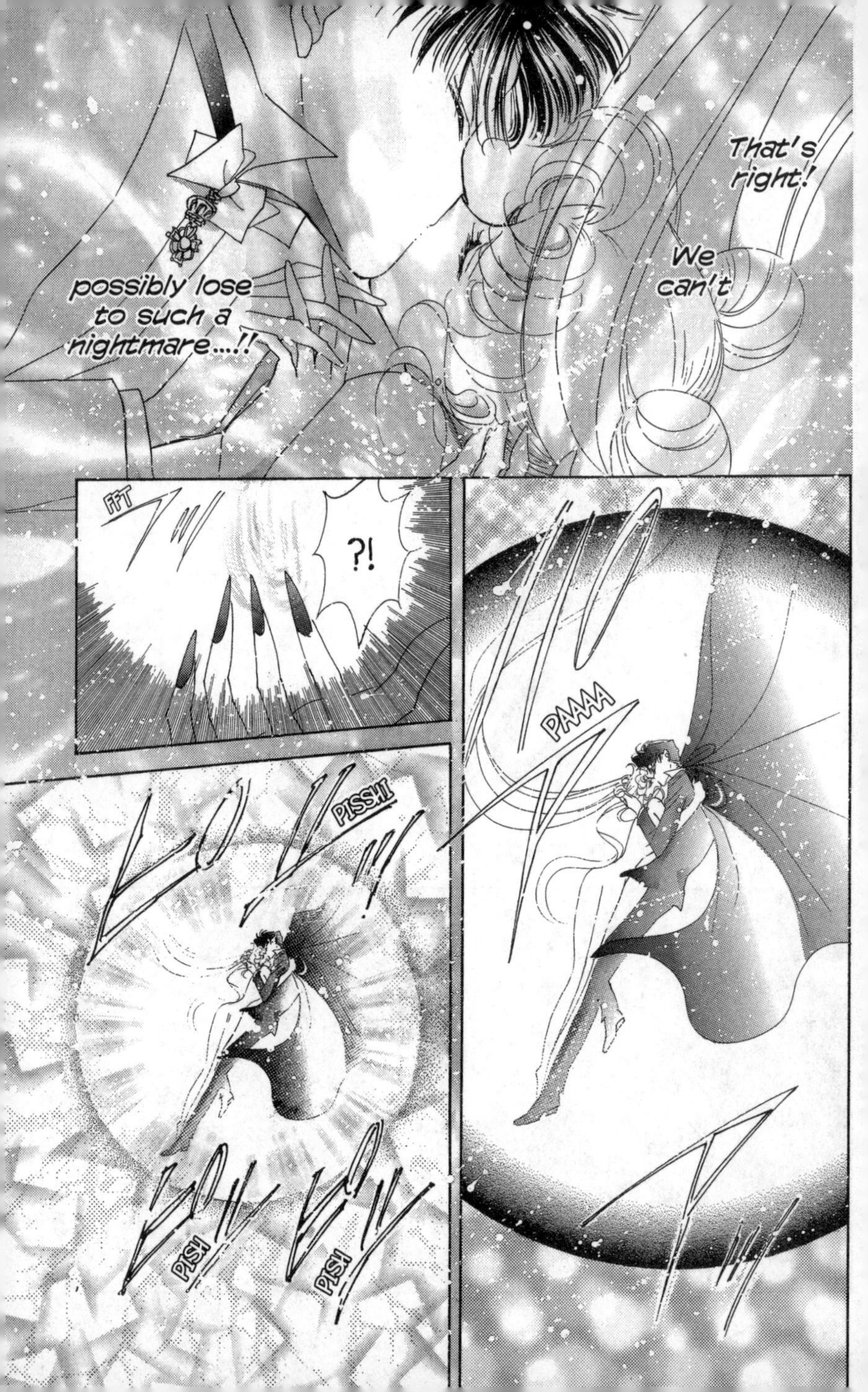
That's right!
We can't
possibly lose to such a nightmare....!!
PAAAA
FFT
?!
PISSH
PISH
PISH

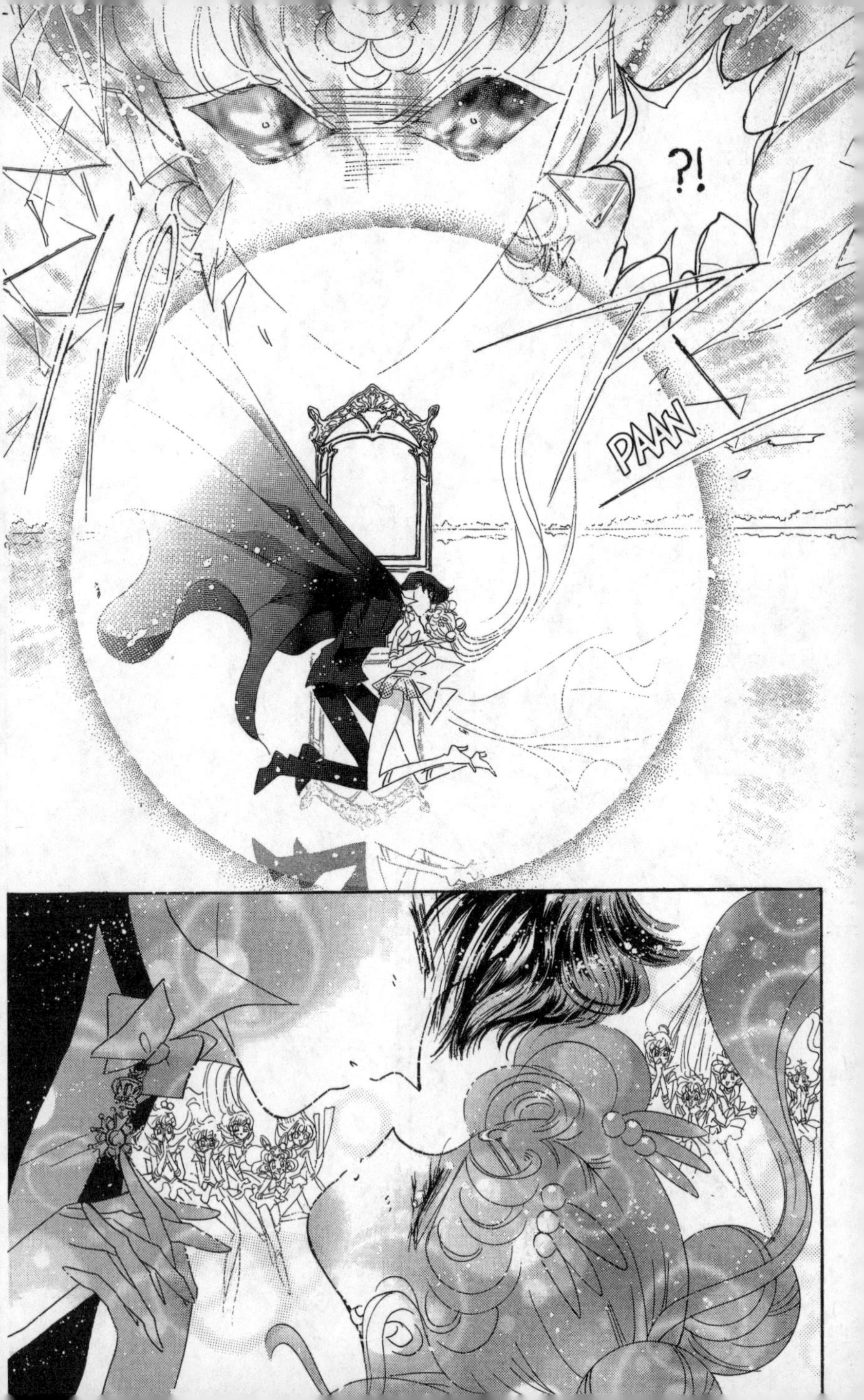
?!
PAAN

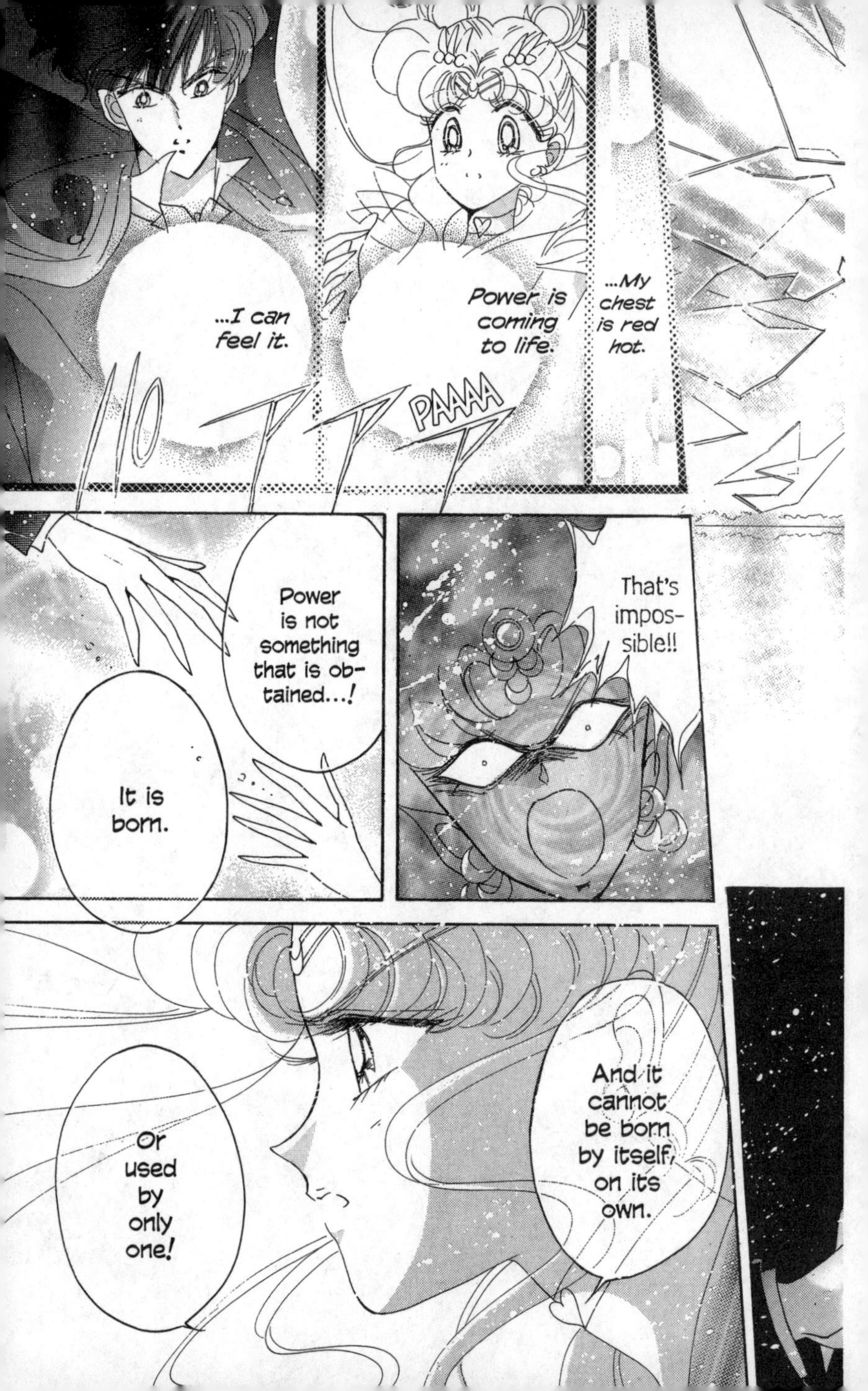
...My chest is red hot.
Power is coming to life.
PAAAA
...I can feel it.
That's impossible!!
Power is not something that is obtained...!
It is born.
And it cannot be born by itself, on its own.
Or used by only one!

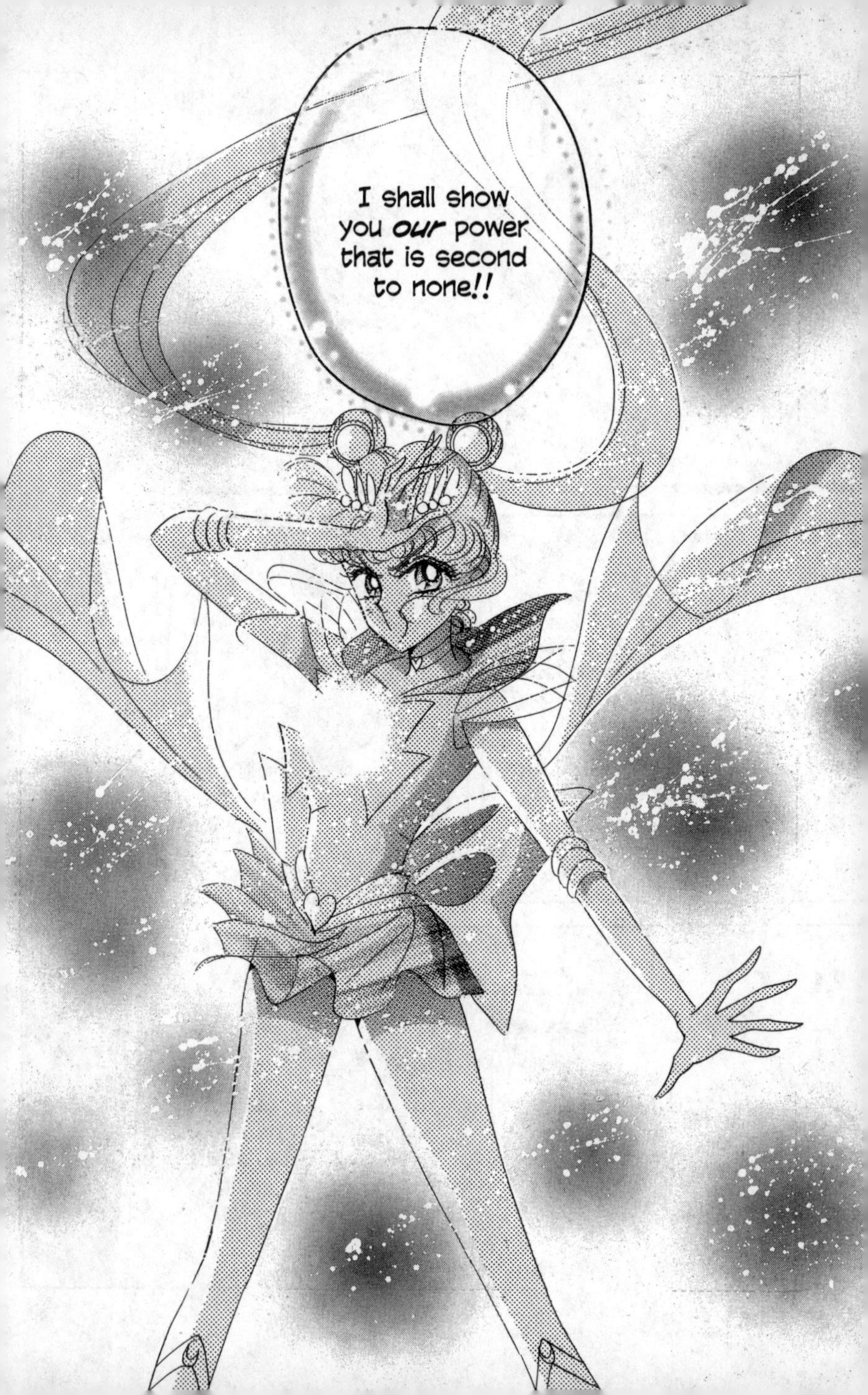
I shall show you *our* power that is second to none!!

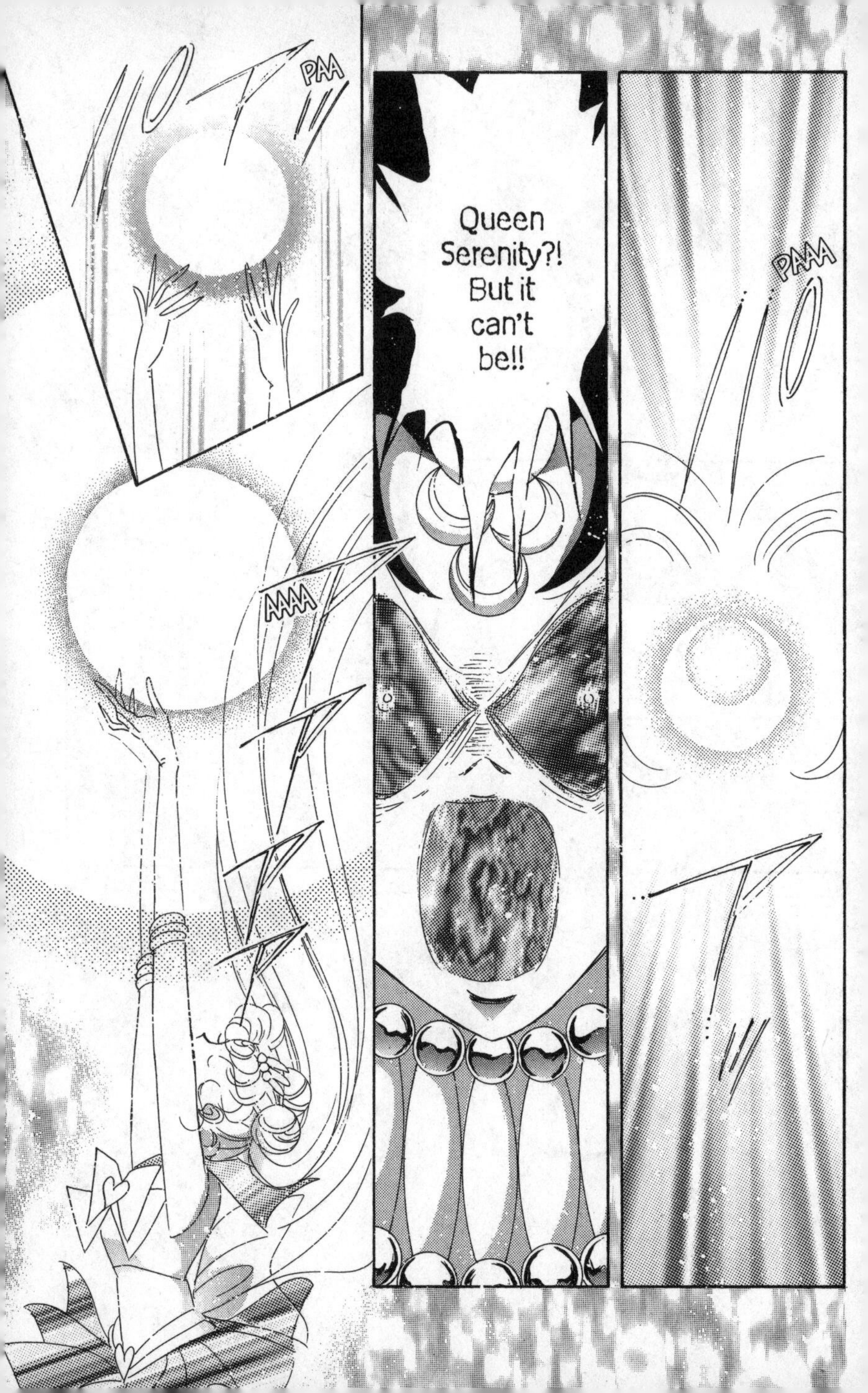
PAAA
Queen Serenity?! But it can't be!!
PAA
AAAA

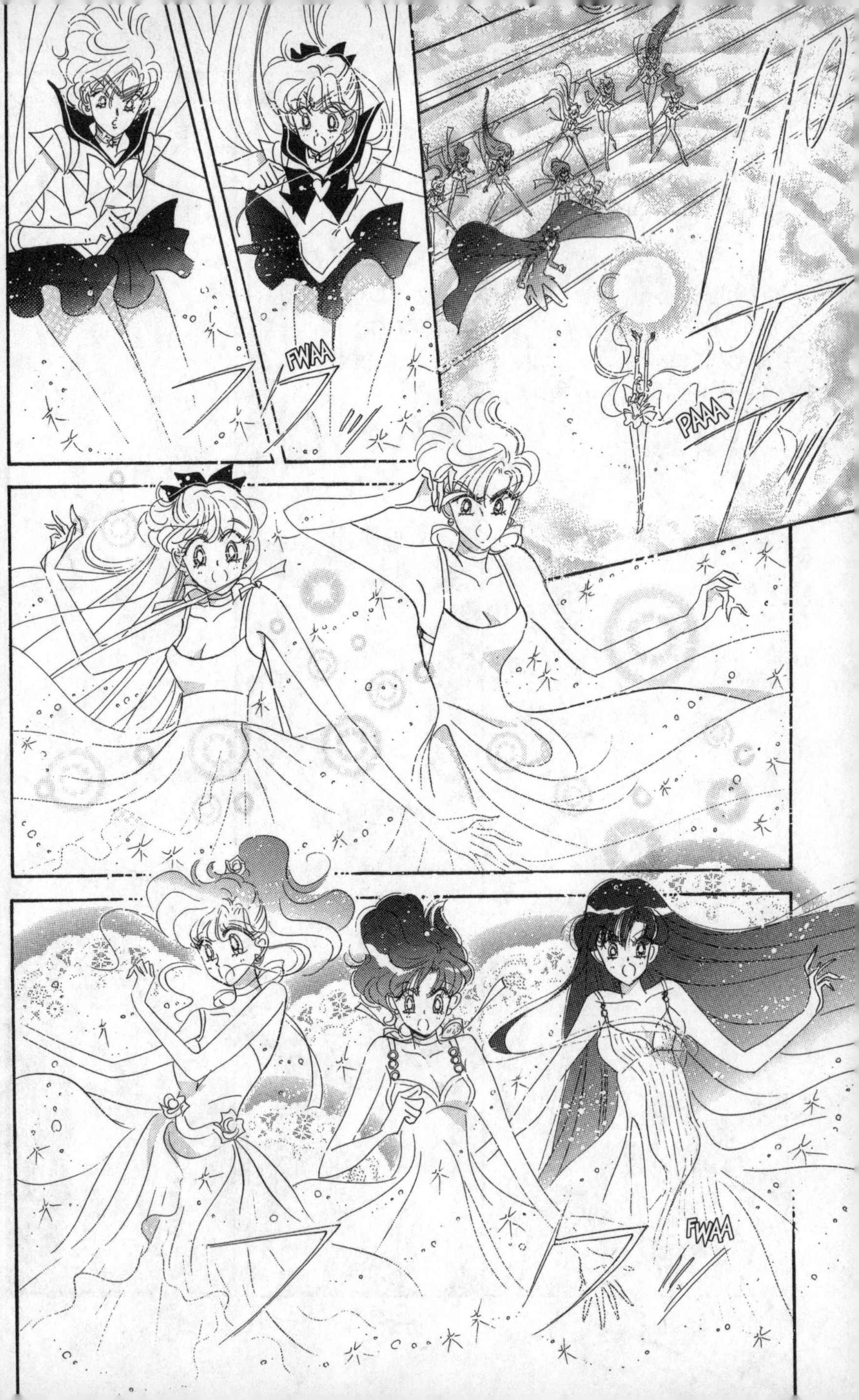
PAAA
FWAA
FWAA

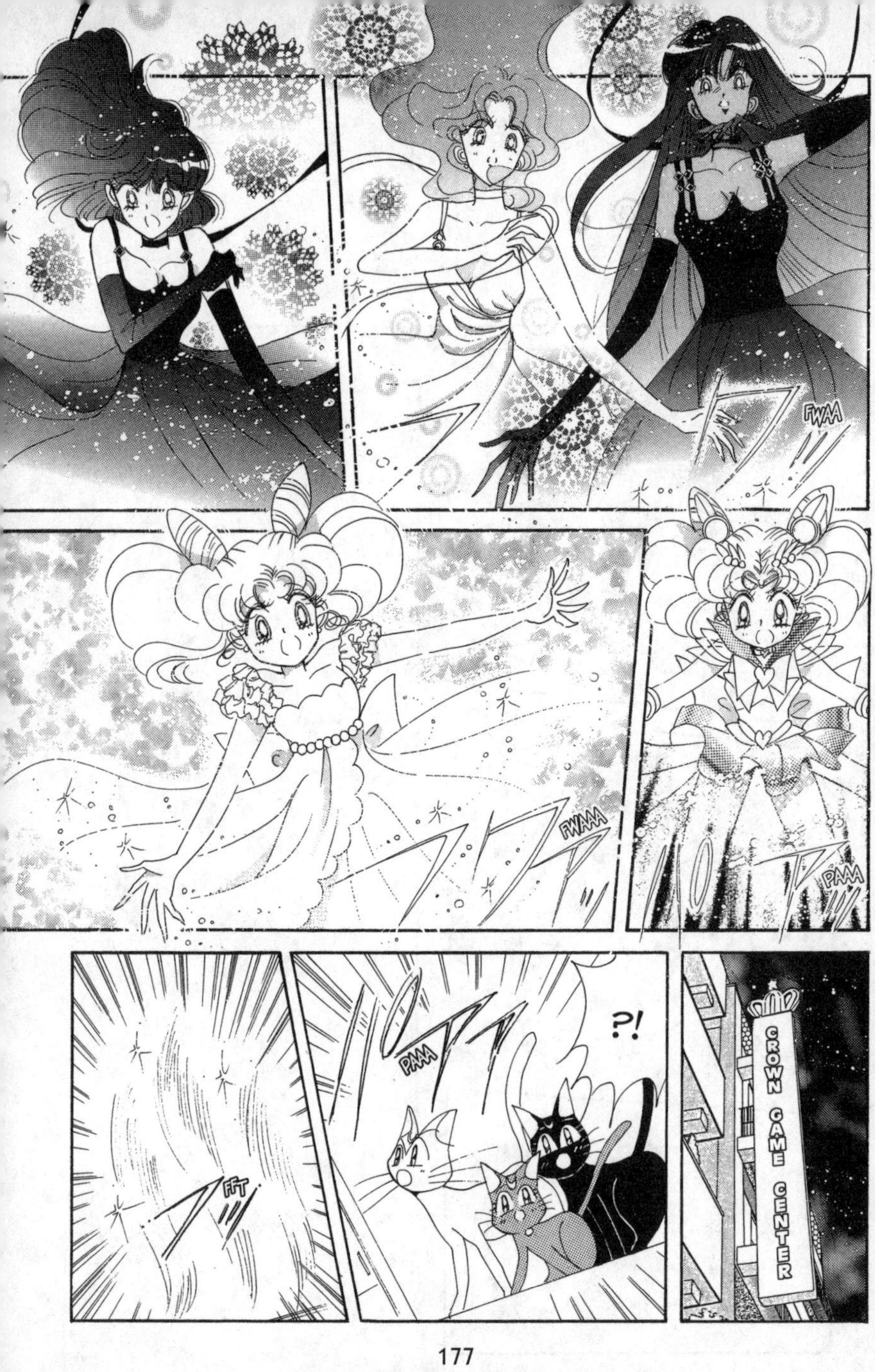
FWAA
PAAA
FWAAA
CROWN GAME CENTER
PAAA
?!
FFT

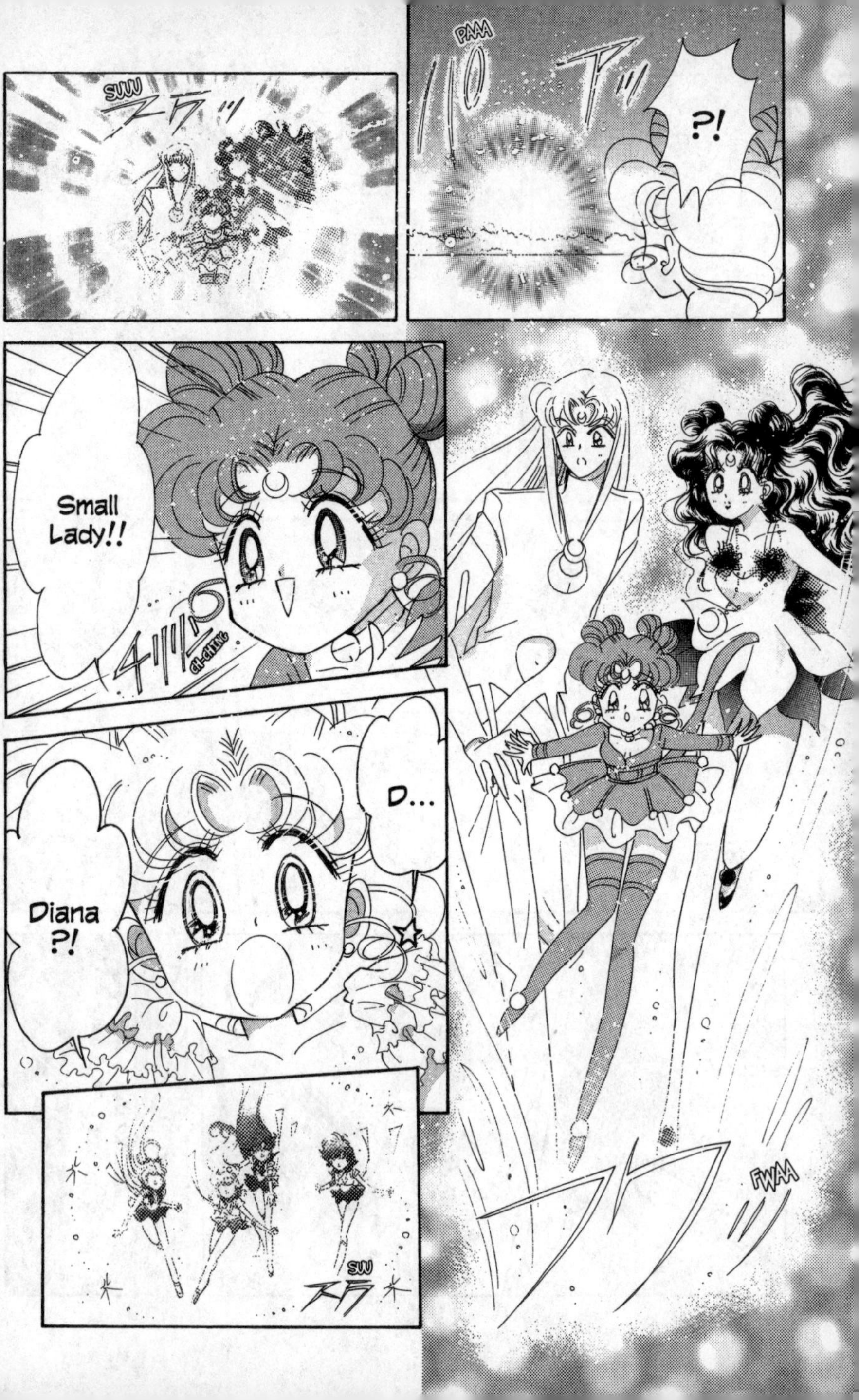
PAAA
?!
SUUU
FWAA
Small Lady!!
CH-CHING
D...
Diana ?!
SUU

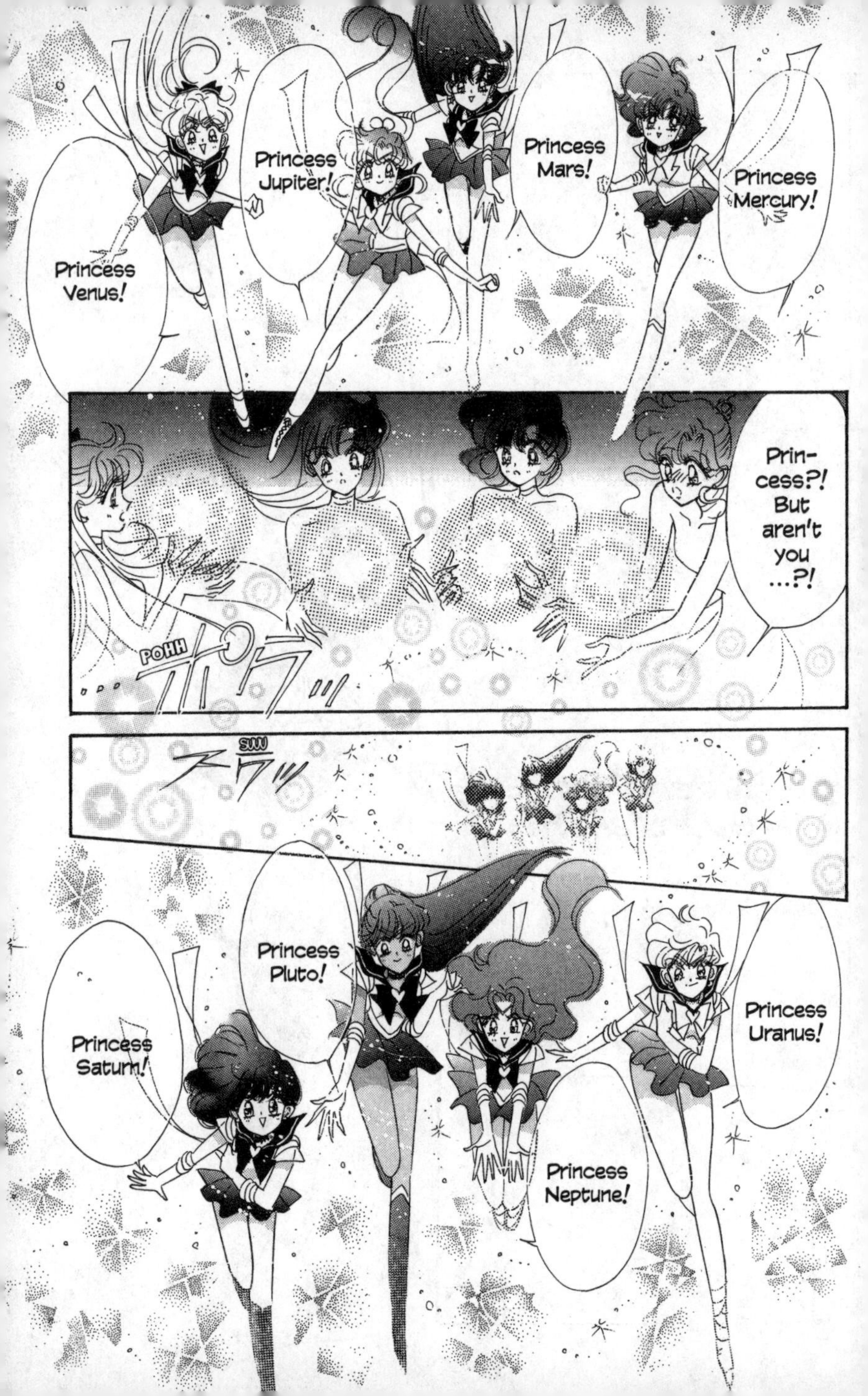
Princess Mercury!
Princess Mars!
Princess Jupiter!
Princess Venus!
Prin-cess?! But aren't you ...?!
POHH
SUUU
Princess Uranus!
Princess Pluto!
Princess Neptune!
Princess Saturn!

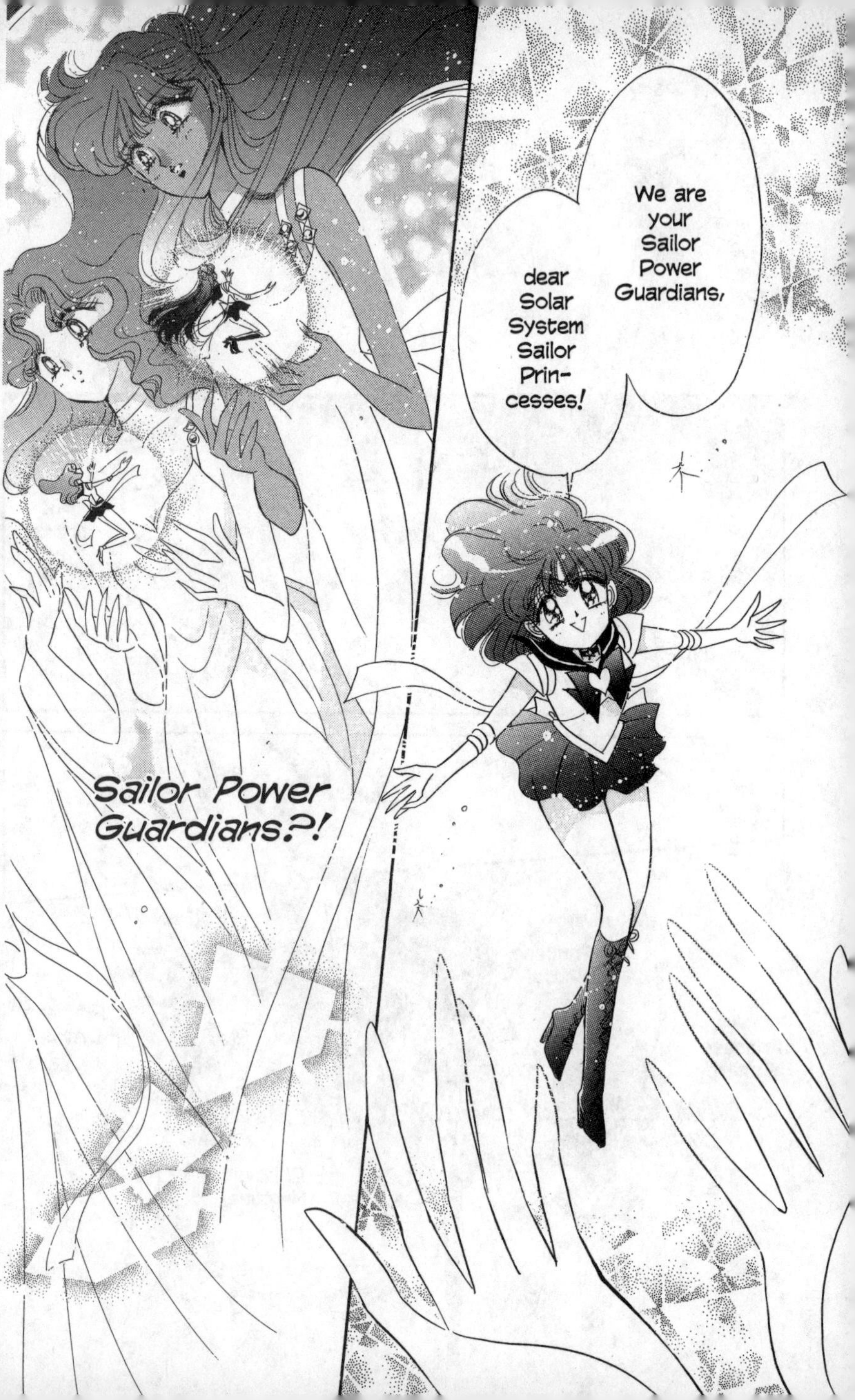
We are your Sailor Power Guardians,
dear Solar System Sailor Prin-cesses!
Sailor Power Guardians?!

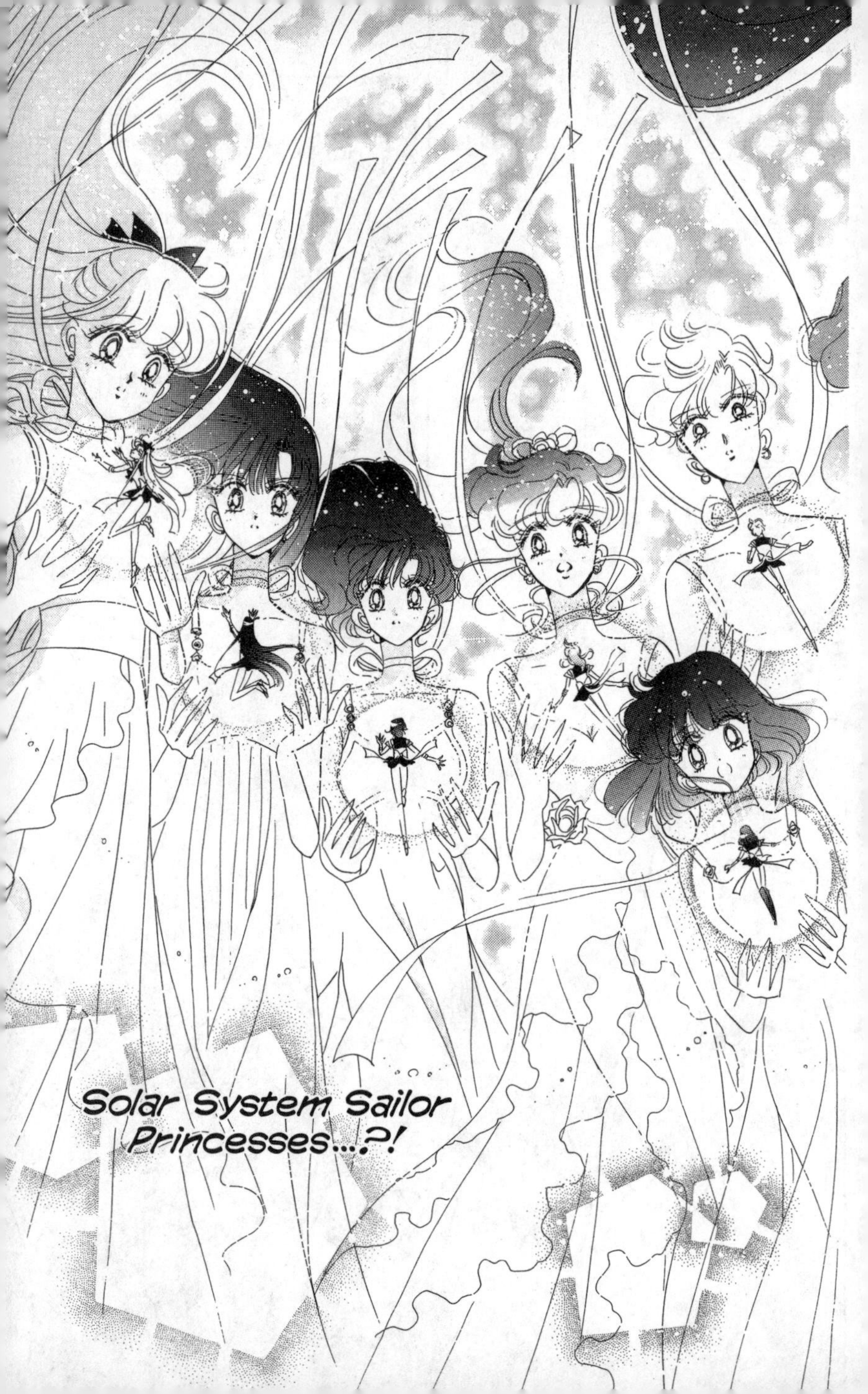
Solar System Sailor Princesses...?!

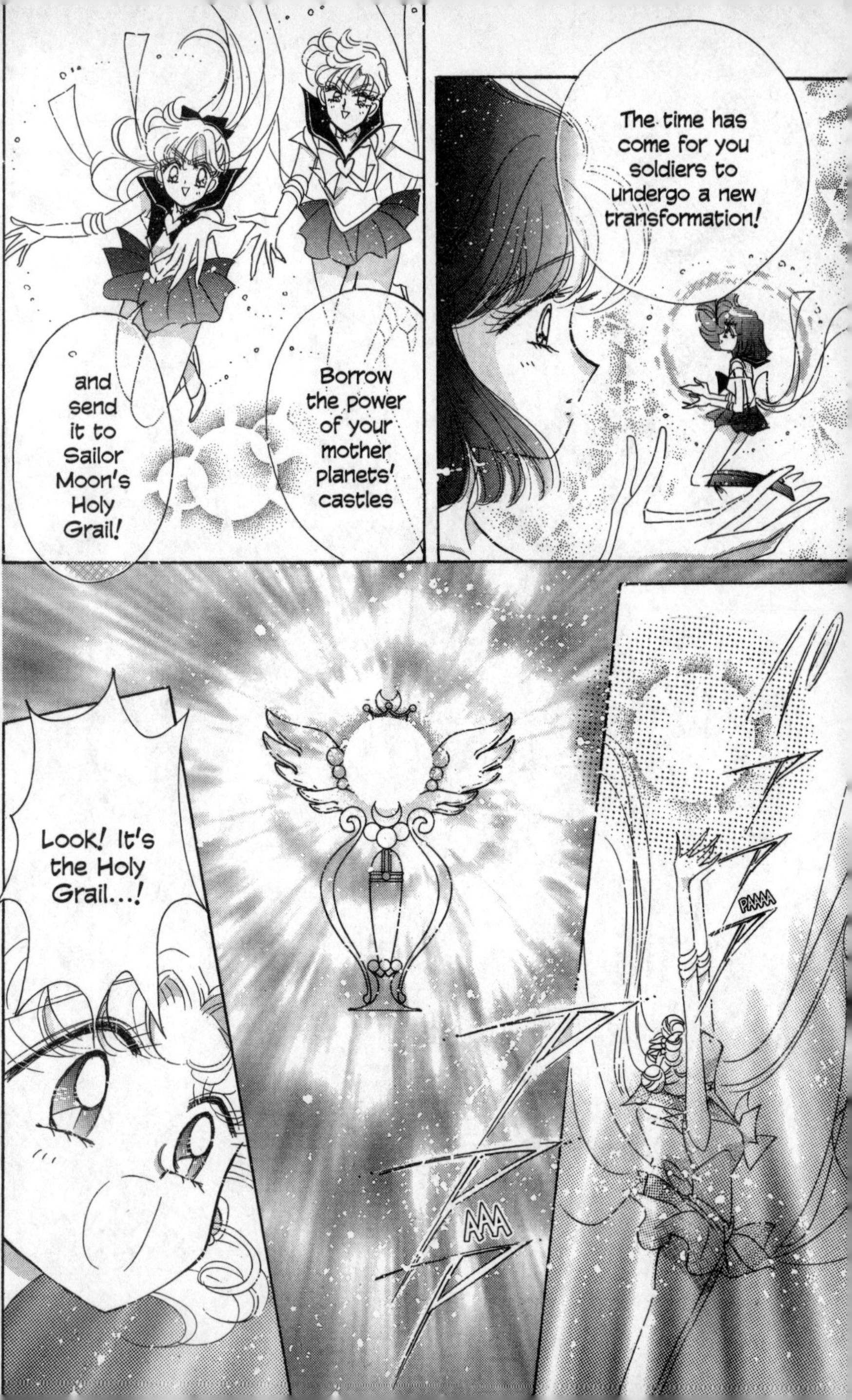
The time has come for you soldiers to undergo a new transformation!
Borrow the power of your mother planets' castles
and send it to Sailor Moon's Holy Grail!
PAAAA
AAA
Look! It's the Holy Grail...!

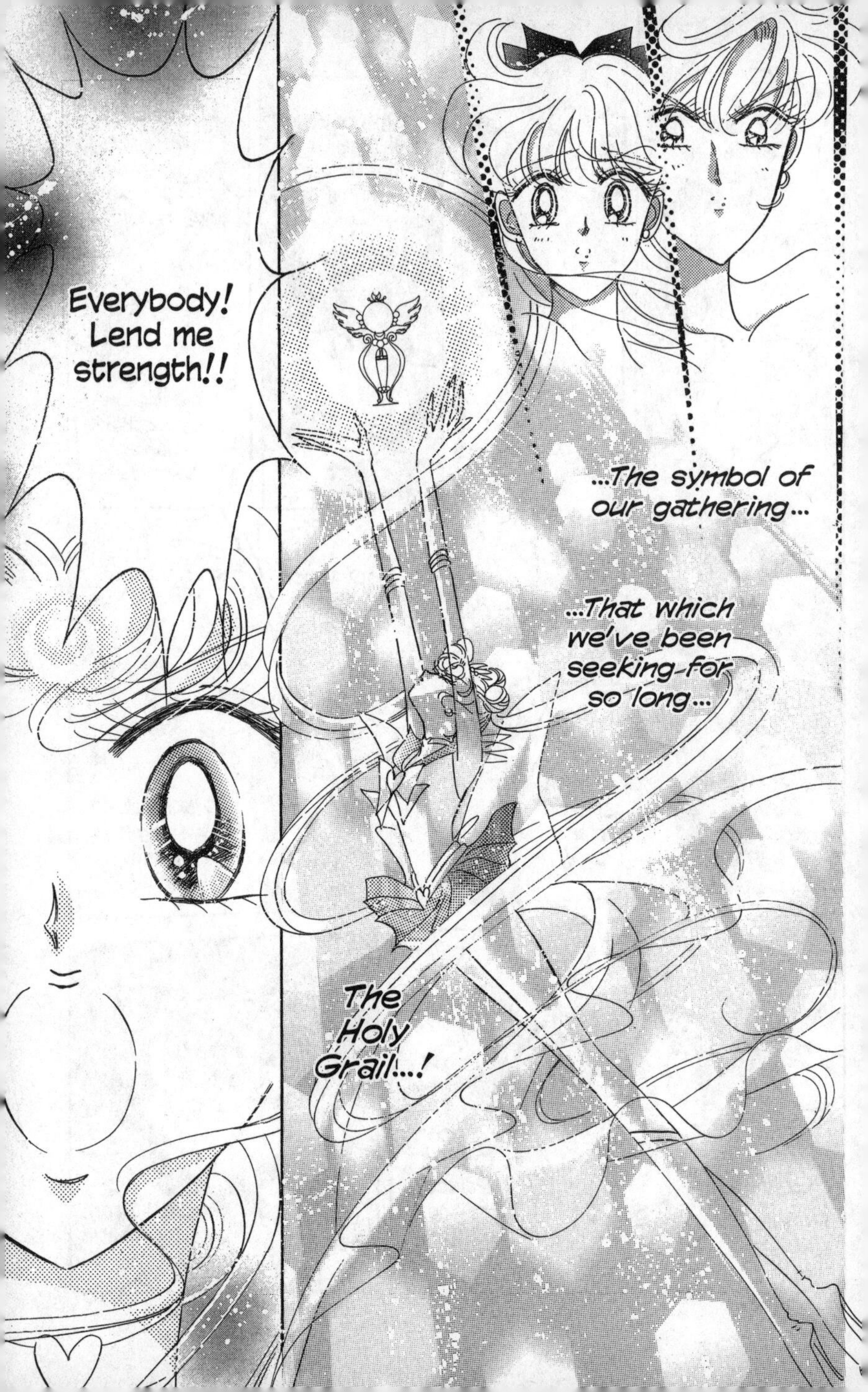
...The symbol of our gathering...
...That which we've been seeking for so long...
The Holy Grail...!
Everybody! Lend me strength!!

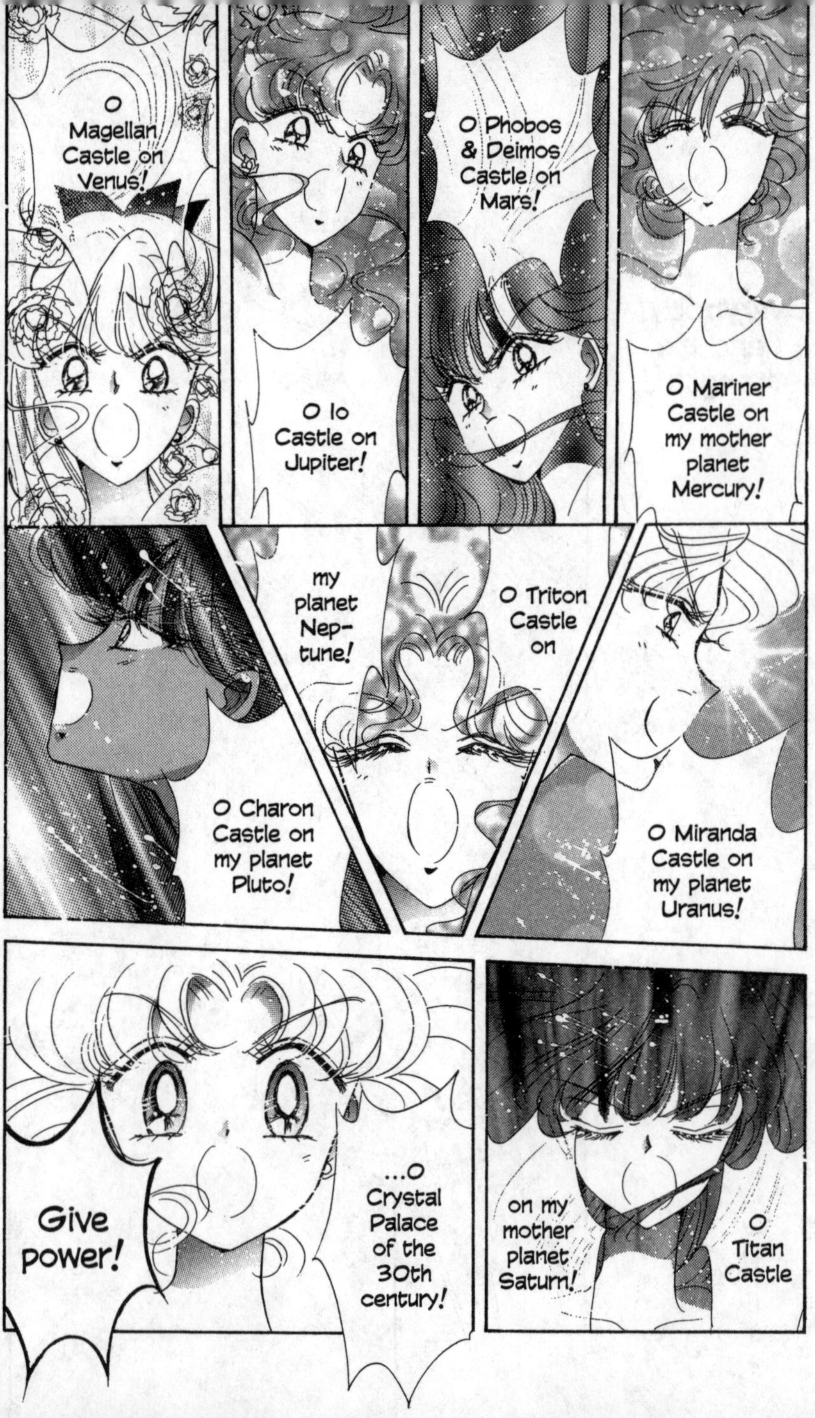
O Mariner Castle on my mother planet Mercury!
O Phobos & Deimos Castle on Mars!
O Io Castle on Jupiter!
O Magellan Castle on Venus!
O Miranda Castle on my planet Uranus!
O Triton Castle on
my planet Nep-tune!
O Charon Castle on my planet Pluto!
O Titan Castle
on my mother planet Saturn!
...O Crystal Palace of the 30th century!
Give power!

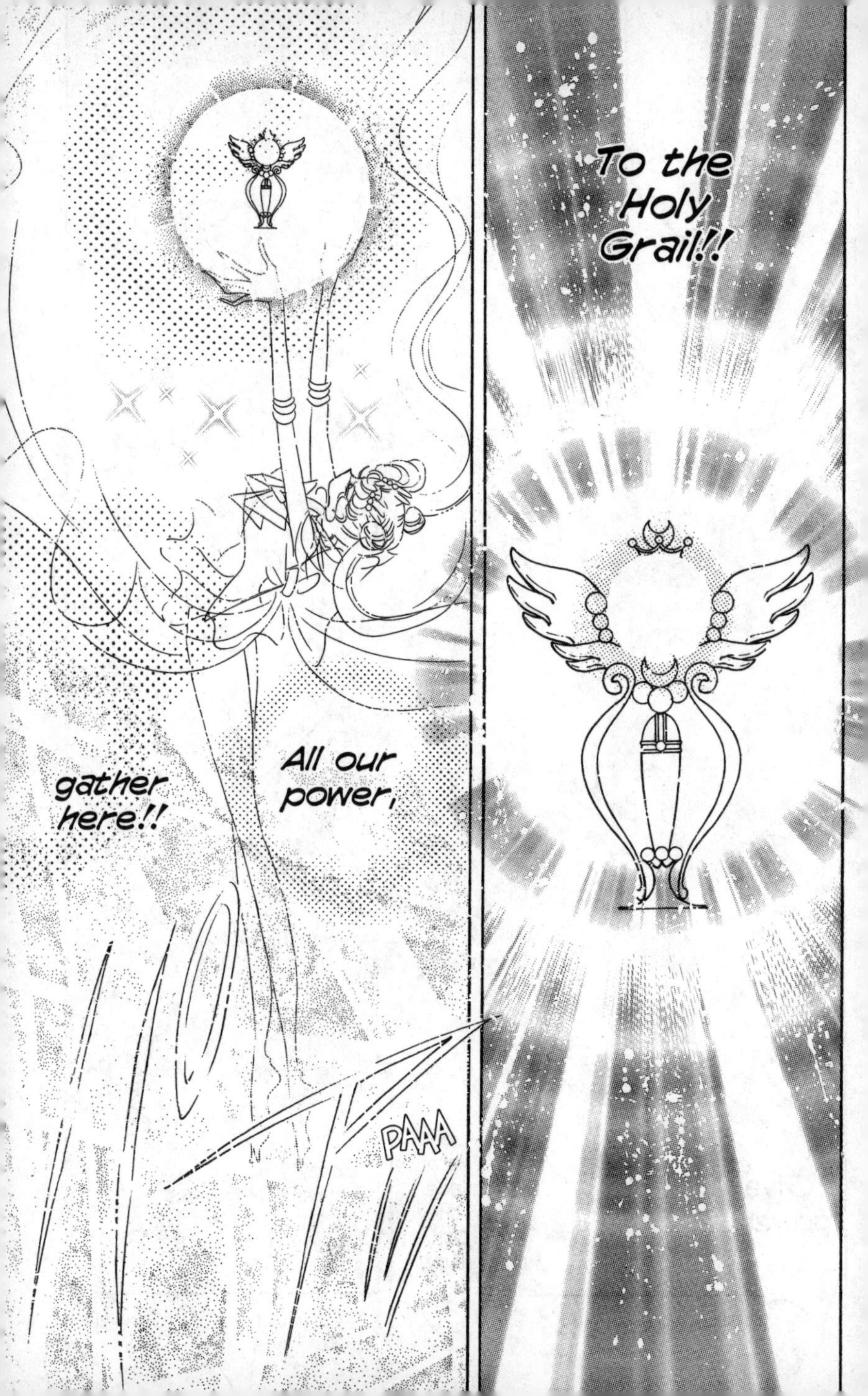
To the Holy Grail!!
All our power,
gather here!!
PAAA

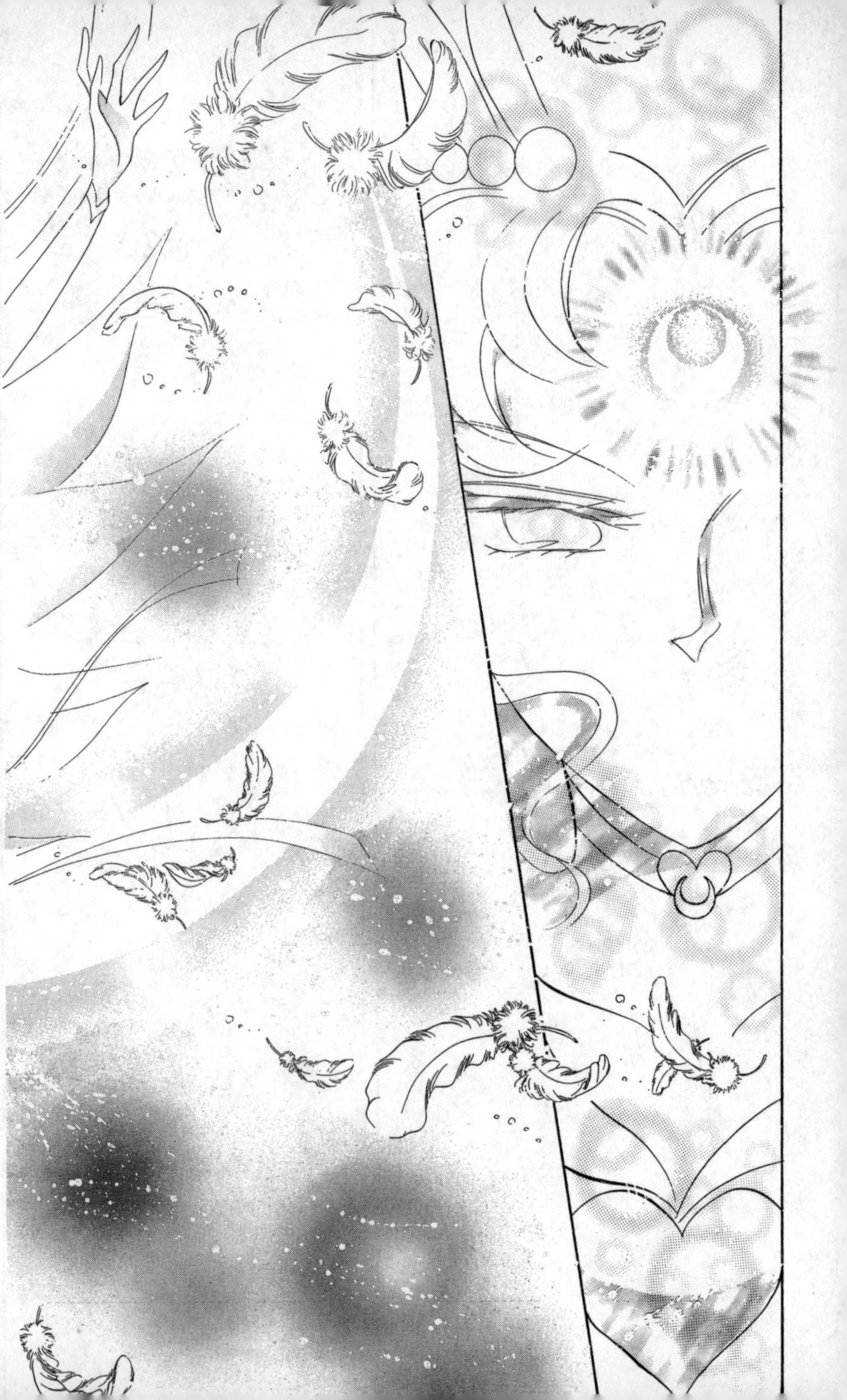

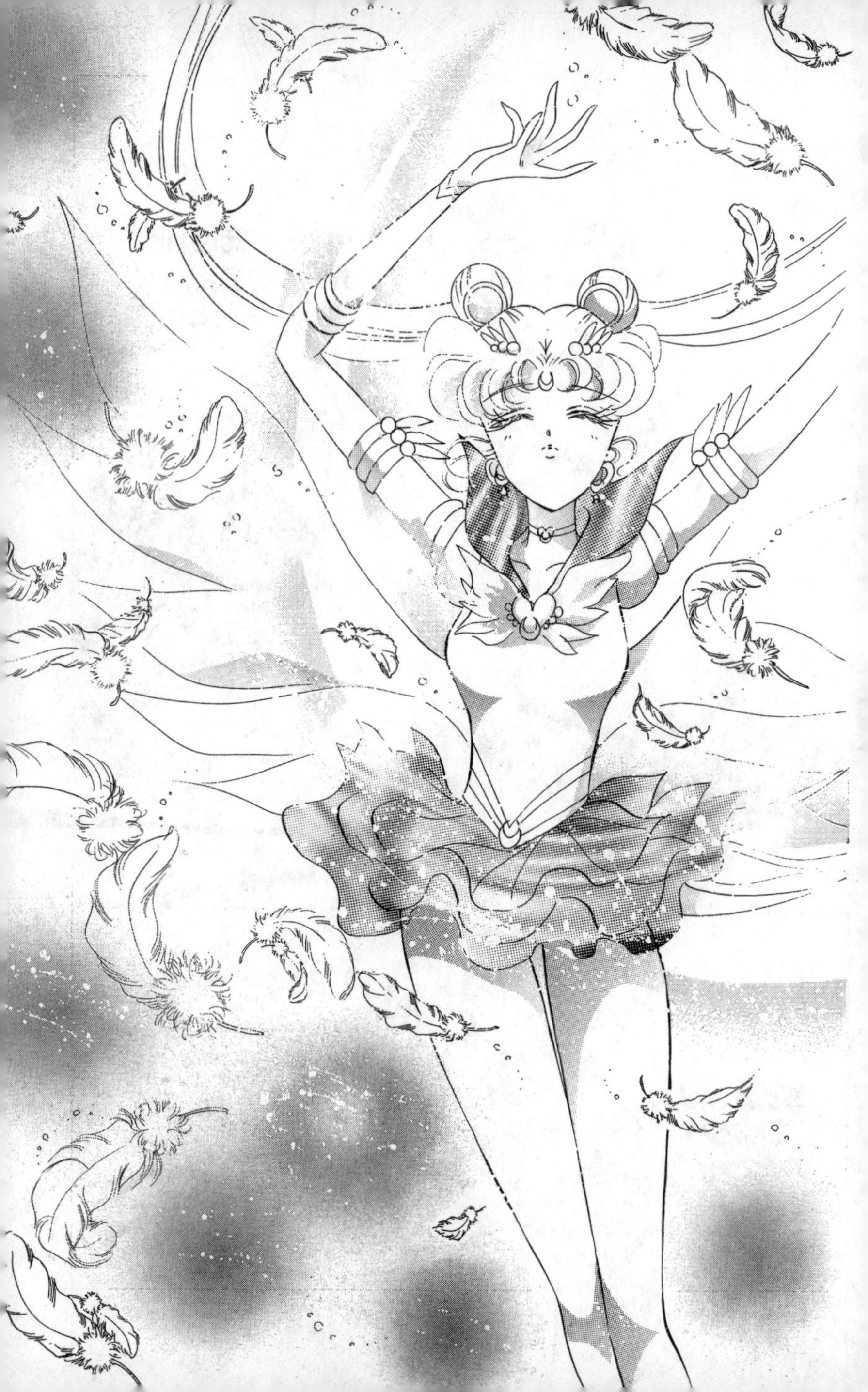

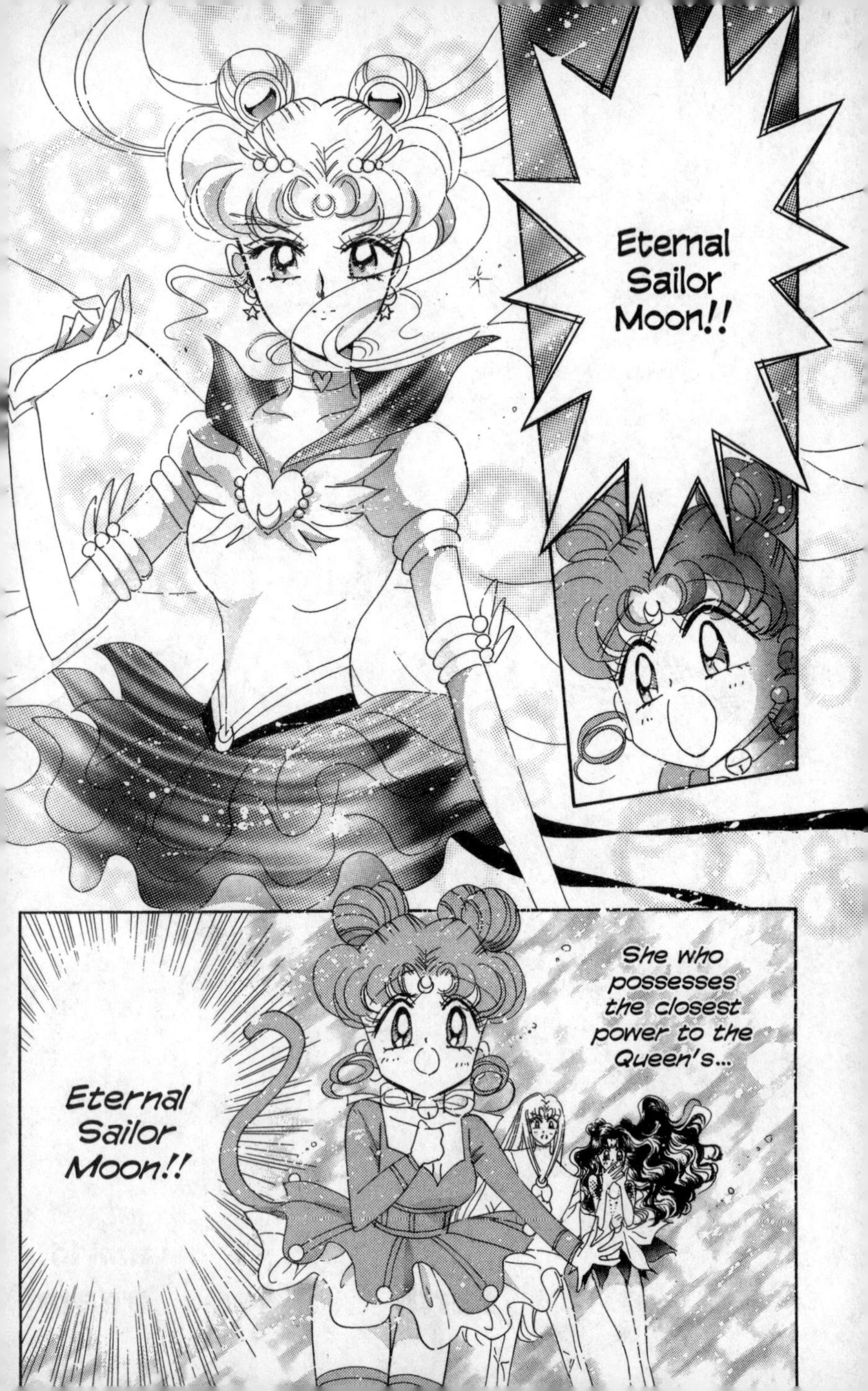
Eternal Sailor Moon!!
She who possesses the closest power to the Queen's...
Eternal Sailor Moon!!

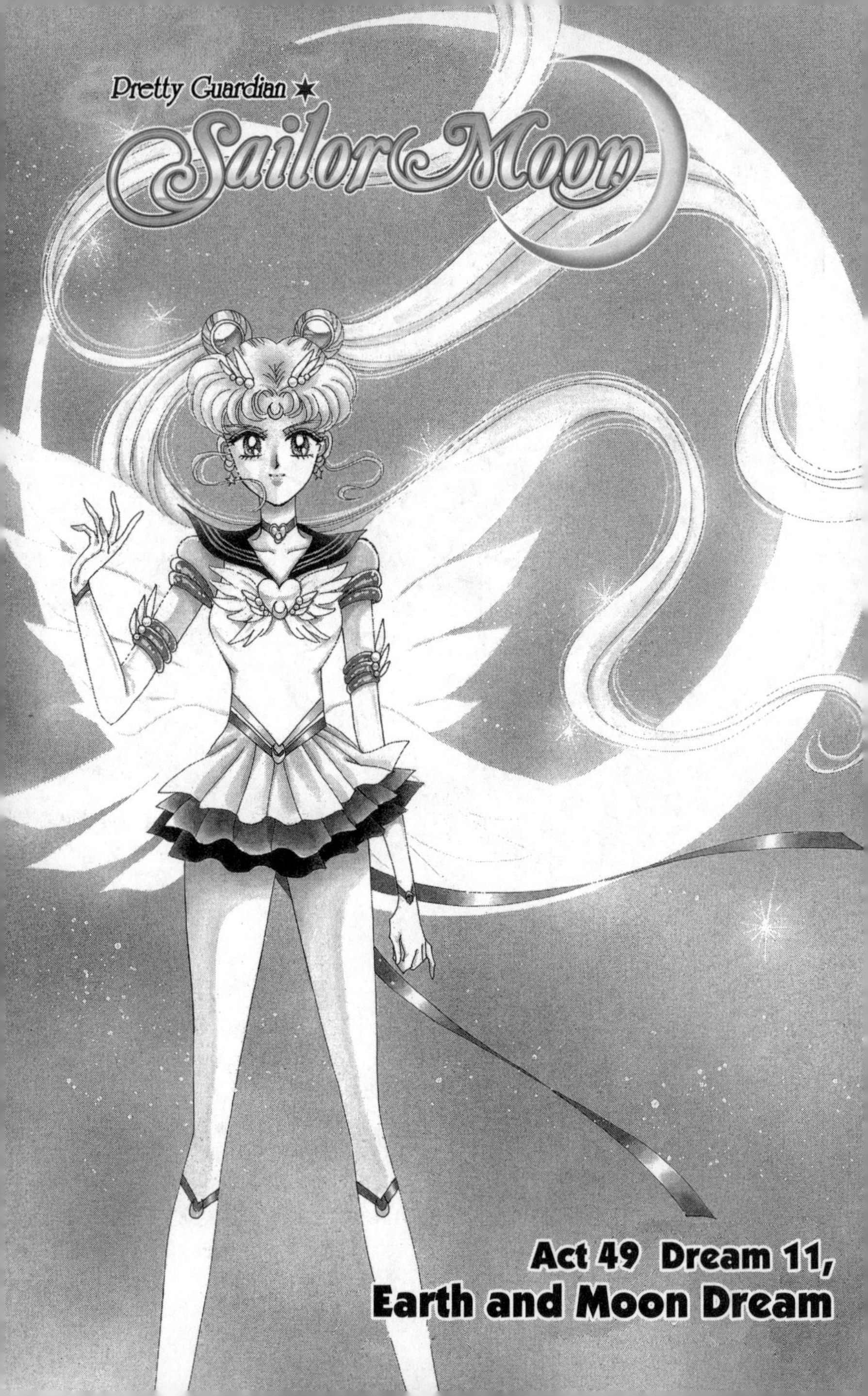
Pretty Guardian ★ Sailor Moon
Act 49 Dream 11,
Earth and Moon Dream

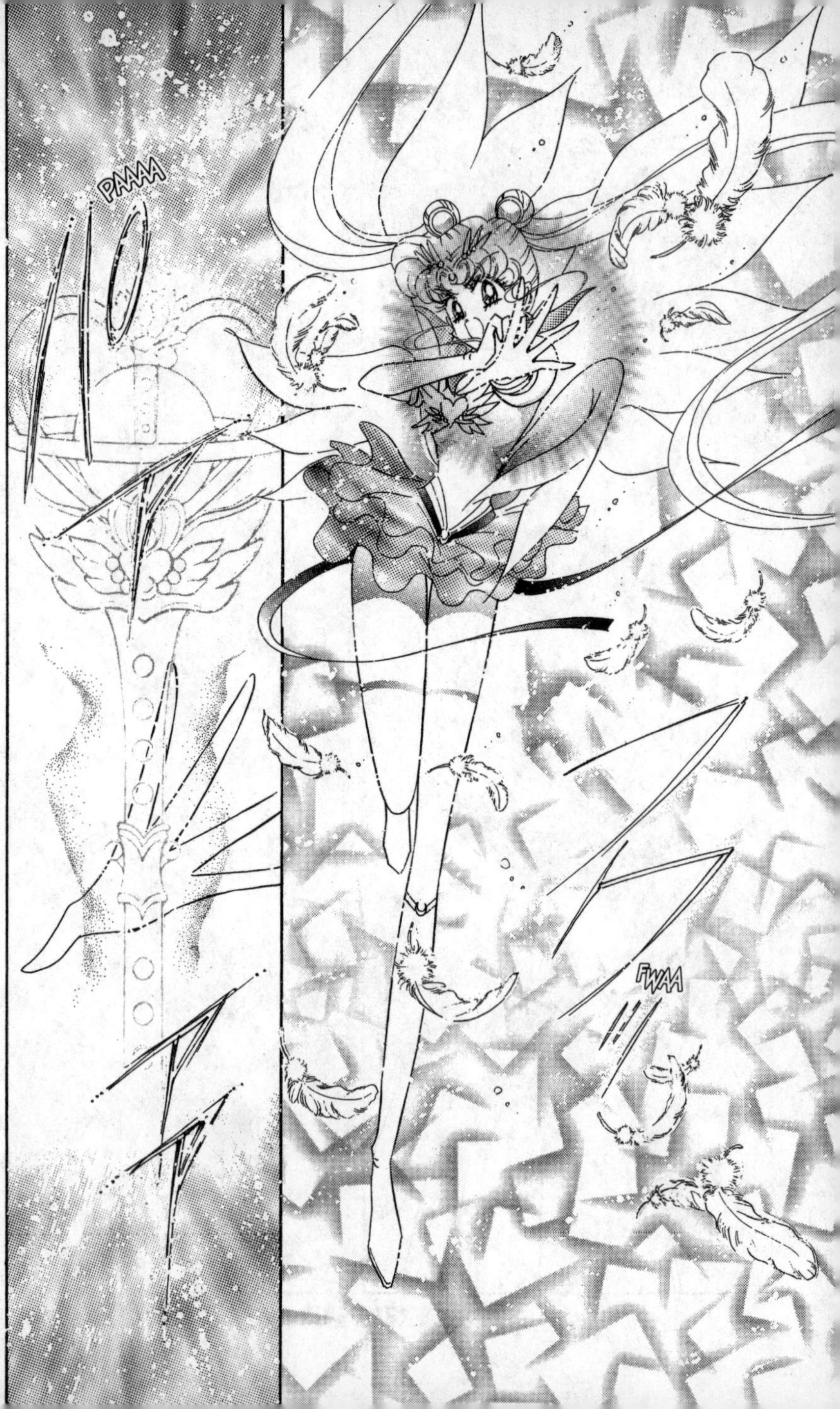
FWAA
PAAAA

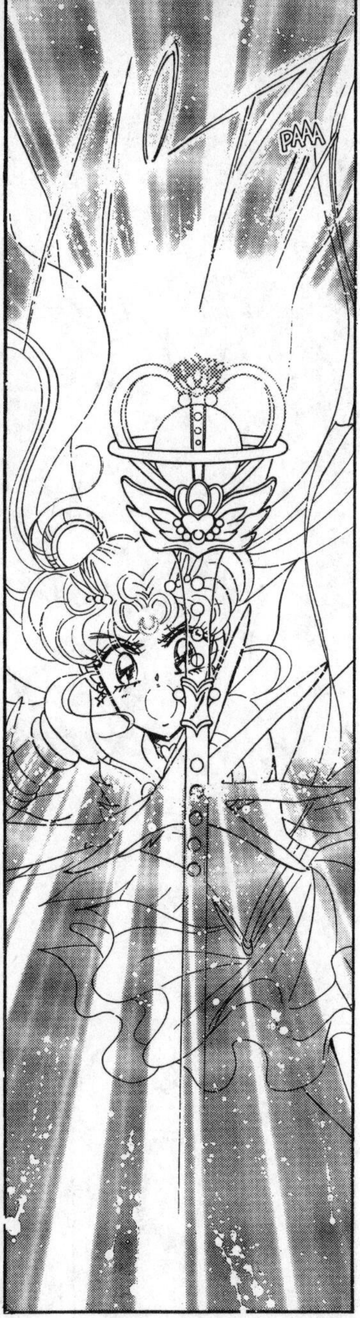
PAAA

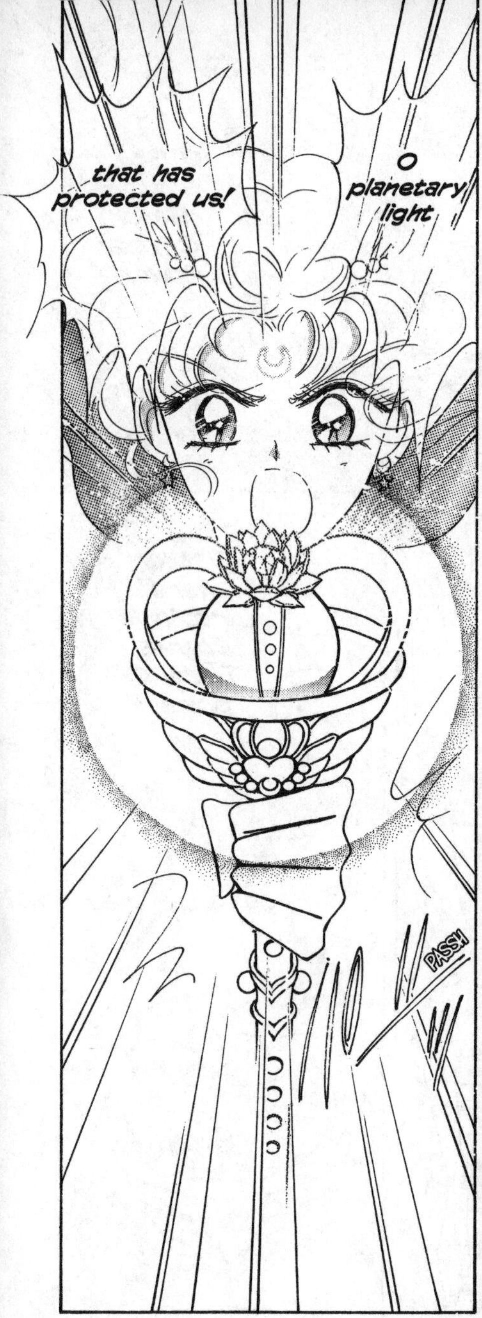
O planetary light
that has protected us!
PASSH

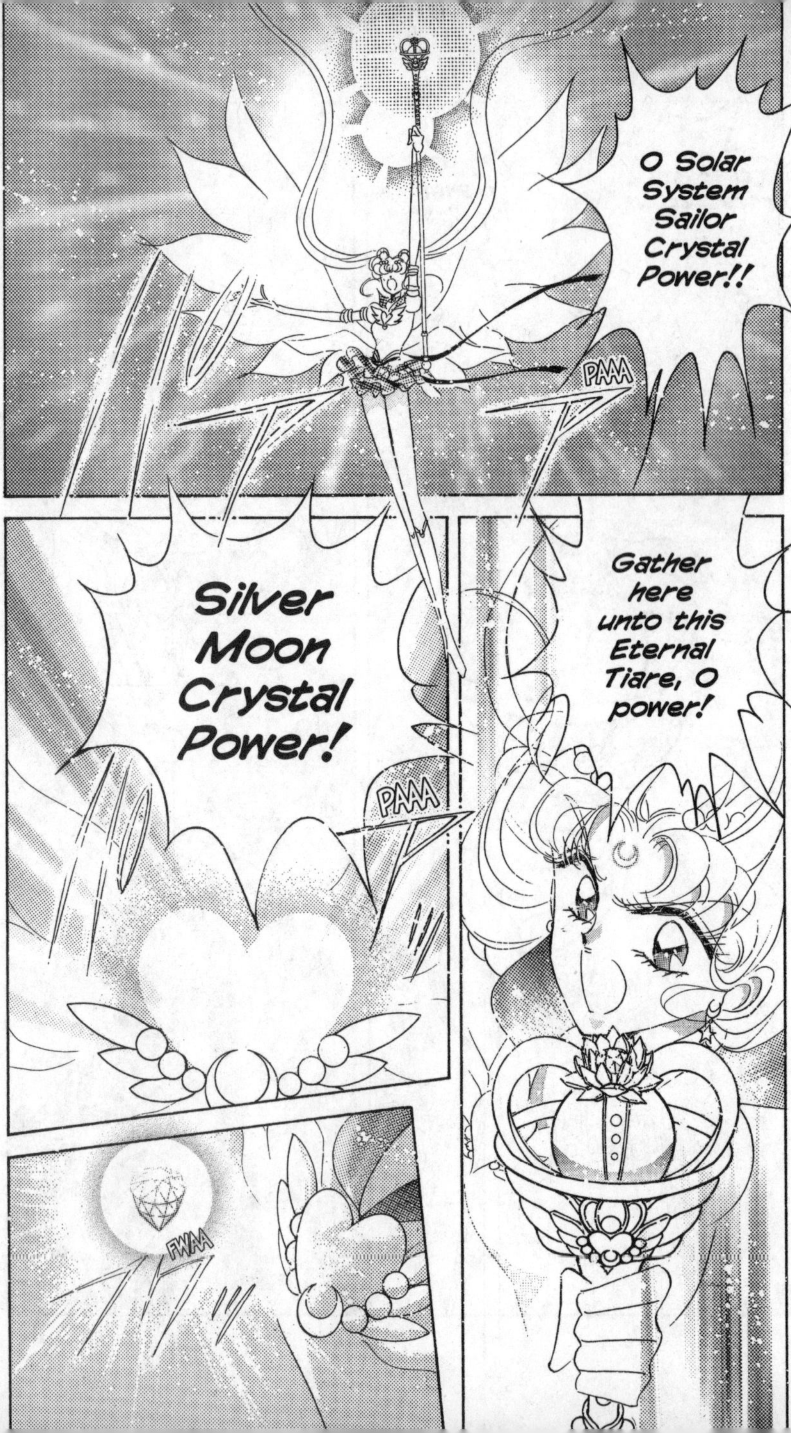
O Solar System Sailor Crystal Power!!
PAAA
Gather here unto this Eternal Tiare, O power!
Silver Moon Crystal Power!
PAAA
FWAA

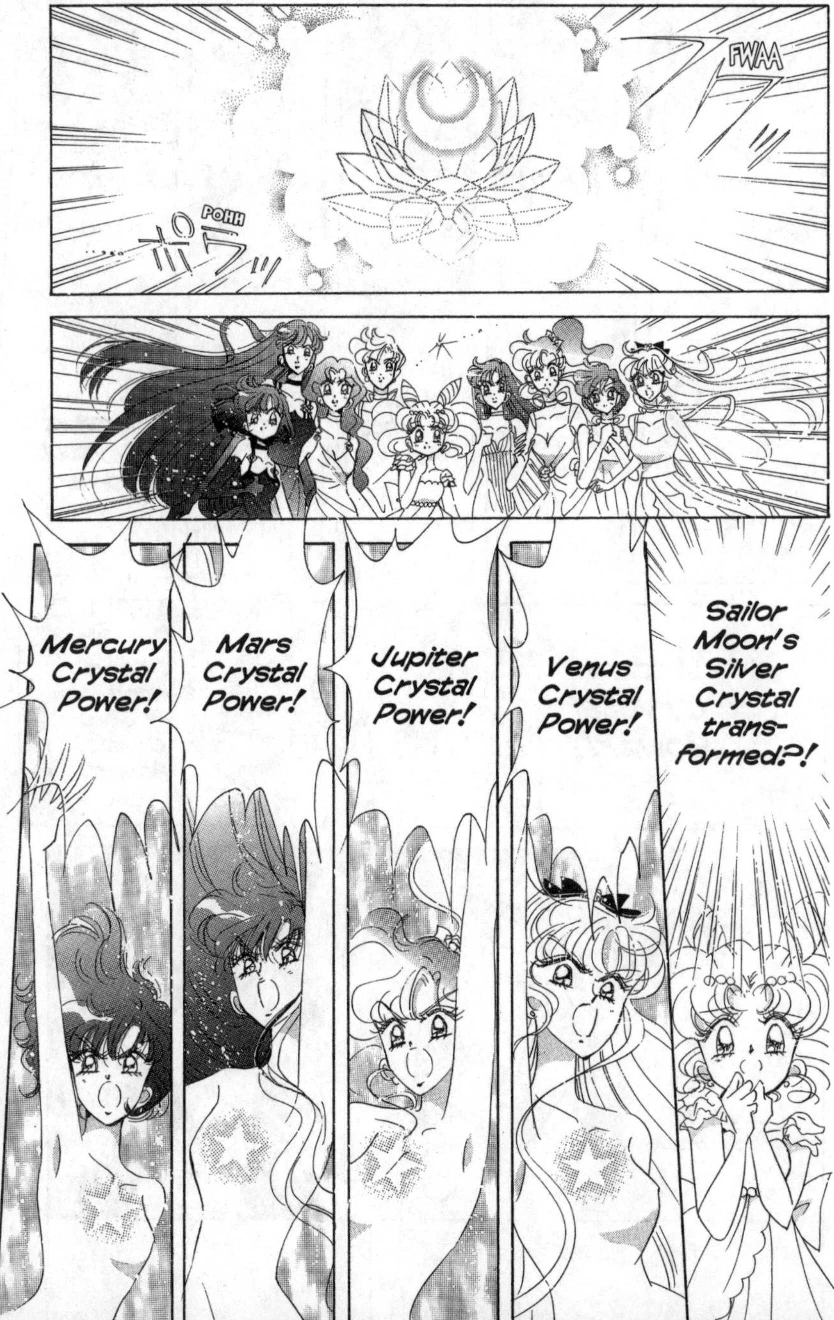
FWAA
POHH
Sailor Moon's Silver Crystal transformed?!
Venus Crystal Power!
Jupiter Crystal Power!
Mars Crystal Power!
Mercury Crystal Power!

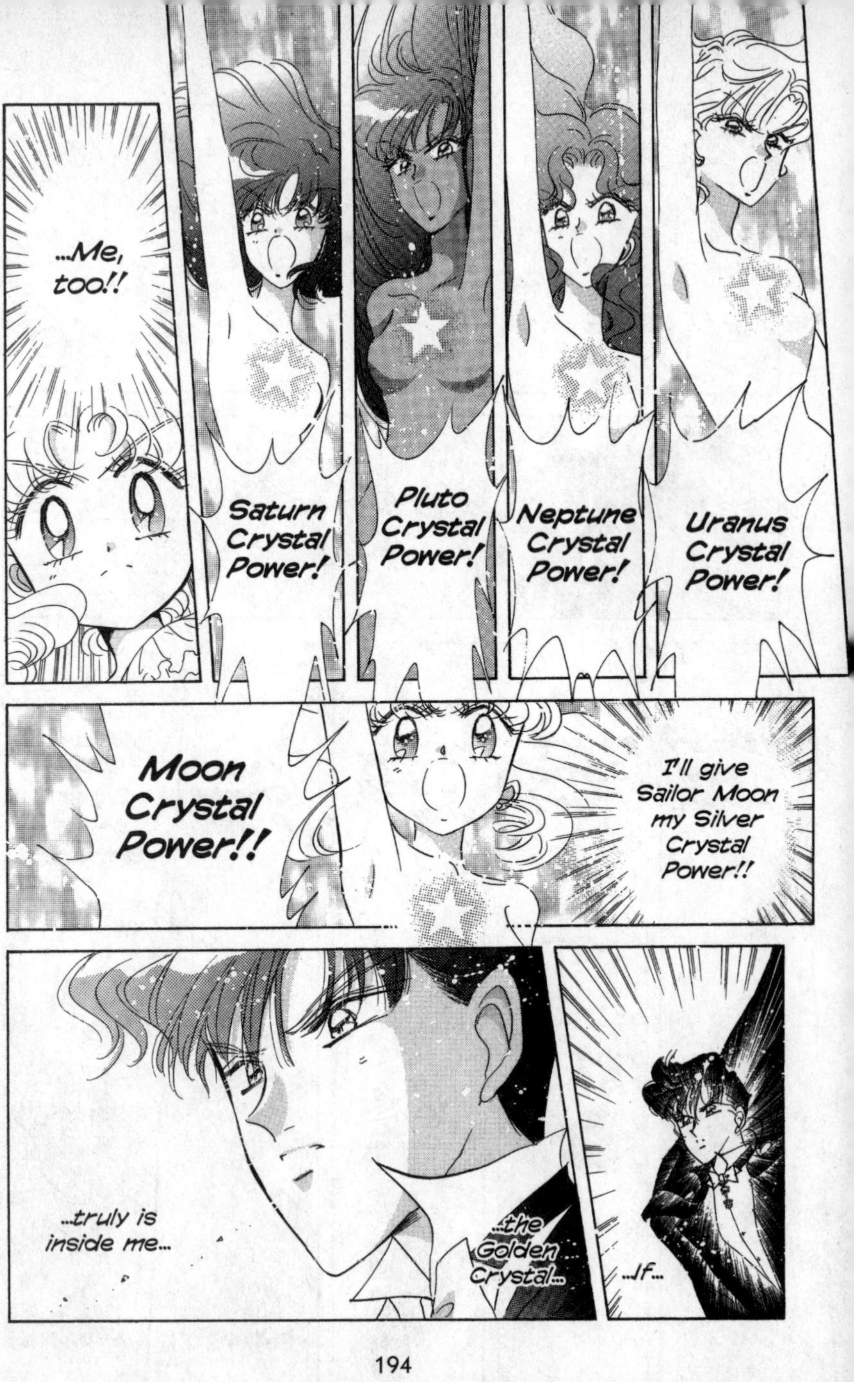
Uranus Crystal Power!
Neptune Crystal Power!
Pluto Crystal Power!
Saturn Crystal Power!
...Me, too!!
I'll give Sailor Moon my Silver Crystal Power!!
Moon Crystal Power!!
...If...
...the Golden Crystal...
...truly is inside me...

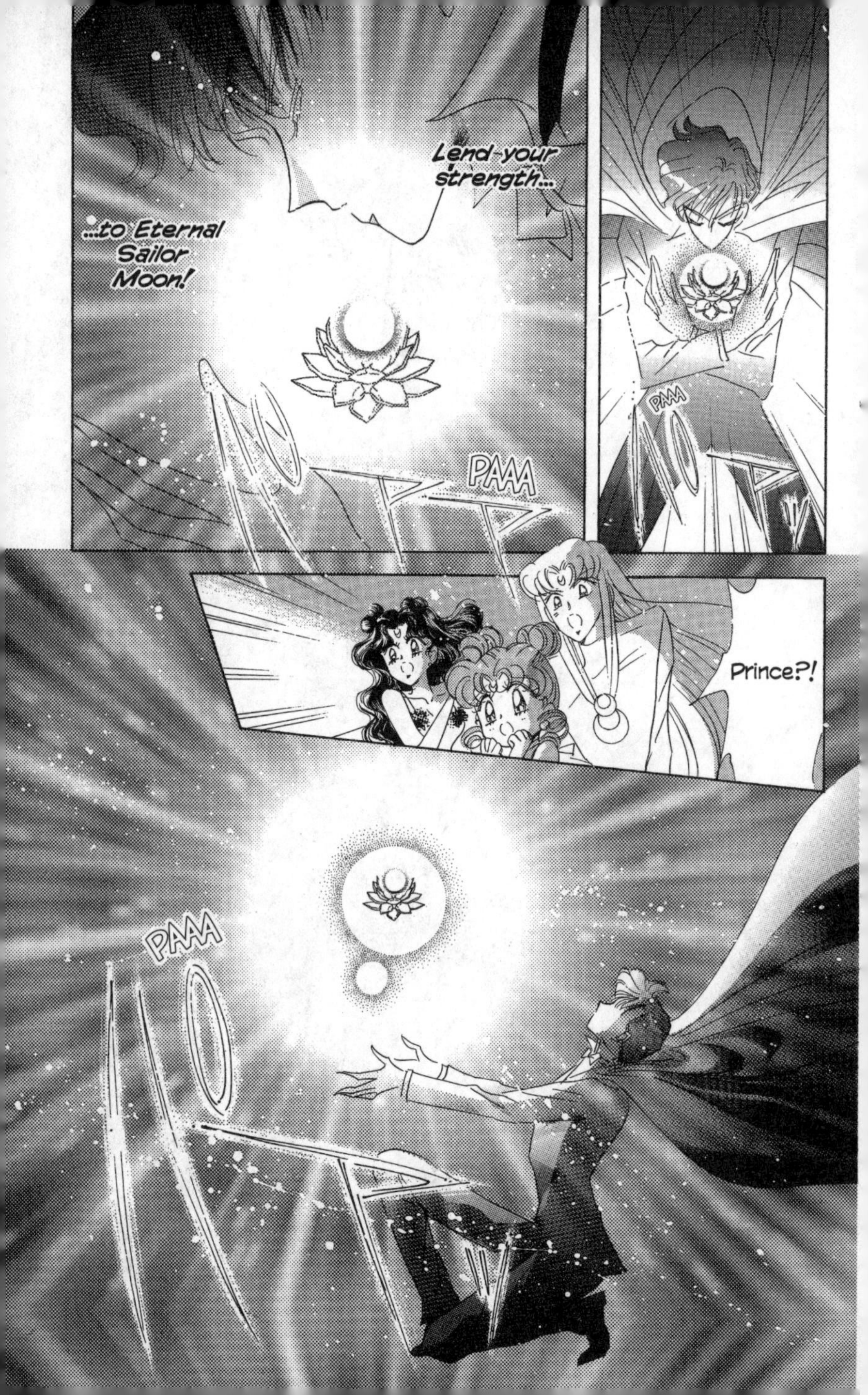
PAAA
Lend your strength...
...to Eternal Sailor Moon!
PAAA
Prince?!
PAAA

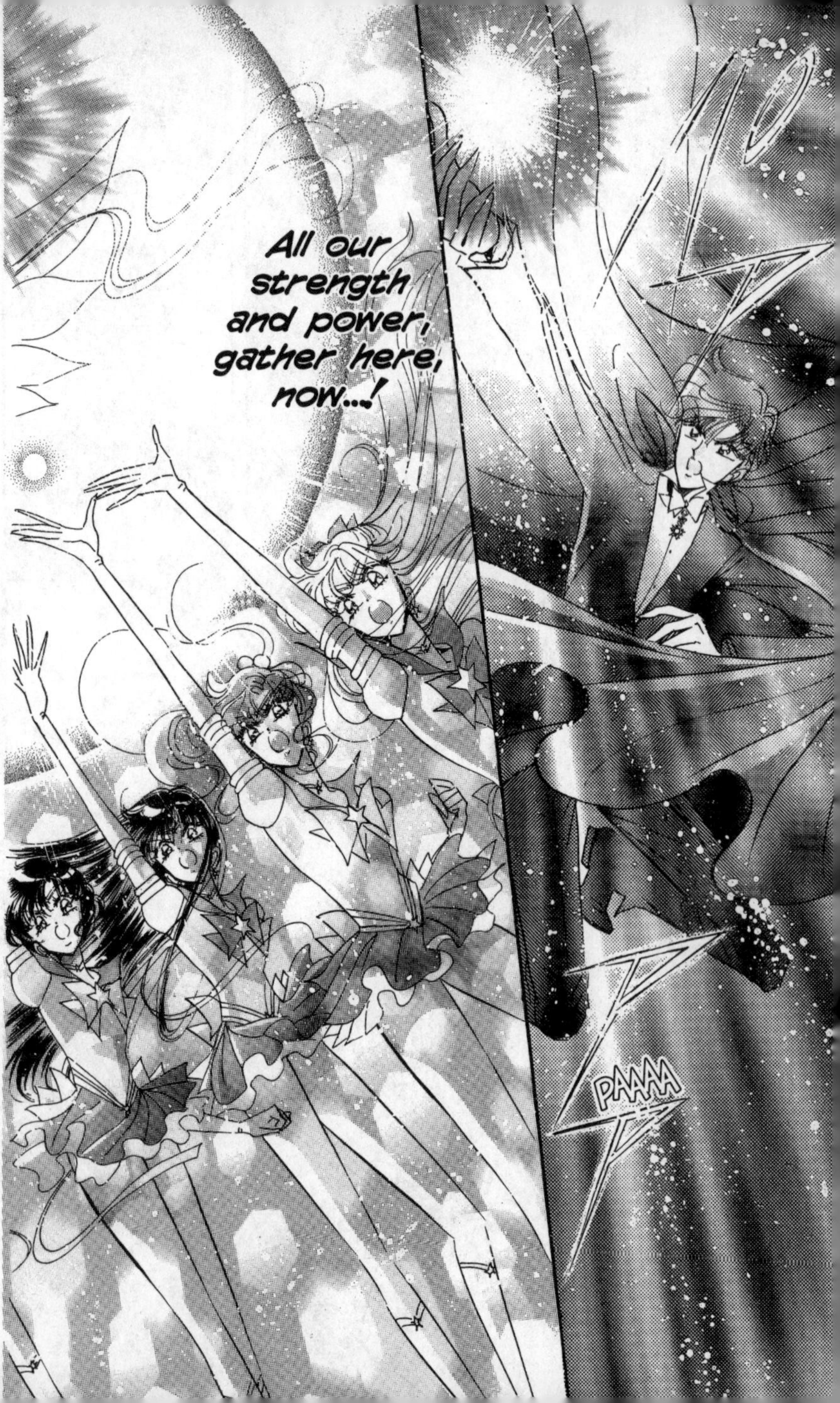
All our strength and power, gather here, now...!
PAAAA

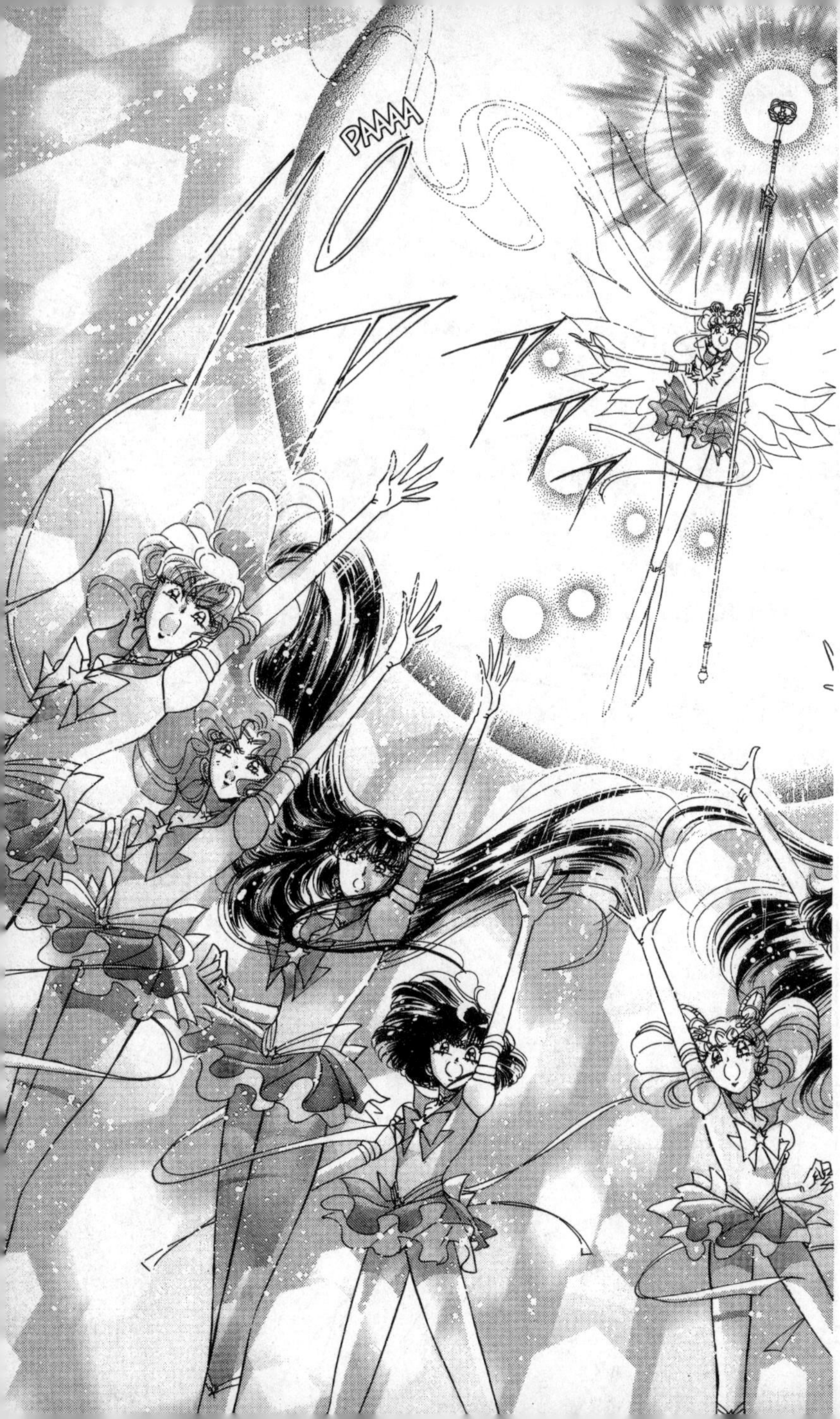
PAAAA

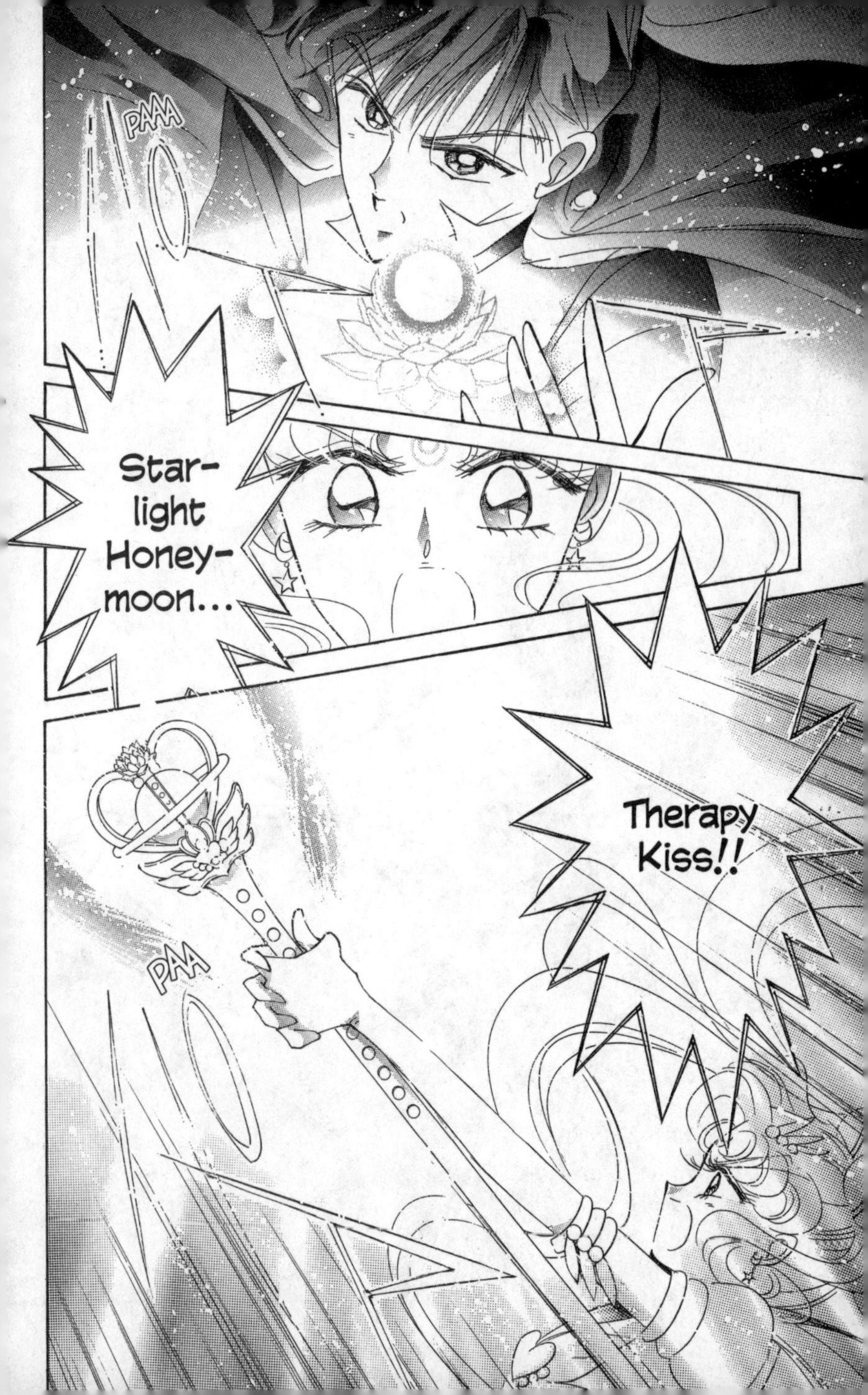
PAAA
Star-light Honey-moon...
Therapy Kiss!!
PAA

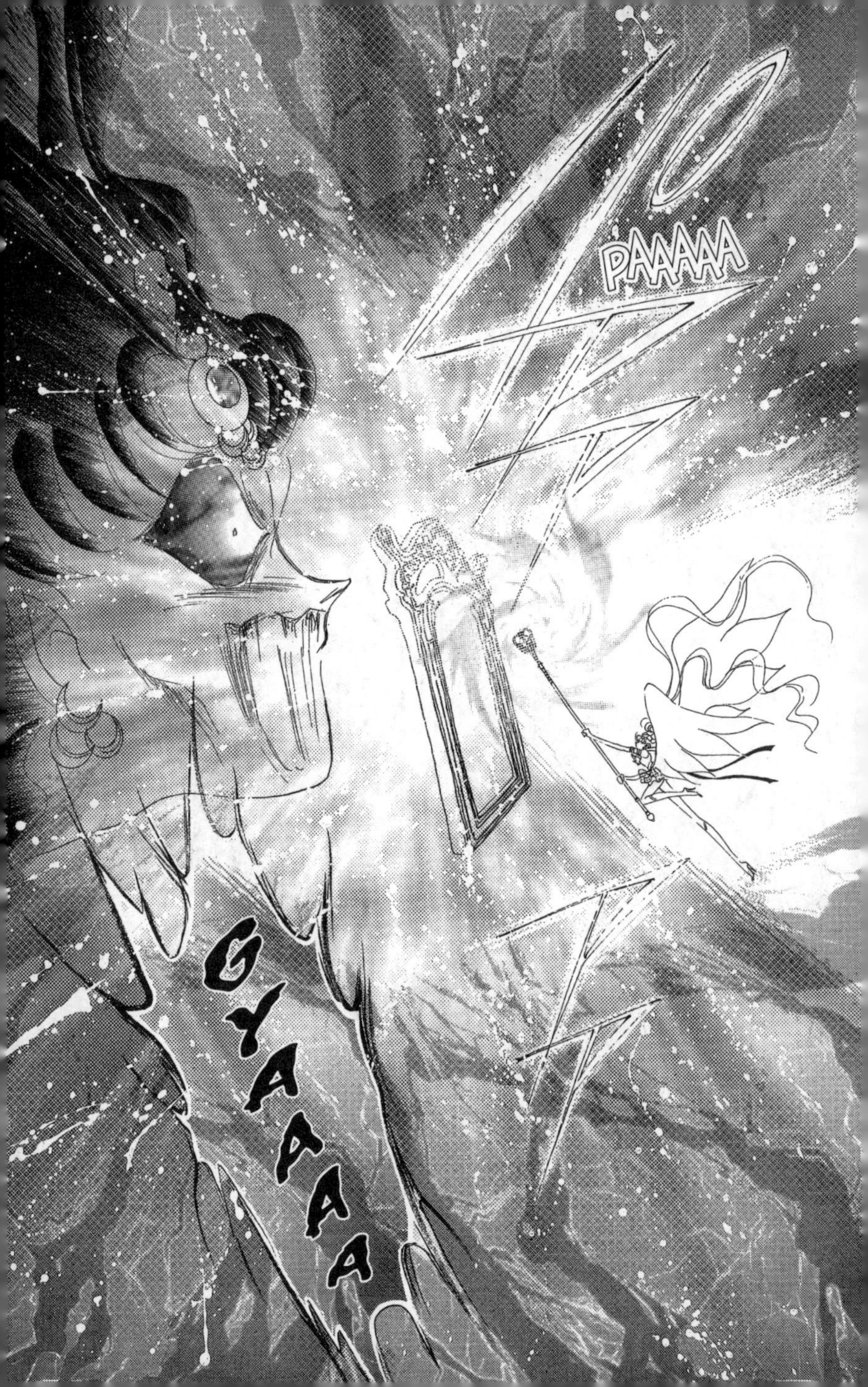
PAAAAA
GYAAAAA

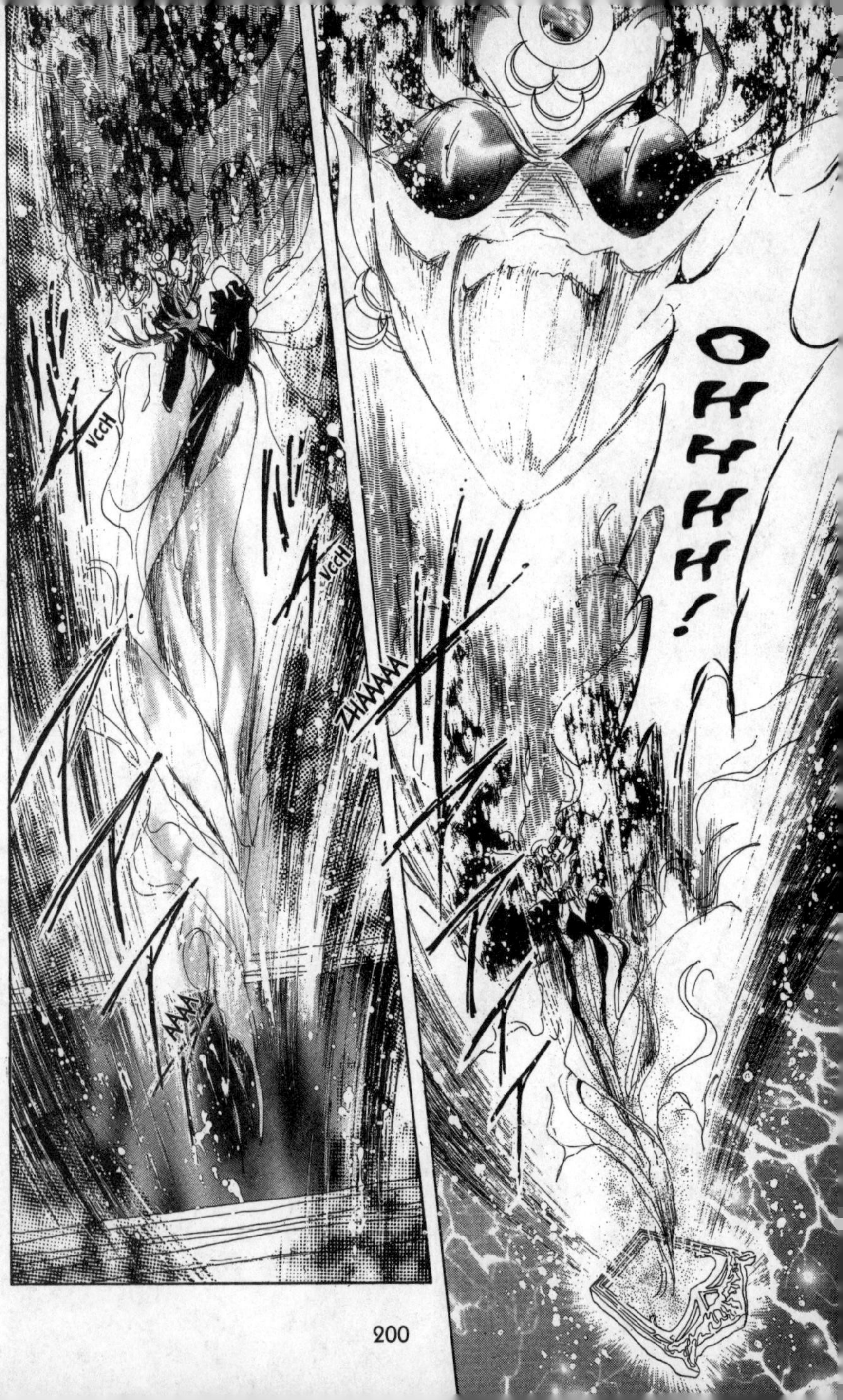
OHHHH!
ZHAAAAA
VCCH
VCCH
AAAA

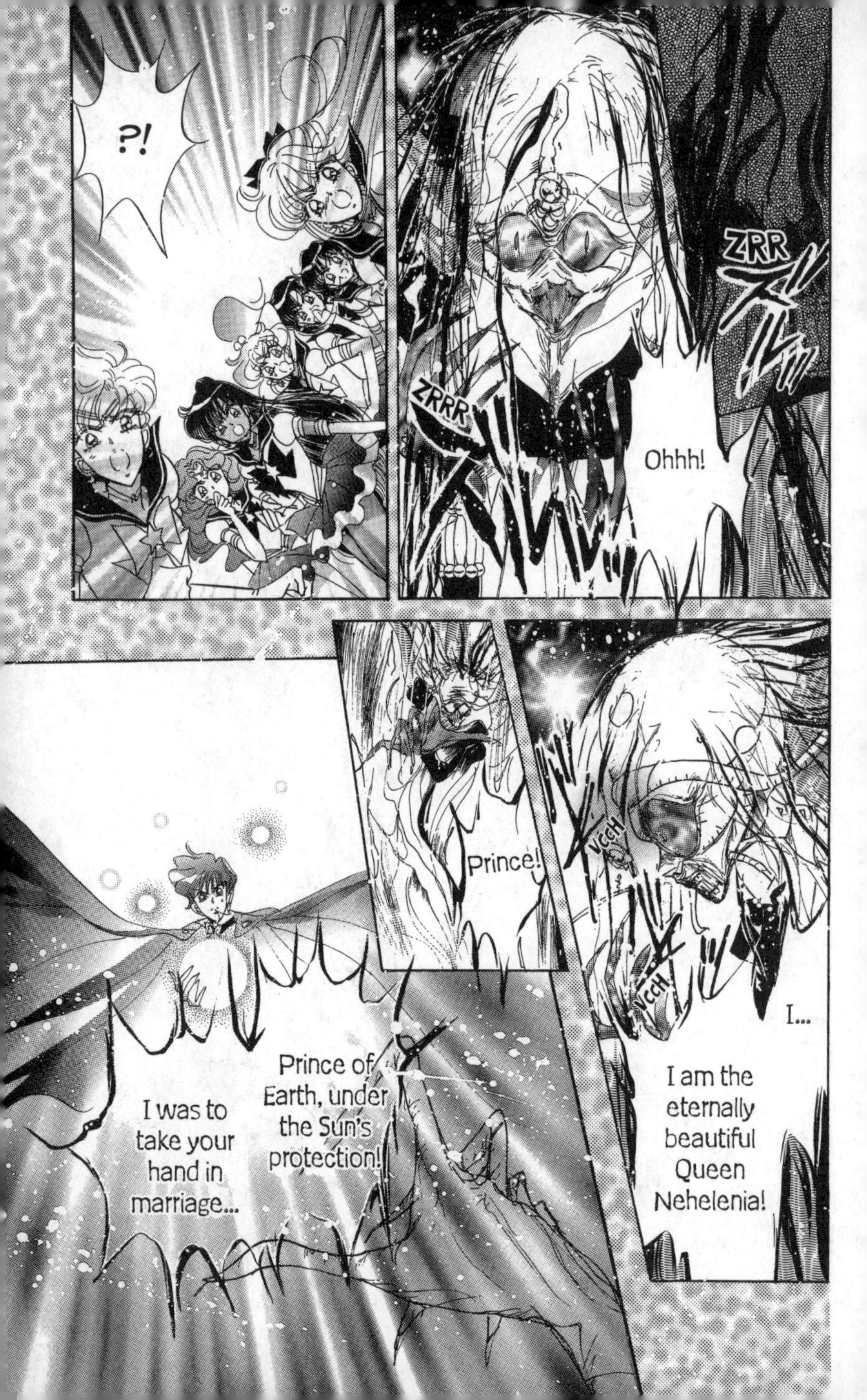
ZRR
ZRRR
Ohhh!
?!
VCCH
VCCH
I...
I am the eternally beautiful Queen Nehelenia!
Prince!
Prince of Earth, under the Sun's protection!
I was to take your hand in marriage...

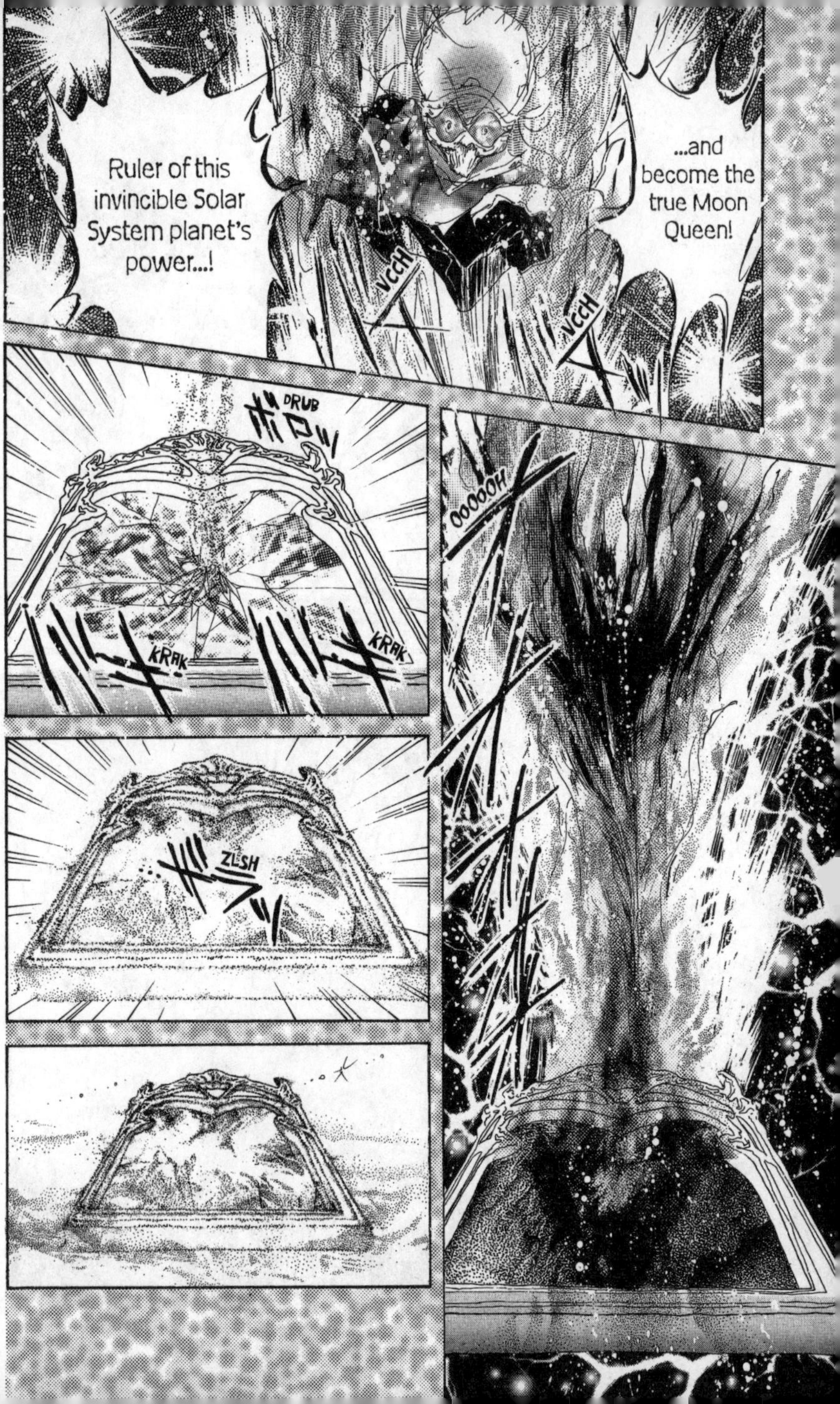
Ruler of this invincible Solar System planet's power...!
...and become the true Moon Queen!
VCCH
VCCH
OOOOOOH
DRUB
KRAK
KRAK
ZLSH

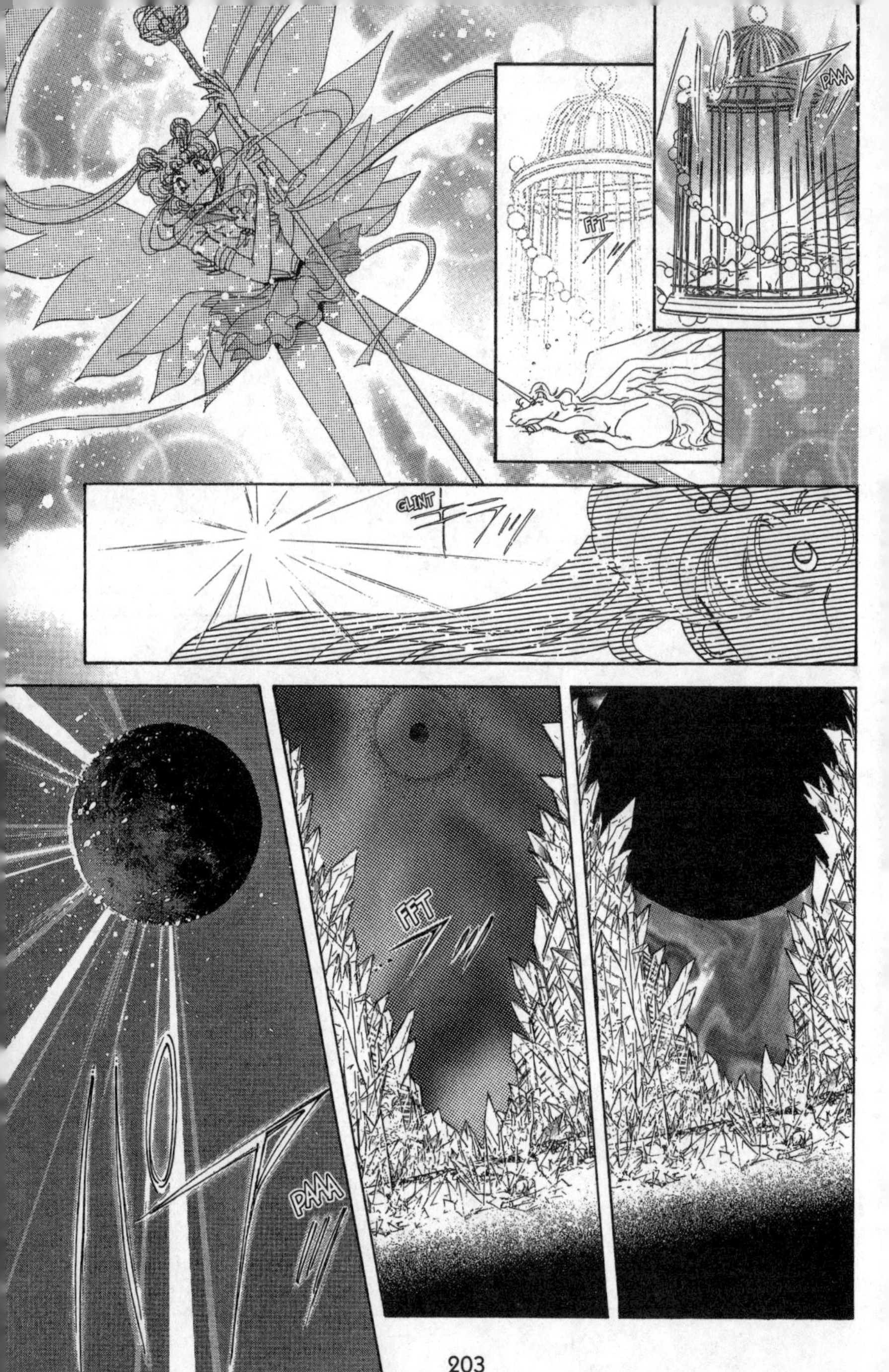
PAAA
FFT
GLINT
FFT
PAAA

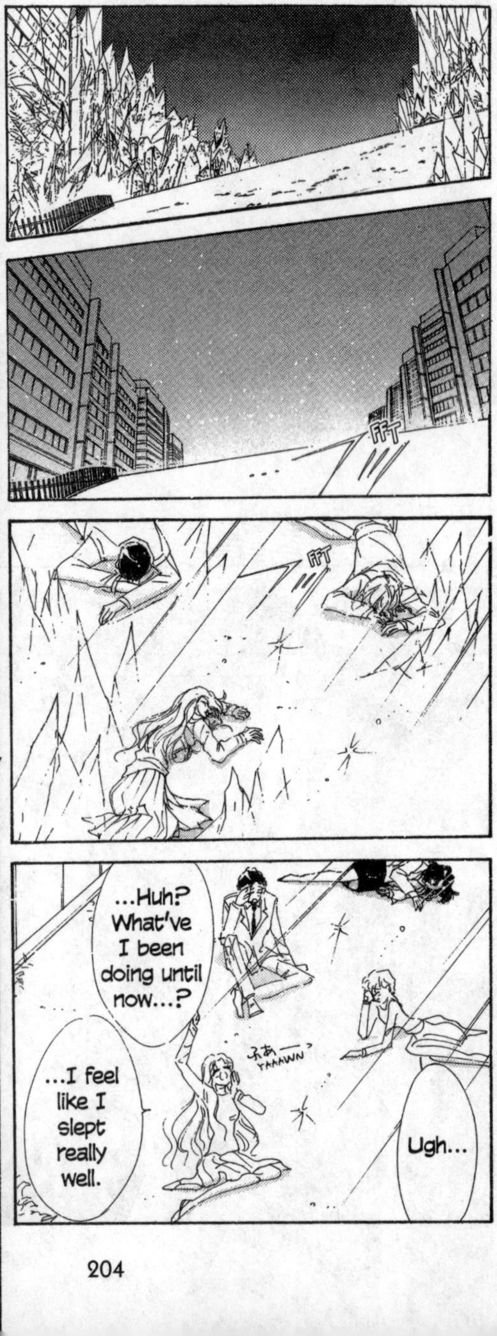
FFT
FFT
...Huh? What've I been doing until now...?
Ugh...
ふあー YAAAWN
...I feel like I slept really well.
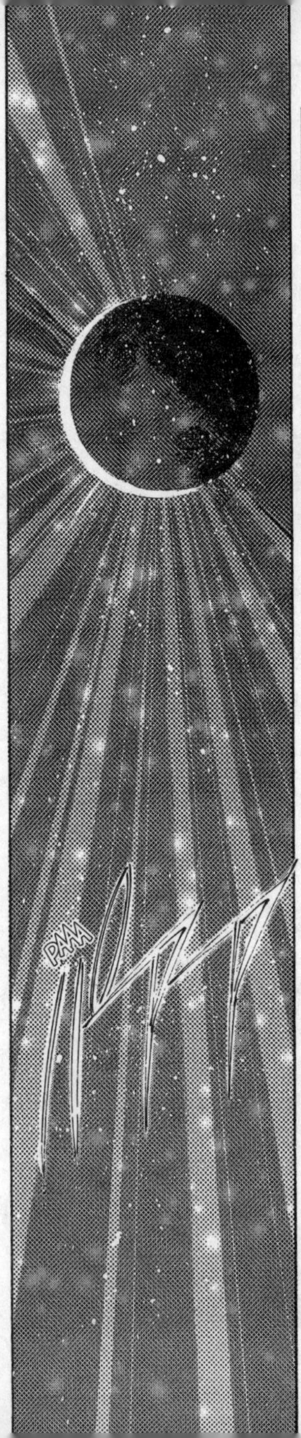
PAAA

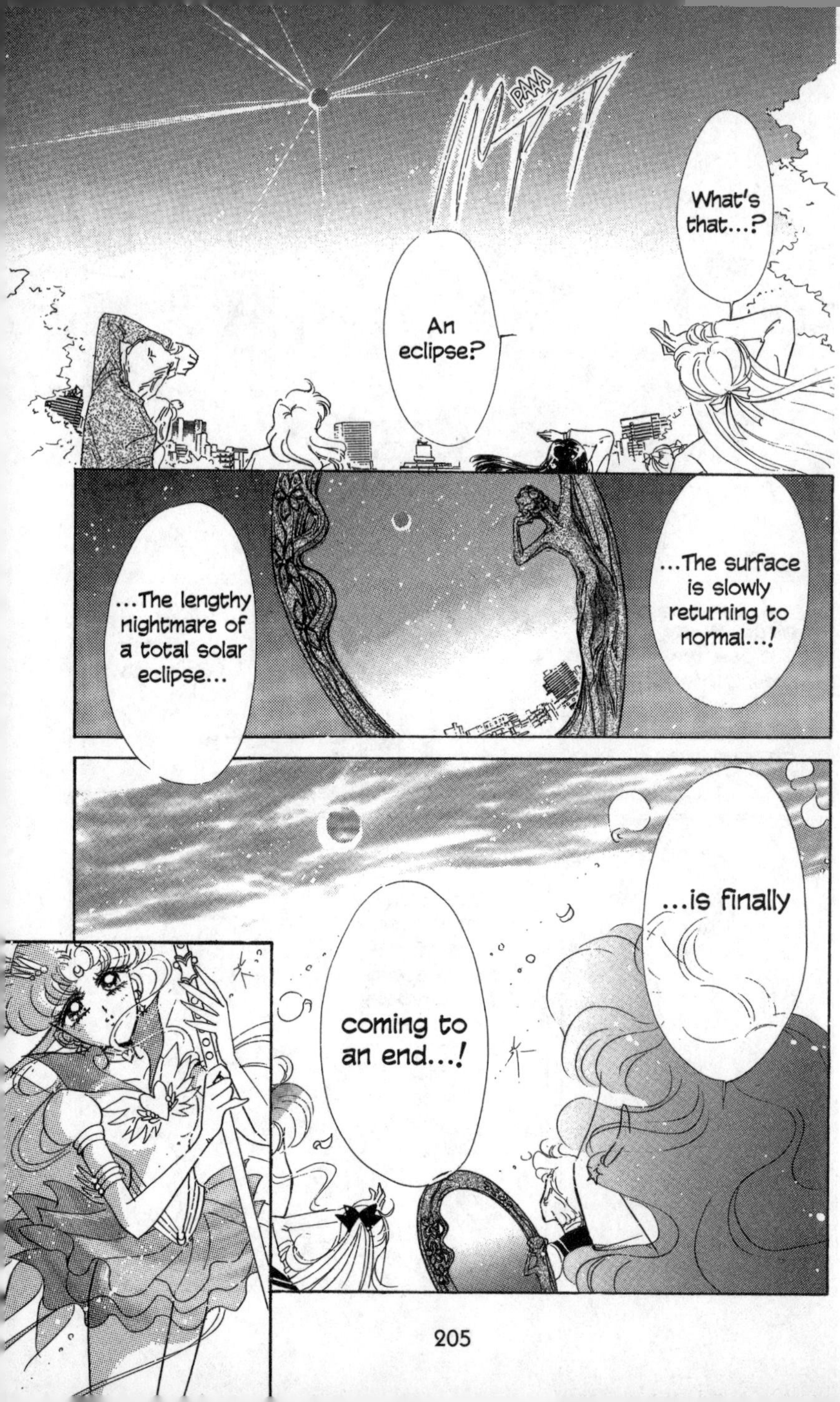
PAAA
What's that...?
An eclipse?
...The surface is slowly returning to normal...!
...The lengthy nightmare of a total solar eclipse...
...is finally
coming to an end...!

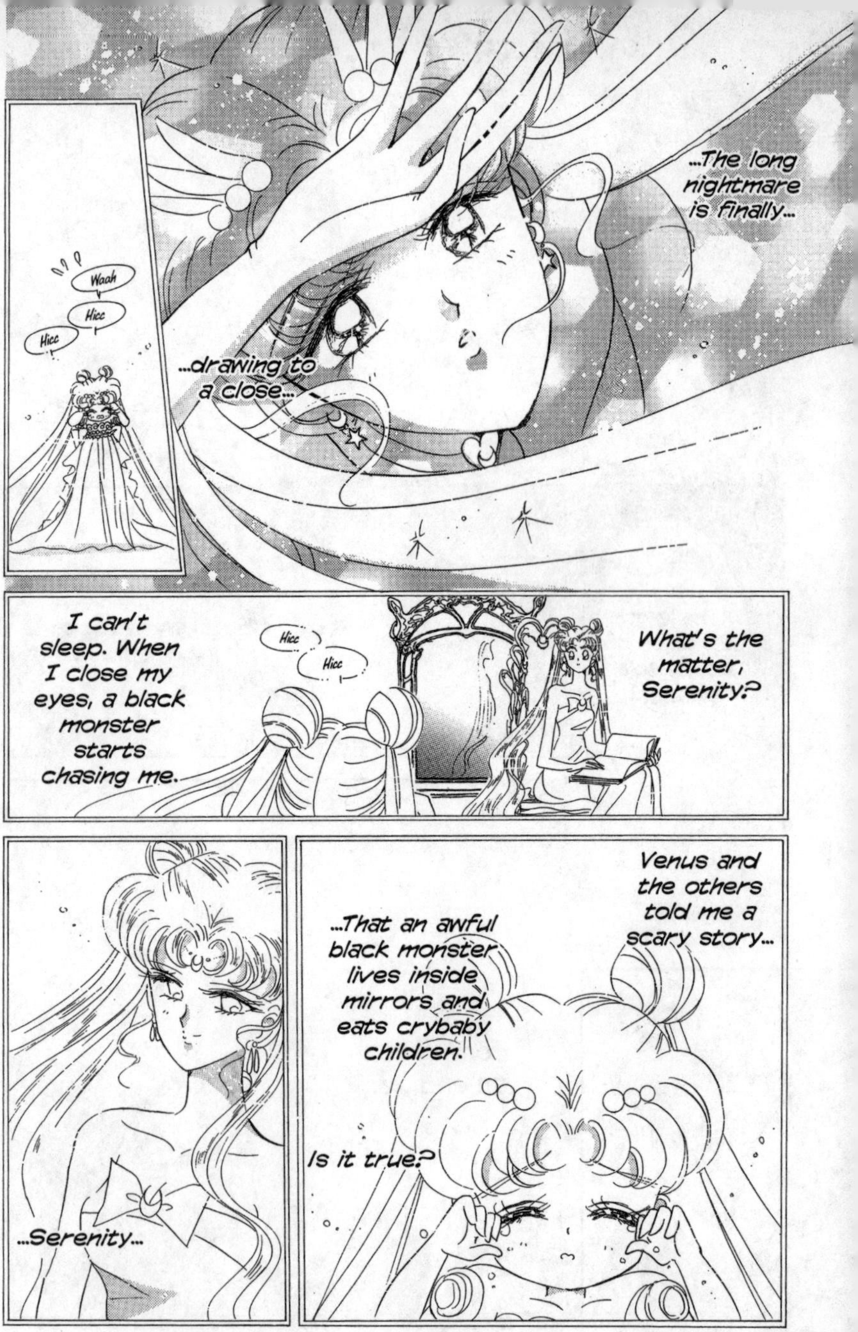
...The long nightmare is finally...
...drawing to a close...
Waah
Hicc
Hicc
What's the matter, Serenity?
Hicc
Hicc
I can't sleep. When I close my eyes, a black monster starts chasing me.
Venus and the others told me a scary story...
...That an awful black monster lives inside mirrors and eats crybaby children.
Is it true?
...Serenity...

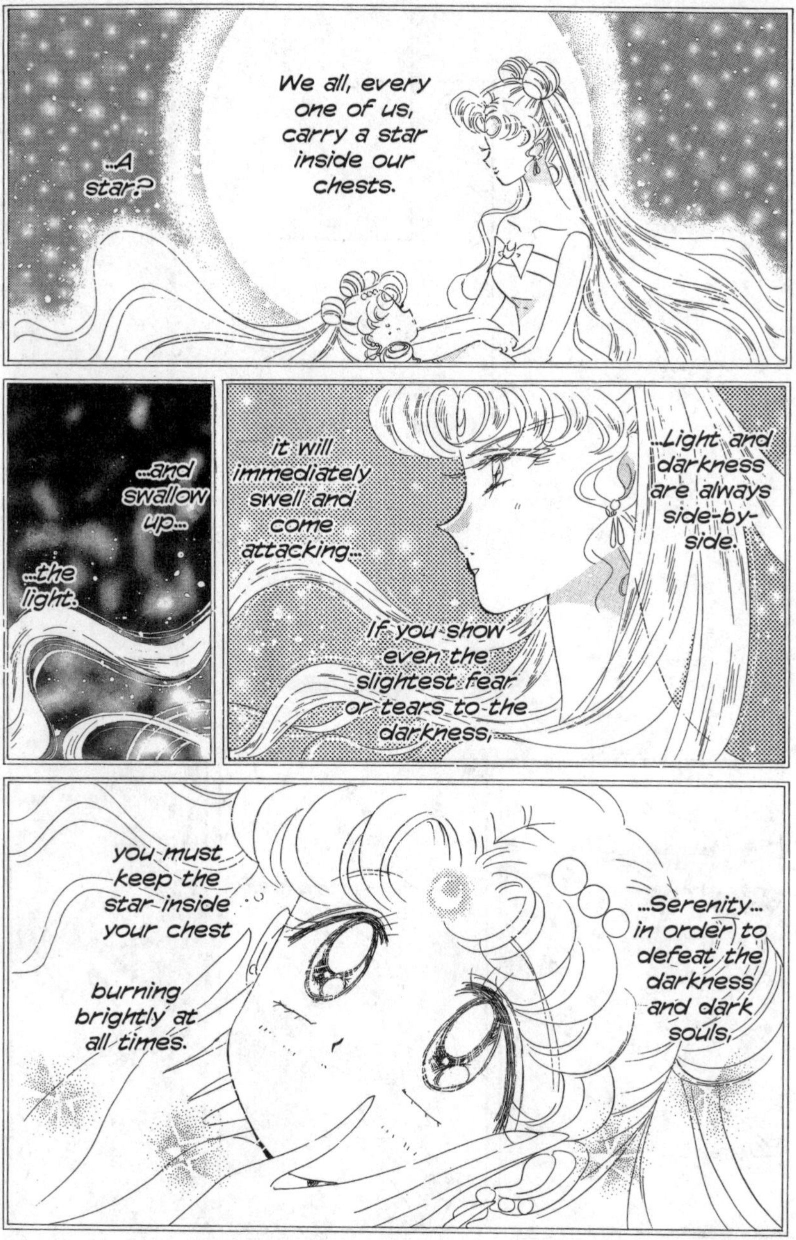
We all, every one of us, carry a star inside our chests.
...A star?
...Light and darkness are always side-by-side.
If you show even the slightest fear or tears to the darkness,
it will immediately swell and come attacking...
...and swallow up...
...the light.
...Serenity... in order to defeat the darkness and dark souls,
you must keep the star inside your chest
burning brightly at all times.

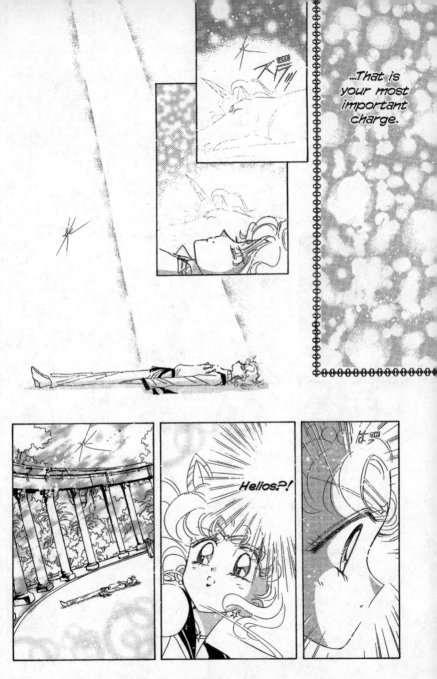

...That is your most important charge.

Helios?!

208

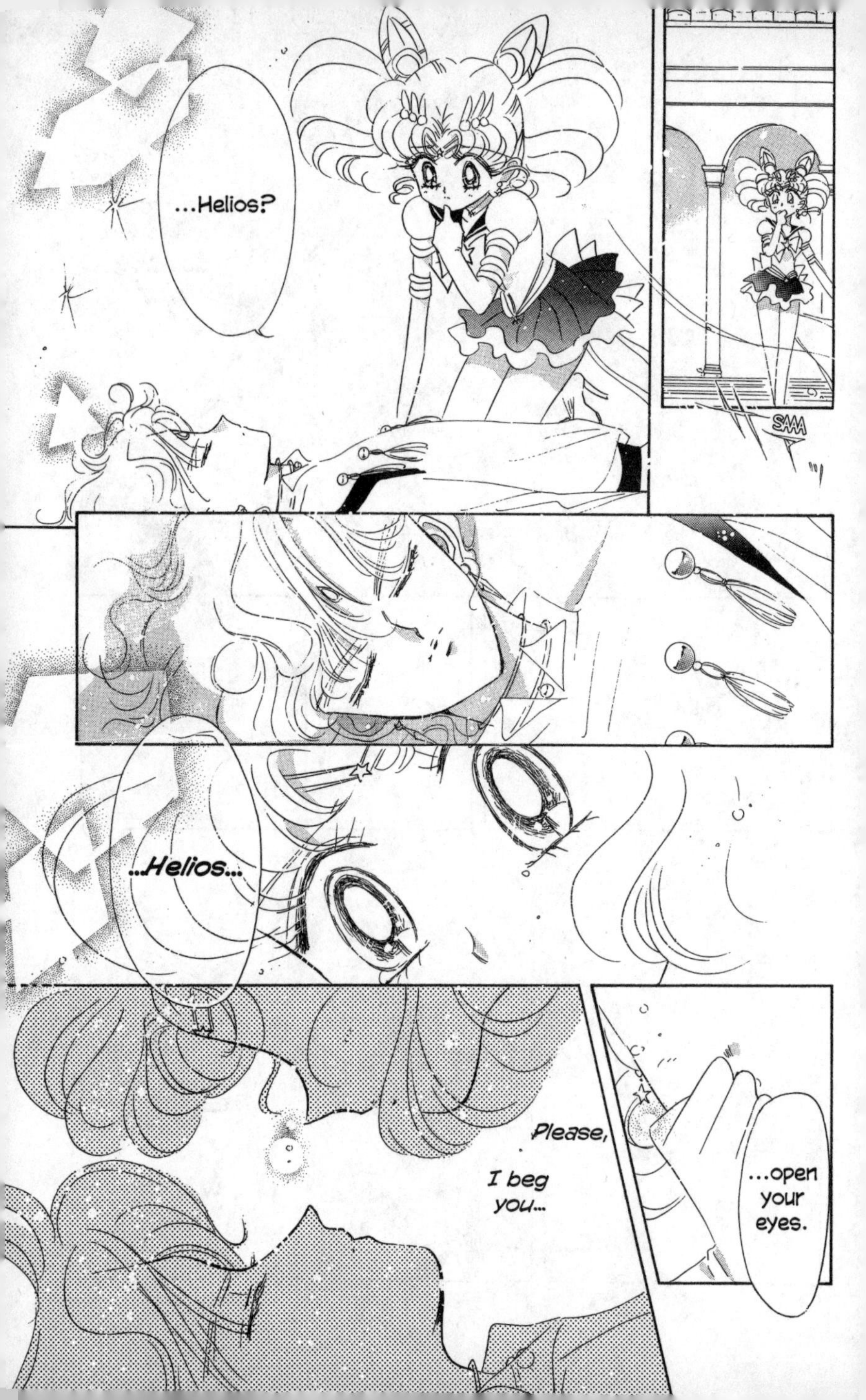
SAAA
...Helios?
..Helios...
...open your eyes.
Please,
I beg you...

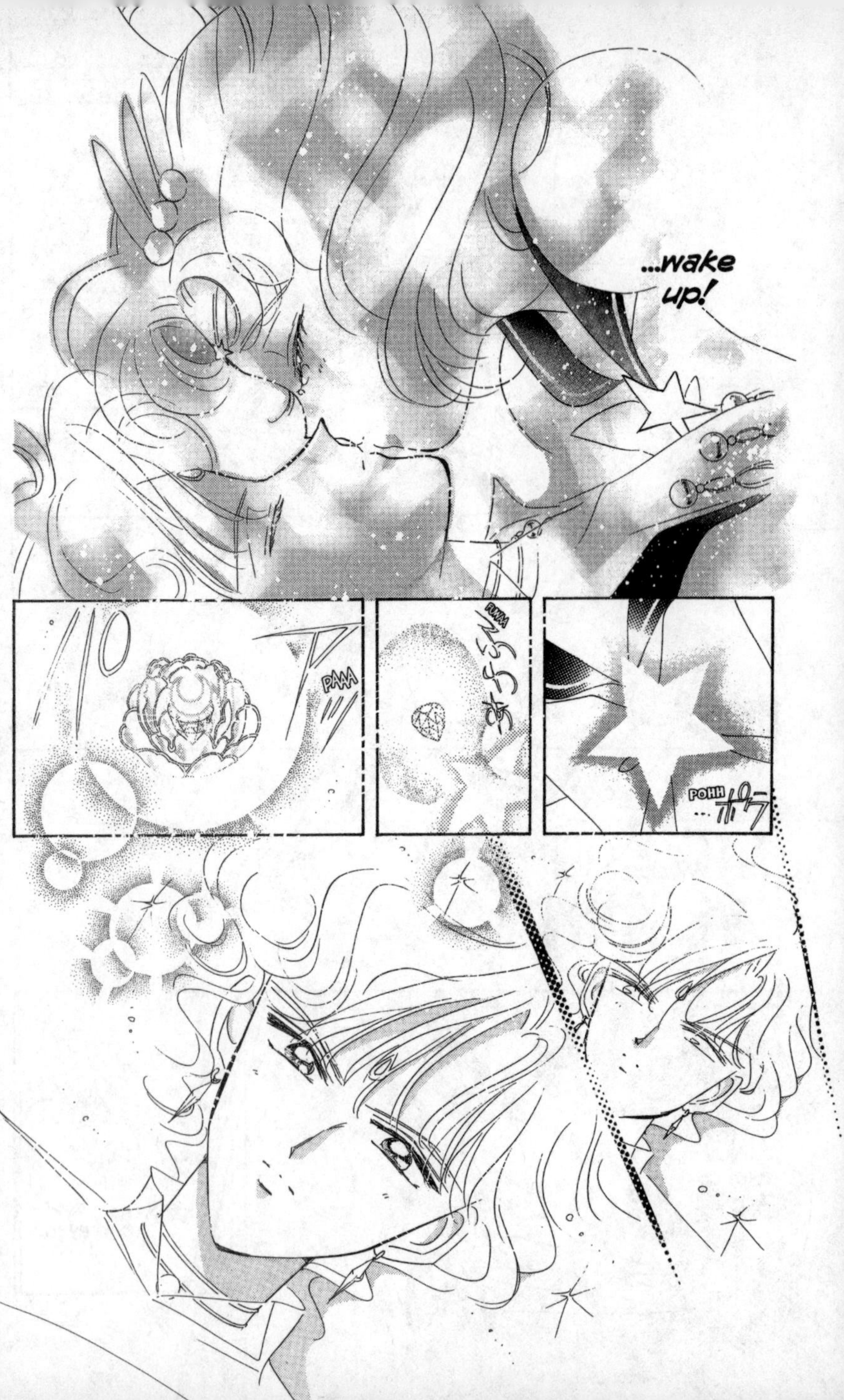
...wake up!
POHH
FUWA
PAAA

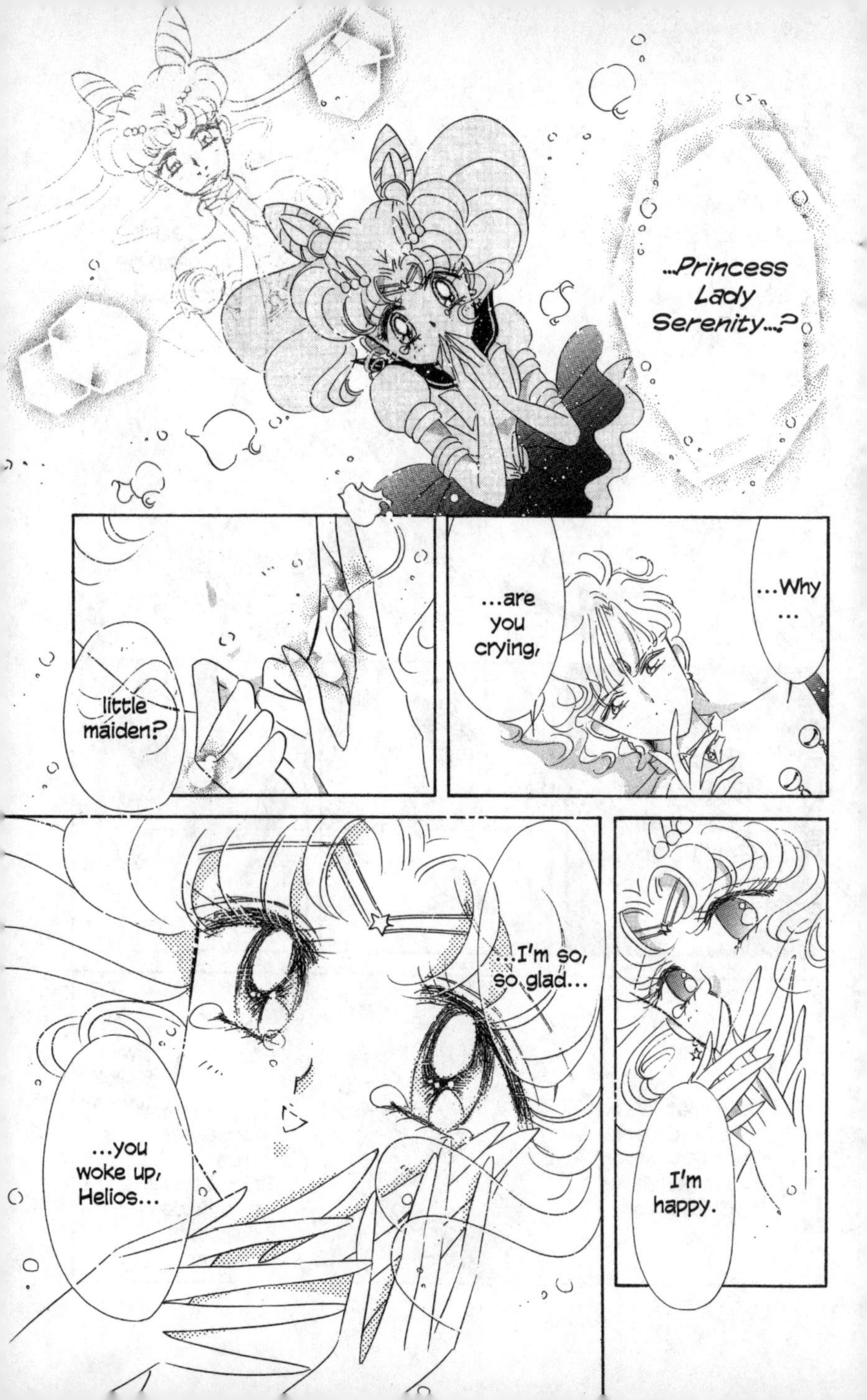
...Princess Lady Serenity...?
...Why ...
...are you crying,
little maiden?
I'm happy.
...I'm so, so glad...
...you woke up, Helios...

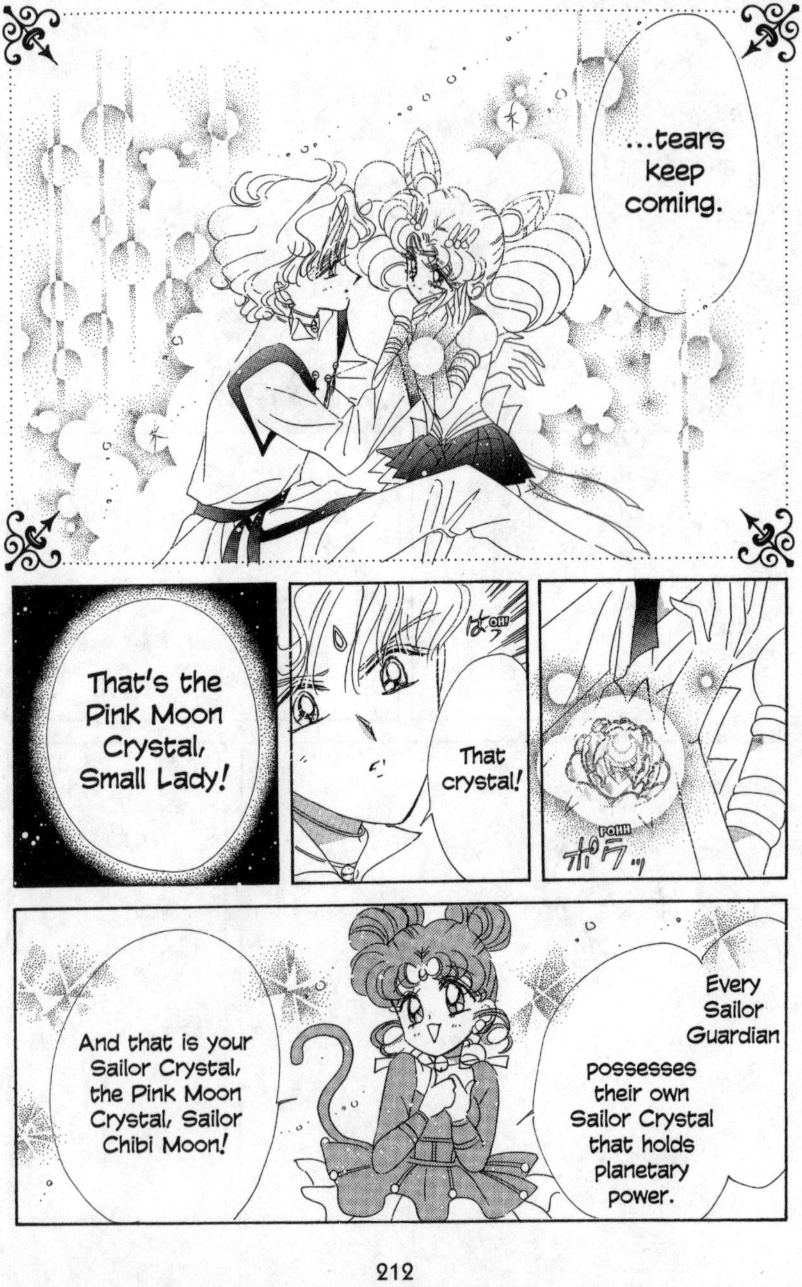
...tears keep coming.
POHN
OH!
That crystal!
That's the Pink Moon Crystal, Small Lady!
Every Sailor Guardian possesses their own Sailor Crystal that holds planetary power.
And that is your Sailor Crystal, the Pink Moon Crystal, Sailor Chibi Moon!

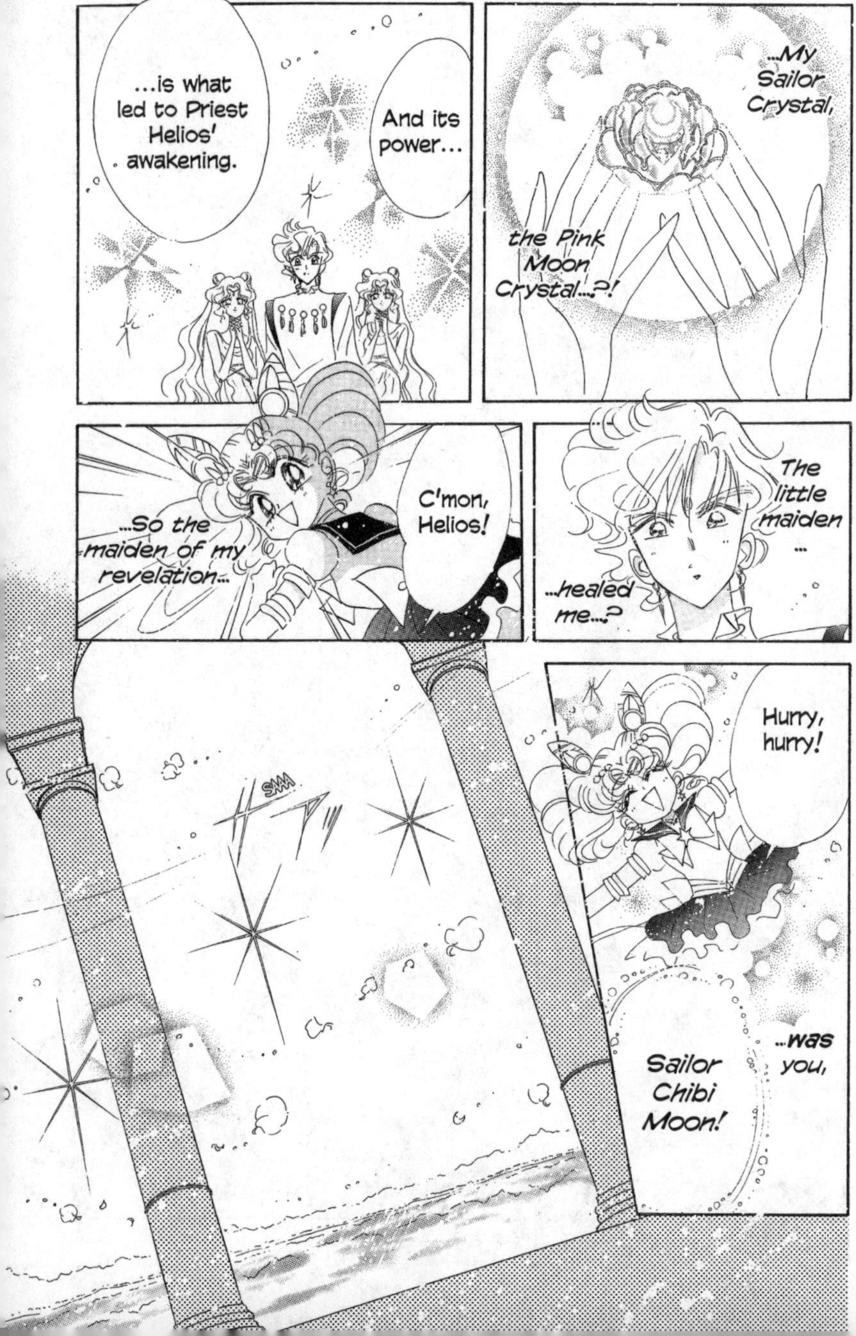
...My Sailor Crystal,
the Pink Moon Crystal...?!
And its power...
...is what led to Priest Helios' awakening.
The little maiden ...
...healed me...?
C'mon, Helios!
...So the maiden of my revelation...
Hurry, hurry!
...was you,
Sailor Chibi Moon!
SAAA

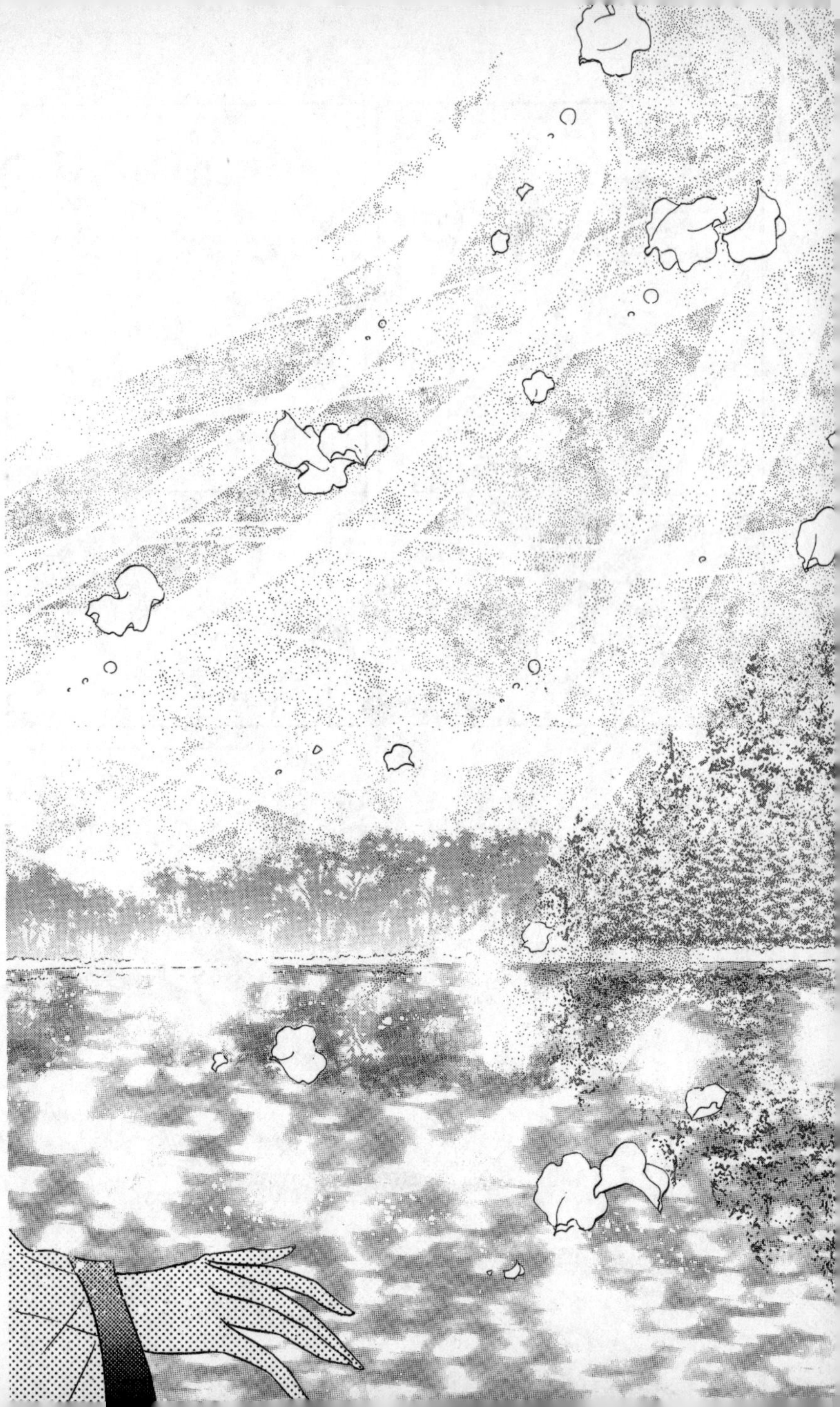

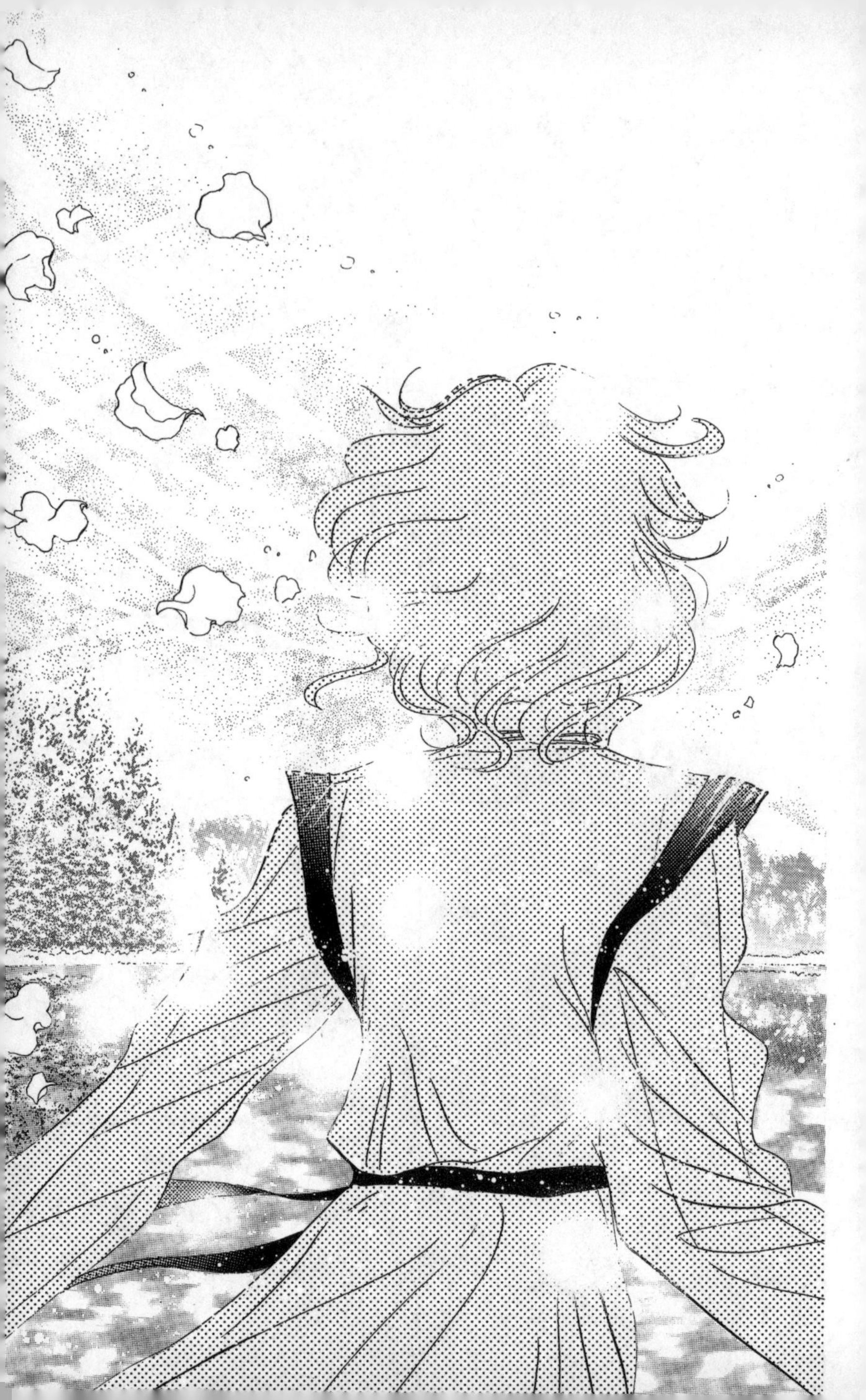

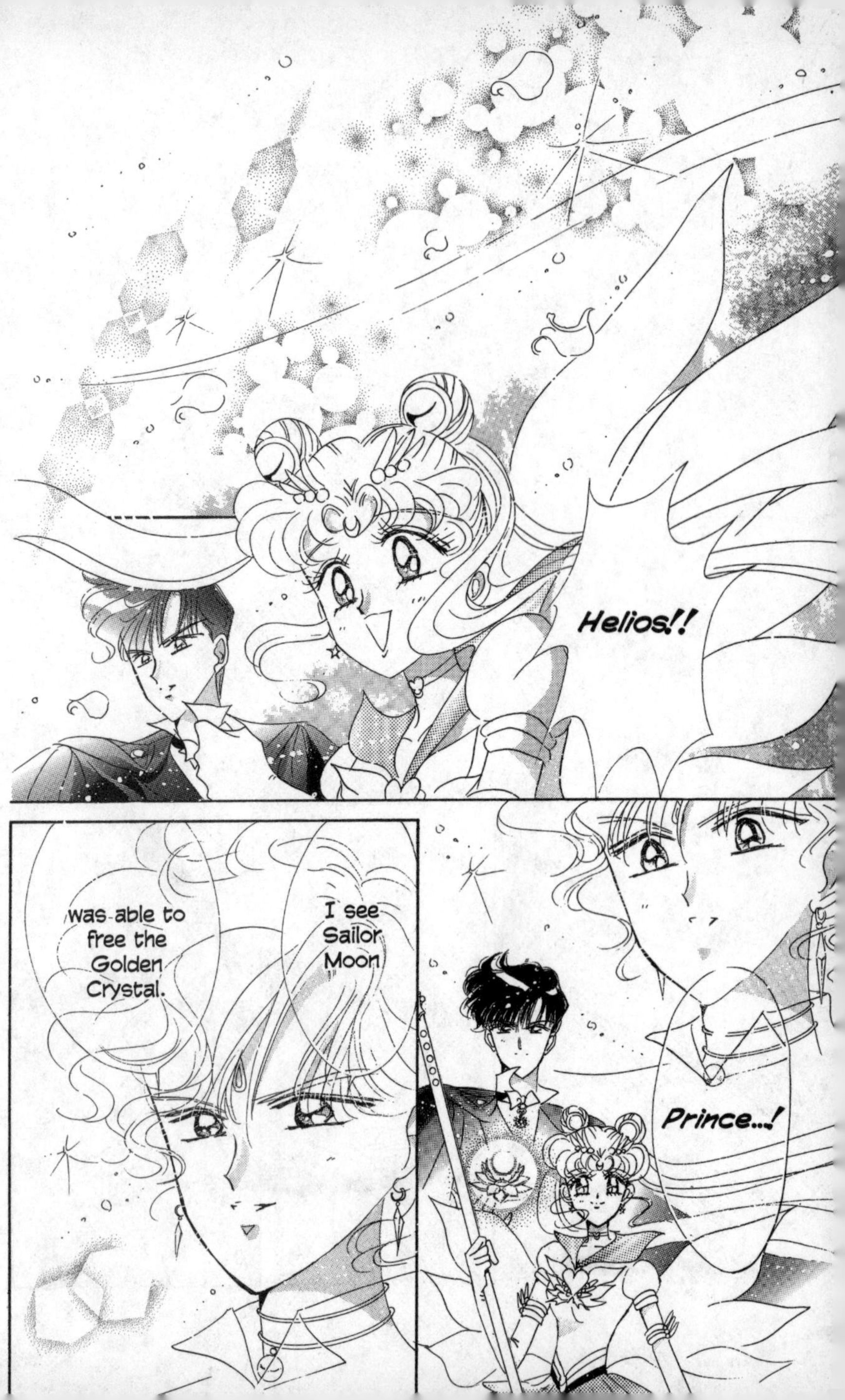
Helios!!
Prince...!
I see Sailor Moon
was able to free the Golden Crystal.

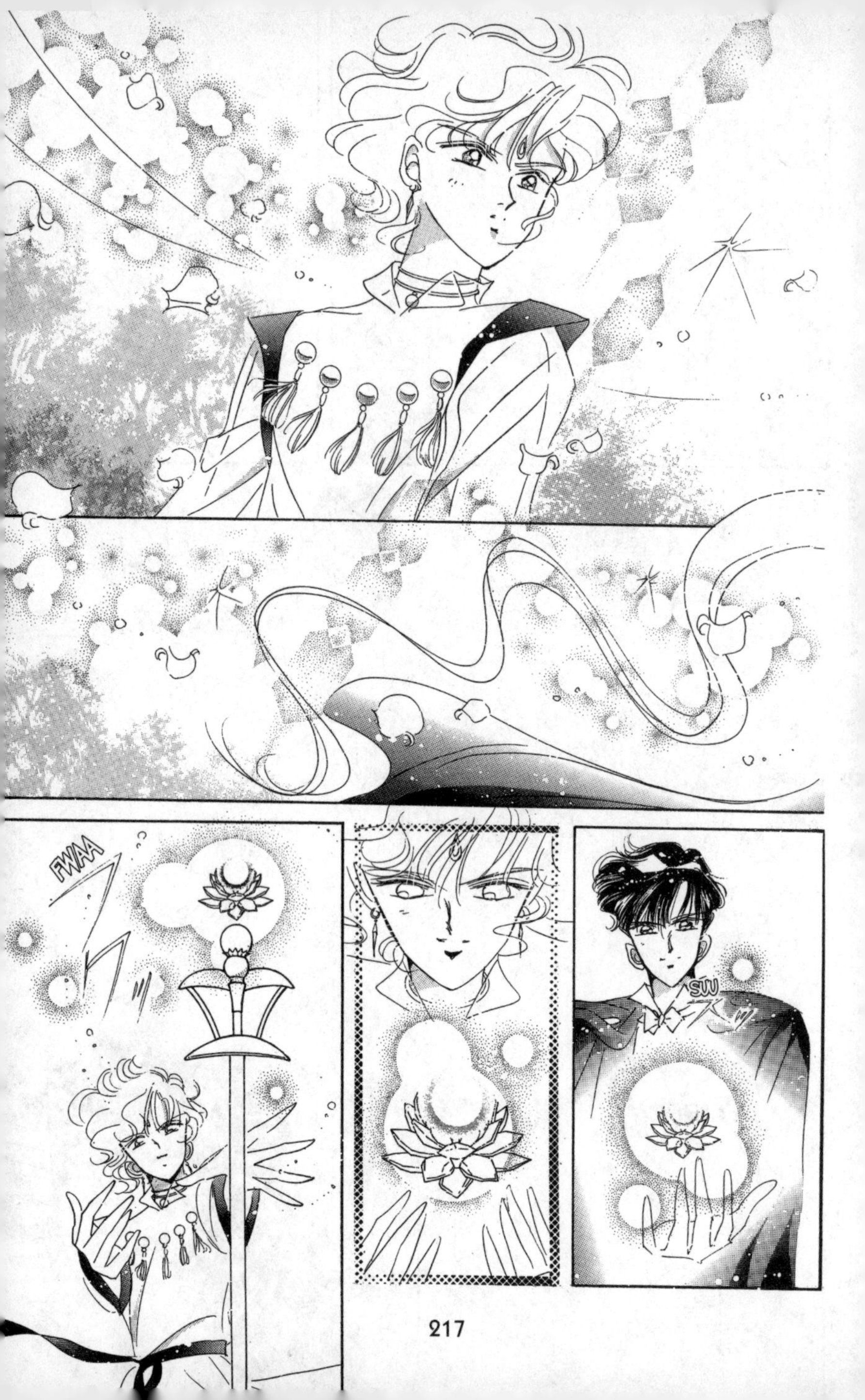
SUU
FWAA

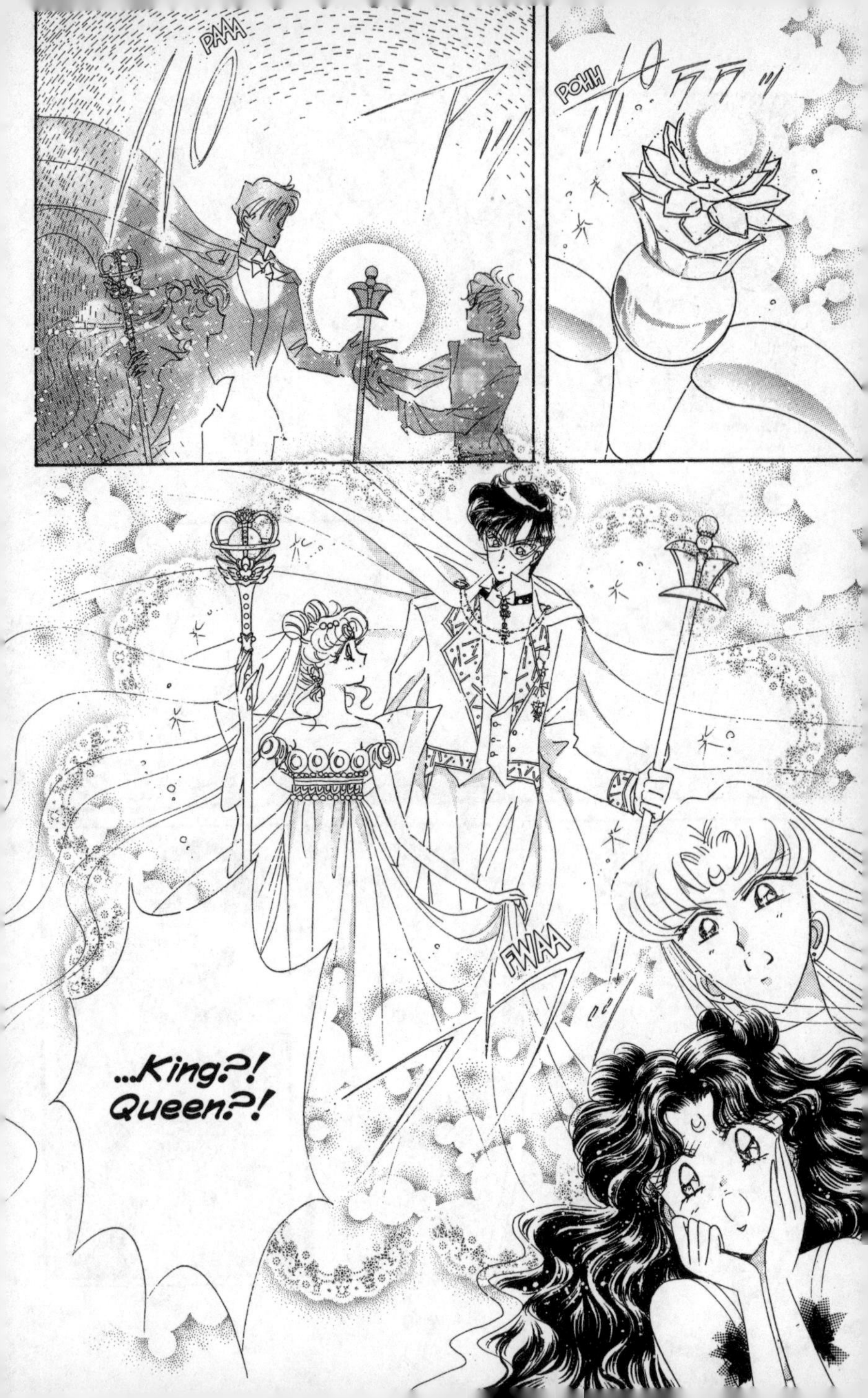
POHH
PAAA
FWAA
...King?!
Queen?!

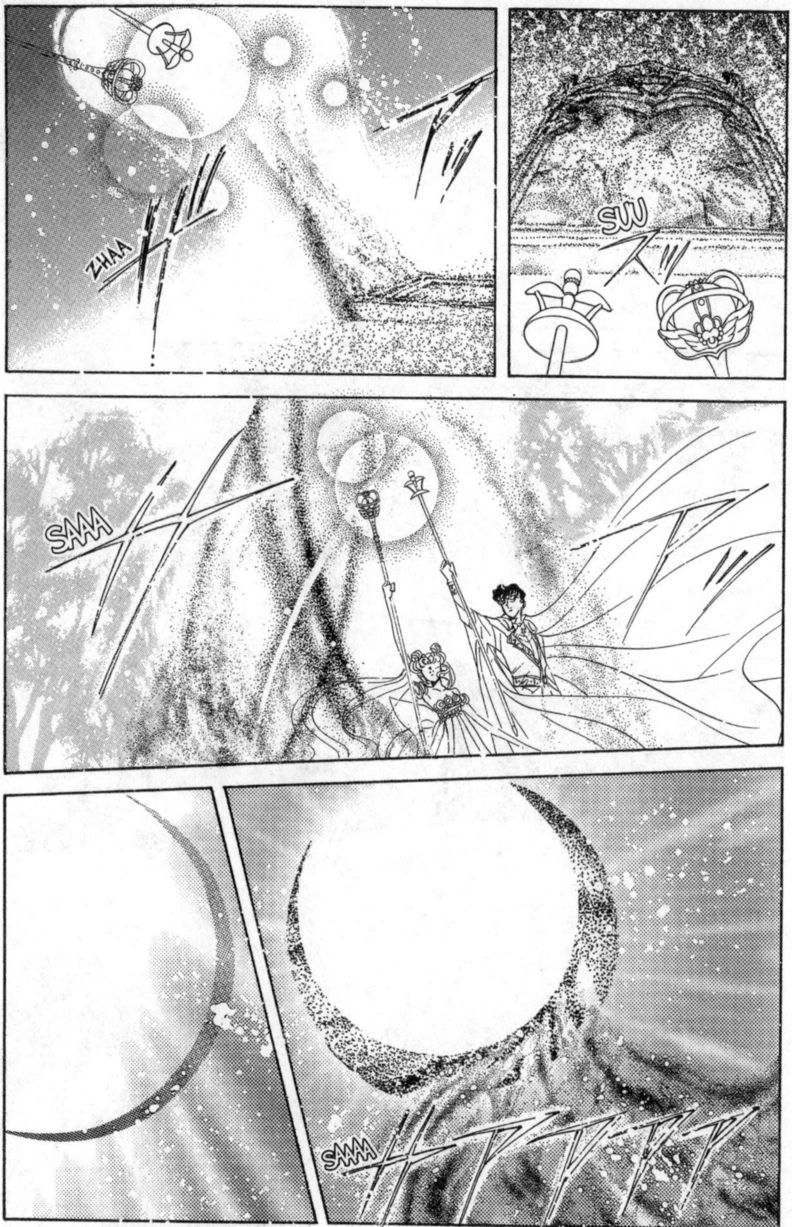
SUU
ZHAA
SAAA
SAAA

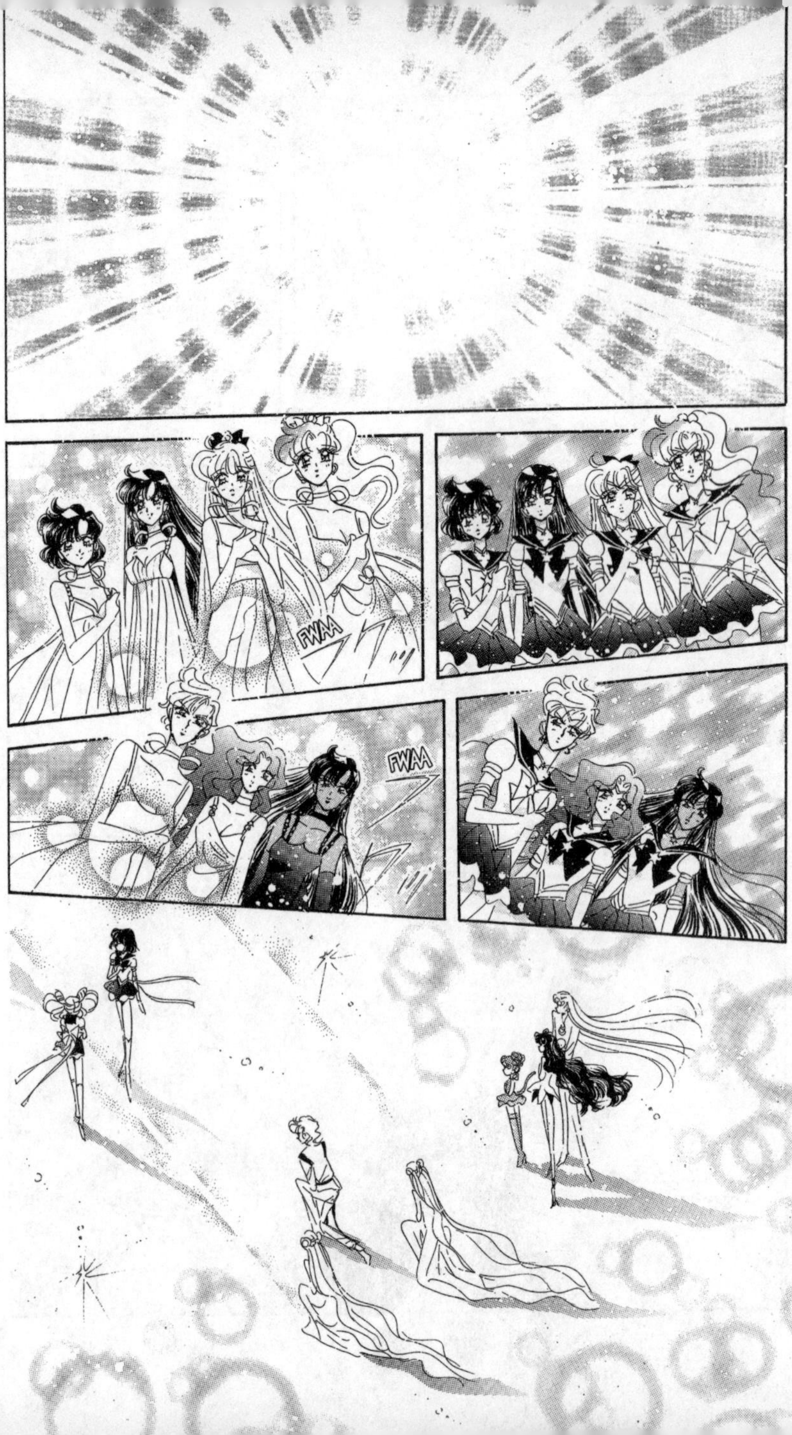
FWAA
FWAA

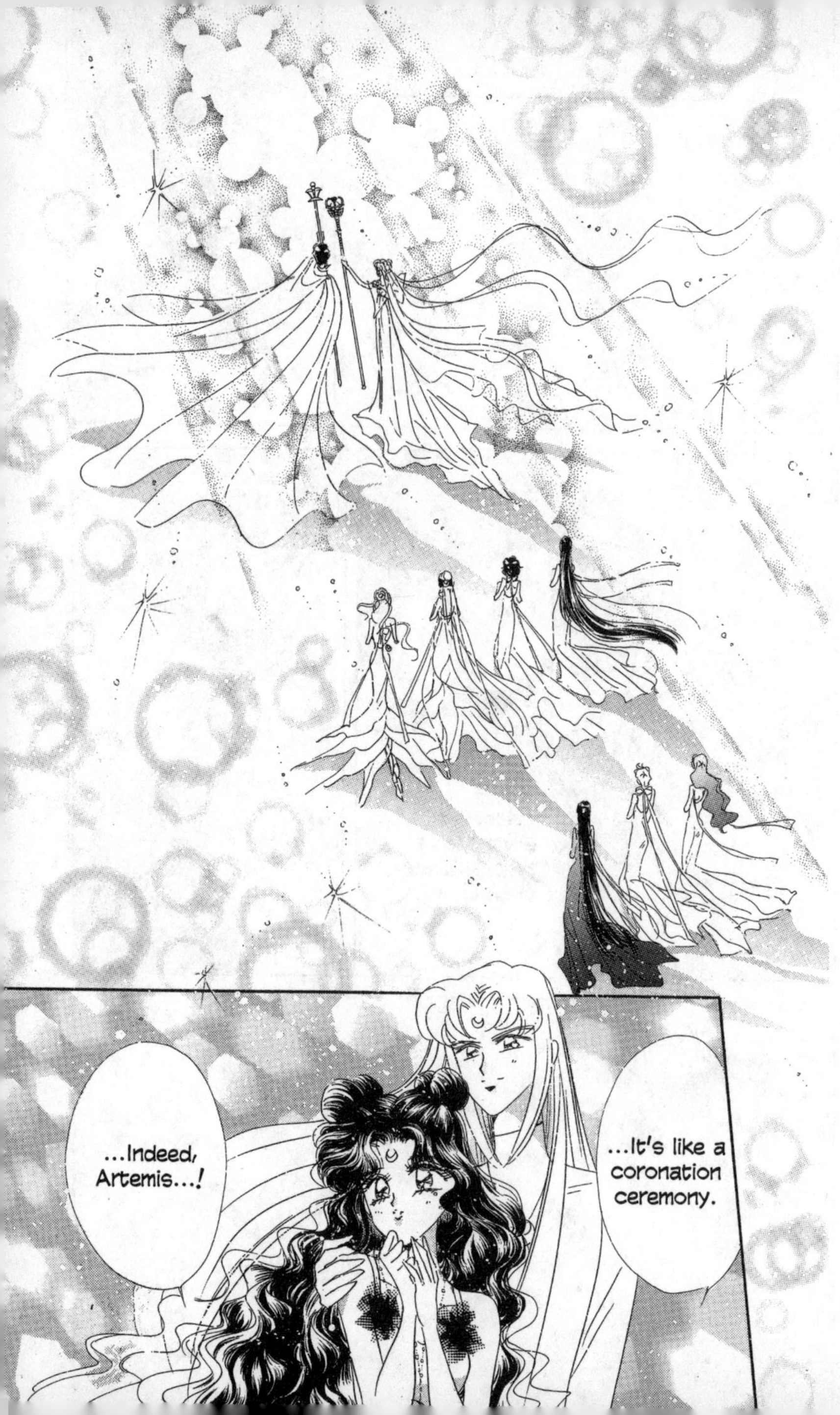
...It's like a coronation ceremony.
...Indeed, Artemis...!

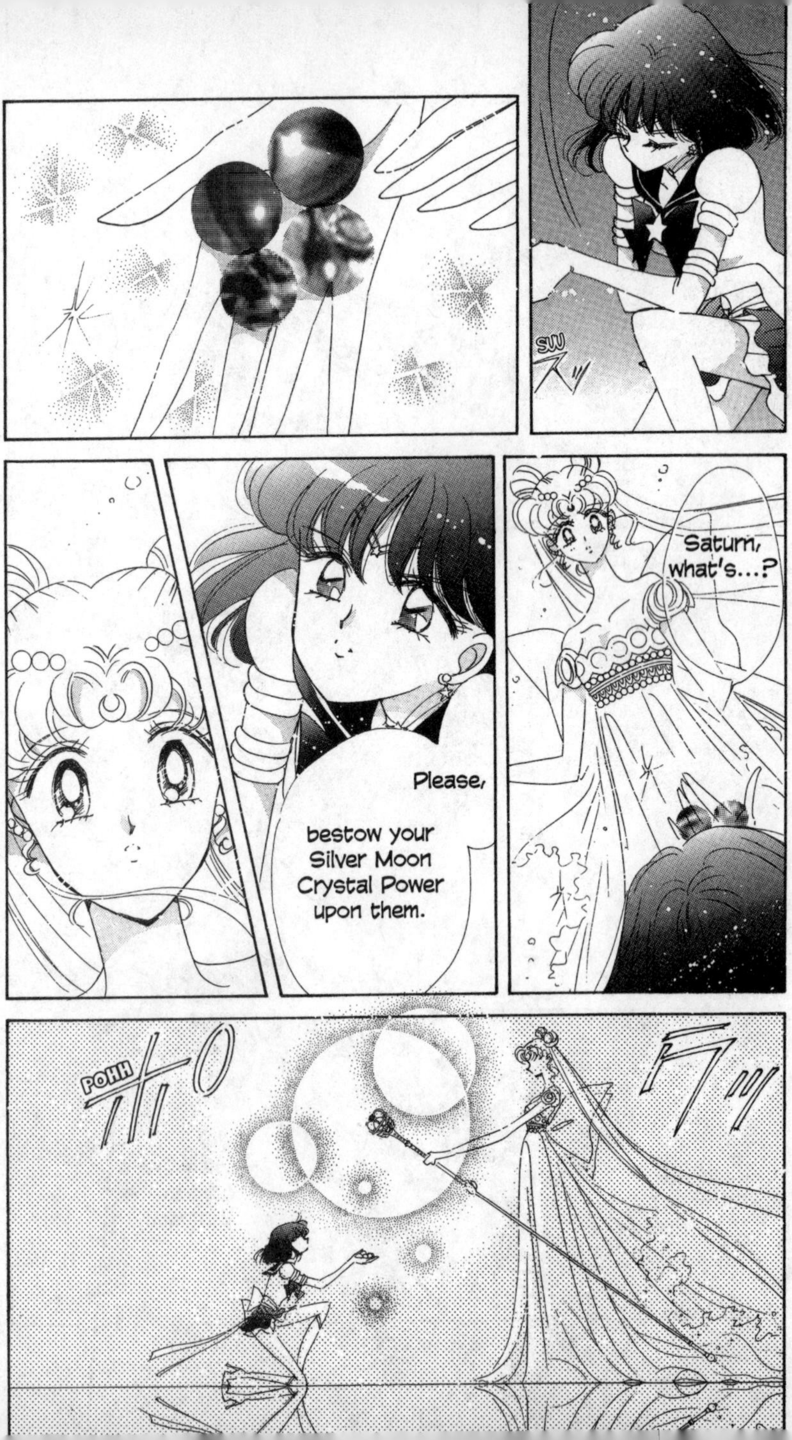
SUU
Saturn, what's...?
Please,
bestow your Silver Moon Crystal Power upon them.
POHH

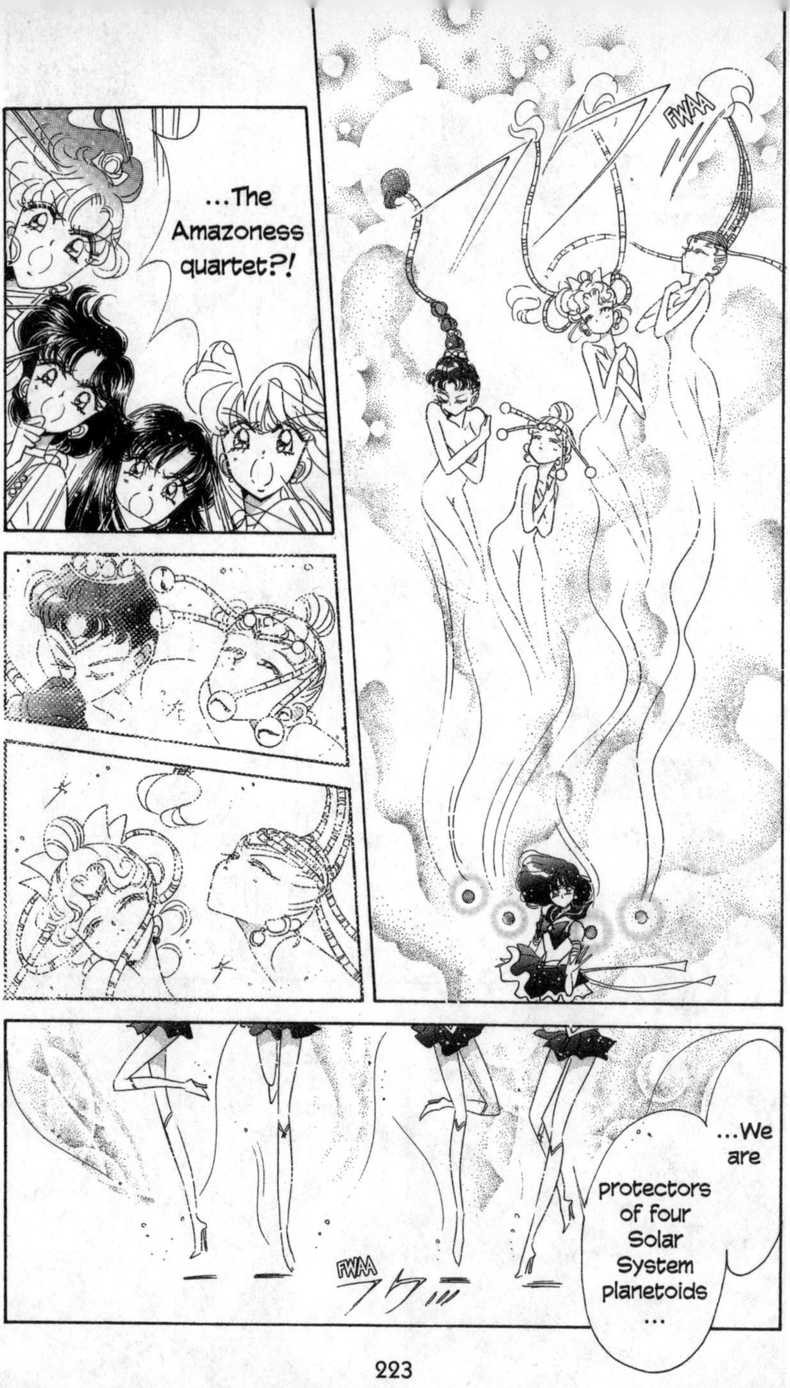
FWAA
...The Amazoness quartet?!
...We are protectors of four Solar System planetoids ...
FWAA

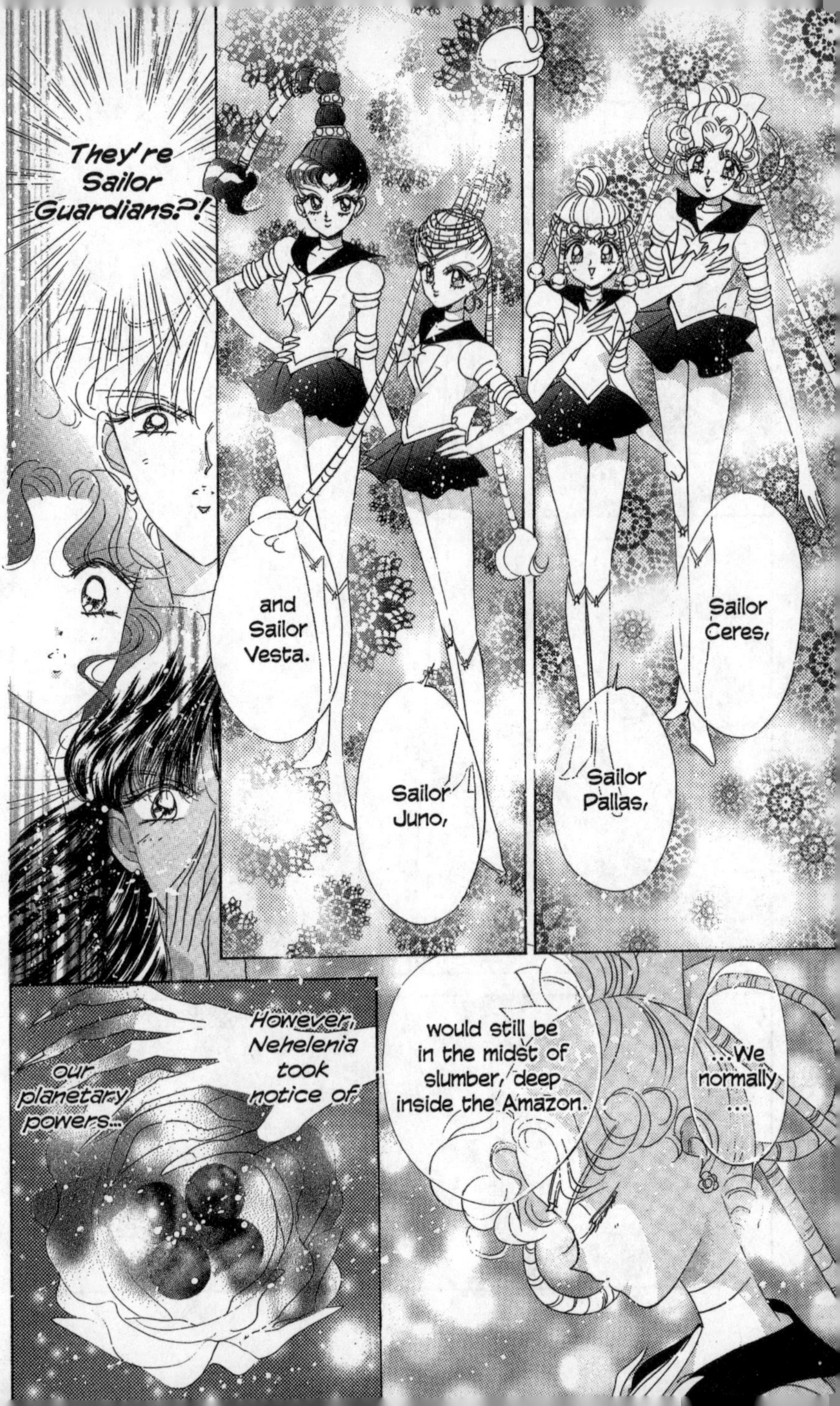
Sailor Ceres,
Sailor Pallas,
Sailor Juno,
and Sailor Vesta.
They're Sailor Guardians?!
...We normally ...
would still be in the midst of slumber, deep inside the Amazon.
However, Nehelenia took notice of
our planetary powers...

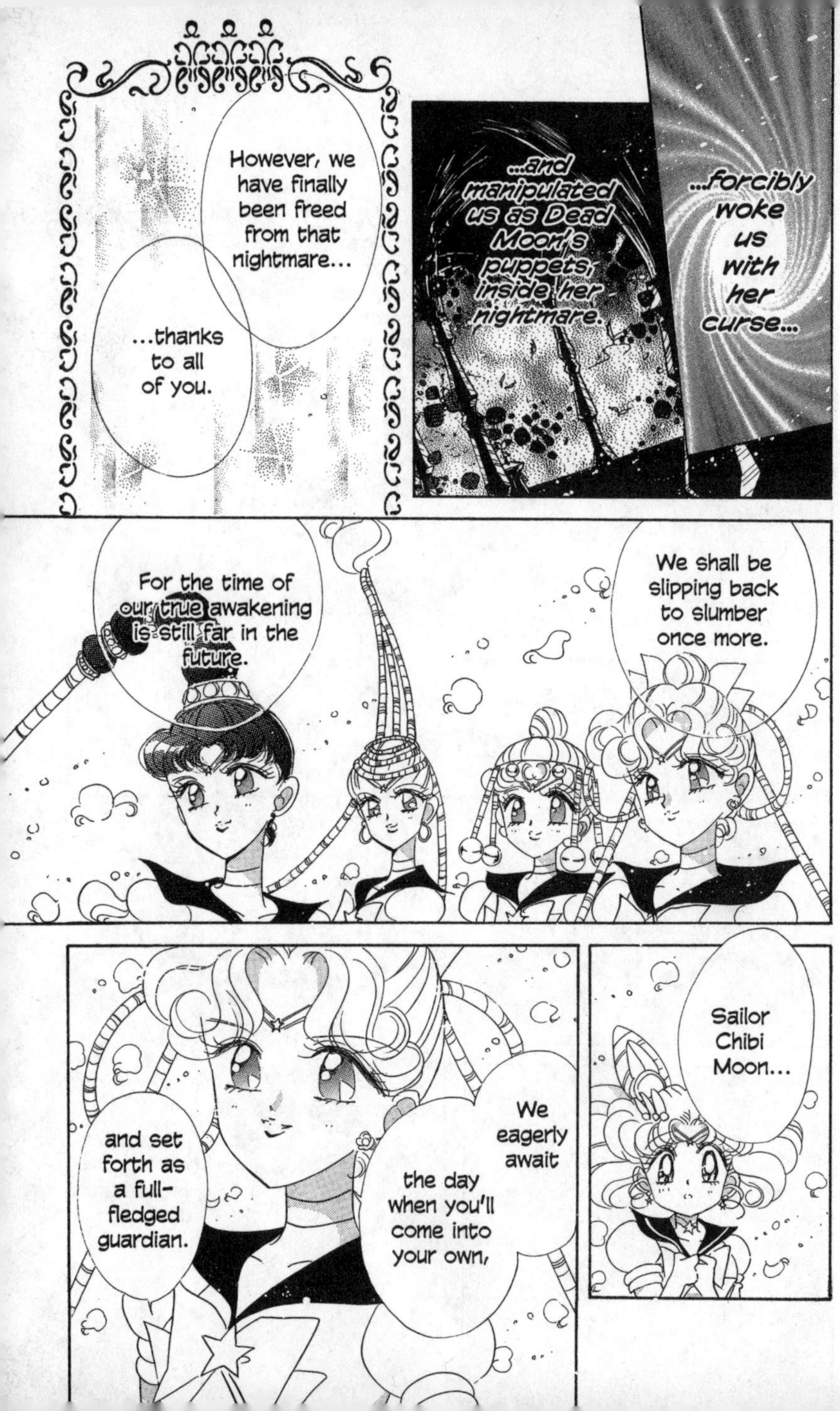
...forcibly woke us with her curse...
...and manipulated us as Dead Moon's puppets, inside her nightmare.
However, we have finally been freed from that nightmare...
...thanks to all of you.
We shall be slipping back to slumber once more.
For the time of our true awakening is still far in the future.
Sailor Chibi Moon...
We eagerly await
the day when you'll come into your own,
and set forth as a full-fledged guardian.

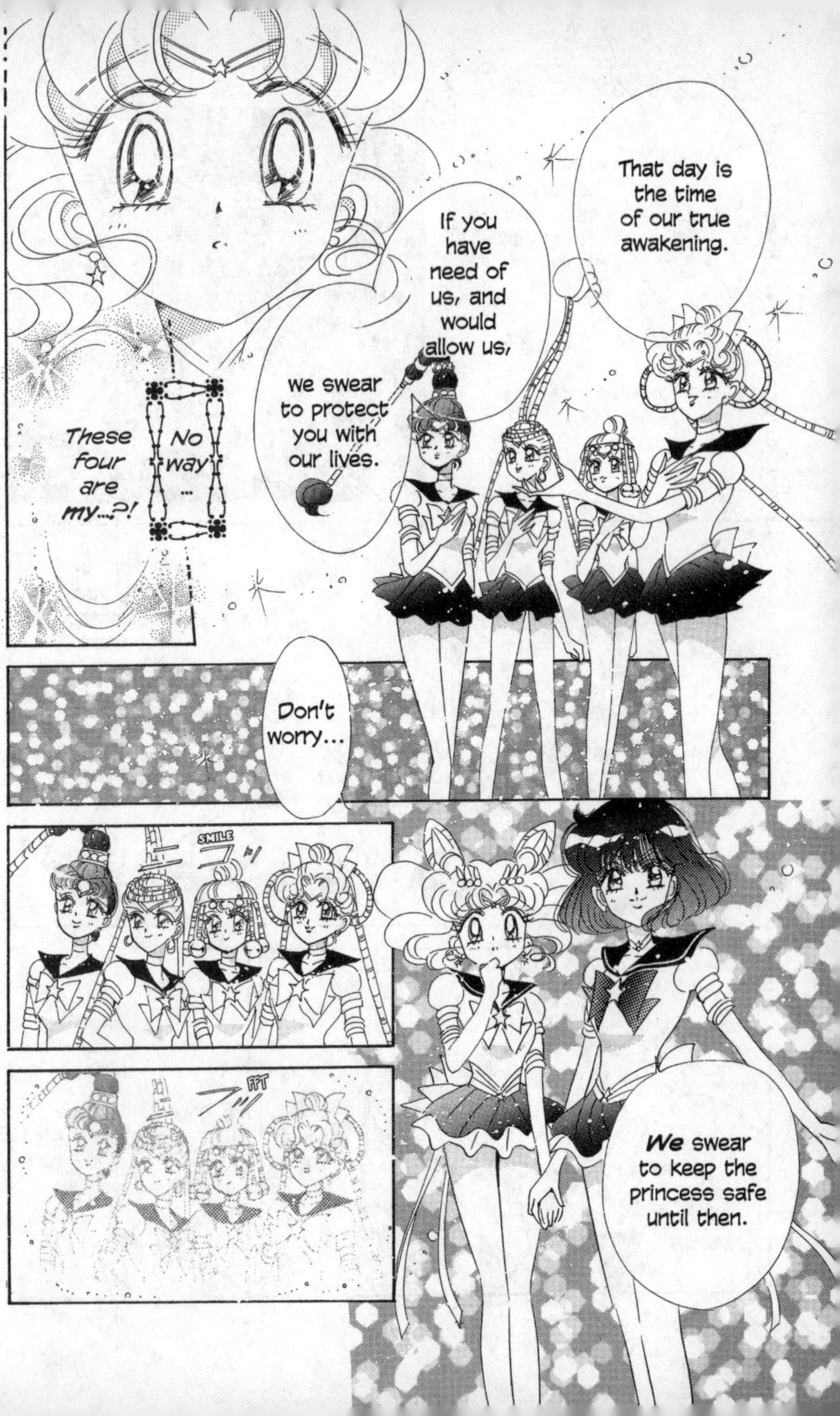
That day is the time of our true awakening.
If you have need of us, and would allow us,
we swear to protect you with our lives.
No way...
These four are *my*...?!
Don't worry...
We swear to keep the princess safe until then.
SMILE
FFT

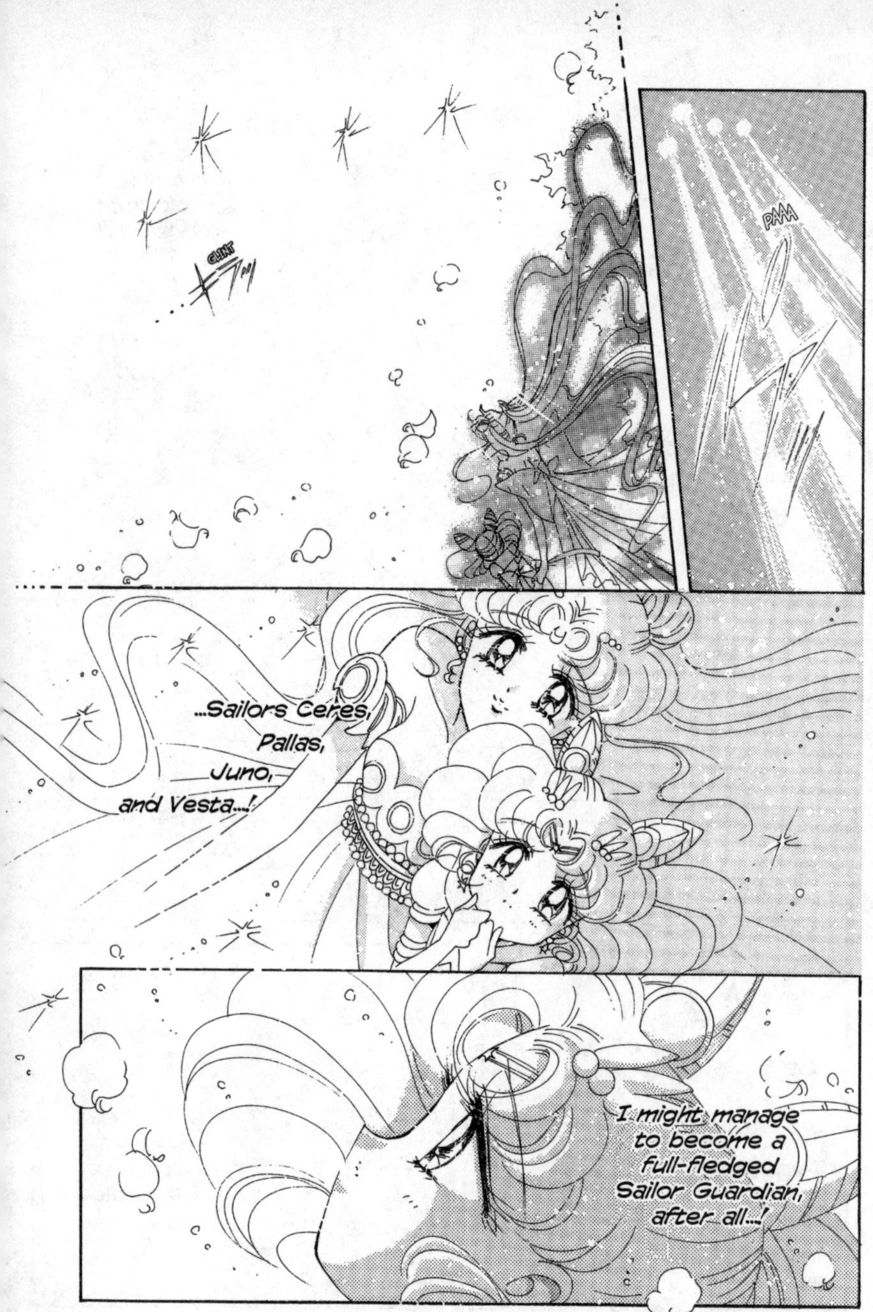
PAAA
CLINT
...Sailors Ceres, Pallas, Juno, and Vesta...!
I might manage to become a full-fledged Sailor Guardian, after all...!

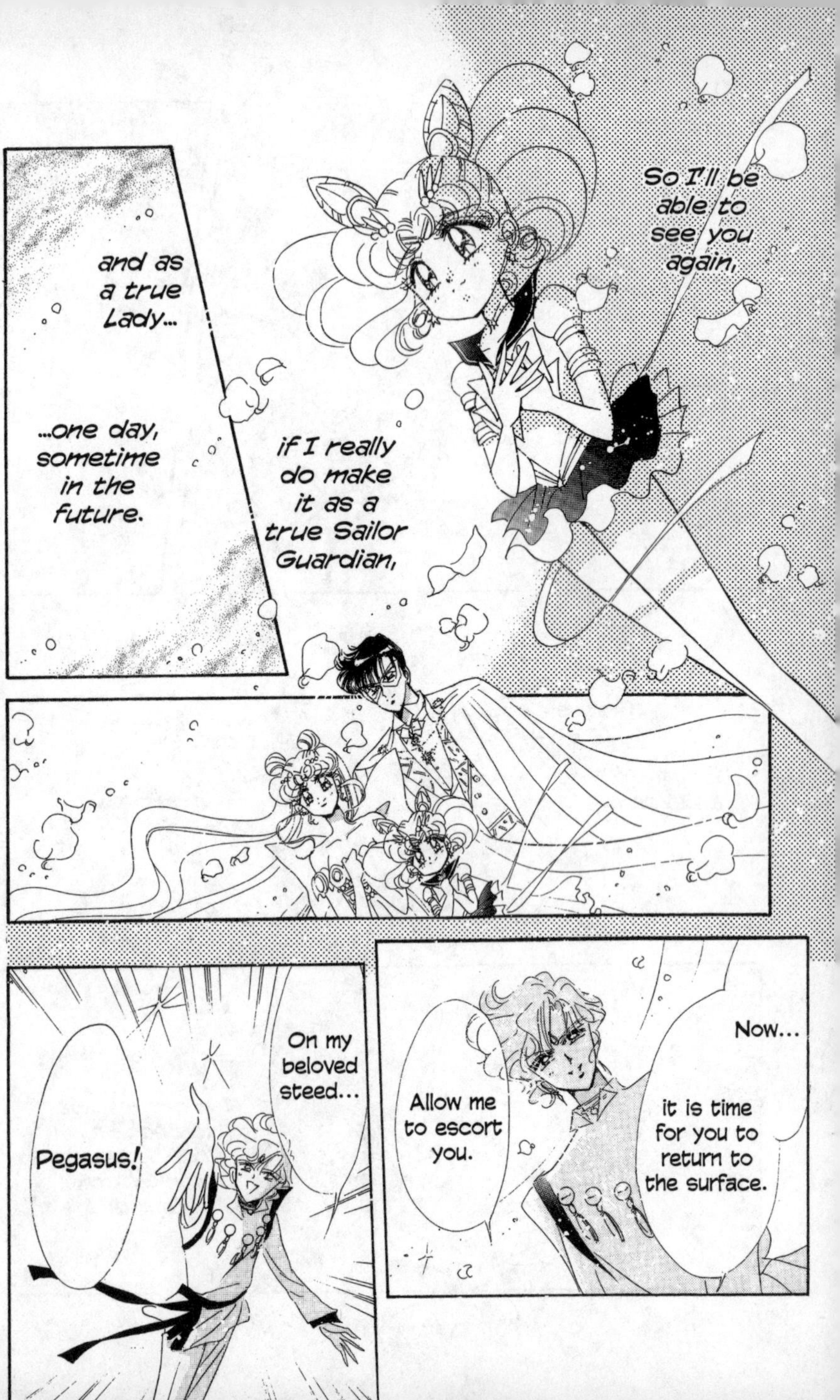
So I'll be able to see you again,
if I really do make it as a true Sailor Guardian,
and as a true Lady...
...one day, sometime in the future.
Now...
it is time for you to return to the surface.
Allow me to escort you.
On my beloved steed...
Pegasus!

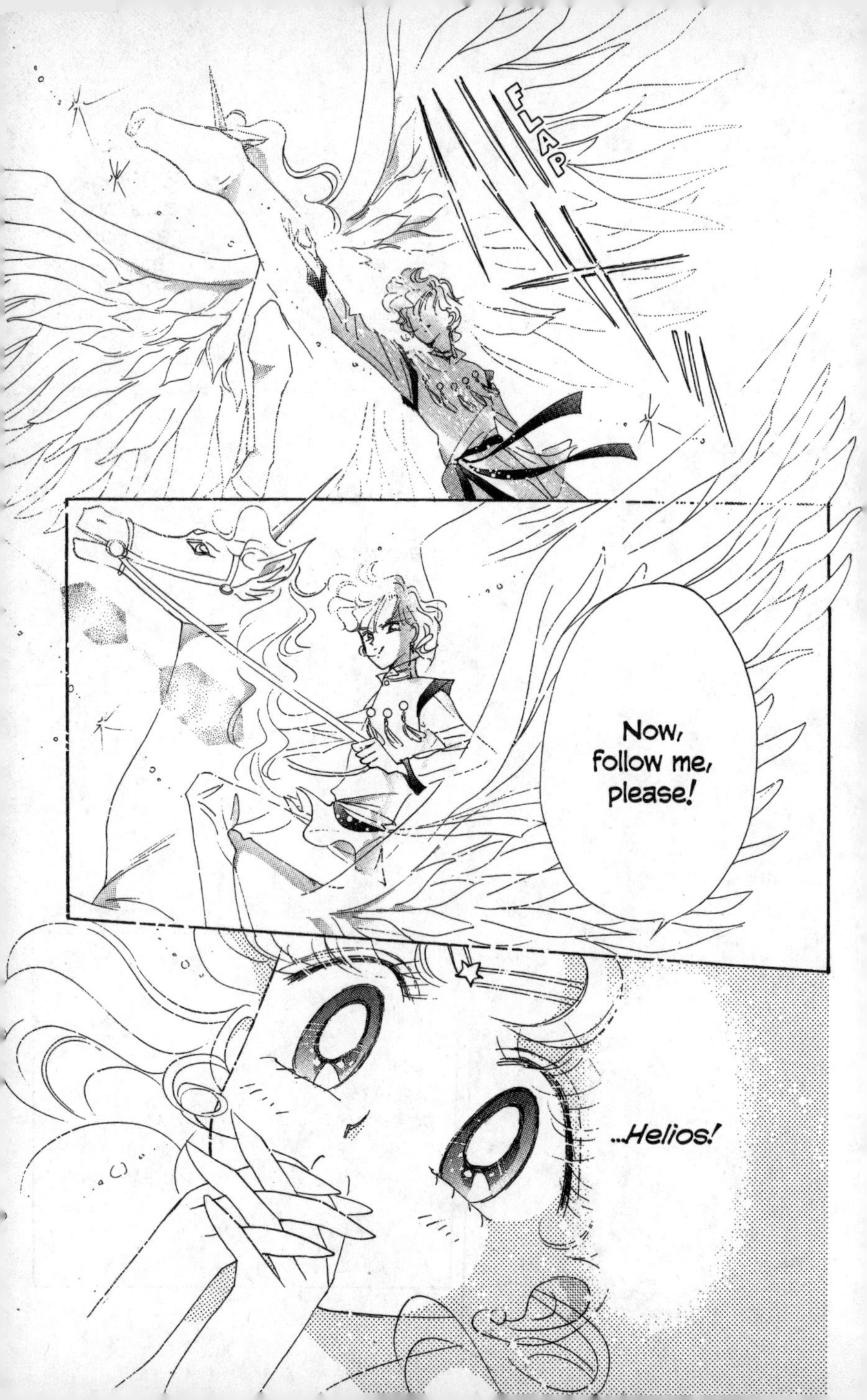
FLAP
Now, follow me, please!
...Helios!

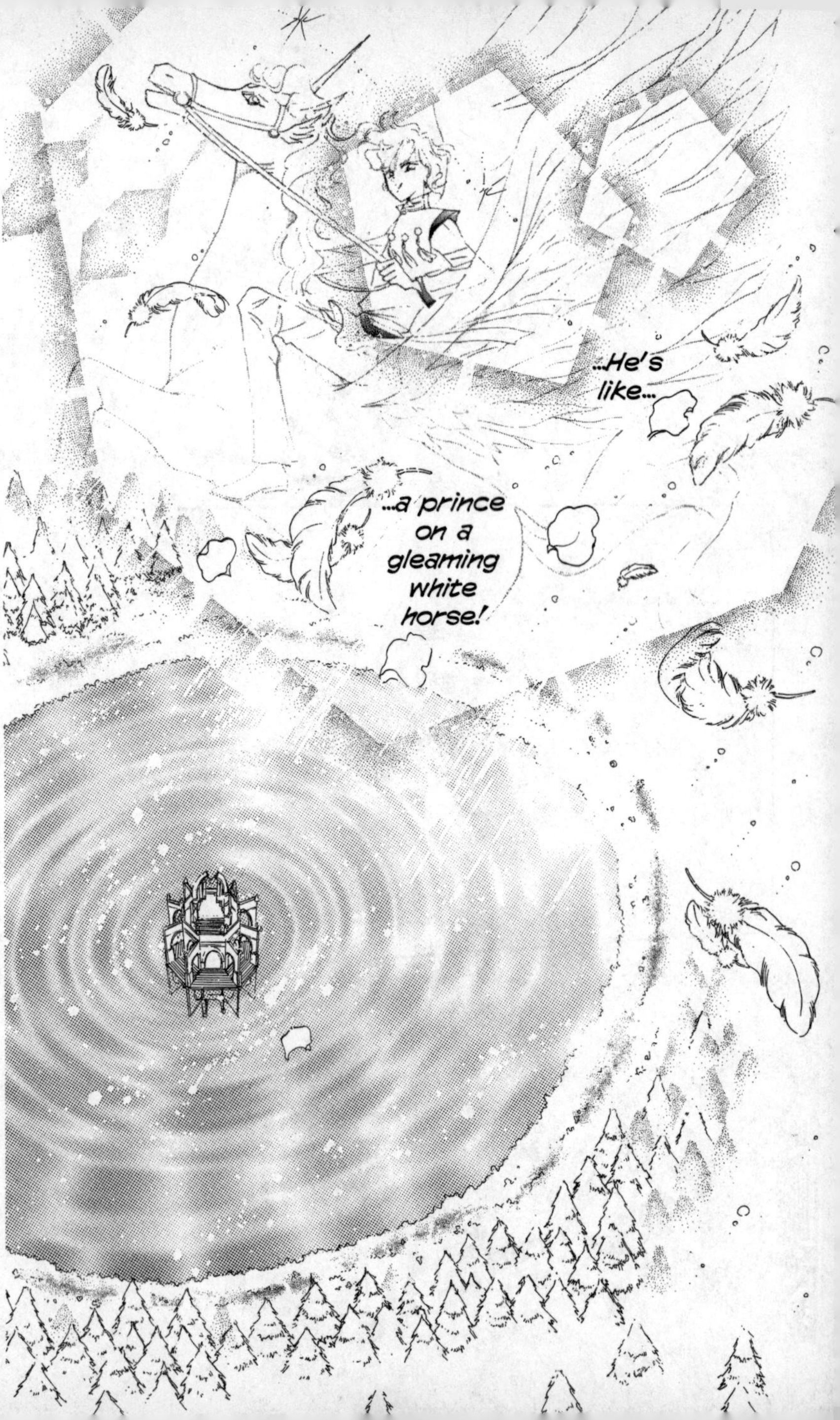
...He's like...
...a prince on a gleaming white horse!

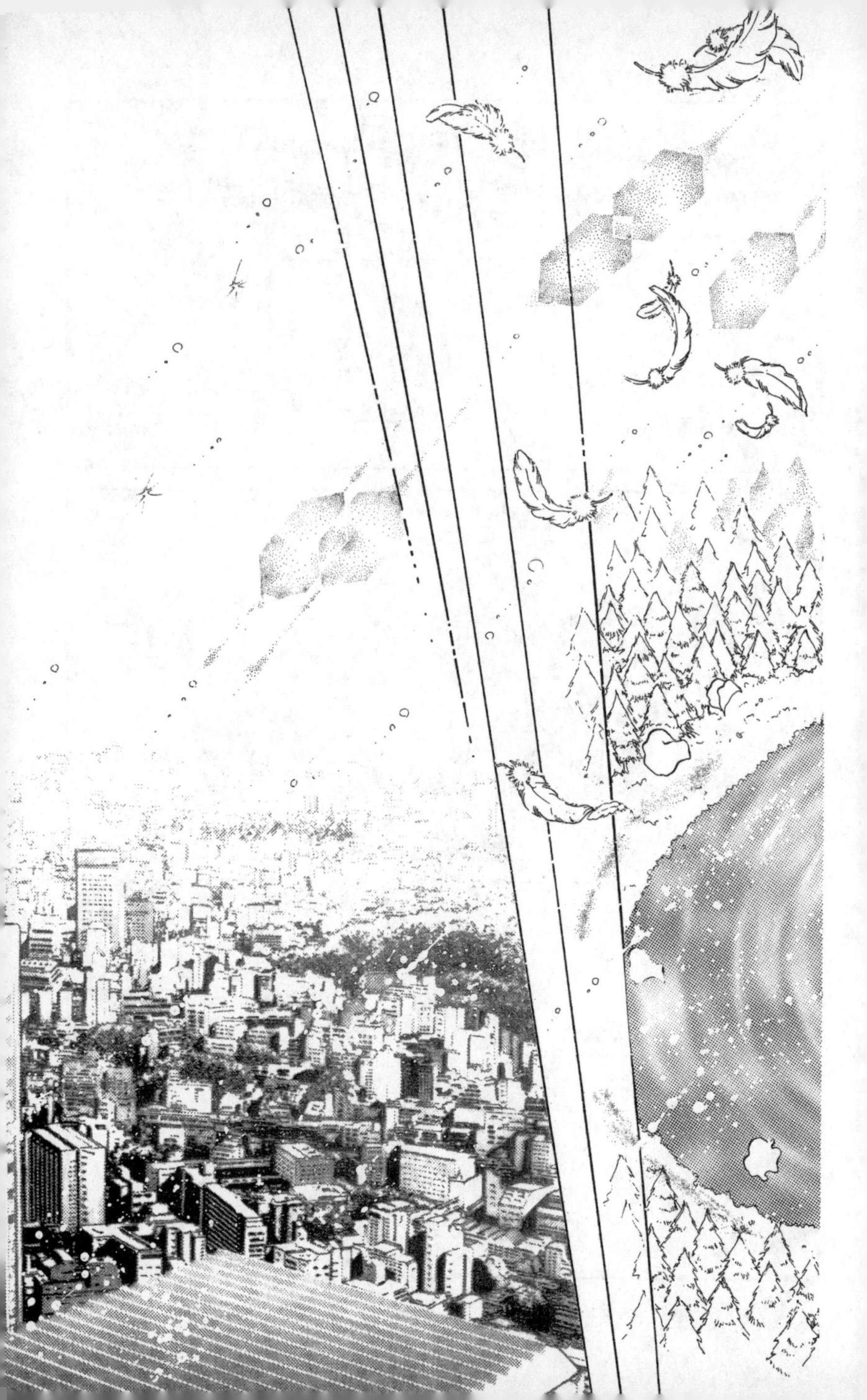

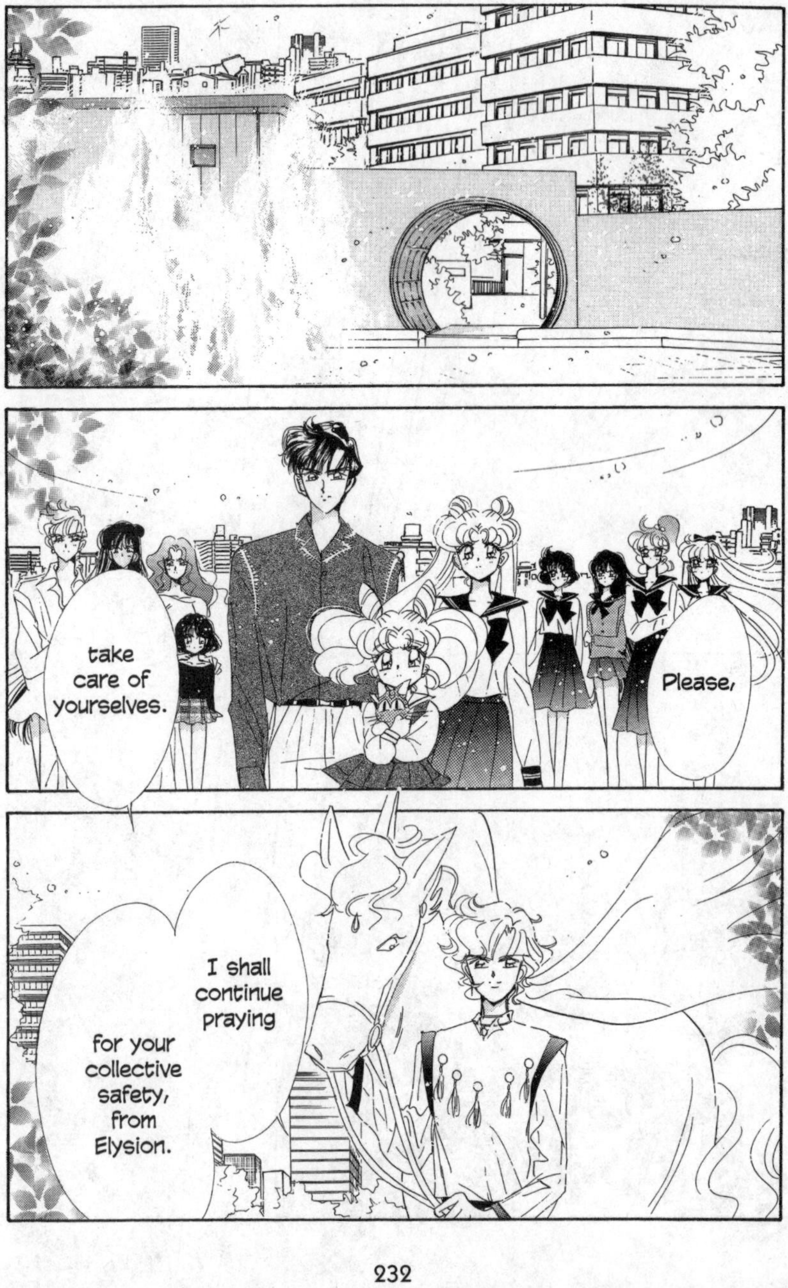
Please,
take care of yourselves.
I shall continue praying
for your collective safety, from Elysion.

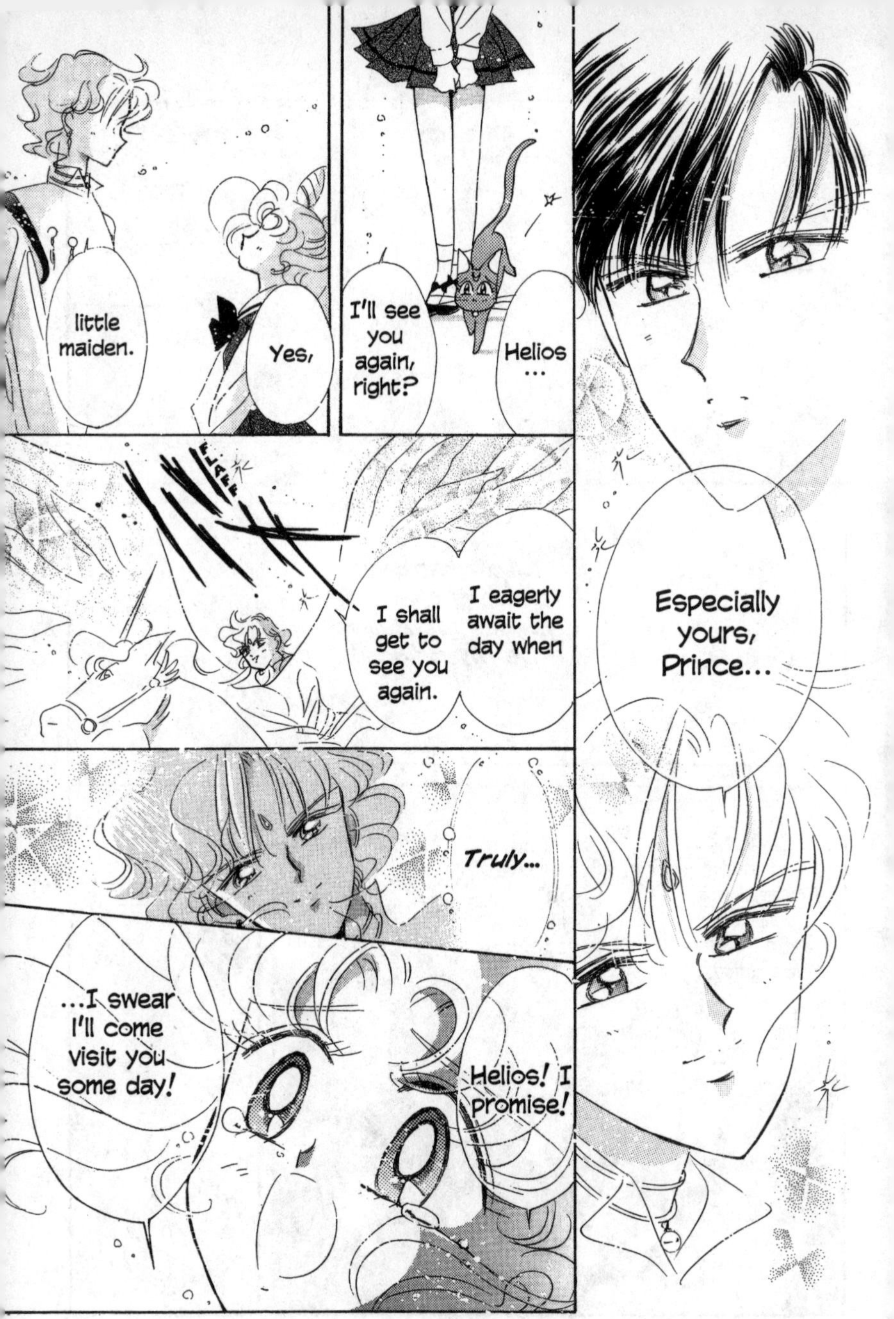
Especially yours, Prince...
Helios...
I'll see you again, right?
Yes,
little maiden.
I eagerly await the day when
I shall get to see you again.
FLAFF
Truly...
Helios! I promise!
...I swear I'll come visit you some day!

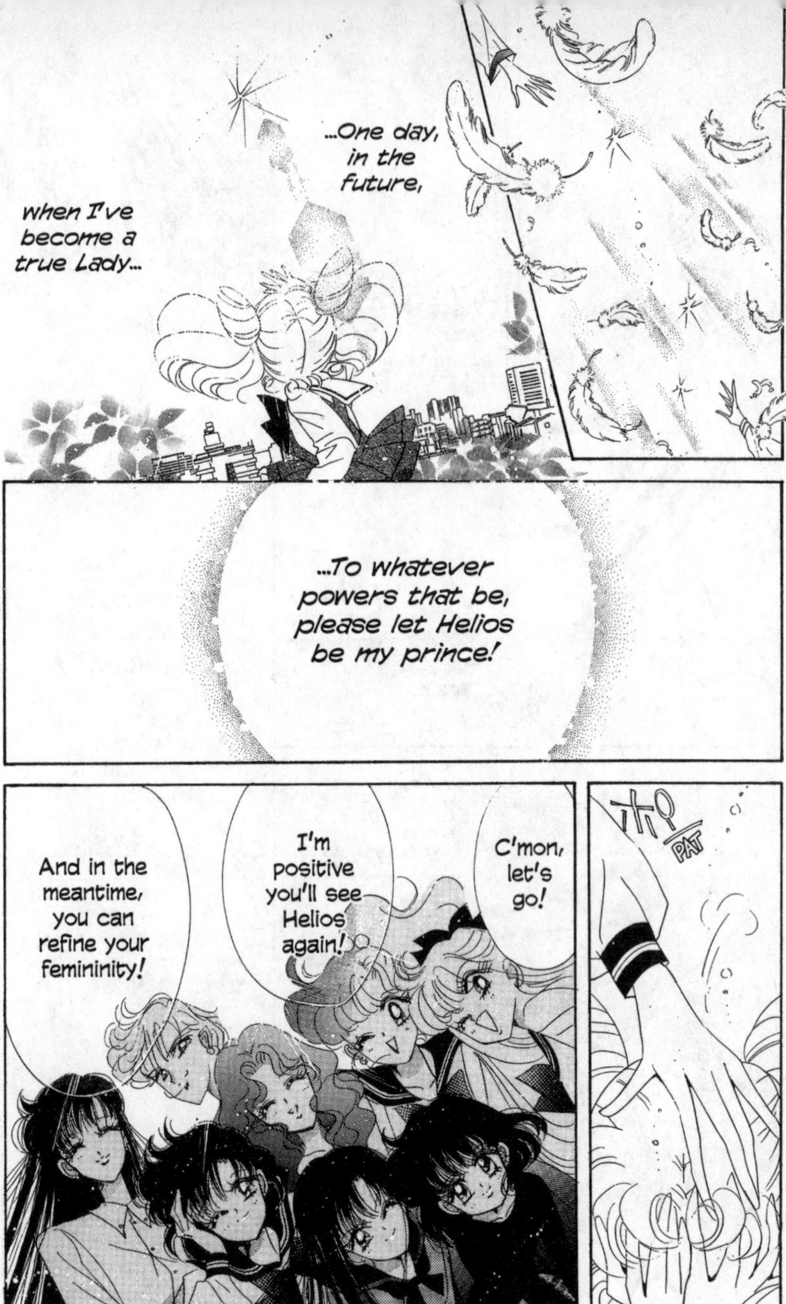
...One day, in the future,
when I've become a true Lady...
...To whatever powers that be, please let Helios be my prince!
PAT
C'mon, let's go!
I'm positive you'll see Helios again!
And in the meantime, you can refine your femininity!

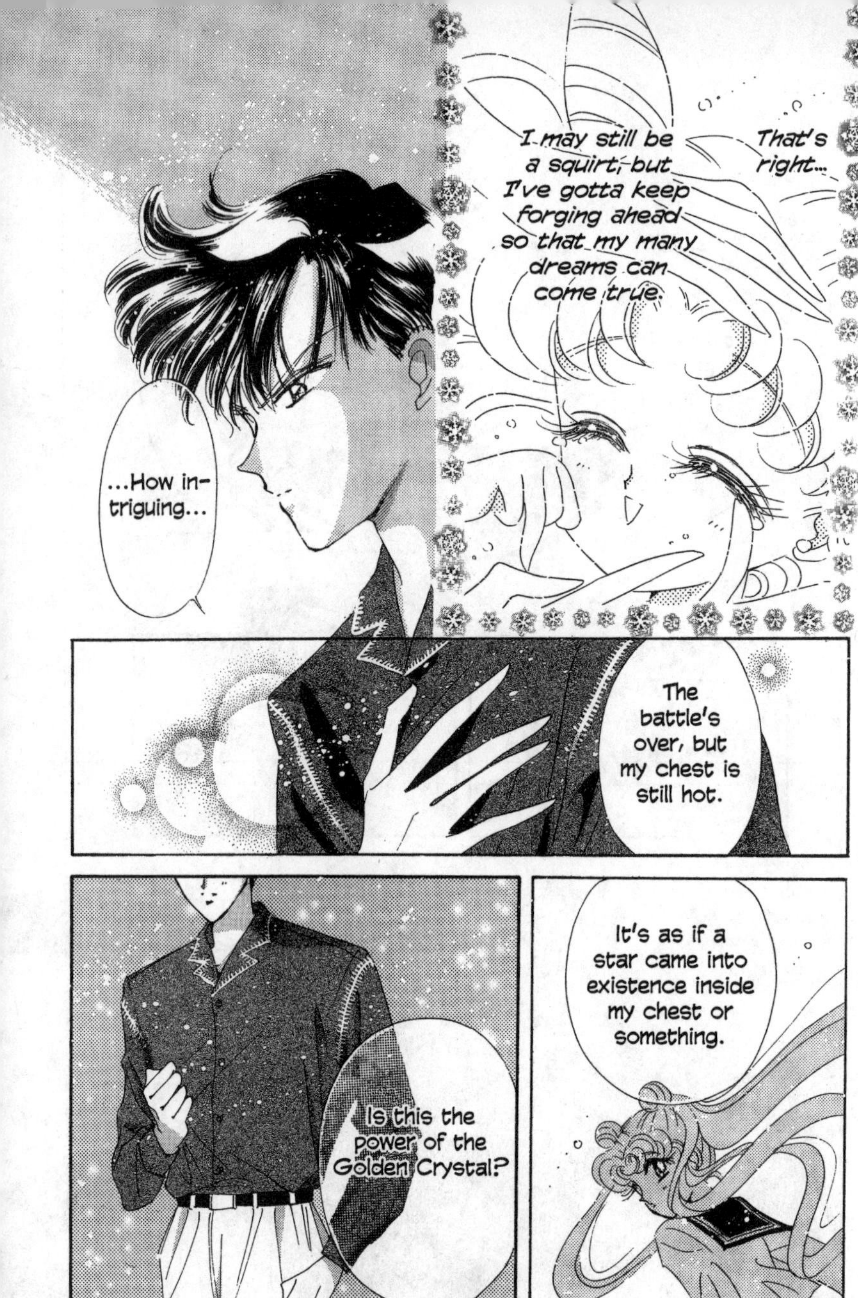
That's right...
I may still be a squirt, but I've gotta keep forging ahead so that my many dreams can come true.
...How intriguing...
The battle's over, but my chest is still hot.
It's as if a star came into existence inside my chest or something.
Is this the power of the Golden Crystal?

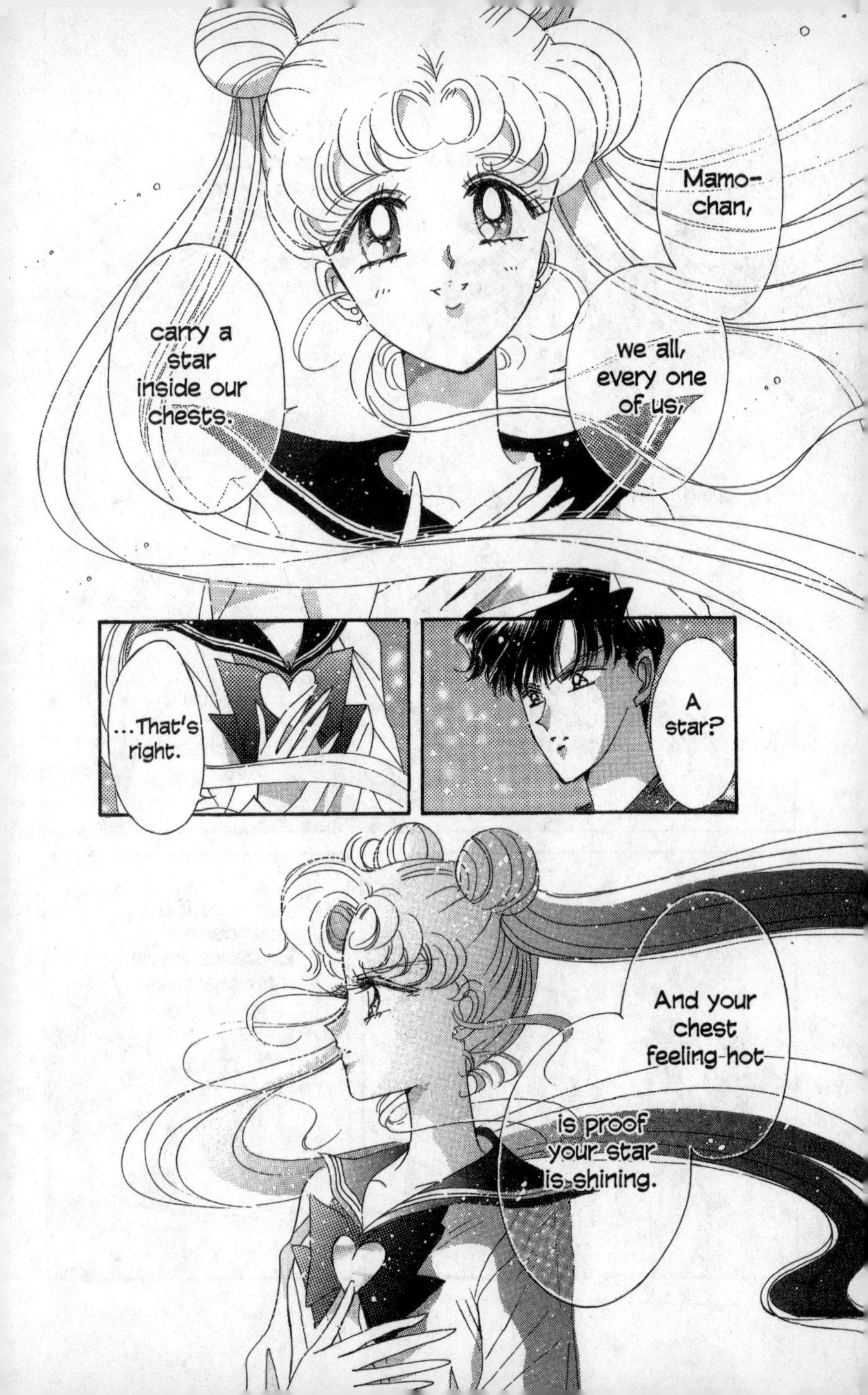
Mamo-chan,
we all, every one of us,
carry a star inside our chests.
A star?
...That's right.
And your chest feeling-hot—
is proof your star is shining.

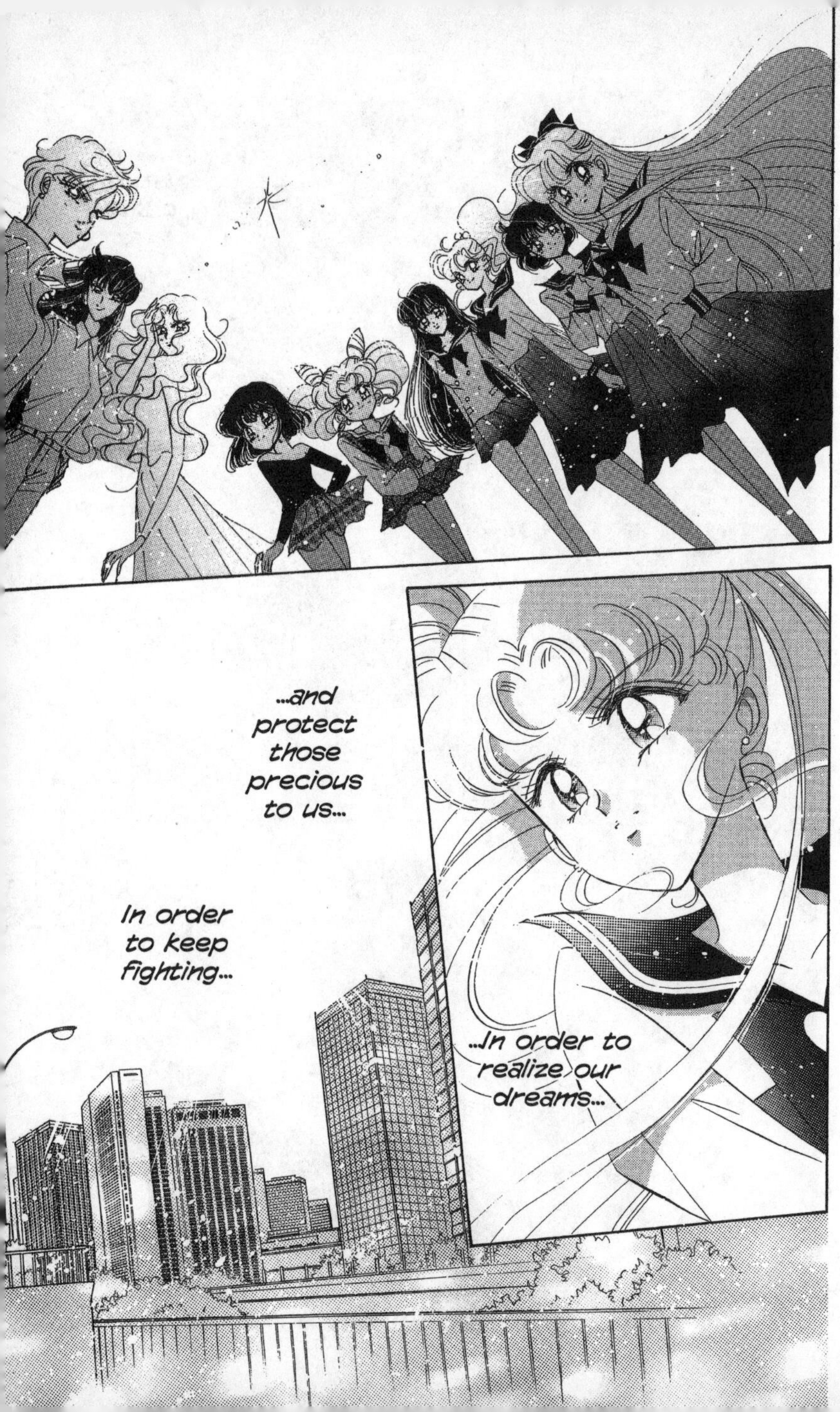
...In order to realize our dreams...
...and protect those precious to us...
In order to keep fighting...

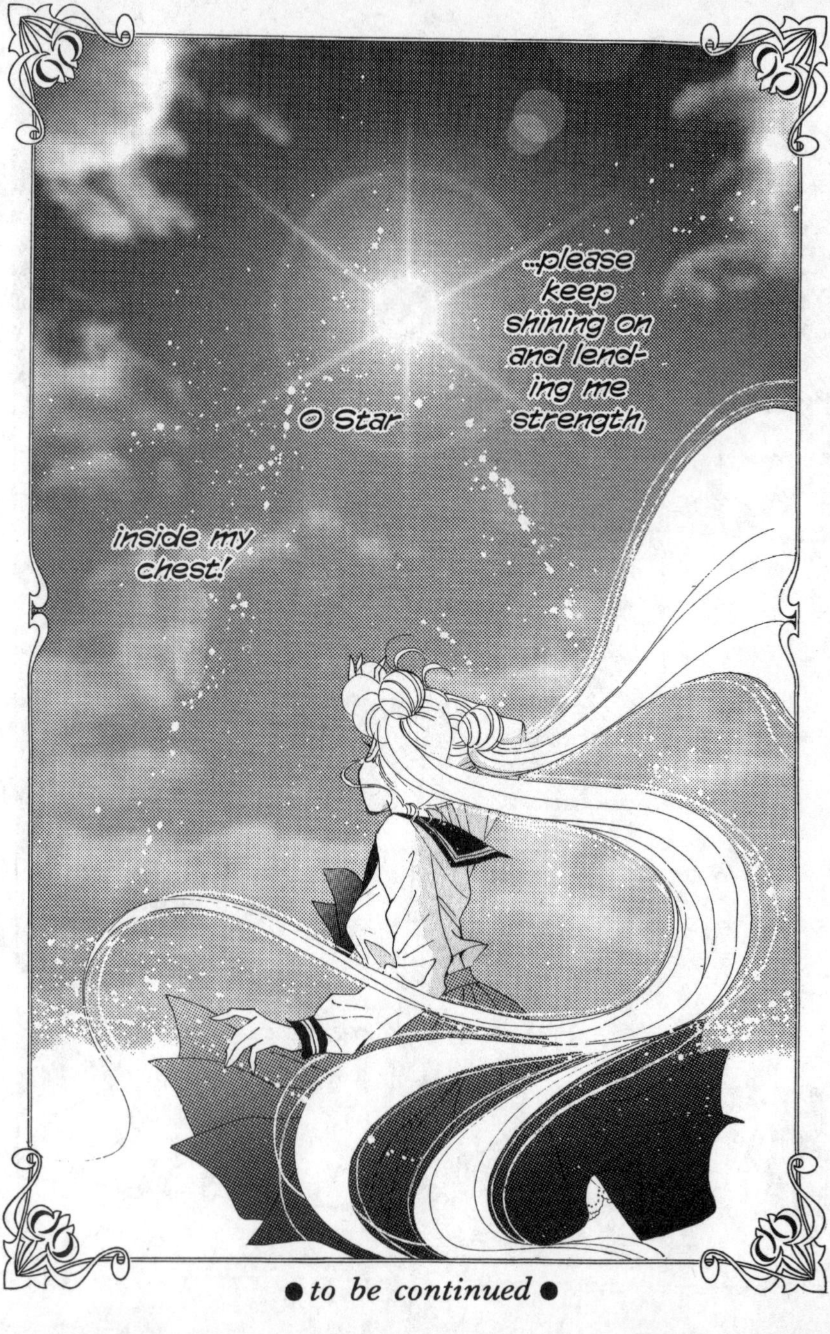
...please keep shining on and lend-ing me strength,
O Star
inside my chest!

●to be continued●

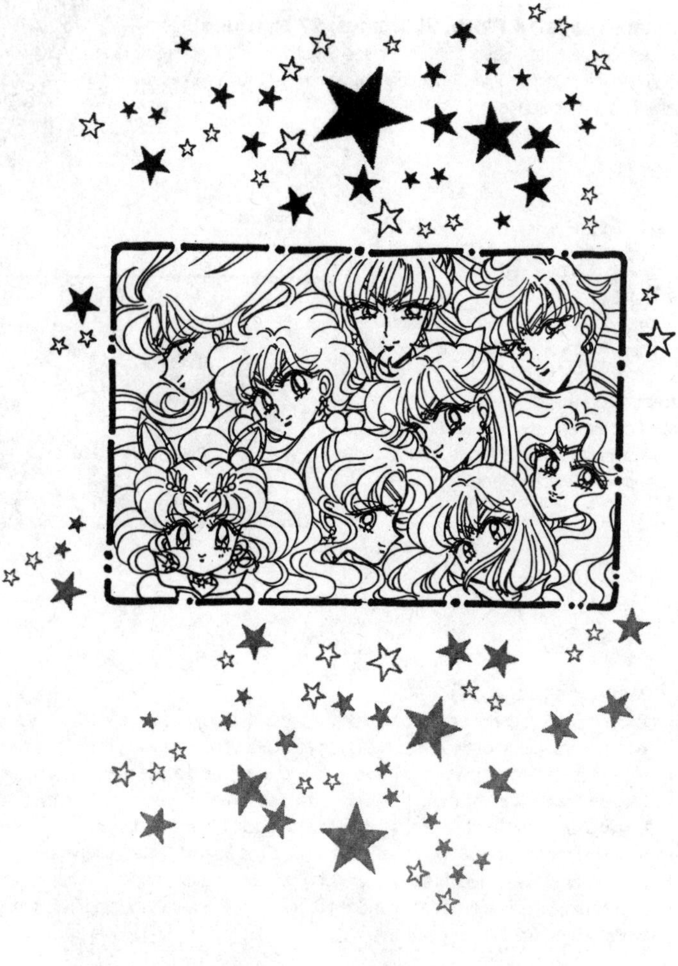

Translation Notes

apanese is a tricky language for most Westerners, and translation is often more art than cience. For your edification and reading pleasure, here are notes on some of the places vhere we could have gone in a different direction with our translation of the work, or vhere a Japanese cultural reference is used.

he three talismans (page 14 Pluto, 20 Uranus, 27 Neptune)

ailor Neptune's Deep Aqua Mirror, Sailor Uranus' Space Sword, and Sailor Pluto's Garnet Orb were likely nspired by and an homage to Japan's Imperial Regalia, which are the Kusanagi sword, the Yata no Kagami mirror), and Yasakani no Magatama jewel.

latto (page 44)

latto are fermented soybeans that are usually eaten s a side dish to rice, more traditionally or commonly n eastern and northern Japan. Its distinctive pungent odor and sticky to slimy consistency leads it to often e used as a comedic element in anime and manga. n this case, PallaPalla's attack serves a function similar o that of glue traps, spider webbing, or tar pits

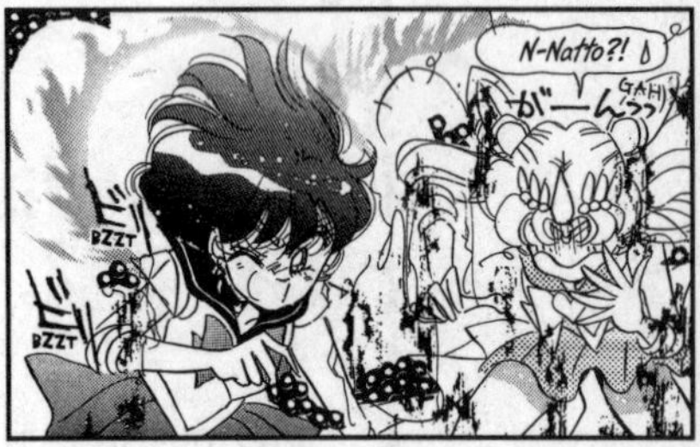
N-Natto?!
GAH
がーん
BZZT
BZZT

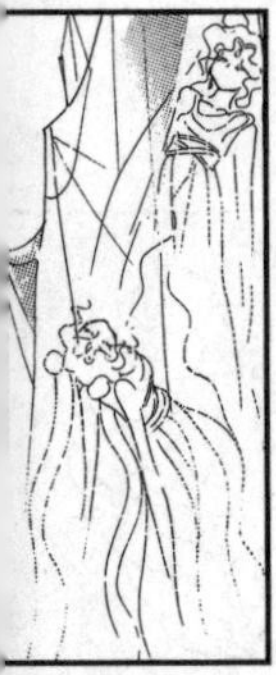

Menaeds (page 64)

The translator first chose to Romanize the Elysion maidens' name/title as "Maenads," which is the name of Dionysus' wild female followers. However, the discrepancy in attributes between the original Maenads and these gentle-seeming Elysion maidens caused the translator pause. It turns out that the "Mae" in Maenads is pronounced "mee", not "may" like the original katakana. In addition, some deeper digging revealed the existence of "Menai" or "Menae," the 50 goddesses of the lunar months who were daughters of the Moon goddess Selene and her great love Endymion, which seemed a lot more apropos, and thus the spelling "Menaeds" was chosen instead.

Nehelenia (page 142)

The name of Dead Moon's queen may be an homage to the goddess Nehalennia who was worshipped around the beginning of the first millennia in the area of what is now the Netherlands and Germany. Not much is known about her other than that she is usually depicted carrying a basket of fruit, with marine symbols, and a large dog at her feet.

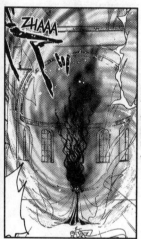

Nehelenia's curse (page 161)

The story of Nehelenia's curse, that of an evil entity showing up to a fete and cursing the object(s) of celebration (in this case Sailor Moon and the Silver Millennium) out of spite for not having been invited, is a common fairy tale motif most reminiscent of the tale of Sleeping Beauty.

Tiare (page 192)

The translator admits to taking a slight liberty Romanizing the name of Sailor Moon's rod, which is literally spelled "tiaru." Several other translations have also been offered, such as "tier" and "tiar", but the translator chose "tiare" because it is the indigenous name of the Tahitian Gardenia, and the top of the rod resembles a flower. However, the actual flower only has a single layer of six petals…

Planetoids (page 223)

Planetoids or minor planets are astronomical objects that orbit our Sun but are neither one of the 8 major planets nor comets. Numbering more than 570,000, they include dwarf planets, asteroids, trojans (objects that share the orbit of one of the major planets), and centaurs (objects that have characteristics of both asteroids and comets), among several others. Ceres, Pallas, Juno, and Vesta were the first four minor planets to be discovered (in that order), and Ceres, Pallas, and Vesta are also the three largest (also in that order). All four are considered asteroids, with Ceres also classified as a dwarf planet, the only one in the inner Solar System.

Alicorn/Unisus/Pegacorn (page 229)

The creature whose form Helios has been cursed into taking is actually a pegasus-unicorn hybrid, a horned steed with wings (or winged steed with a horn). The original "Pegasus" turns out to Helios' beloved steed.

Elysion (pages 214-215)

More commonly spelled Elysium or Elysian Fields, Elysion is a fictional place in the afterlife that first appears in ancient Greek mythology. Originally located on the western fringe of Earth, separate from the underworld, and reserved for heroes and those related to the gods, it would later become more analogous to Paradise and the Christian heaven. In Virgil's Aeneid and Dante's Divine Comedy, Elysium is part of the underworld and is located deep below Earth's surface. Here in Sailor Moon, Elysion is described as a paradise-like place deep inside Earth where the Golden Kingdom, realm of Earth's rulers, once stood.

Preview of *Sailor Moon 11*

We're pleased to present you with a preview from
Pretty Guardian Sailor Moon 11. Please check our
website (www.kodanshacomics.com to see when
this volume will be available.

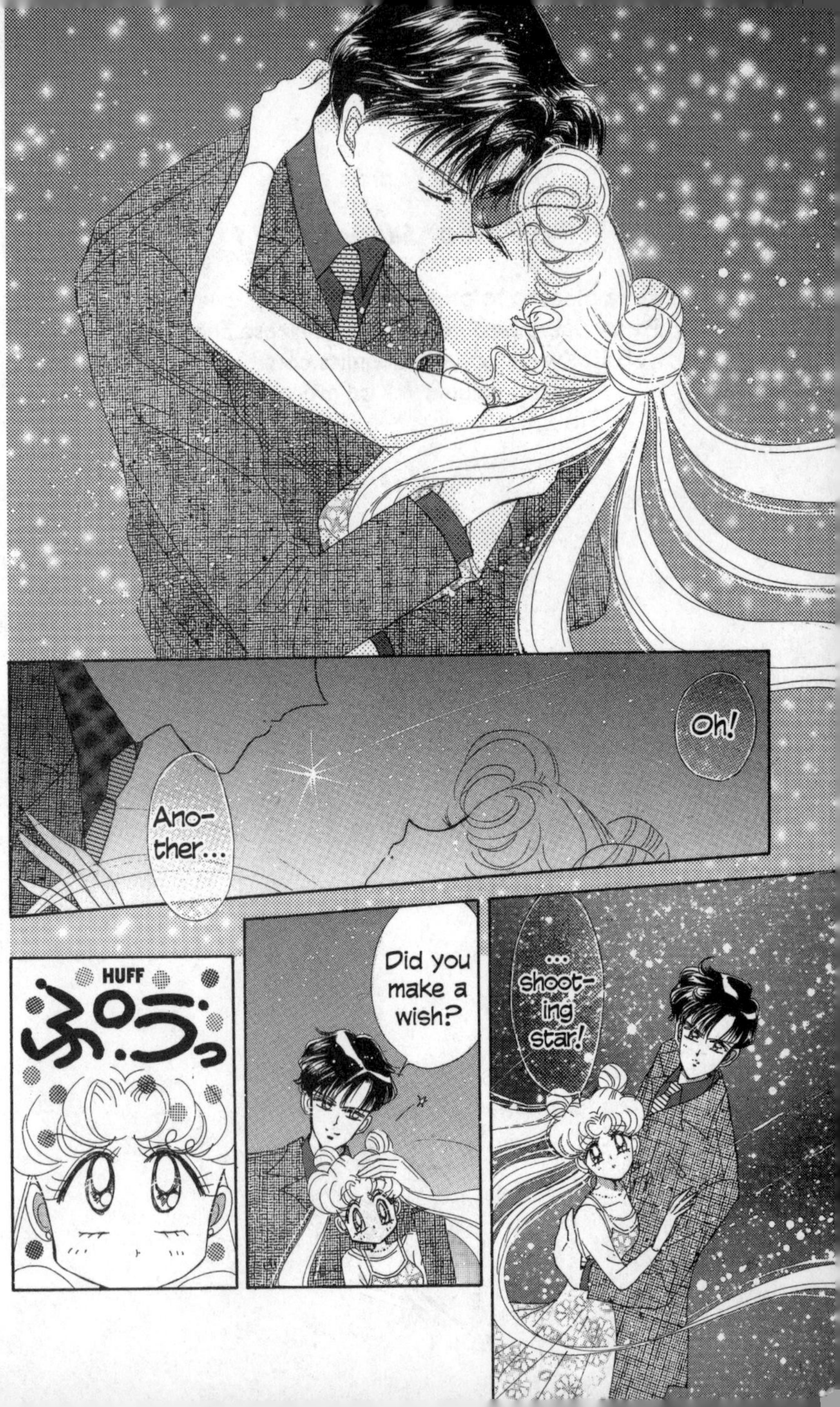

Oh!
Ano-ther...
...shoot-ing star!
Did you make a wish?
HUFF
ぷうっ

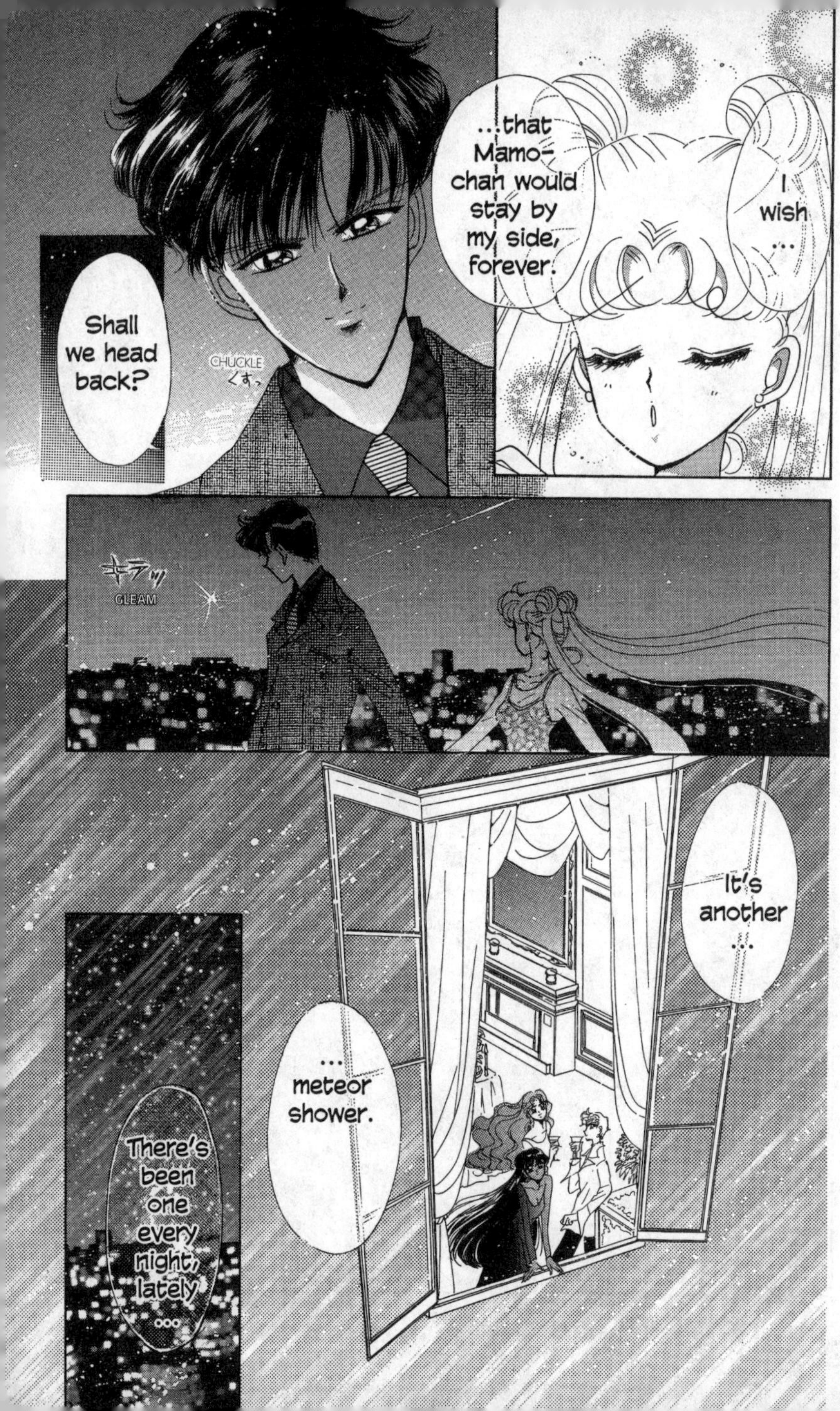
I wish...
...that Mamo-chan would stay by my side, forever.
Shall we head back?
CHUCKLE
くすっ
キラッ
GLEAM
It's another...
...meteor shower.
There's been one every night, lately...

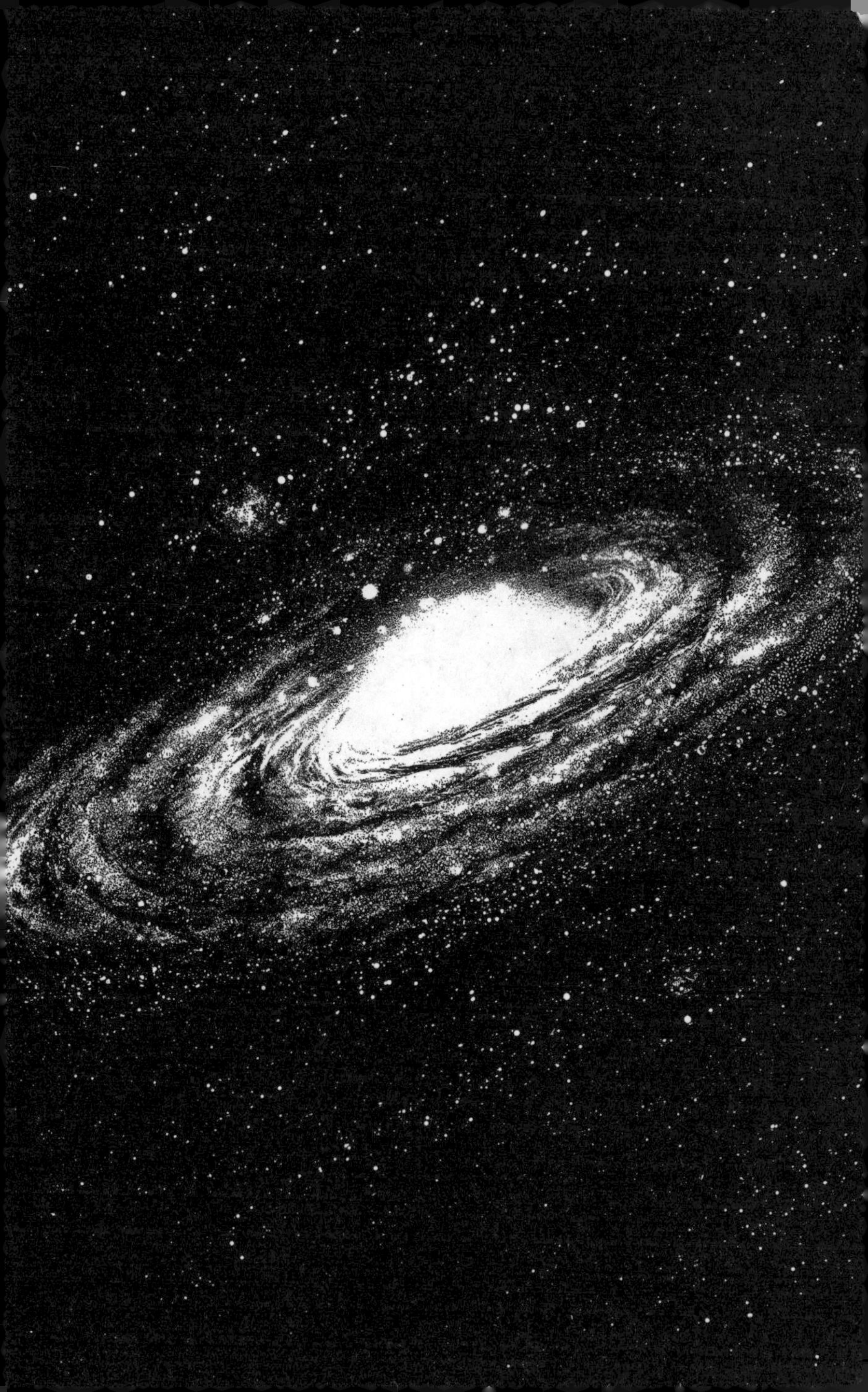

A Kodansha Trade Paperback Original.

Published in the United States by Kodansha Comics, an imprint
of Kodansha USA Publishing, LLC, New York.

Publication rights for this English edition arranged through
Kodansha Ltd., Tokyo.

First published in Japan in 2004 by Kodansha Ltd., Tokyo, as
Bishoujosenshi Sailor Moon Shinsoban, volume 10.

ISBN 978-1-61262-006-0

Printed in Canada

www.kodansha.us

9 8 7 6 5

Translator/Adapter: Mari Morimoto
Lettering: Jennifer Skarupa

TOMARE!
STOP

You're going the wrong way!

Manga is a completely different type of reading experience.

To start at the beginning, Go to the end!

That's right! Authentic manga is read the traditional Japanese way—from right to left, exactly the opposite of how American books are read. It's easy to follow: Just go to the other end of the book and read each page—and each panel—from right side to left side, starting at the top right. Now you're experiencing manga as it was meant to be!